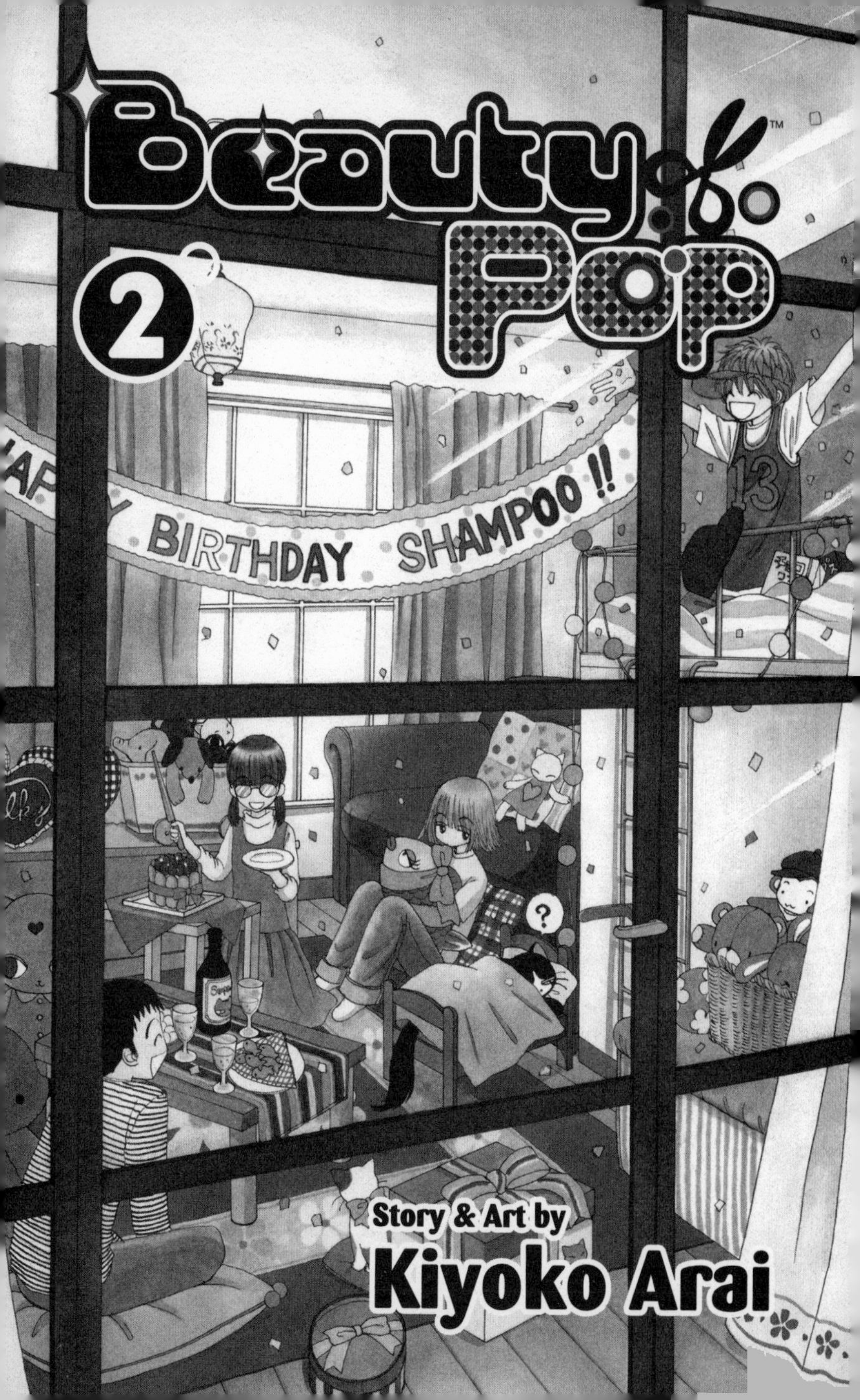
Beauty Pop™
2
AP
Y BIRTHDAY SHAMPOO !!
Story & Art by
Kiyoko Arai

Beauty Pop

Characters 2

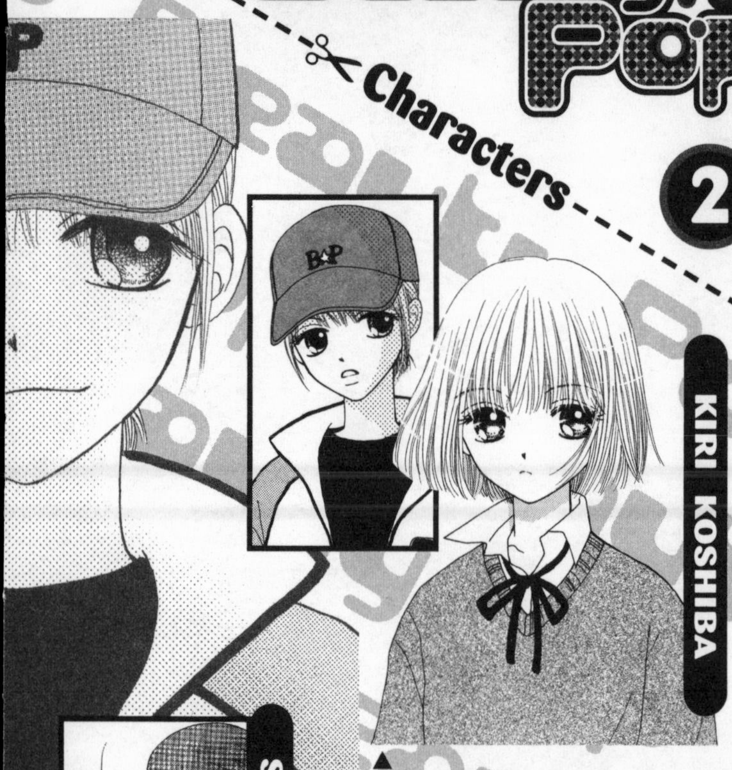

KIRI KOSHIBA

▲ She's absentminded and seems self-centered, but she really cares for her friends and has a strong sense of justice. Kiri also has exceptional haircutting techniques.

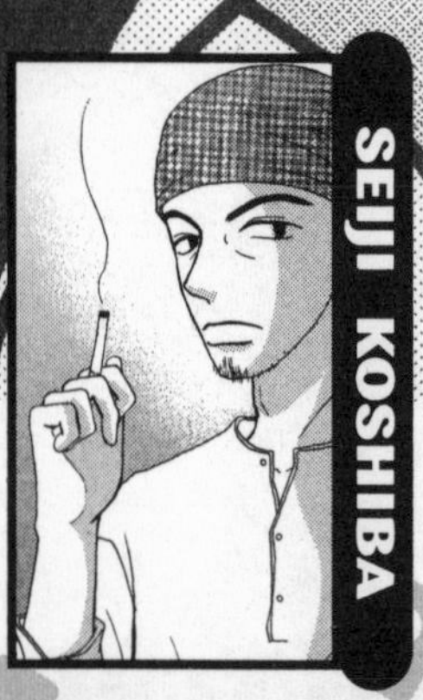

SEIJI KOSHIBA

◀ Seiji is Kiri's father. He owns the Koshiba Beauty Salon and is Kiri's haircutting teacher.

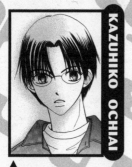

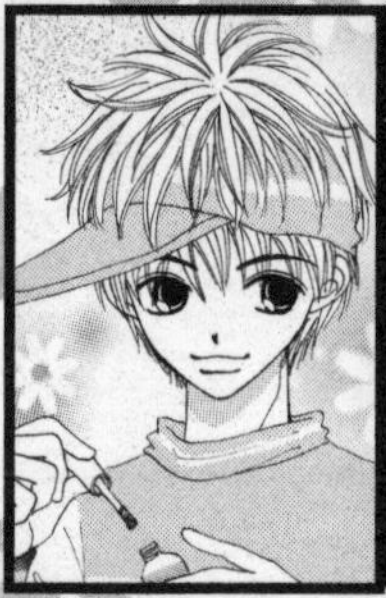
KEI MINAMI

▲
Kei is cheerful and loves to eat snacks. He's in charge of nail art in the Scissors Project.

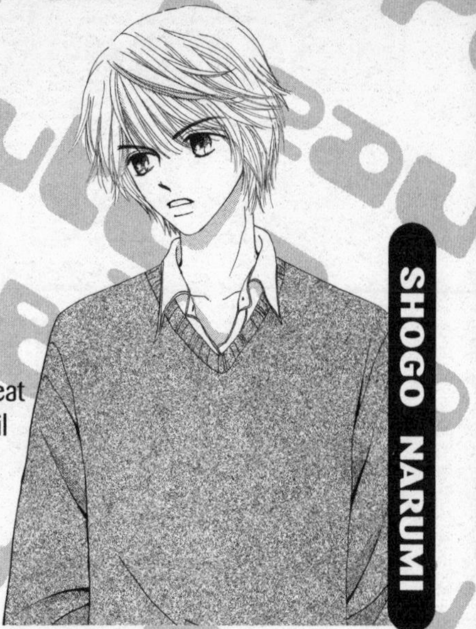
SHOGO NARUMI

▲
Shogo is the leader of the Scissors Project. He's a hothead. His father is the owner of Salon de Narumi, the best beauty salon in the industry. Shogo aspires to be the top beautician in Japan, but…

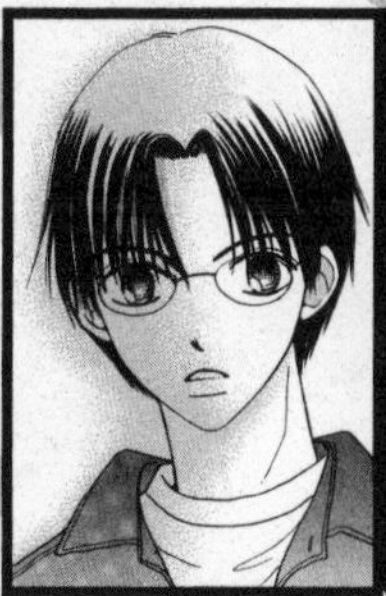
KAZUHIKO OCHIAI

▲
He's the Scissors Project's consultant for overall beauty. His father is the president of a cosmetics company.

Story So Far

Kiri is in her first year of high school. At Kiri's school, there are three boys who created a club called the Scissors Project, and they are famous for doing makeovers on girls. But because Kiri worked wonders on girls that the boys had rejected, she was made to compete in a haircutting battle against them at the Cultural Festival! Kiri transformed the nappy-haired Yorozuya-san…

Beauty Pop 2

CONTENTS

Beauty Pop.....7

Bonus Story: Dreams
Come True.....132

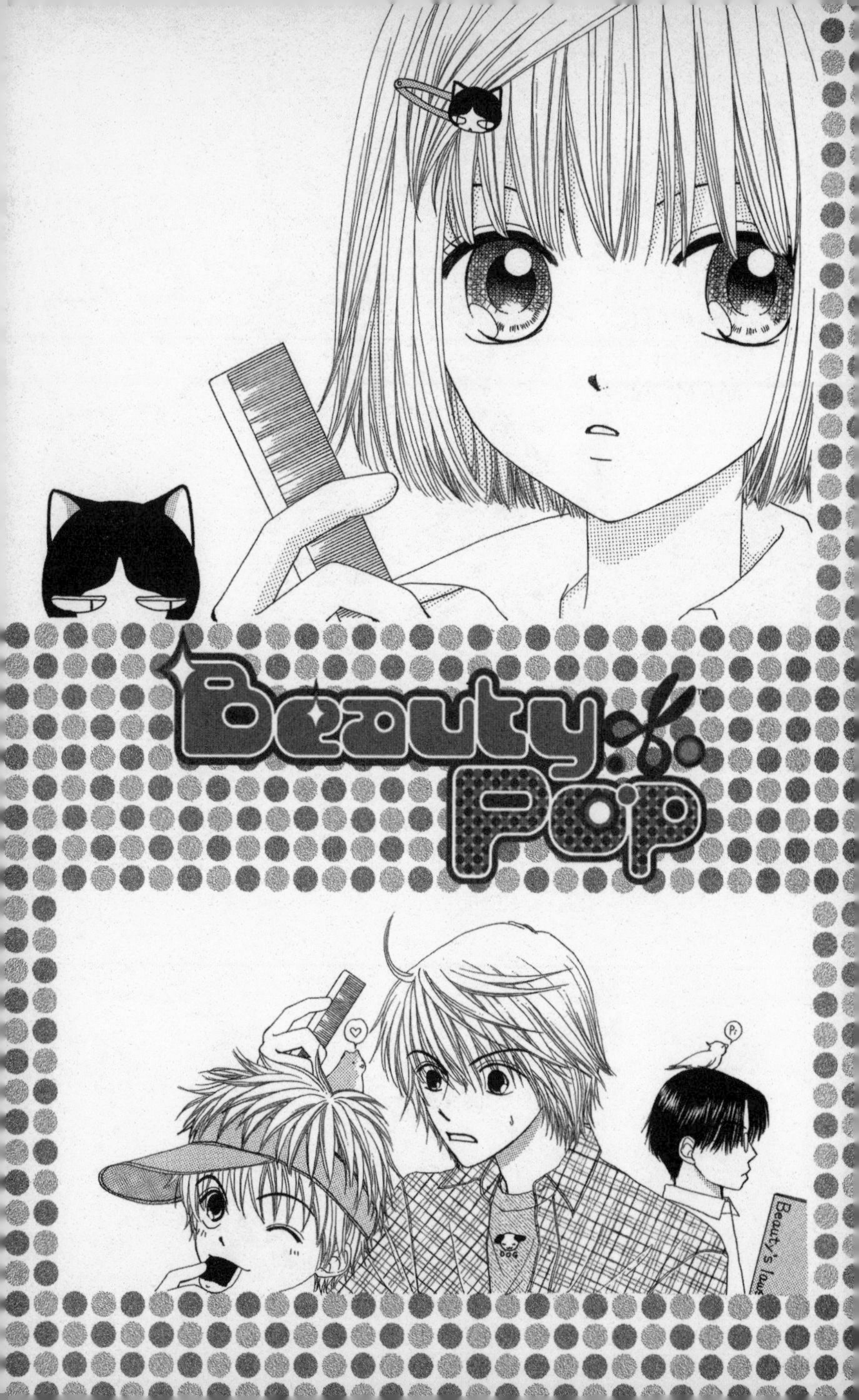
Beauty Pop

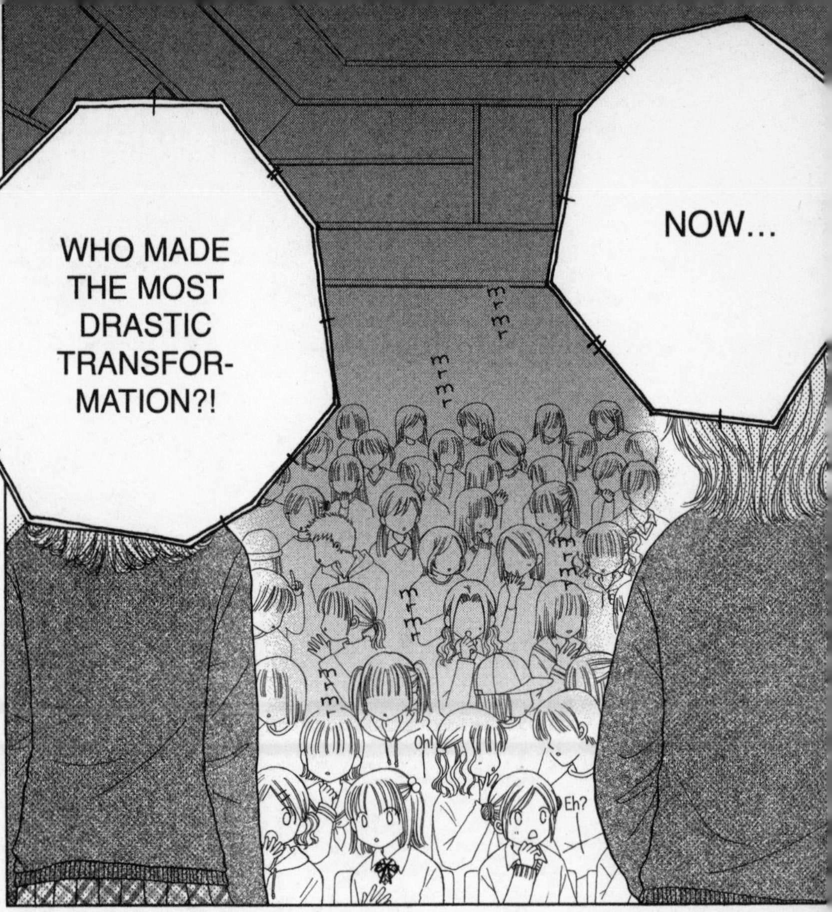
NOW...
WHO MADE THE MOST DRASTIC TRANSFOR-MATION?!
mrmr
mrmr
mrmr
mrmr
mrmr
Oh!
Eh?

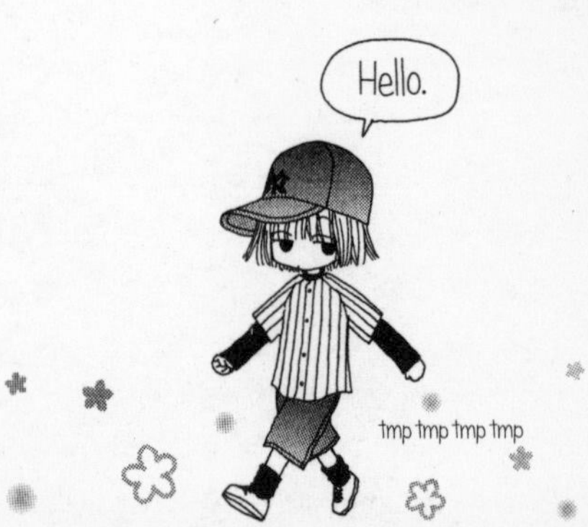
Hello.
tmp tmp tmp tmp

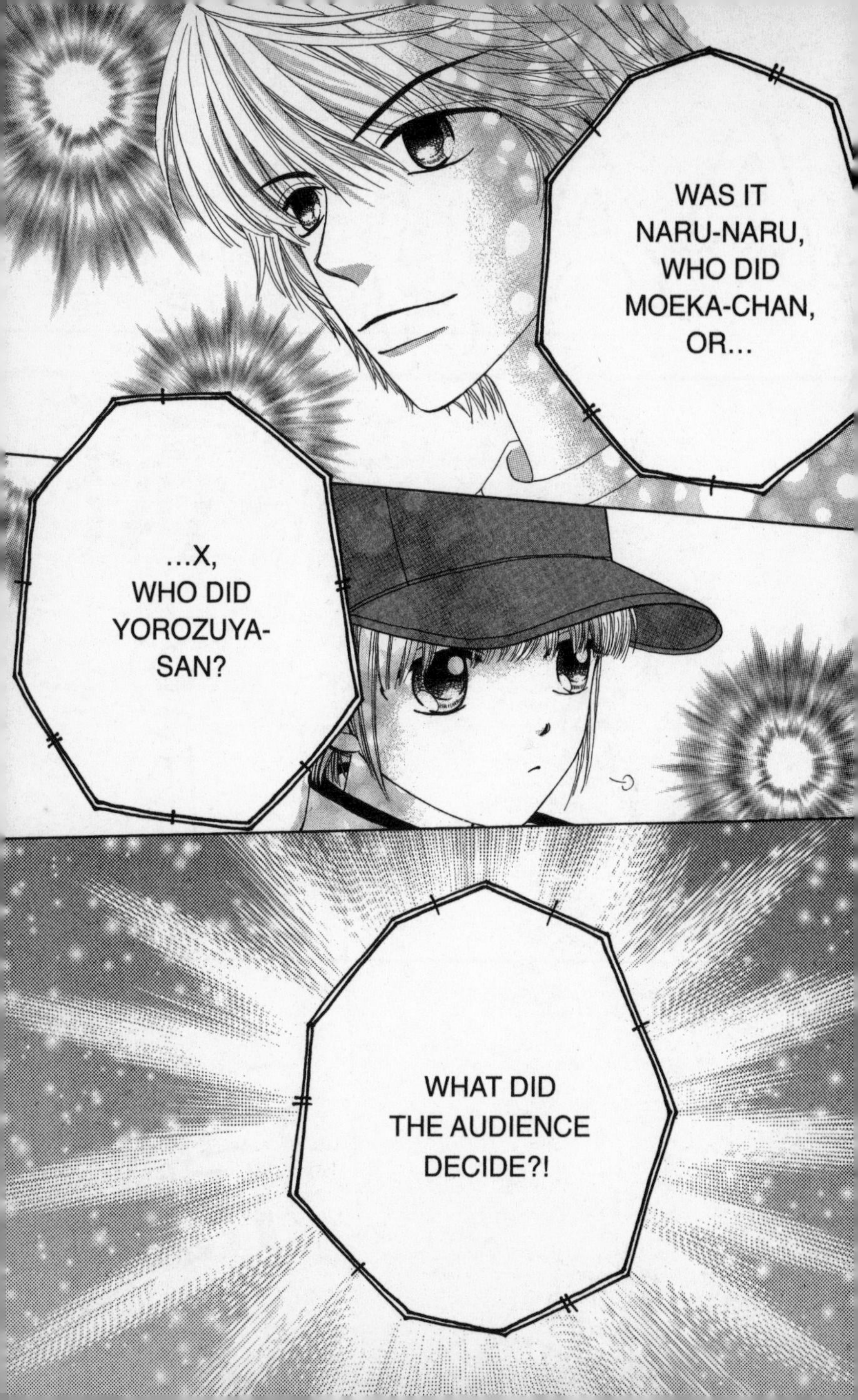
WAS IT NARU-NARU, WHO DID MOEKA-CHAN, OR...
...X, WHO DID YOROZUYA-SAN?
WHAT DID THE AUDIENCE DECIDE?!

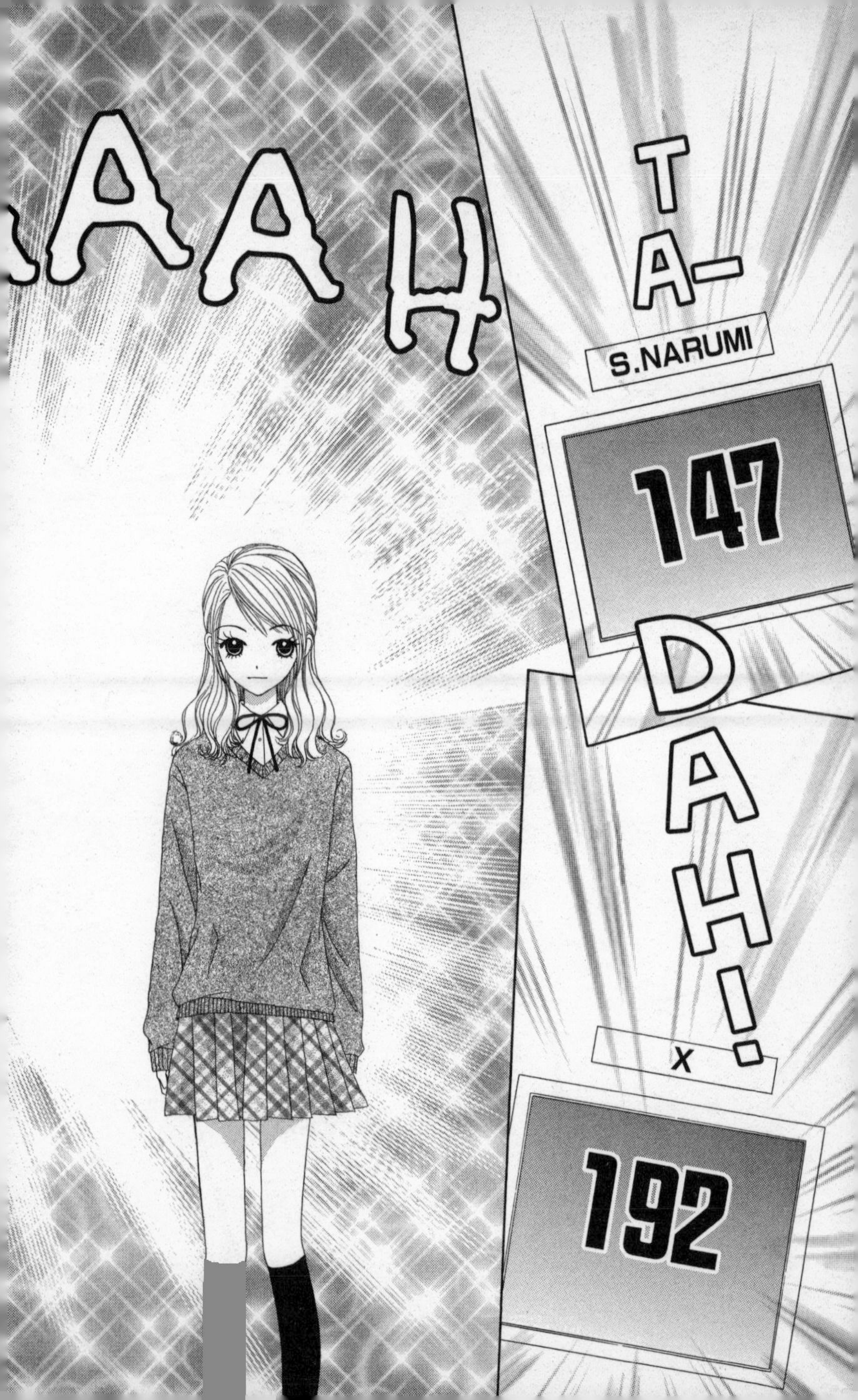

TA-
S.NARUMI
147
DAH!
X
192
AAH

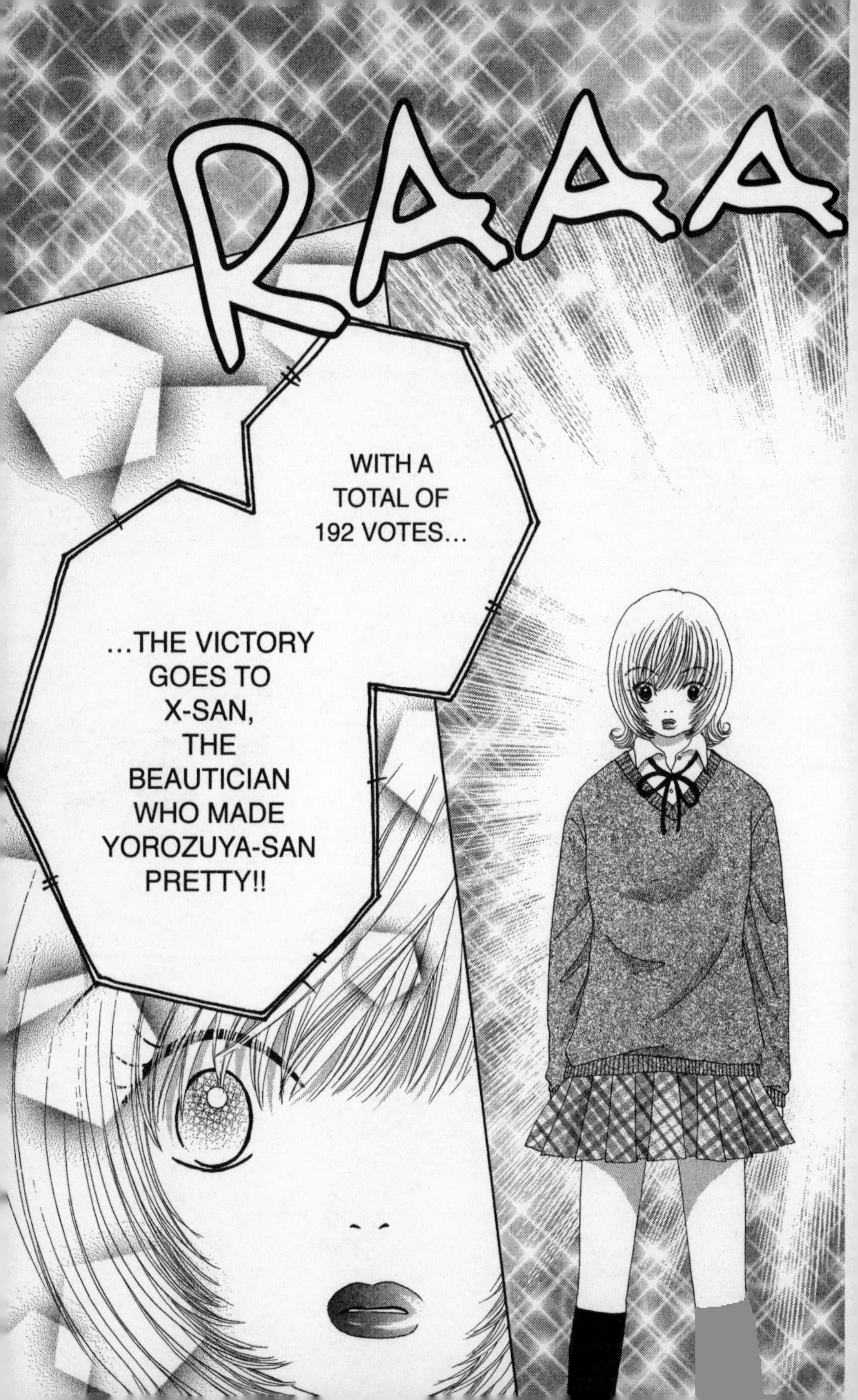
RAAA
WITH A TOTAL OF 192 VOTES...
...THE VICTORY GOES TO X-SAN, THE BEAUTICIAN WHO MADE YOROZUYA-SAN PRETTY!!

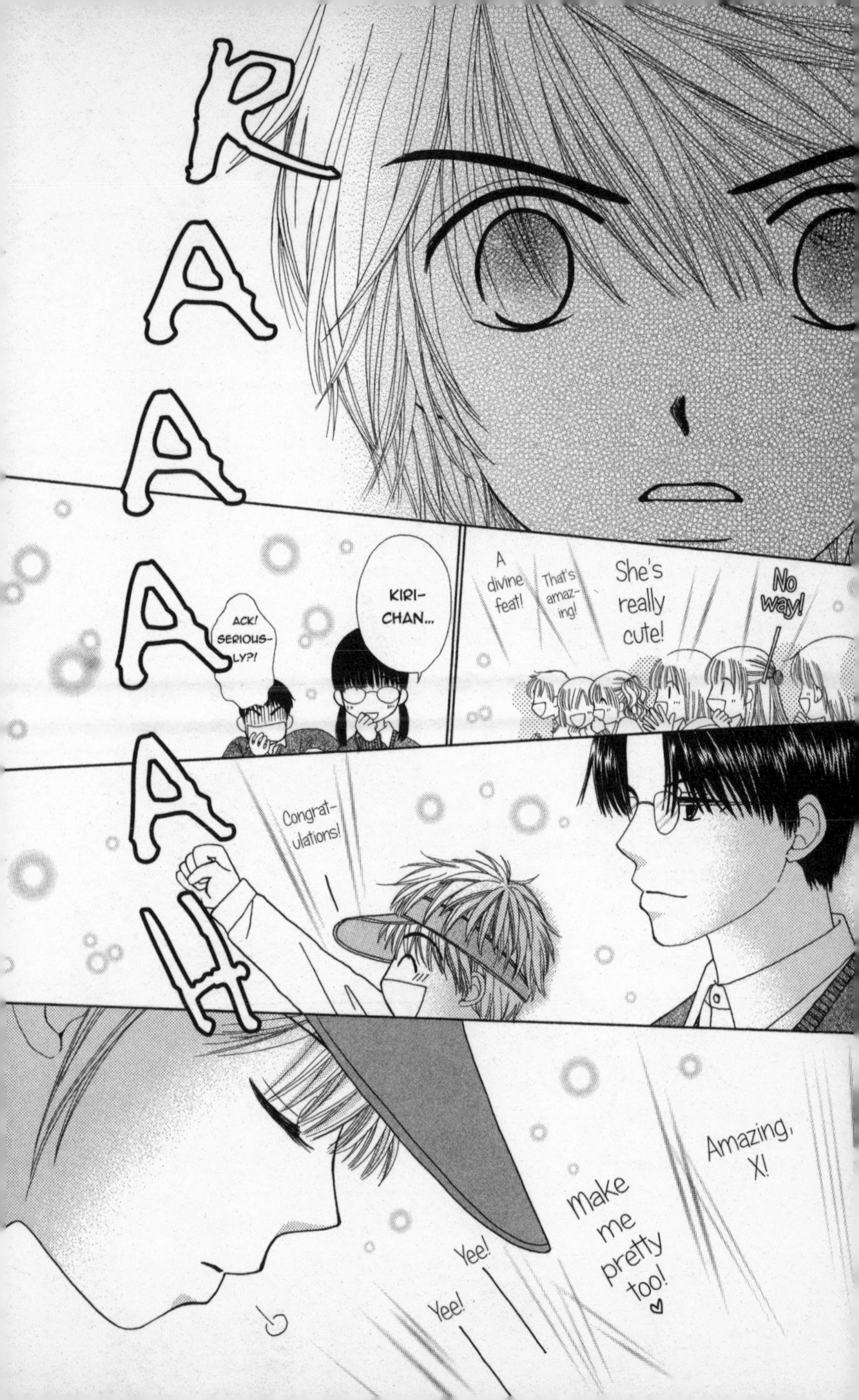
RAAAAH
No way!
She's really cute!
That's amazing!
A divine feat!
KIRI-CHAN...
ACK! SERIOUSLY?!
Congratulations!
Amazing, X!
Make me pretty too!
Yee!
Yee!

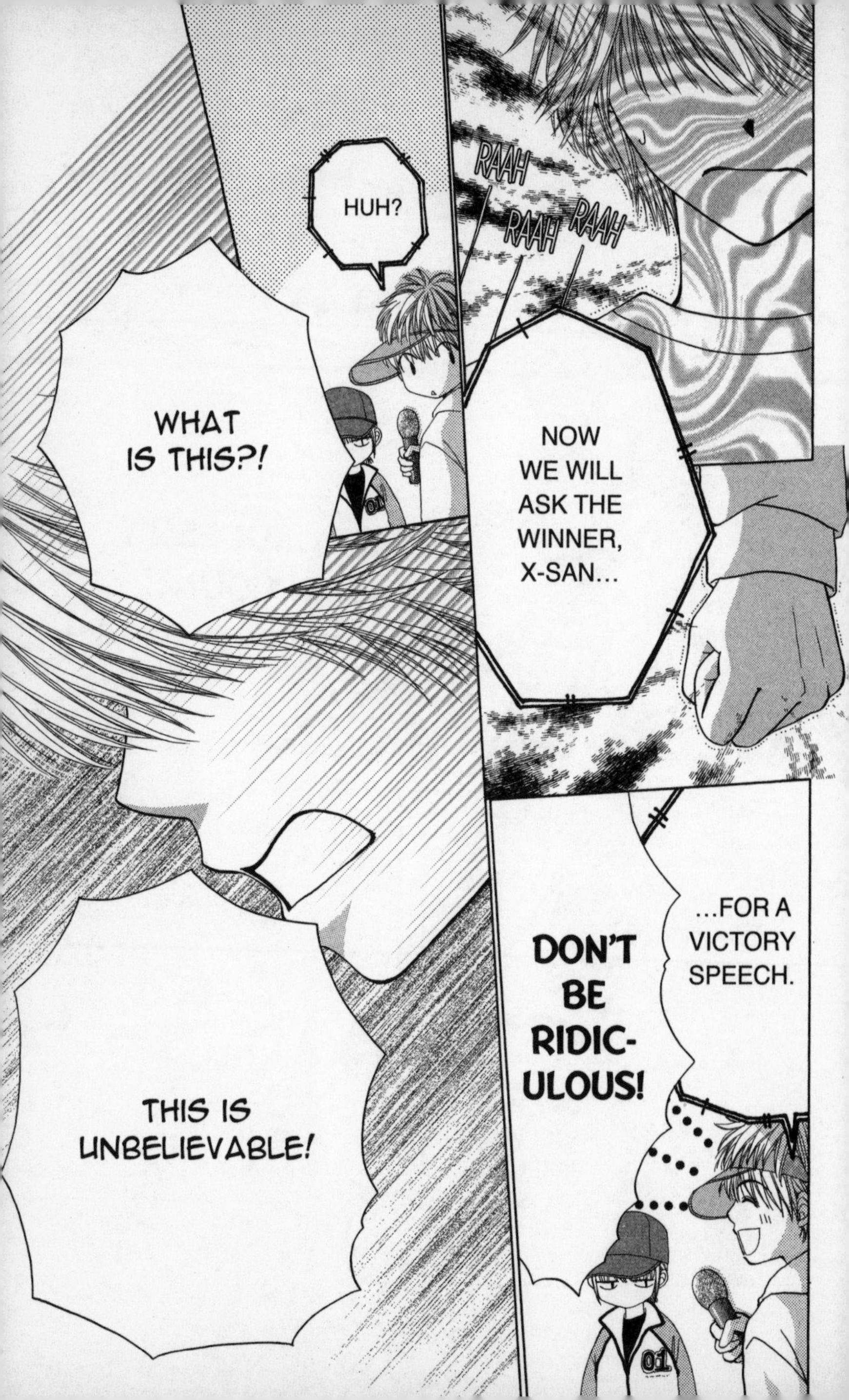
RAAH
RAAH
RAAH
NOW WE WILL ASK THE WINNER, X-SAN...
...FOR A VICTORY SPEECH.
DON'T BE RIDIC-ULOUS!
HUH?
WHAT IS THIS?!
THIS IS UNBELIEVABLE!

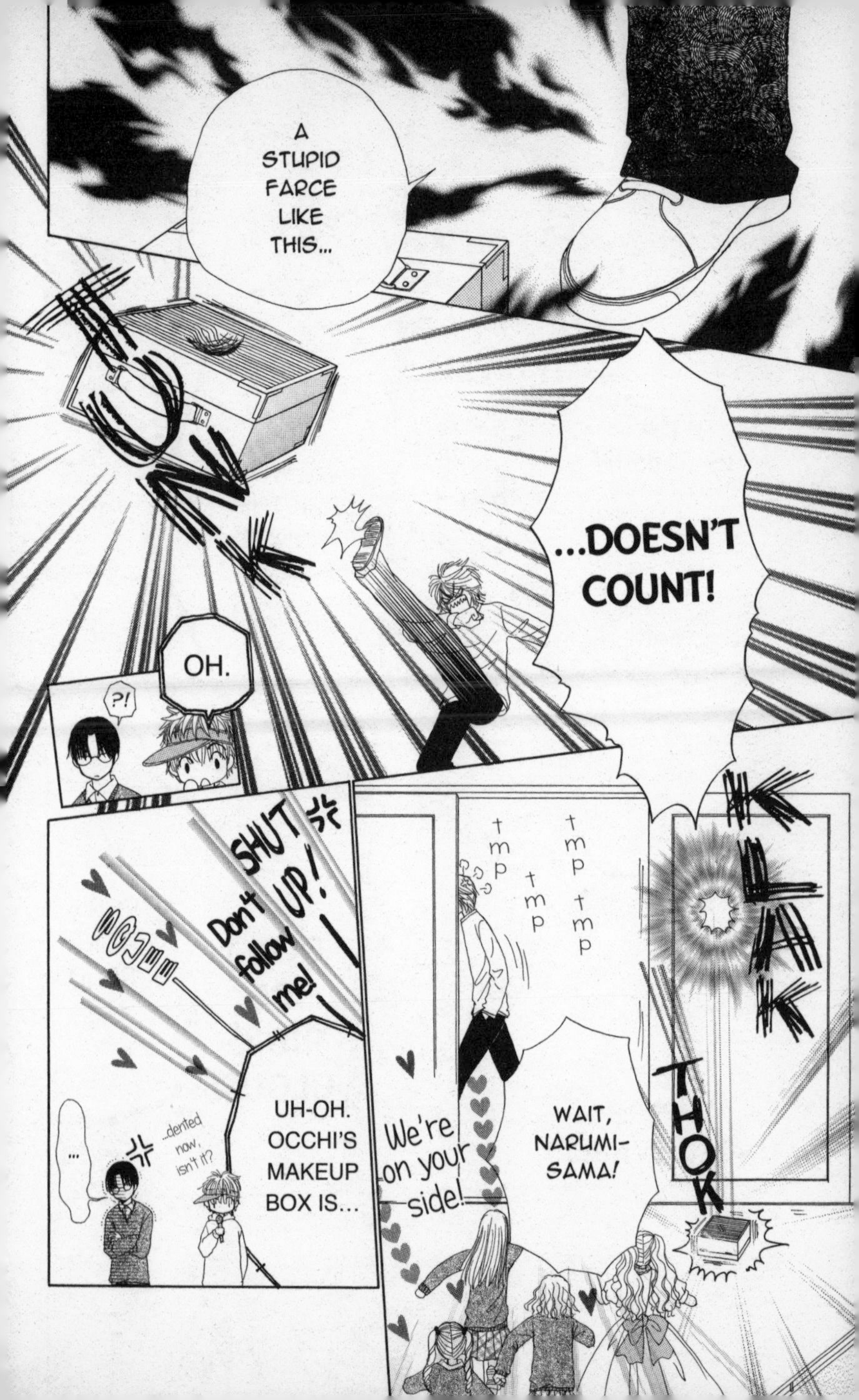
A STUPID FARCE LIKE THIS...
...DOESN'T COUNT!
OH.
?!
THOK
WAIT, NARUMI-SAMA!
We're on your side!
tmp tmp tmp tmp tmp
SHUT UP!
Don't follow me!
UH-OH. OCCHI'S MAKEUP BOX IS...
...dented now, isn't it?
...

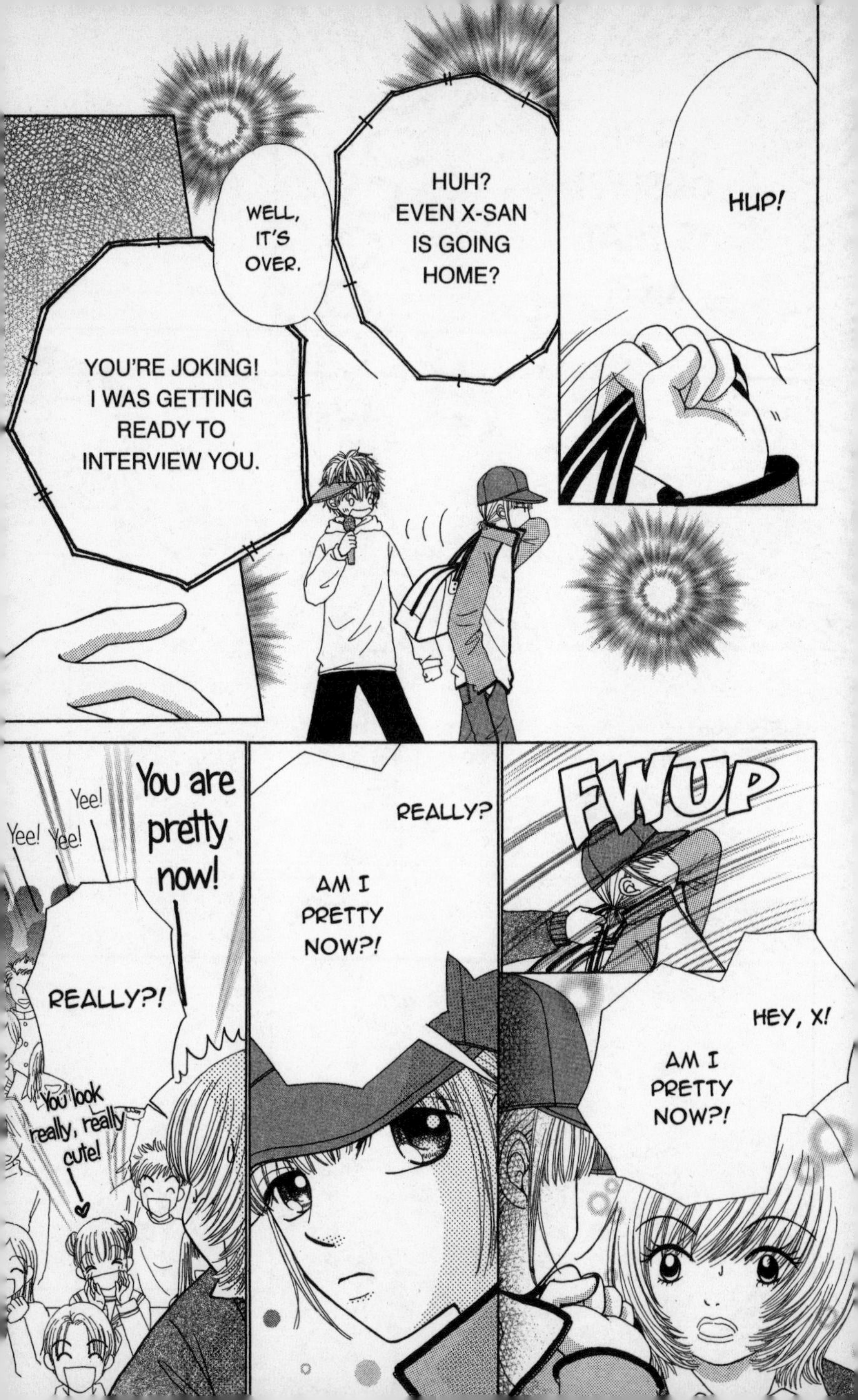
HUP!
HUH? EVEN X-SAN IS GOING HOME?
WELL, IT'S OVER.
YOU'RE JOKING! I WAS GETTING READY TO INTERVIEW YOU.
FWUP
HEY, X!
AM I PRETTY NOW?!
REALLY?
AM I PRETTY NOW?!
You are pretty now!
Yee!
Yee!
Yee!
REALLY?!
You look really, really cute!

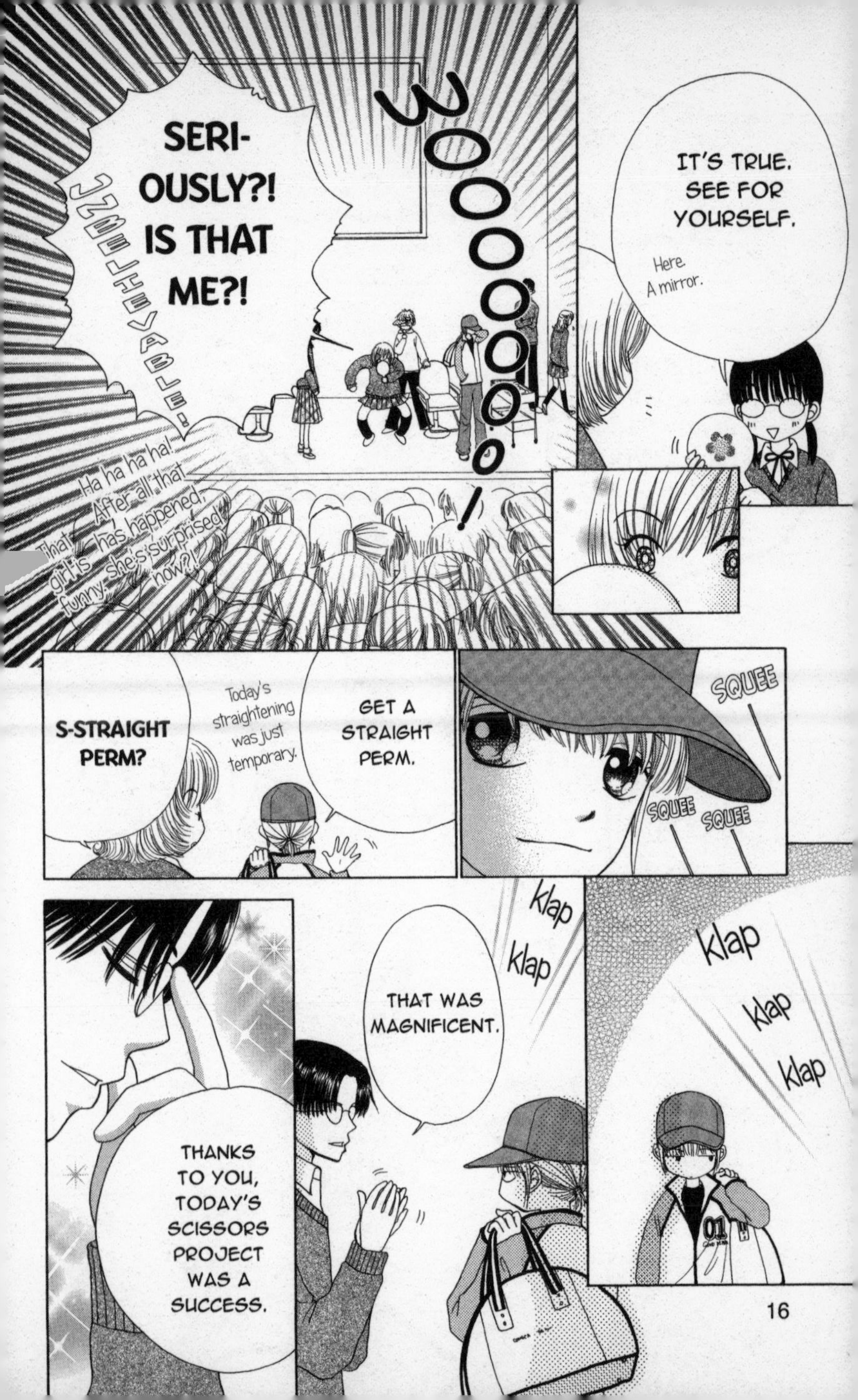
IT'S TRUE. SEE FOR YOURSELF.
Here. A mirror.
SERI-OUSLY?! IS THAT ME?!
UNBELIEVABLE!
WOOOOOOOO!
Ha ha ha ha! That girl's funny. After all that has happened, she's surprised now?!
SQUEE
SQUEE SQUEE
GET A STRAIGHT PERM.
Today's straightening was just temporary.
S-STRAIGHT PERM?
Klap
klap
klap
klap
klap
THAT WAS MAGNIFICENT.
THANKS TO YOU, TODAY'S SCISSORS PROJECT WAS A SUCCESS.

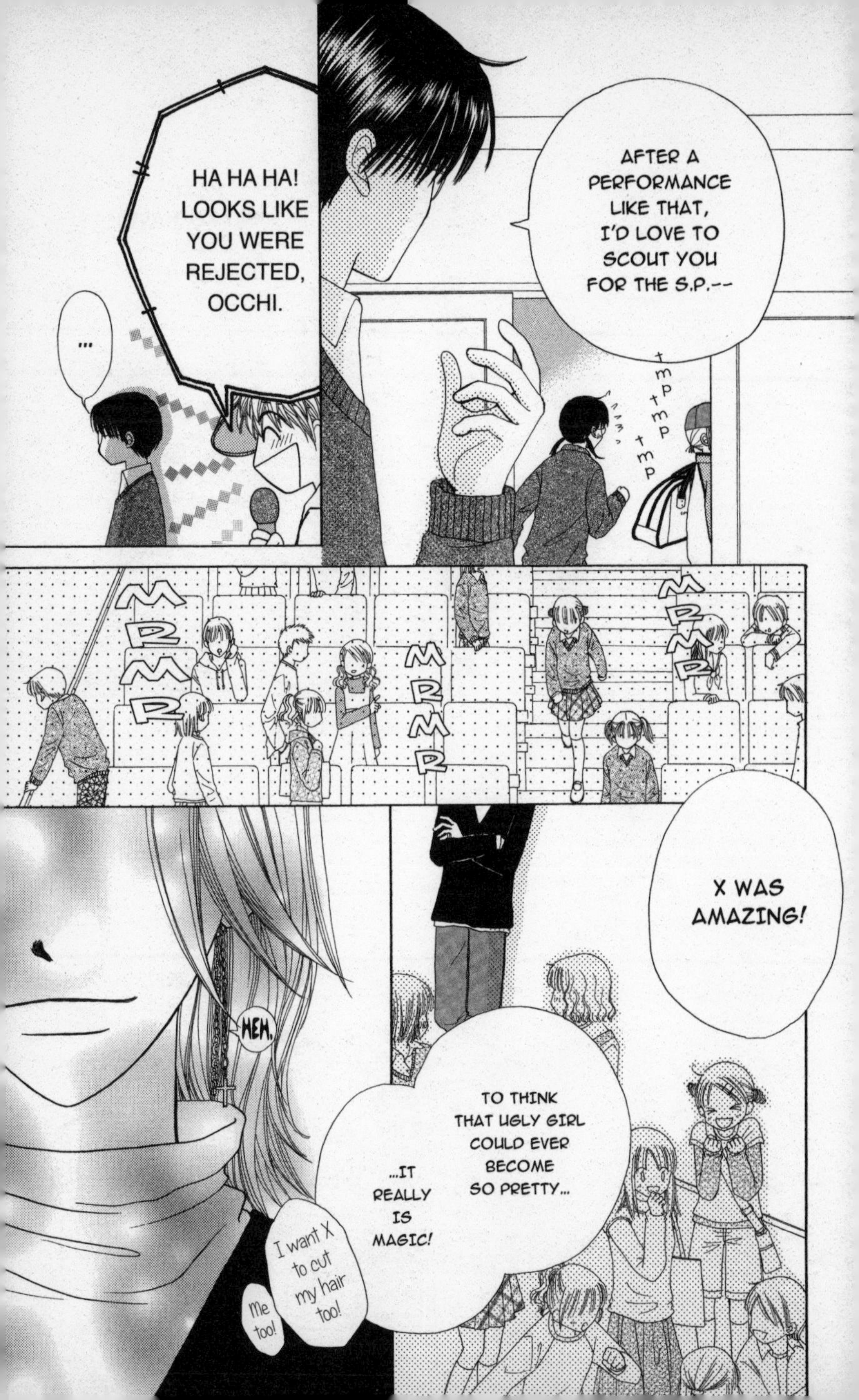
AFTER A PERFORMANCE LIKE THAT, I'D LOVE TO SCOUT YOU FOR THE S.P.--
tmp tmp tmp tmp
HA HA HA! LOOKS LIKE YOU WERE REJECTED, OCCHI.
...
MRMR
MRMR
MRMR
X WAS AMAZING!
TO THINK THAT UGLY GIRL COULD EVER BECOME SO PRETTY...
...IT REALLY IS MAGIC!
I want X to cut my hair too!
Me too!
HEH.

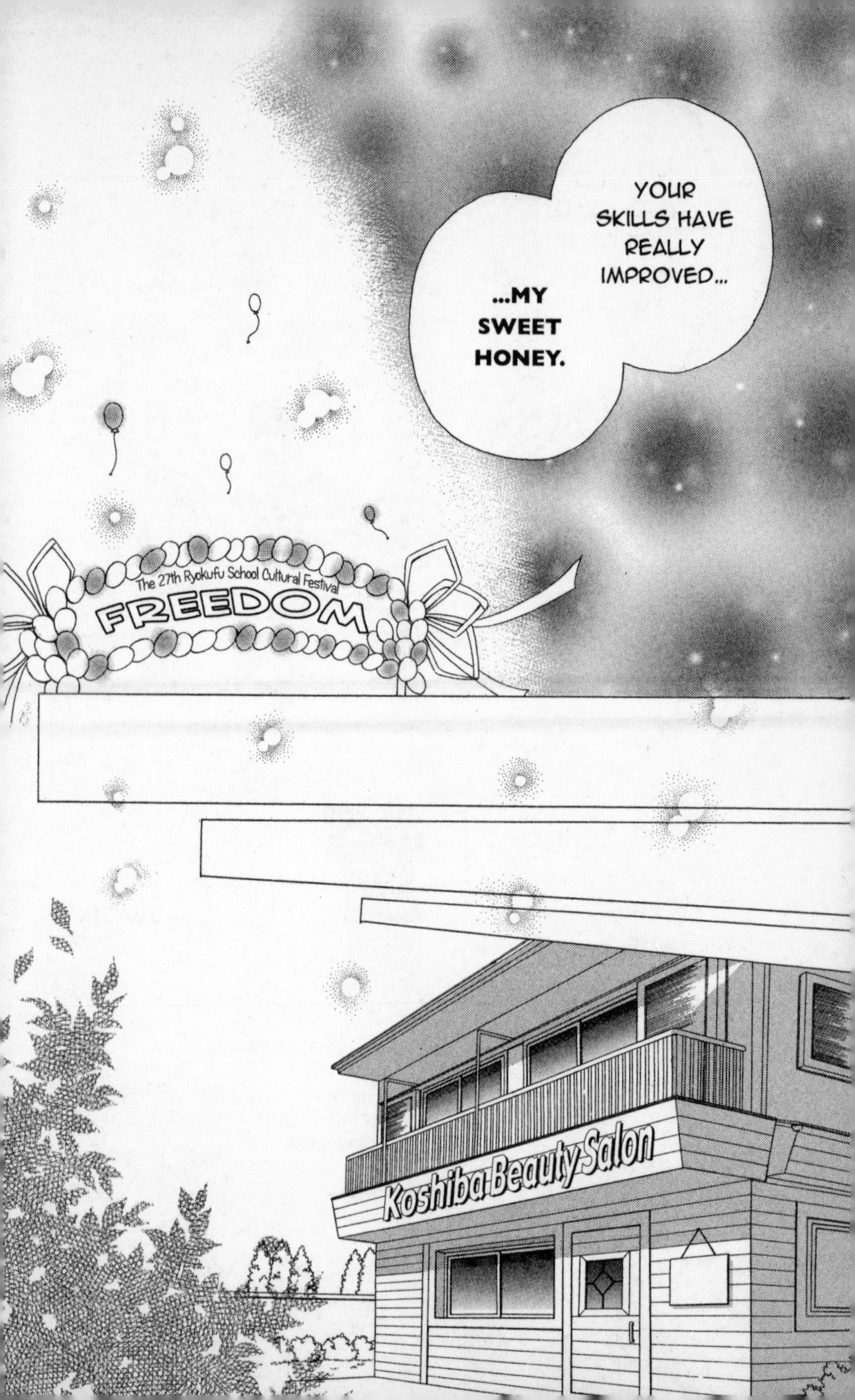
YOUR SKILLS HAVE REALLY IMPROVED...
...MY SWEET HONEY.
The 27th Ryokufu School Cultural Festival
FREEDOM
Koshiba Beauty Salon

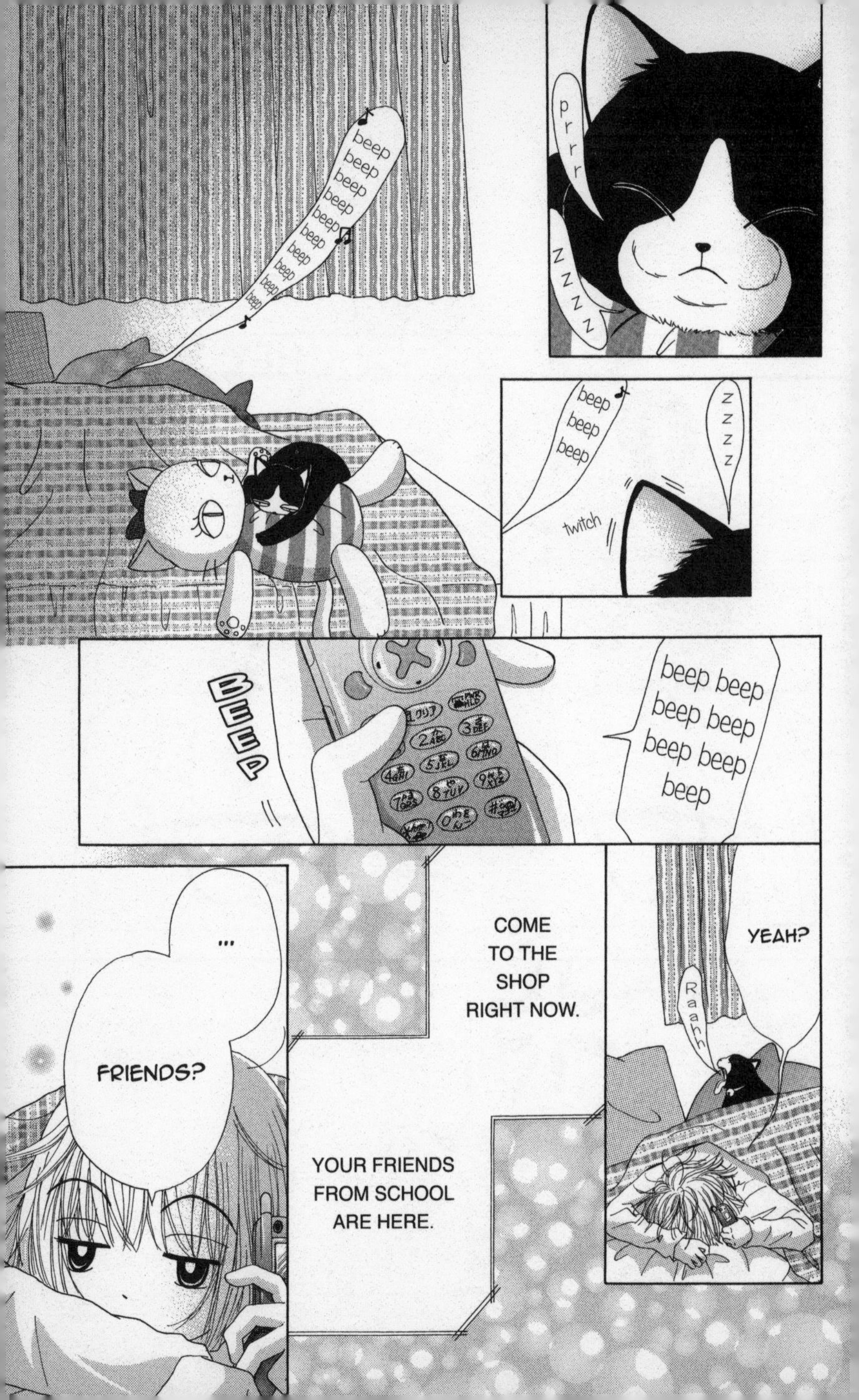
prrr
ZZZZ
beep beep beep beep beep beep beep beep beep beep
ZZZZ
beep beep beep
twitch
beep beep beep beep beep beep beep
BEEP
YEAH?
Raahn
COME TO THE SHOP RIGHT NOW.
YOUR FRIENDS FROM SCHOOL ARE HERE.
...
FRIENDS?

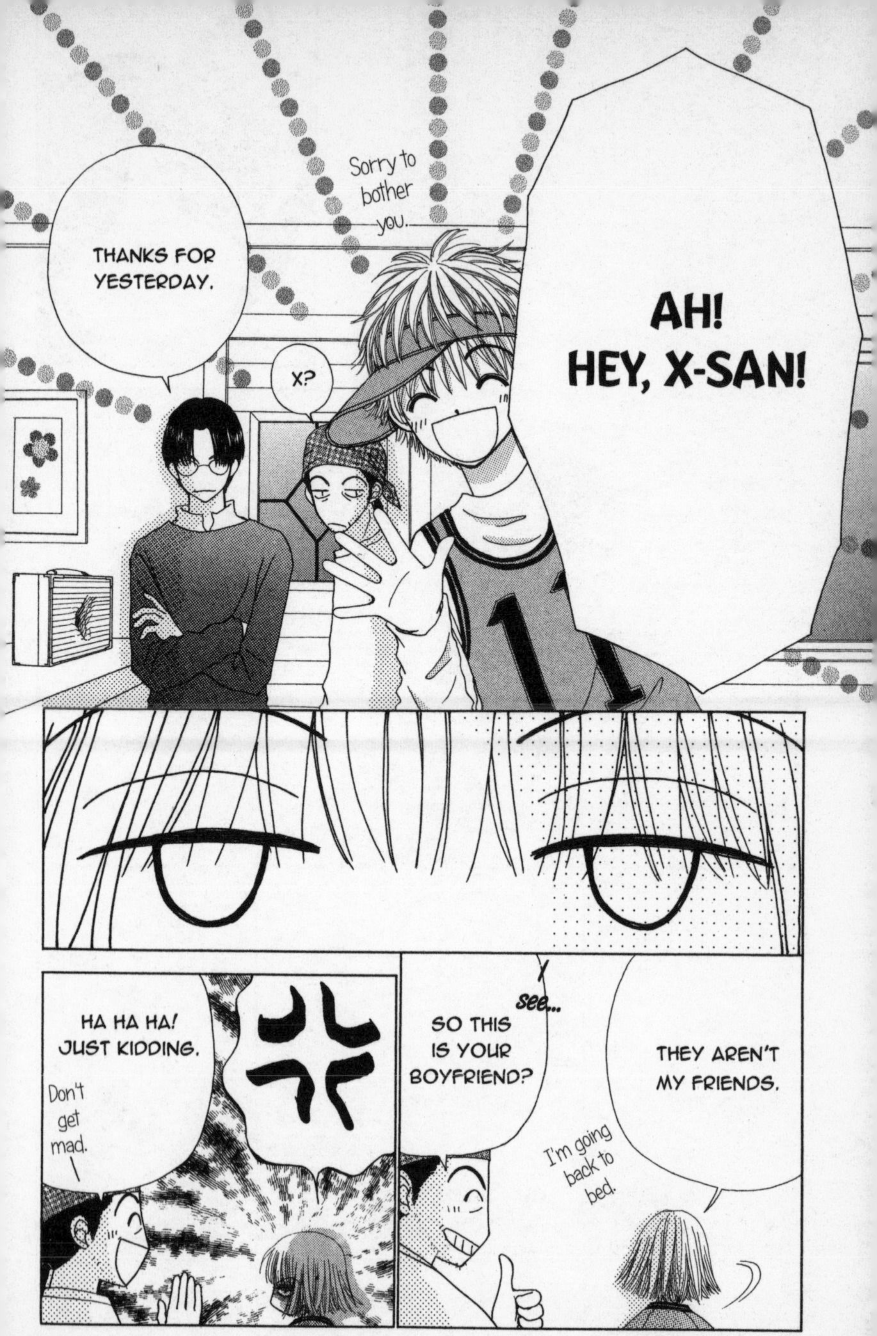
AH! HEY, X-SAN!
Sorry to bother you.
THANKS FOR YESTERDAY.
X?
THEY AREN'T MY FRIENDS.
I'm going back to bed.
I see...
SO THIS IS YOUR BOYFRIEND?
HA HA HA! JUST KIDDING.
Don't get mad.

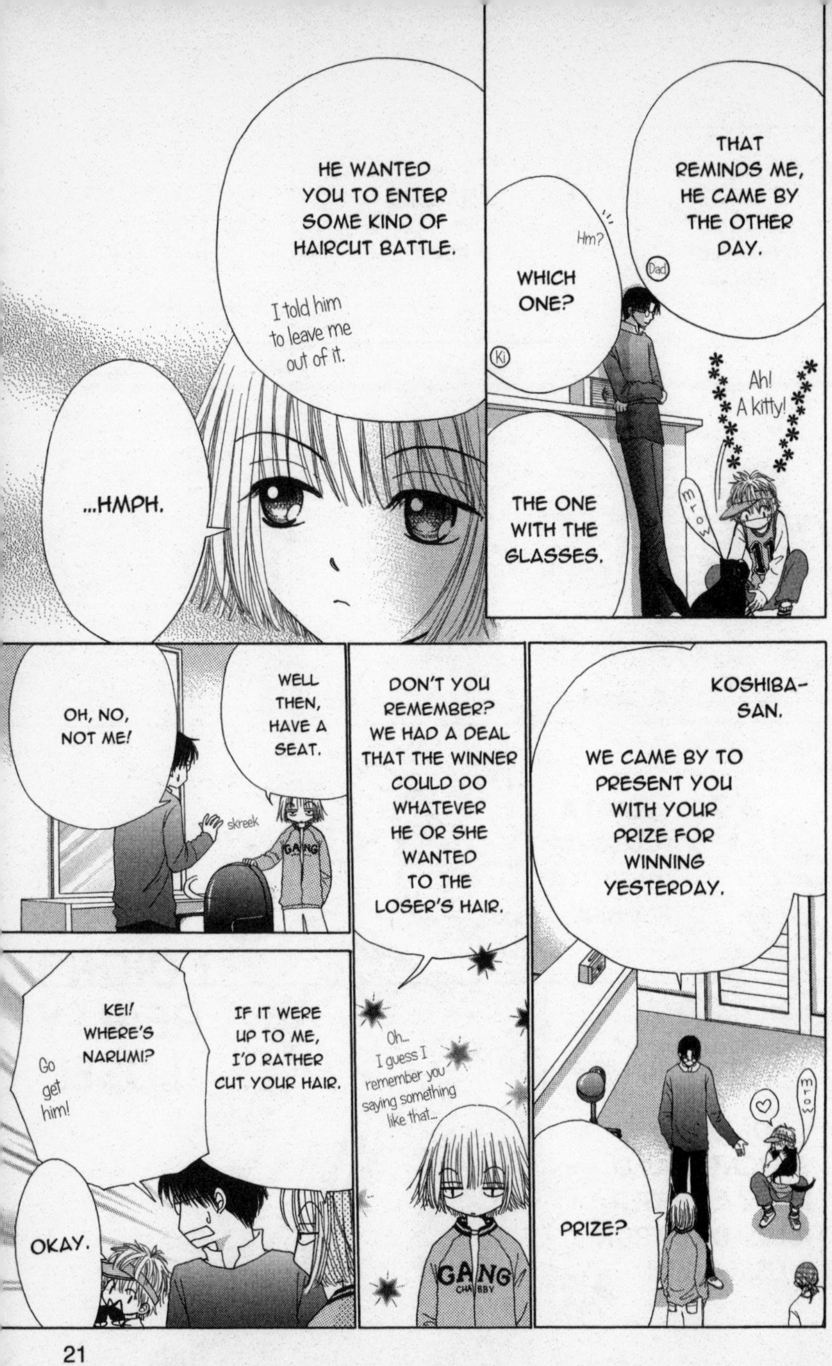
THAT REMINDS ME, HE CAME BY THE OTHER DAY.
Dad
Hm?
WHICH ONE?
Ki
Ah! A kitty!
mrow
THE ONE WITH THE GLASSES.
HE WANTED YOU TO ENTER SOME KIND OF HAIRCUT BATTLE.
I told him to leave me out of it.
...HMPH.
KOSHIBA-SAN.
WE CAME BY TO PRESENT YOU WITH YOUR PRIZE FOR WINNING YESTERDAY.
mrow
PRIZE?
DON'T YOU REMEMBER? WE HAD A DEAL THAT THE WINNER COULD DO WHATEVER HE OR SHE WANTED TO THE LOSER'S HAIR.
Oh... I guess I remember you saying something like that...
GANG
WELL THEN, HAVE A SEAT.
OH, NO, NOT ME!
skreek
GANG
IF IT WERE UP TO ME, I'D RATHER CUT YOUR HAIR.
KEI! WHERE'S NARUMI?
Go get him!
OKAY.

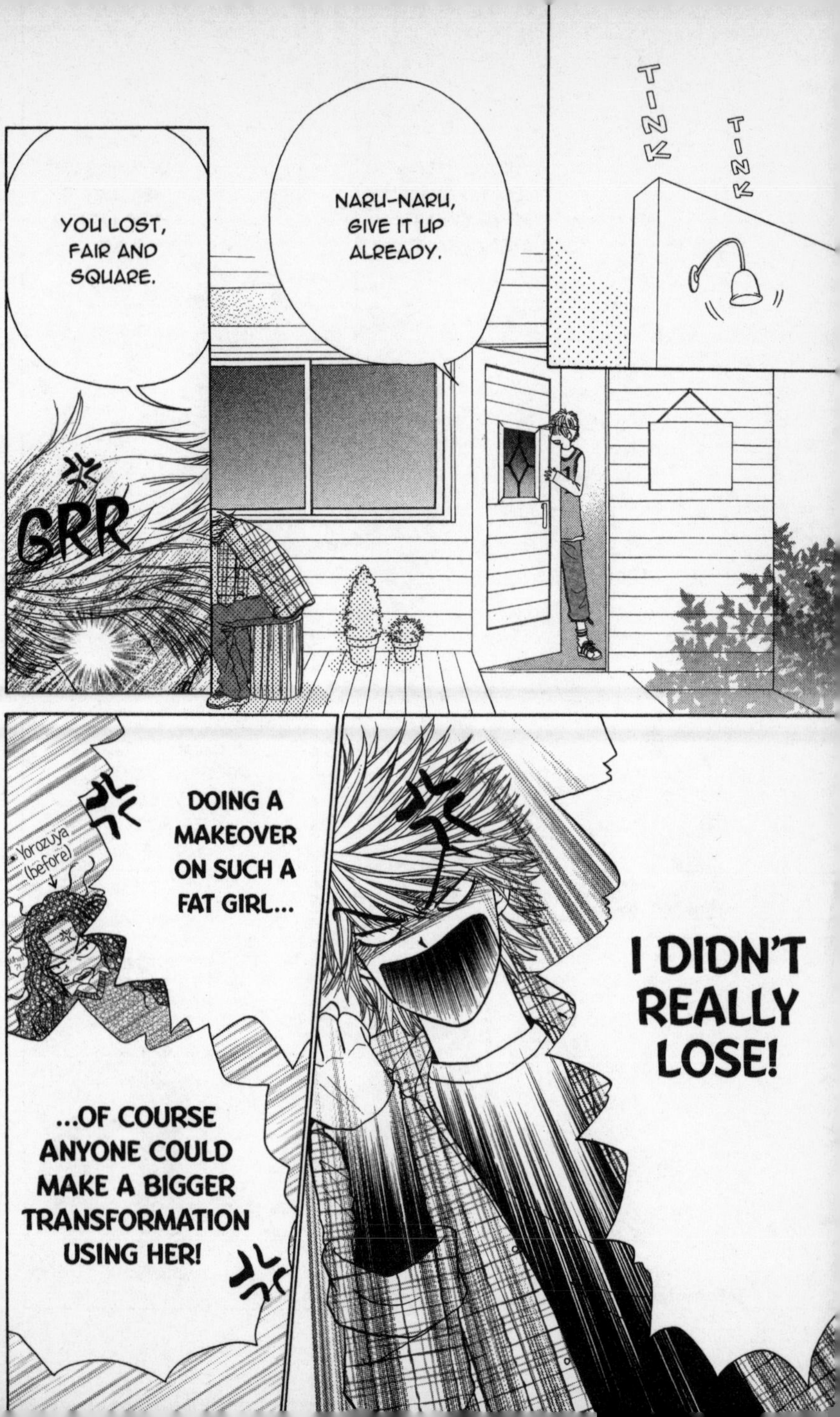
TINK
TINK
NARU-NARU, GIVE IT UP ALREADY.
YOU LOST, FAIR AND SQUARE.
GRR
I DIDN'T REALLY LOSE!
DOING A MAKEOVER ON SUCH A FAT GIRL...
Yorozuya (before)
...OF COURSE ANYONE COULD MAKE A BIGGER TRANSFORMATION USING HER!

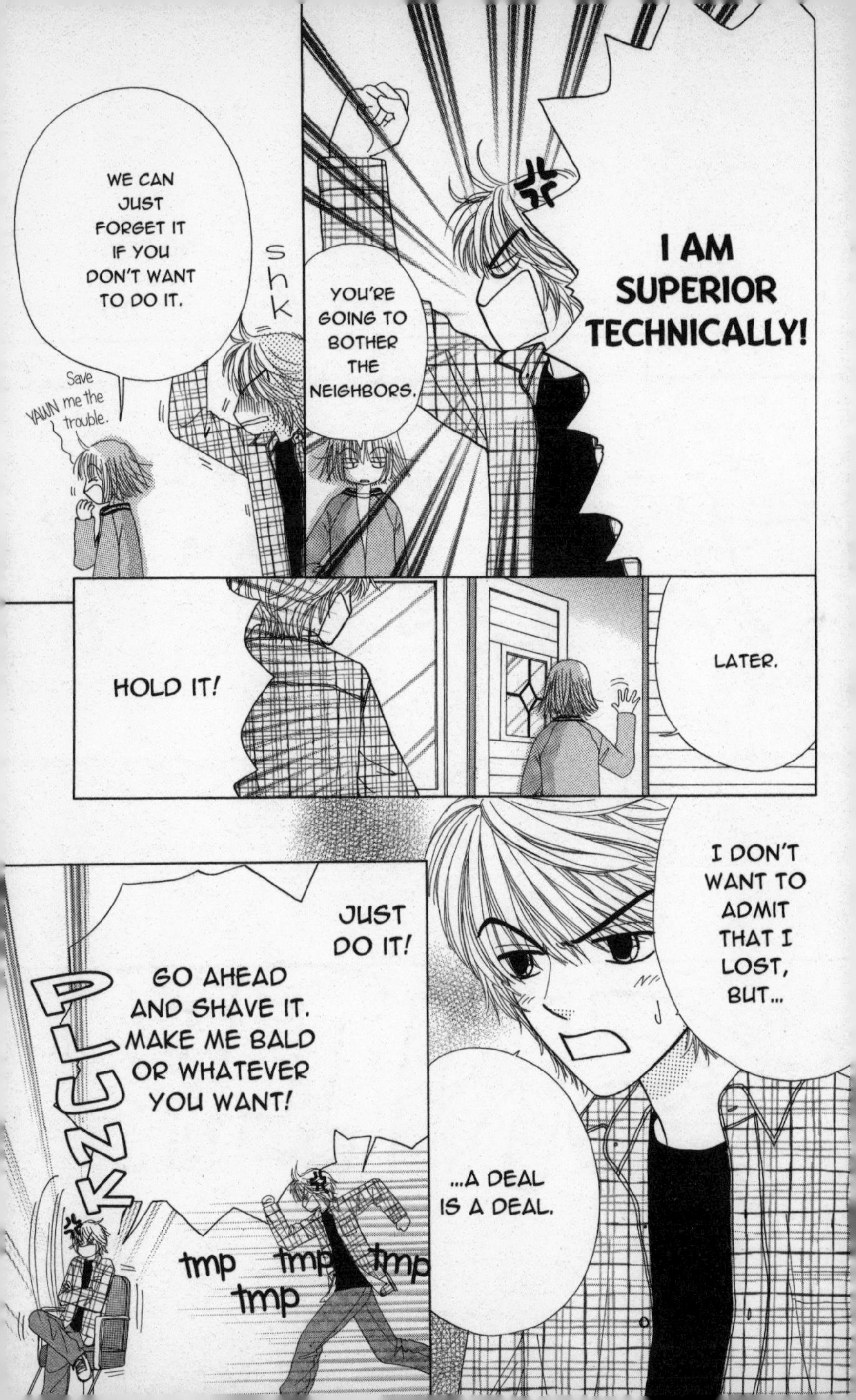
I AM SUPERIOR TECHNICALLY!
YOU'RE GOING TO BOTHER THE NEIGHBORS.
shk
WE CAN JUST FORGET IT IF YOU DON'T WANT TO DO IT.
YAWN
Save me the trouble.
LATER.
HOLD IT!
I DON'T WANT TO ADMIT THAT I LOST, BUT...
...A DEAL IS A DEAL.
JUST DO IT!
GO AHEAD AND SHAVE IT. MAKE ME BALD OR WHATEVER YOU WANT!
PLUNK
tmp tmp tmp tmp

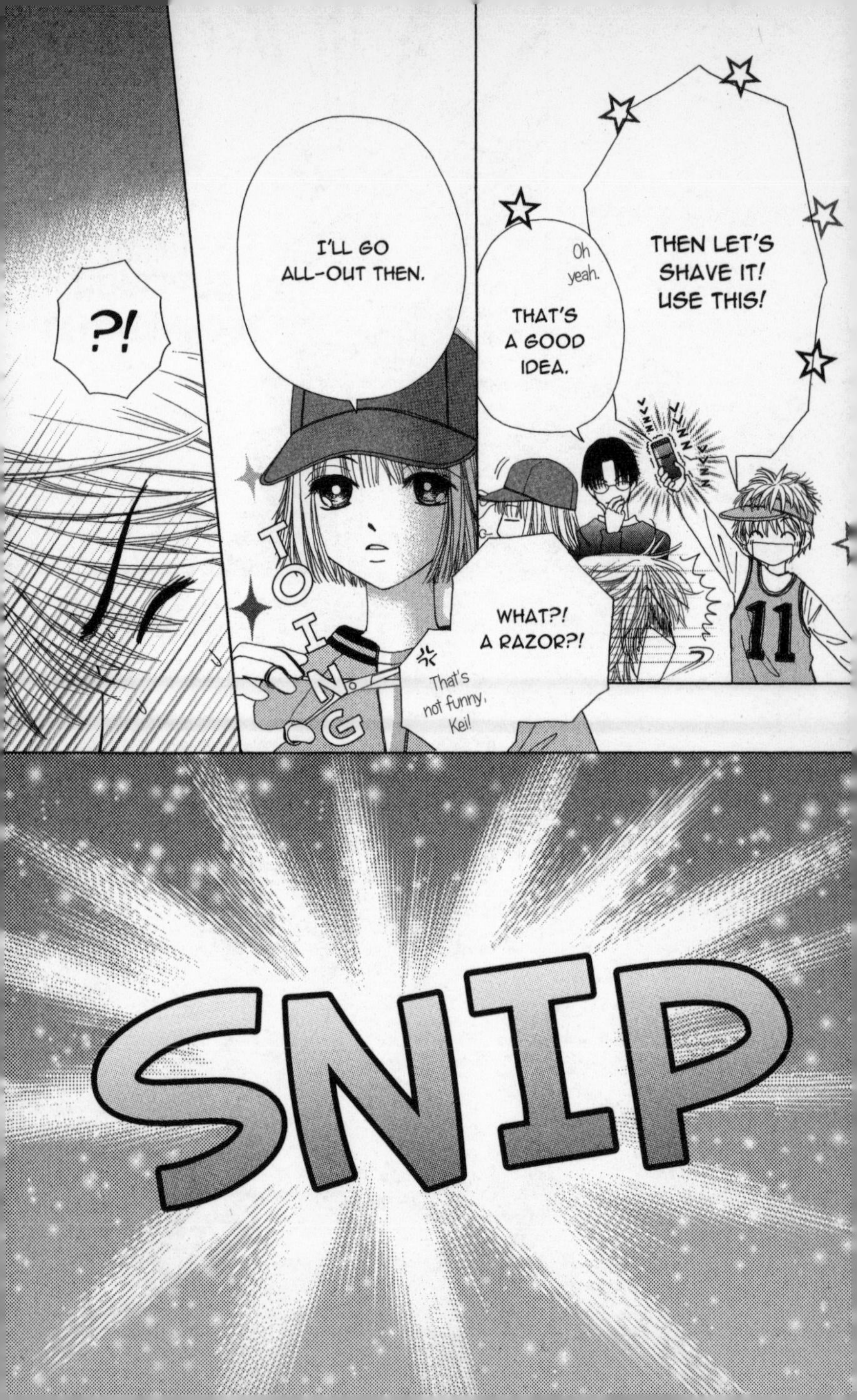
THEN LET'S SHAVE IT! USE THIS!
Oh yeah.
THAT'S A GOOD IDEA.
WHAT?! A RAZOR?!
That's not funny, Kei!
I'LL GO ALL-OUT THEN.
TOING
?!
SNIP

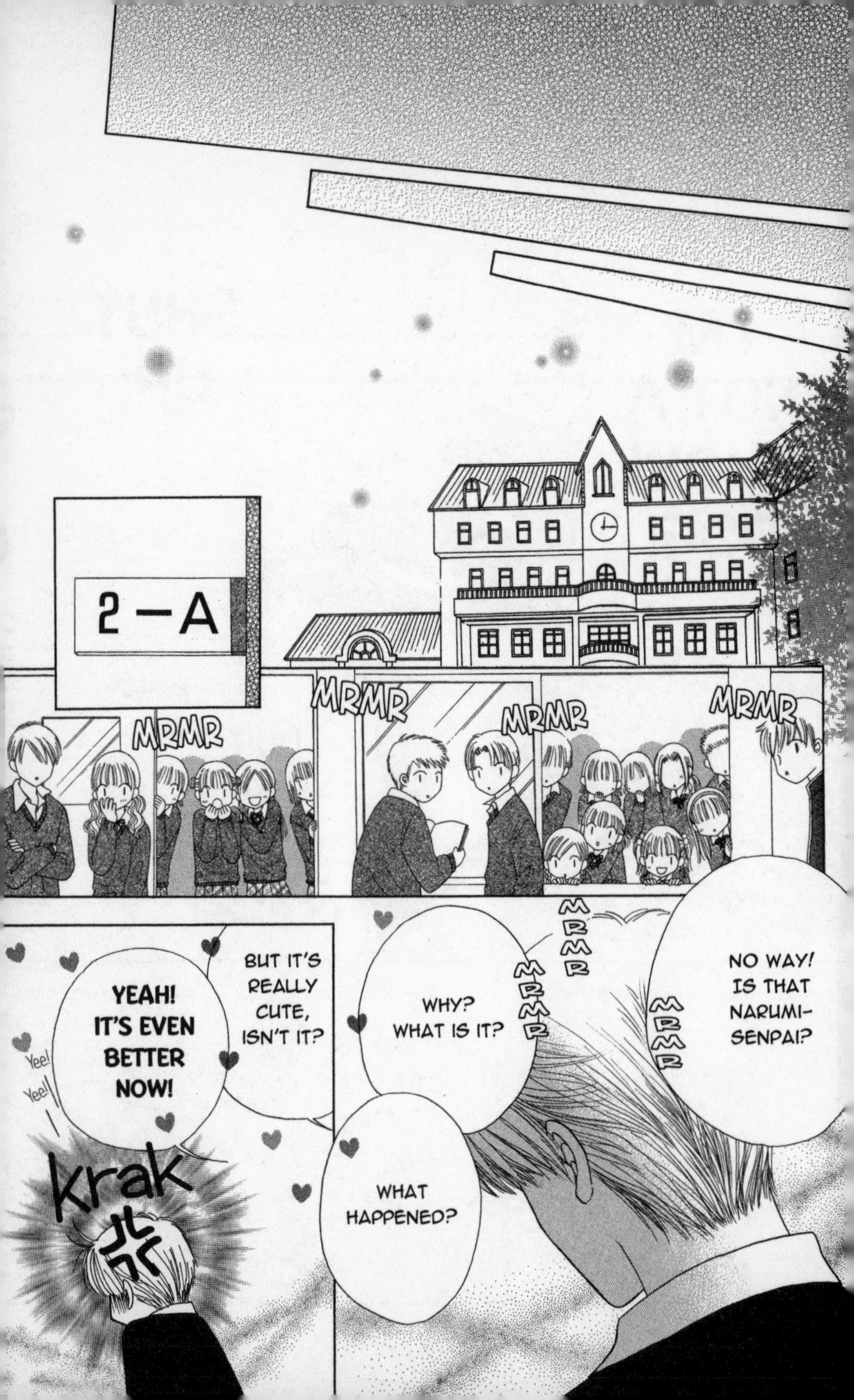
MRMR
MRMR
MRMR
2-A
MRMR
NO WAY! IS THAT NARUMI-SENPAI?
MRMR
MRMR
MRMR
WHY? WHAT IS IT?
WHAT HAPPENED?
BUT IT'S REALLY CUTE, ISN'T IT?
YEAH! IT'S EVEN BETTER NOW!
Yee! Yee!
Krak

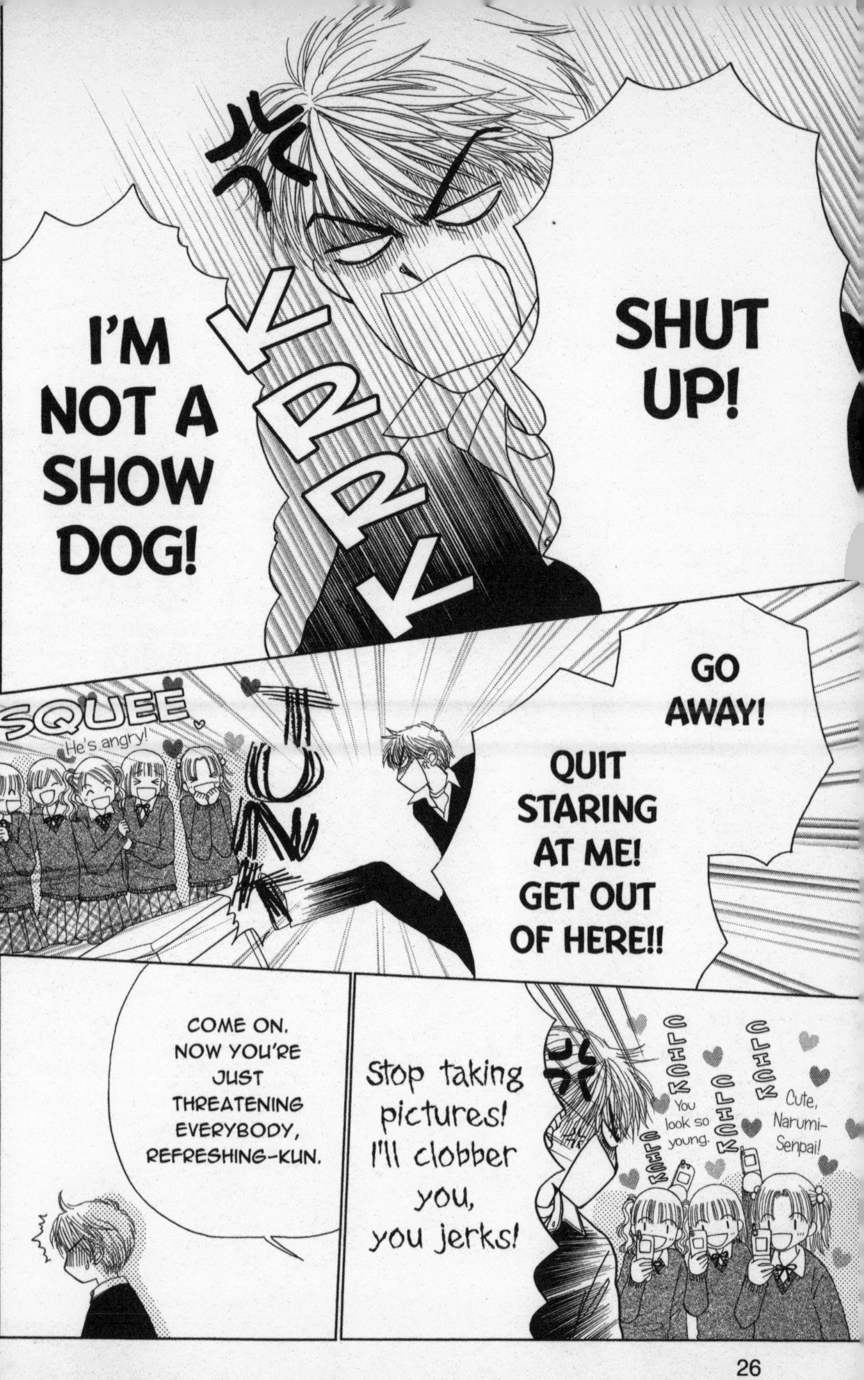
SHUT UP!
I'M NOT A SHOW DOG!
GO AWAY!
QUIT STARING AT ME! GET OUT OF HERE!!
SQUEE
He's angry!
Stop taking pictures! I'll clobber you, you jerks!
CLICK
CLICK
Cute, Narumi-Senpai!
You look so young.
CLICK
CLICK
COME ON. NOW YOU'RE JUST THREATENING EVERYBODY, REFRESHING-KUN.

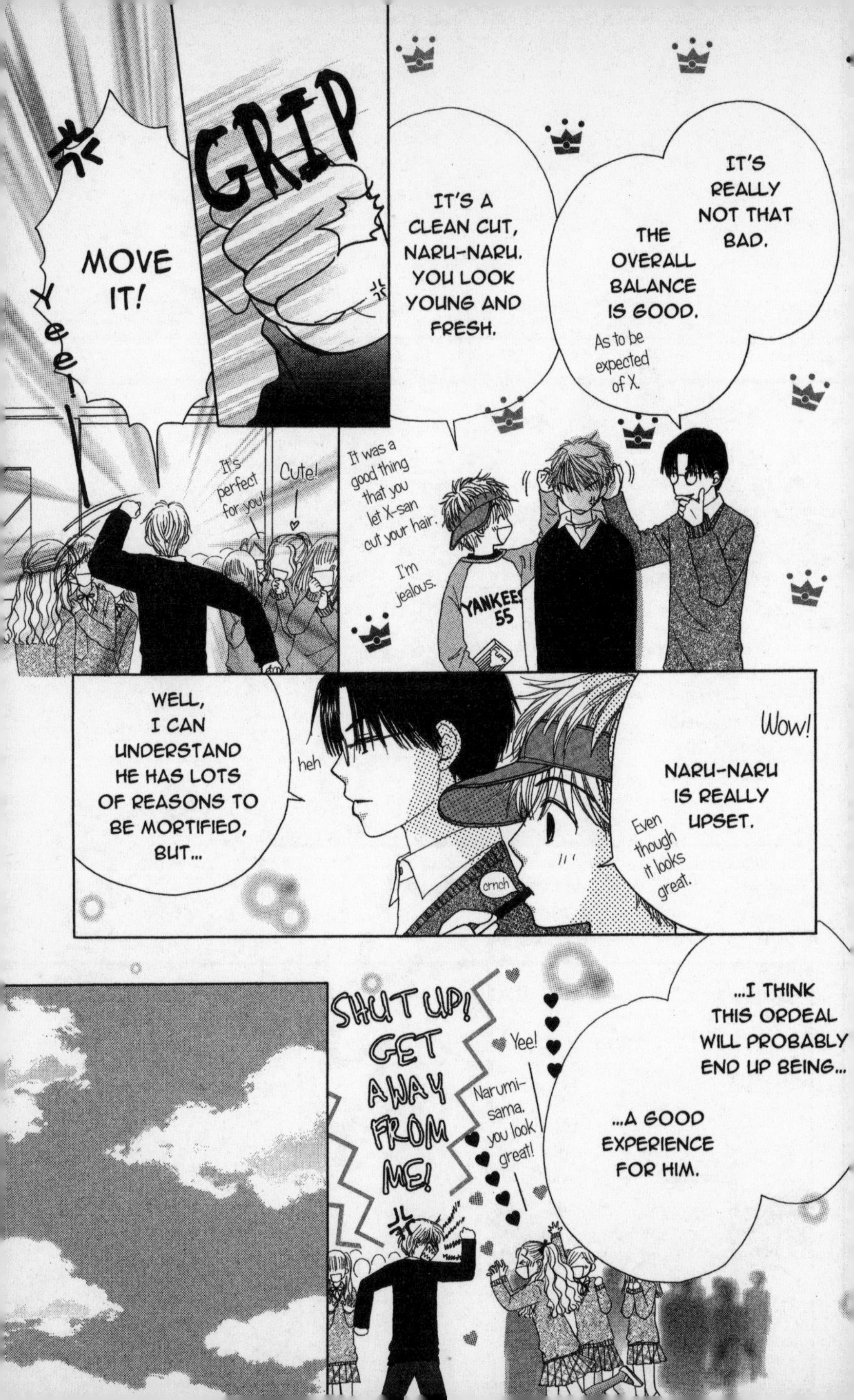
IT'S REALLY NOT THAT BAD.
THE OVERALL BALANCE IS GOOD.
As to be expected of X.
IT'S A CLEAN CUT, NARU-NARU. YOU LOOK YOUNG AND FRESH.
It was a good thing that you let X-san cut your hair.
I'm jealous.
YANKEES 55
GRIP
MOVE IT!
Yeee!
It's perfect for you!
Cute!
Wow!
NARU-NARU IS REALLY UPSET.
Even though it looks great.
crnch
heh
WELL, I CAN UNDERSTAND HE HAS LOTS OF REASONS TO BE MORTIFIED, BUT...
...I THINK THIS ORDEAL WILL PROBABLY END UP BEING...
...A GOOD EXPERIENCE FOR HIM.
Yee!
Narumi-sama, you look great!
SHUT UP! GET AWAY FROM ME!

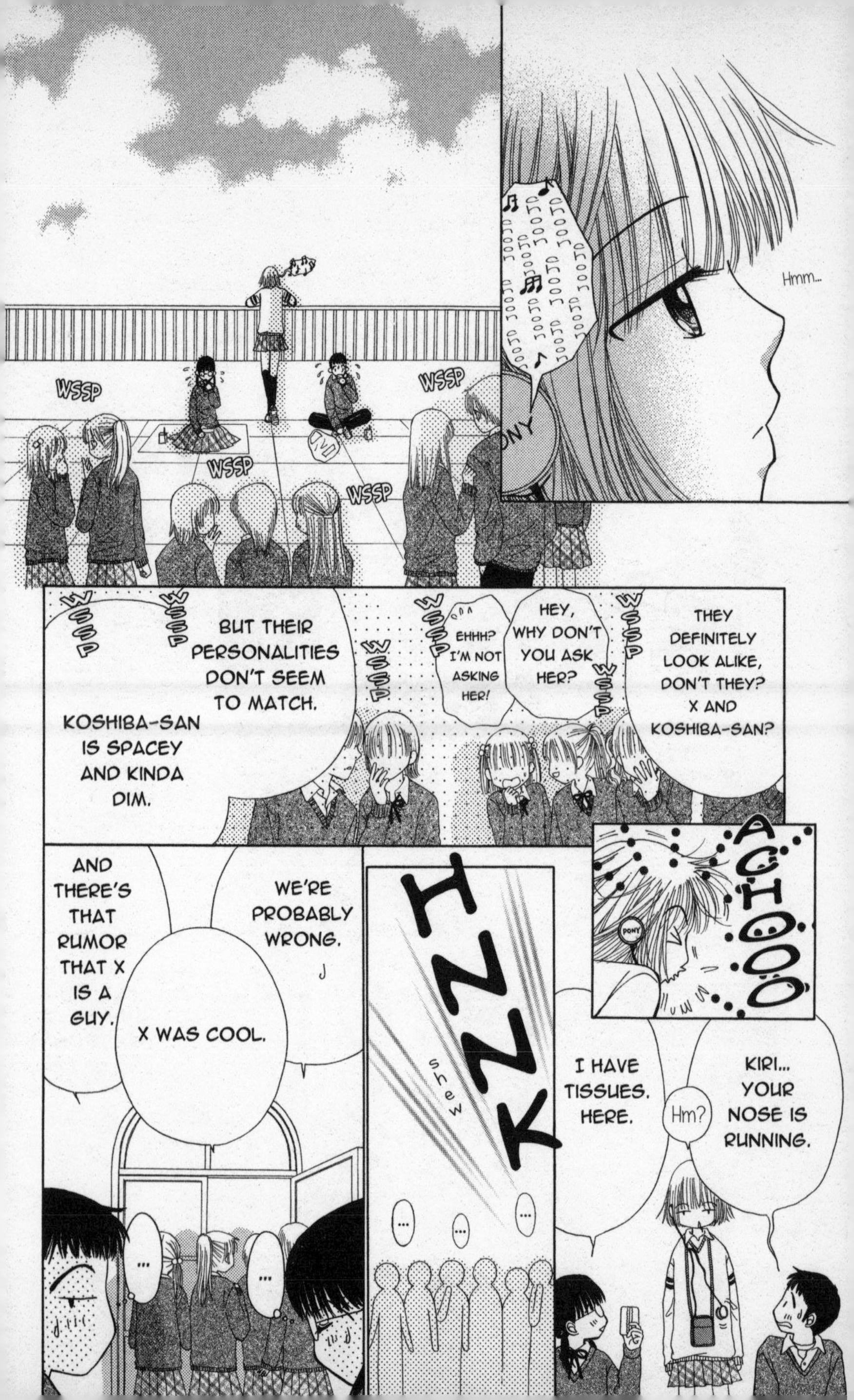
Hmm...
PONY
WSSP
WSSP
WSSP
WSSP
THEY DEFINITELY LOOK ALIKE, DON'T THEY? X AND KOSHIBA-SAN?
WSSP
HEY, WHY DON'T YOU ASK HER?
WSSP
EHHH? I'M NOT ASKING HER!
WSSP
WSSP
BUT THEIR PERSONALITIES DON'T SEEM TO MATCH.
KOSHIBA-SAN IS SPACEY AND KINDA DIM.
ACHOOOO
PONY
KIRI... YOUR NOSE IS RUNNING.
Hm?
I HAVE TISSUES. HERE.
HNNK
shew
...
...
...
WE'RE PROBABLY WRONG.
AND THERE'S THAT RUMOR THAT X IS A GUY.
X WAS COOL.
...
...

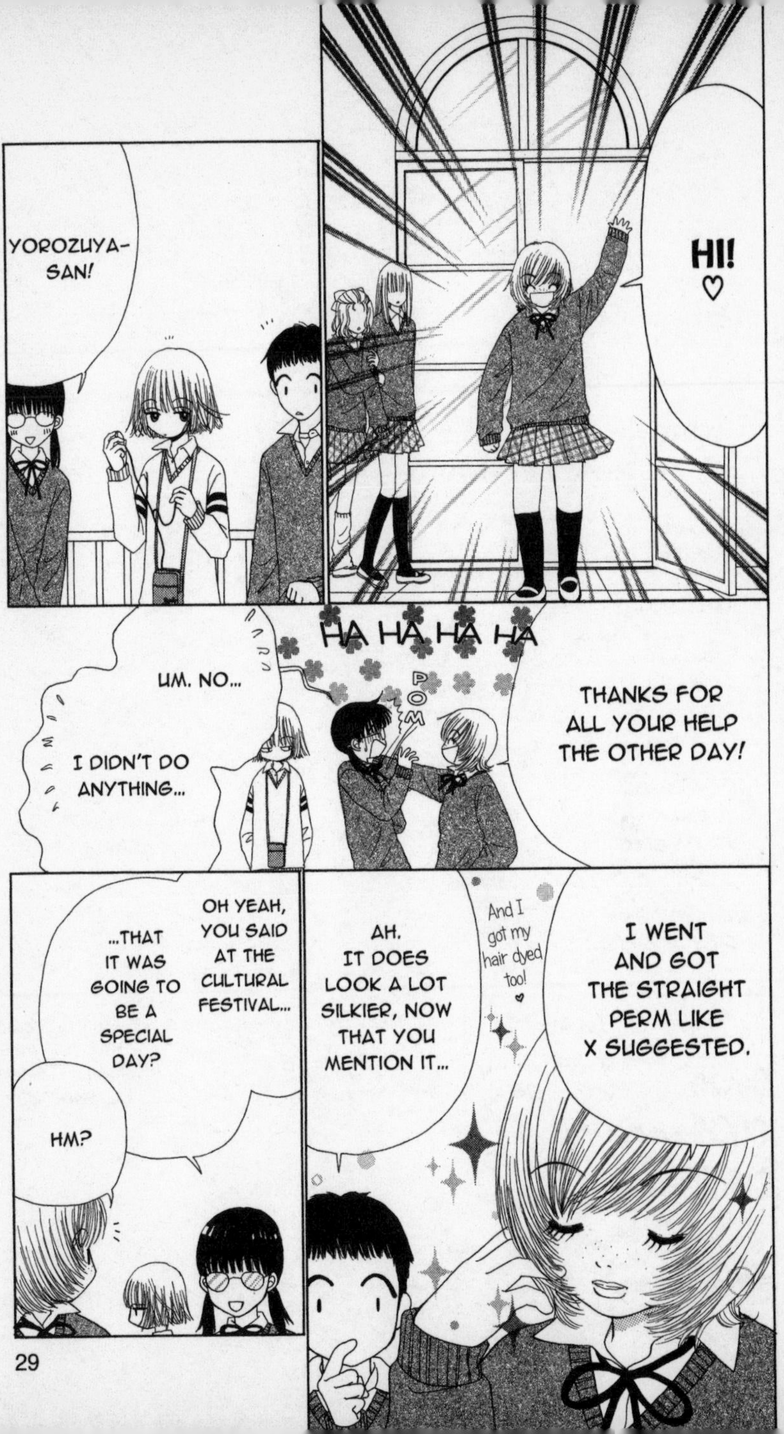
HI! ♡
YOROZUYA-SAN!
THANKS FOR ALL YOUR HELP THE OTHER DAY!
HA HA HA HA
POM
UM. NO...
I DIDN'T DO ANYTHING...
I WENT AND GOT THE STRAIGHT PERM LIKE X SUGGESTED.
And I got my hair dyed too! ♡
AH. IT DOES LOOK A LOT SILKIER, NOW THAT YOU MENTION IT...
OH YEAH, YOU SAID AT THE CULTURAL FESTIVAL...
...THAT IT WAS GOING TO BE A SPECIAL DAY?
HM?

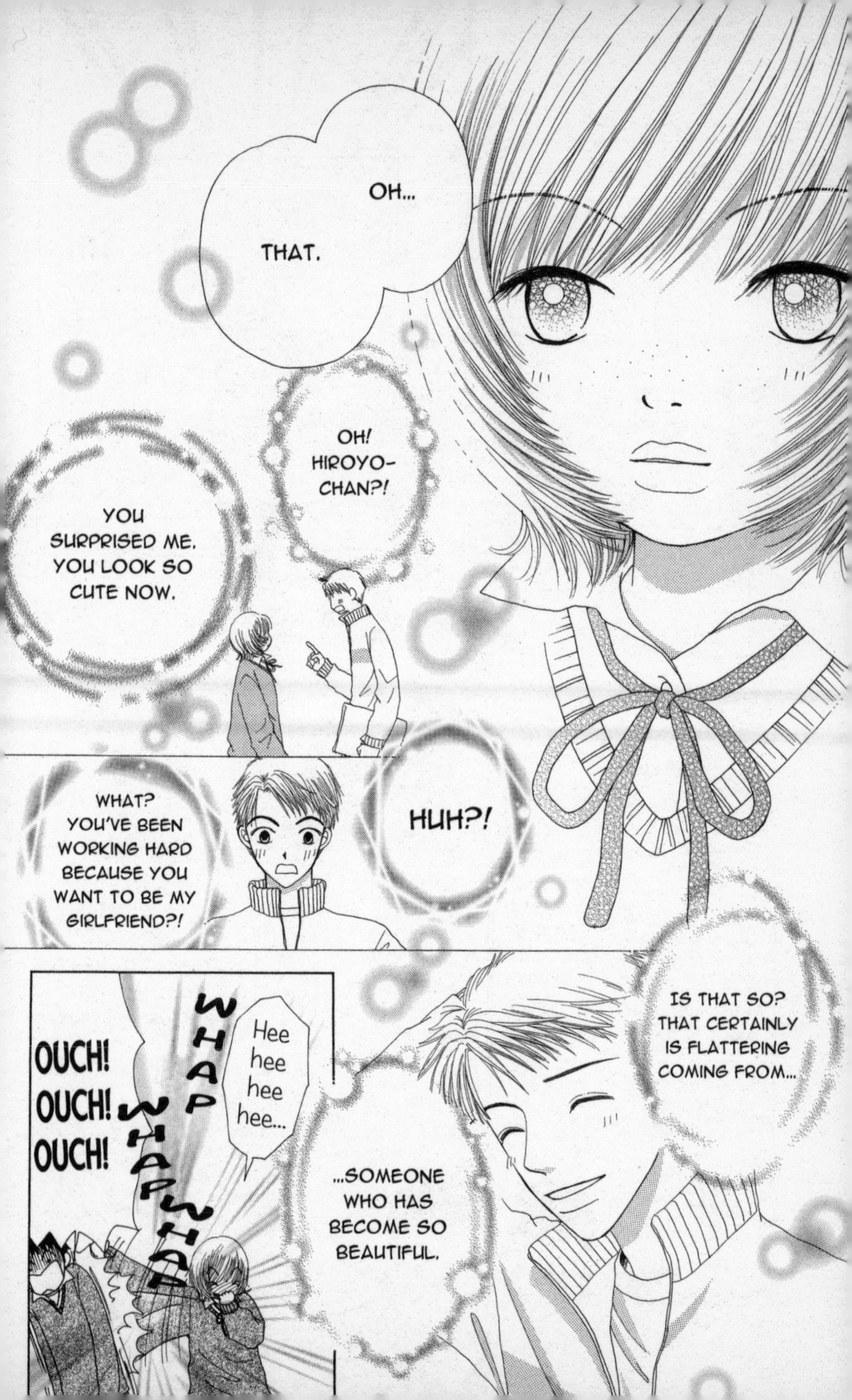
OH...
THAT.
OH! HIROYO-CHAN?!
YOU SURPRISED ME. YOU LOOK SO CUTE NOW.
HUH?!
WHAT? YOU'VE BEEN WORKING HARD BECAUSE YOU WANT TO BE MY GIRLFRIEND?!
IS THAT SO? THAT CERTAINLY IS FLATTERING COMING FROM...
...SOMEONE WHO HAS BECOME SO BEAUTIFUL.
Hee hee hee hee...
WHAP
WHAP WHAP
OUCH! OUCH! OUCH!

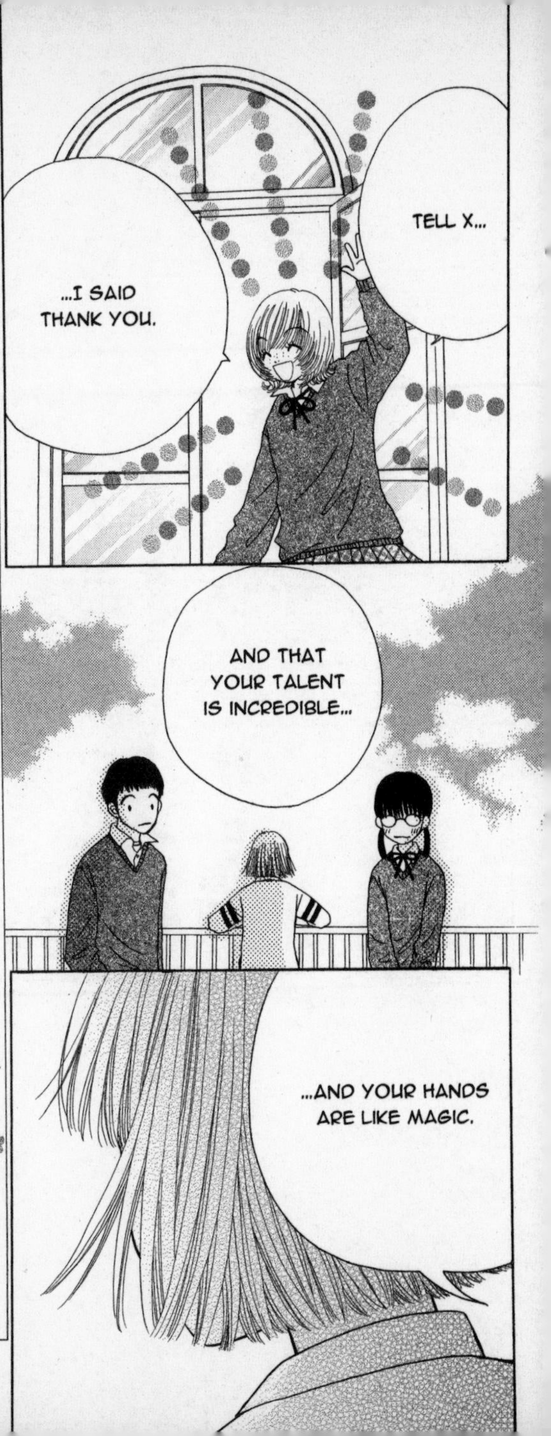
TELL X...
...I SAID THANK YOU.
AND THAT YOUR TALENT IS INCREDIBLE...
...AND YOUR HANDS ARE LIKE MAGIC.

K's Club Talk

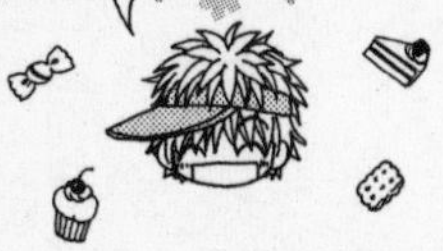

Hello everyone!
This is Kiyoko Arai. I adopted a dog in January of this year (2004) and because of that, I've received lots of email from readers who also have dogs! Sometimes they even include a photo--it's really very cute!! Before I was only collecting cat stuff, but as expected, I've been getting a lot more dog items lately ——!!

I was worried about whether the cats would get along with Kanon (the dog), but they are doing just fine. Maybe it's because Kanon is really outgoing and seems to like other people even more than me-- the owner. Really...
How am I supposed to feel?

When I said "Kanon, come here"...

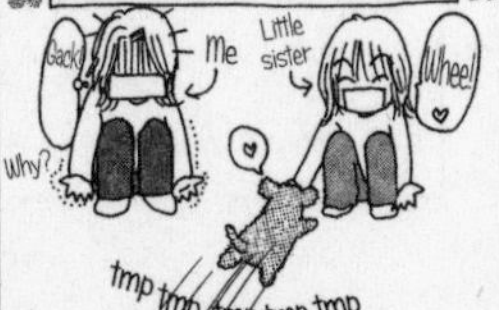
Gack
Me
Little sister
Whee!
Why?
tmp tmp tmp tmp

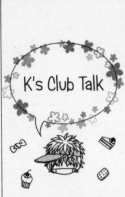

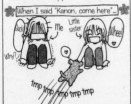

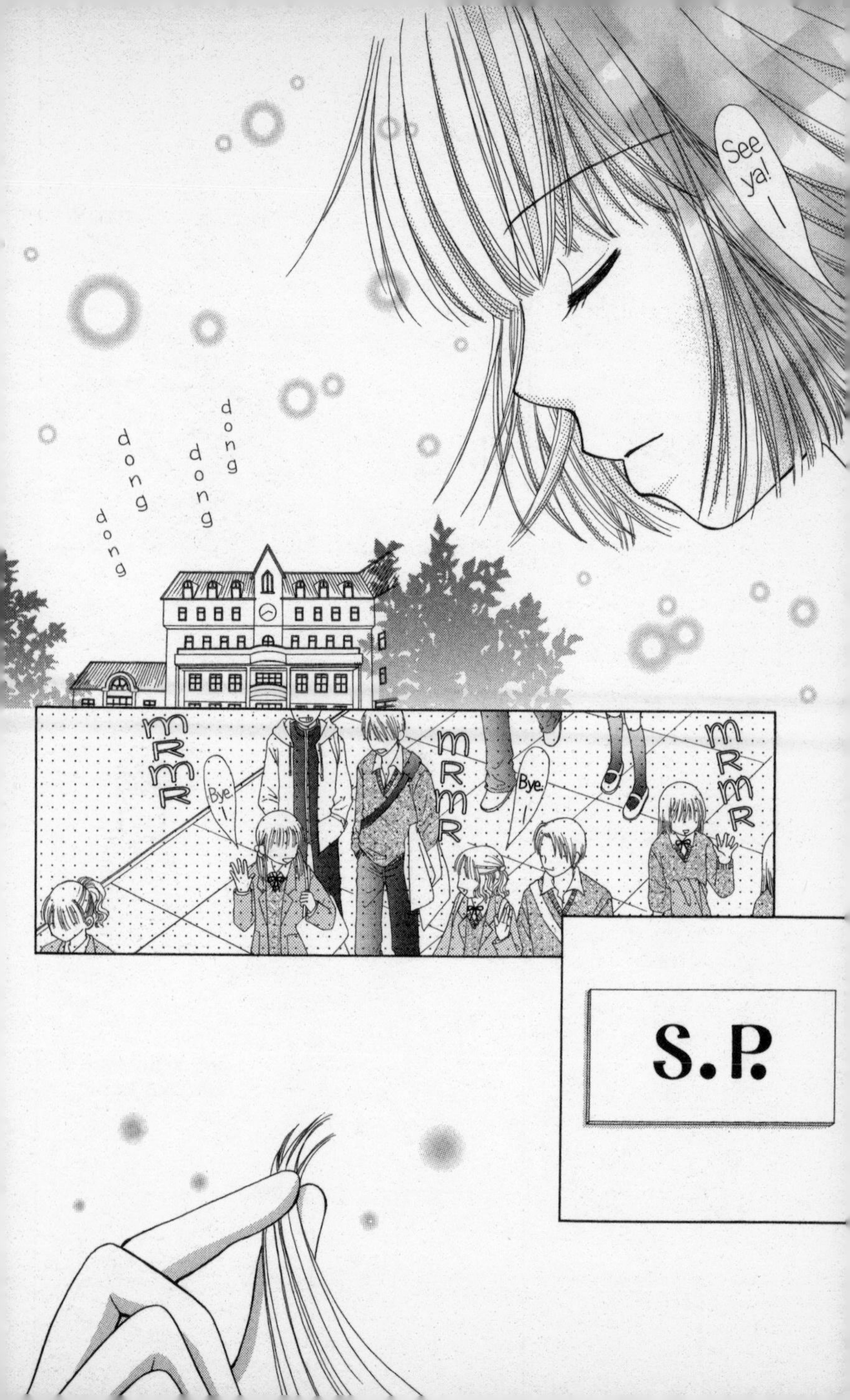
See ya!
dong dong dong
MRMR
Bye.
MRMR
Bye.
MRMR
S.P.

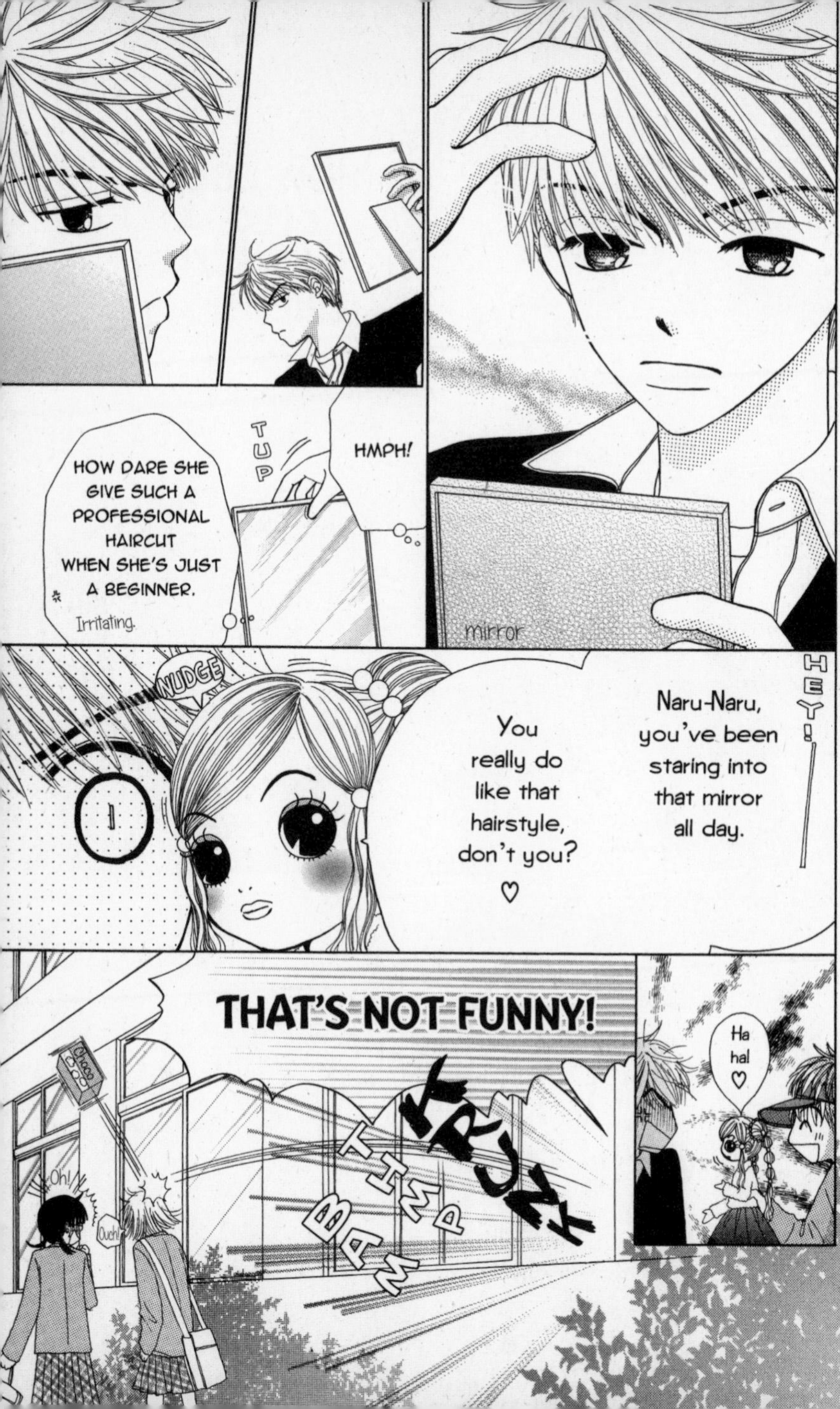
mirror
HMPH!
TUP
HOW DARE SHE GIVE SUCH A PROFESSIONAL HAIRCUT WHEN SHE'S JUST A BEGINNER.
Irritating.
HEY!
Naru-Naru, you've been staring into that mirror all day.
You really do like that hairstyle, don't you? ♡
NUDGE
Ha ha! ♡
THAT'S NOT FUNNY!
KRUNK
THMP
BAM
Choco
Oh!
Ouch!

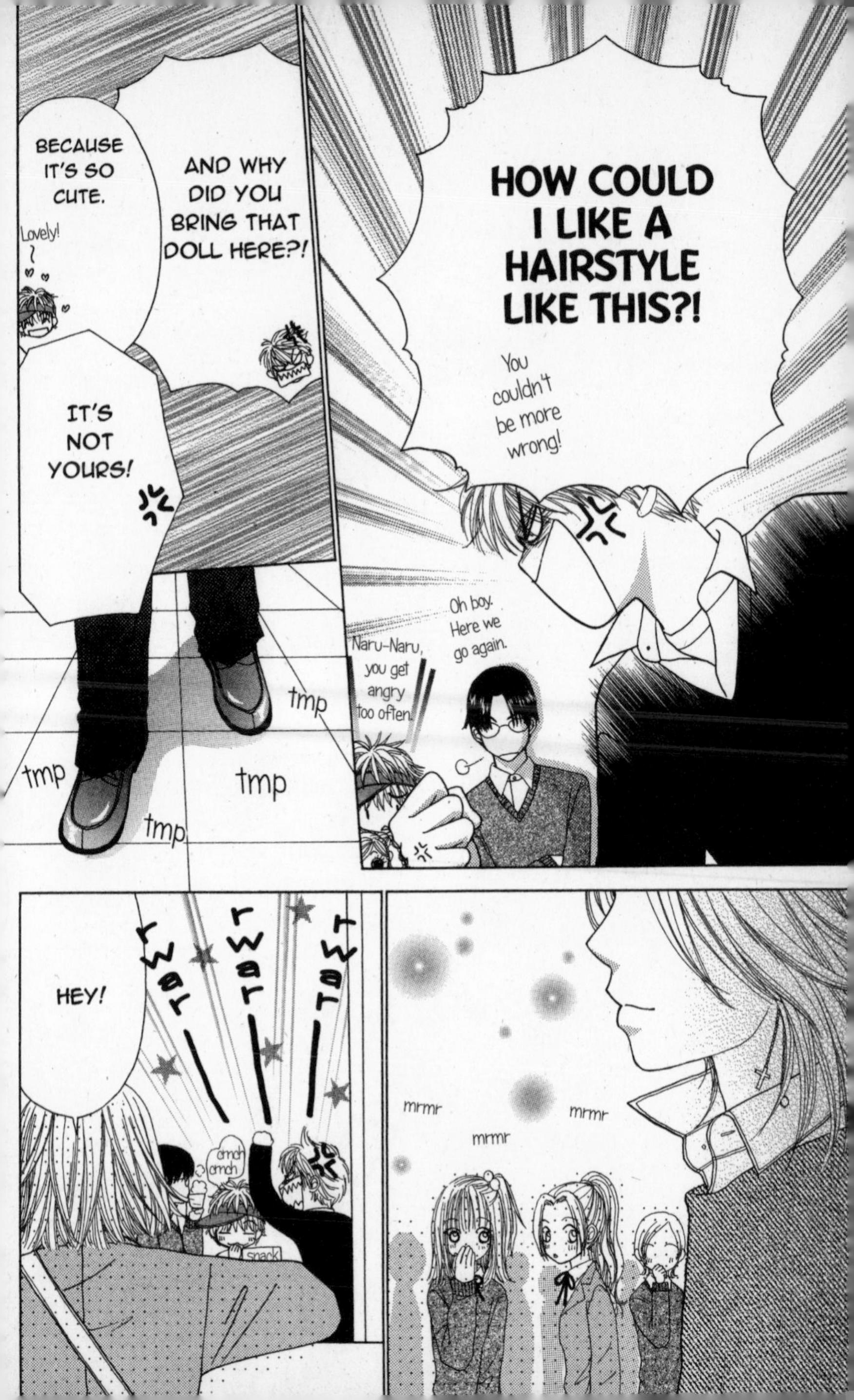
HOW COULD I LIKE A HAIRSTYLE LIKE THIS?!
You couldn't be more wrong!
Oh boy. Here we go again.
Naru-Naru, you get angry too often.
AND WHY DID YOU BRING THAT DOLL HERE?!
BECAUSE IT'S SO CUTE.
Lovely!
IT'S NOT YOURS!
tmp
tmp
tmp
tmp
mrmr
mrmr
mrmr
HEY!
rwar—
rwar—
rwar—
omch omch
snack

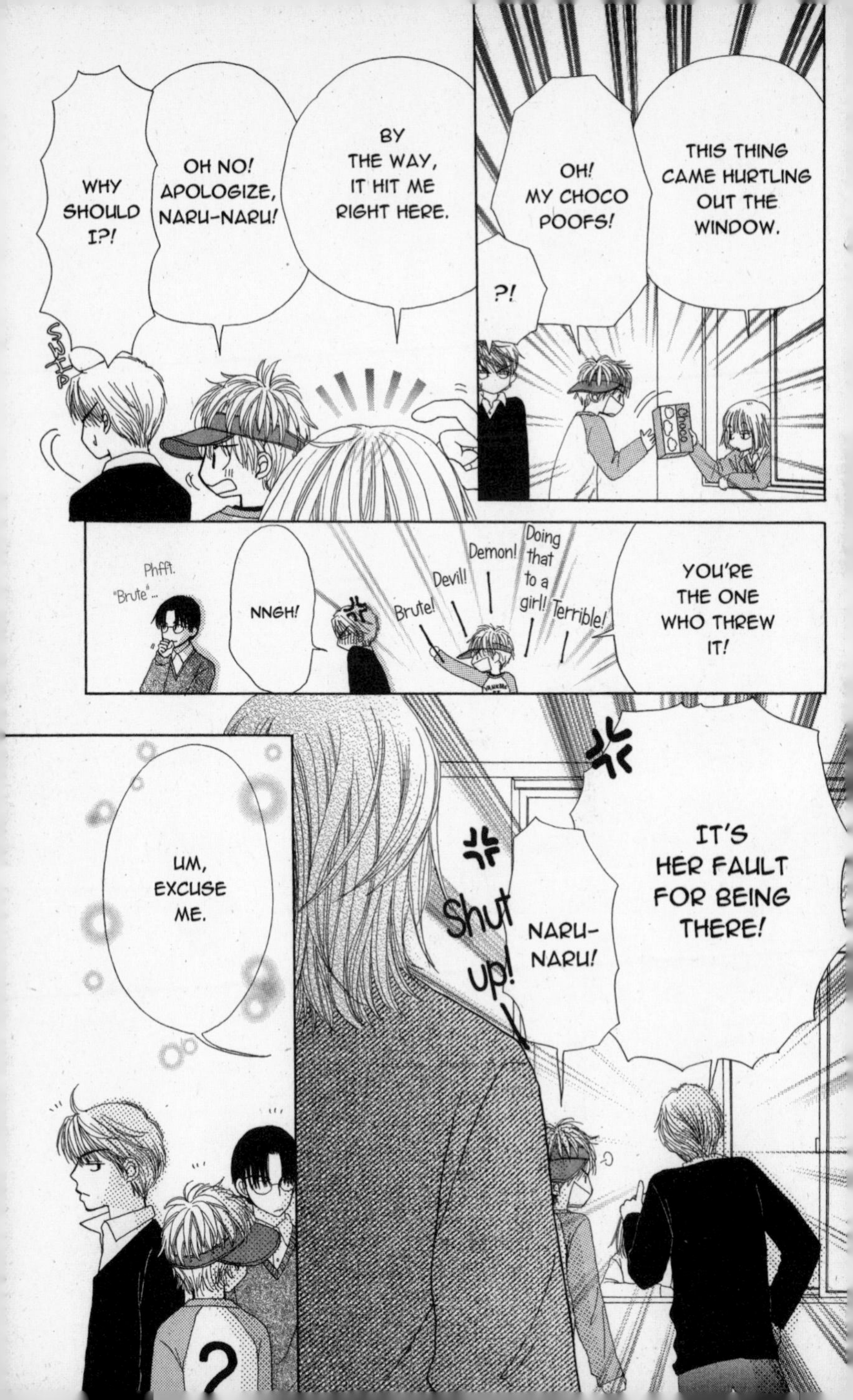
THIS THING CAME HURTLING OUT THE WINDOW.
OH! MY CHOCO POOFS!
Choco
?!
BY THE WAY, IT HIT ME RIGHT HERE.
OH NO! APOLOGIZE, NARU-NARU!
WHY SHOULD I?!
YOU'RE THE ONE WHO THREW IT!
Terrible!
Doing that to a girl!
Demon!
Devil!
Brute!
NNGH!
Phfft.
"Brute"...
IT'S HER FAULT FOR BEING THERE!
NARU-NARU!
Shut up!
UM, EXCUSE ME.
?

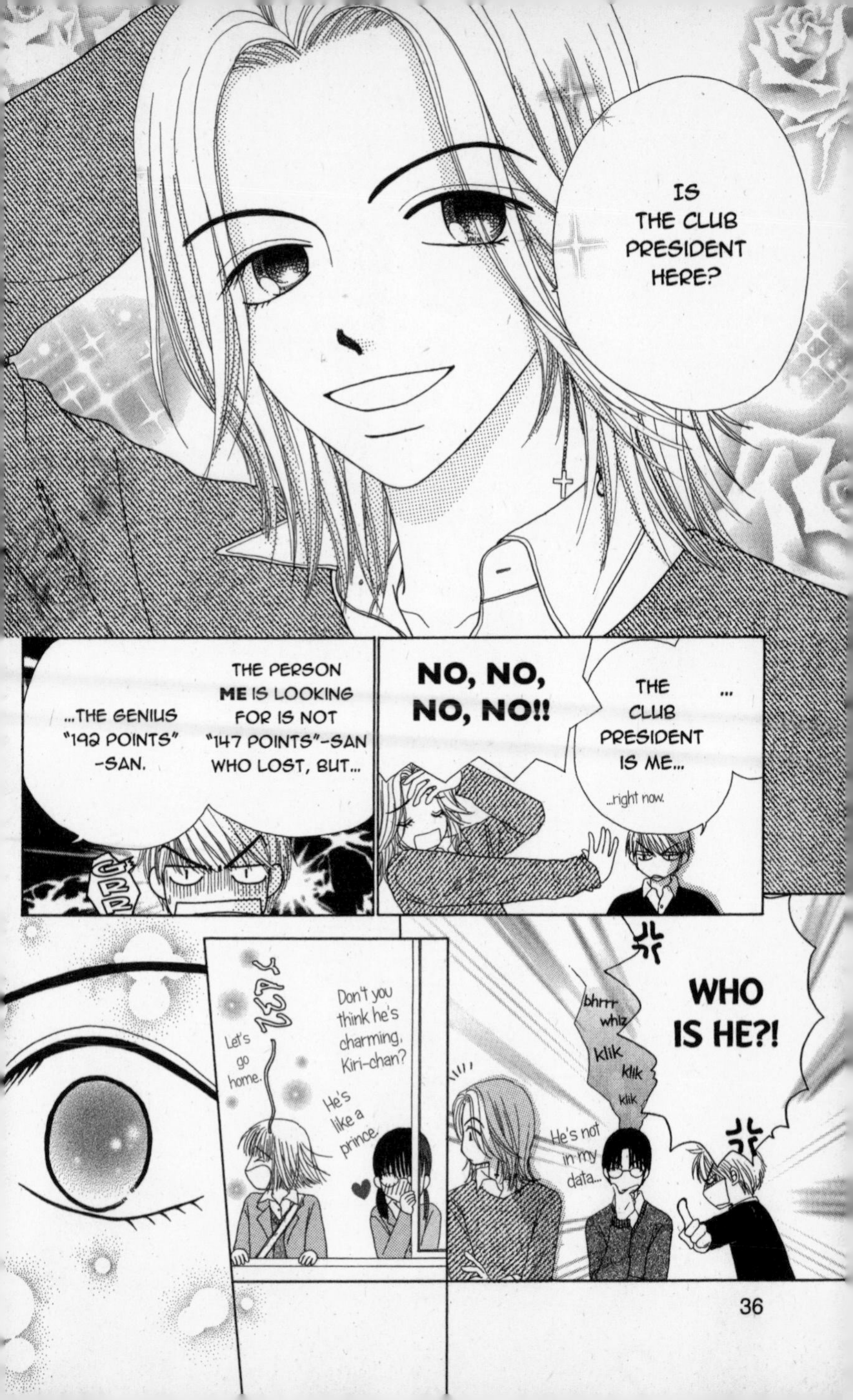
IS THE CLUB PRESIDENT HERE?
...
THE CLUB PRESIDENT IS ME...
...right now.
NO, NO, NO, NO!!
THE PERSON ME IS LOOKING FOR IS NOT "147 POINTS"-SAN WHO LOST, BUT...
...THE GENIUS "192 POINTS" -SAN.
WHO IS HE?!
bhrrr whiz klik klik klik
He's not in my data...
Don't you think he's charming, Kiri-chan?
He's like a prince.
Let's go home.

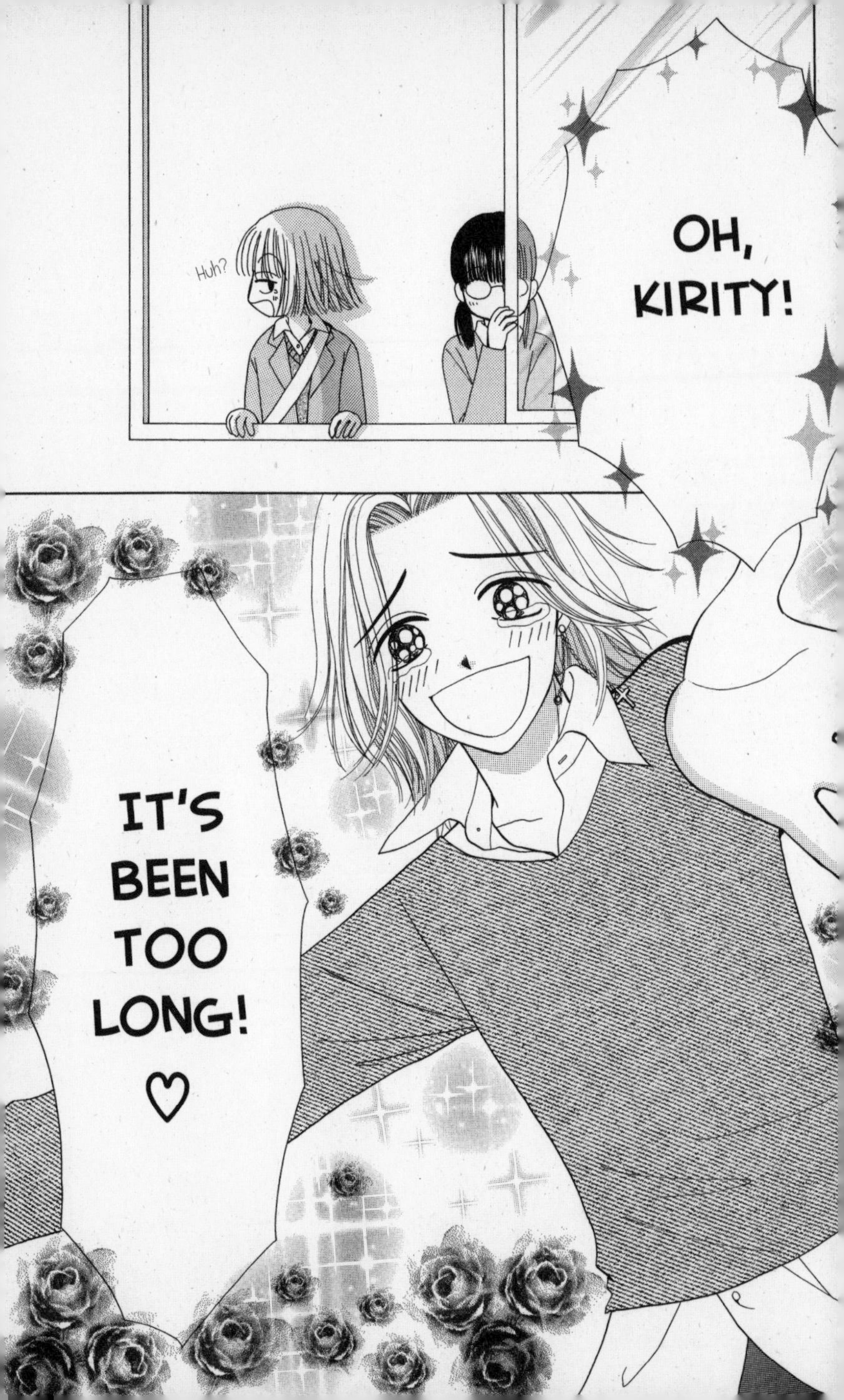
Huh?
OH, KIRITY!
IT'S BEEN TOO LONG! ♡

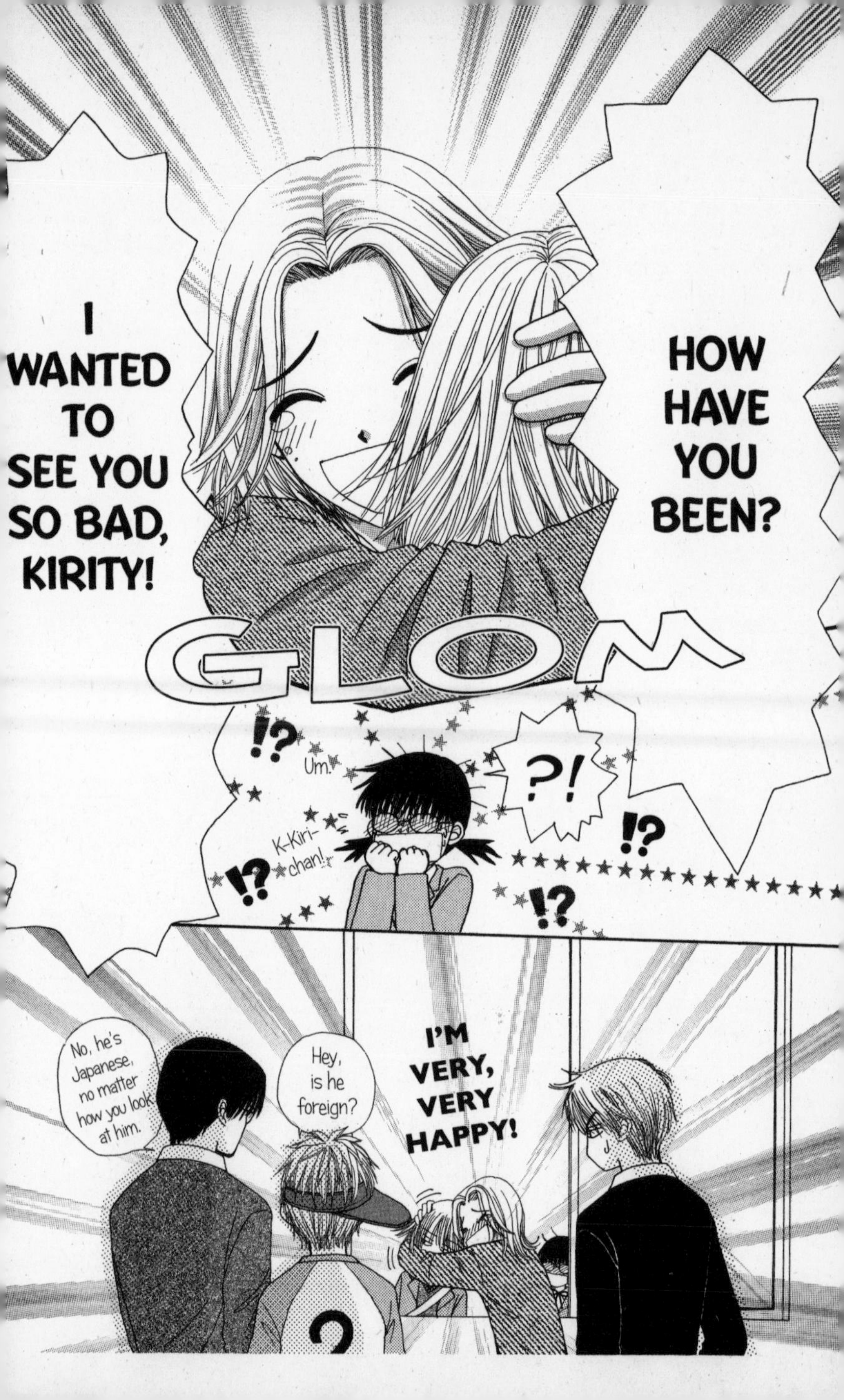
HOW HAVE YOU BEEN?
I WANTED TO SEE YOU SO BAD, KIRITY!
GLOM
?!
!?
Um.
!?
K-Kiri-chan!
!?
!?
I'M VERY, VERY HAPPY!
Hey, is he foreign?
No, he's Japanese, no matter how you look at him.
?

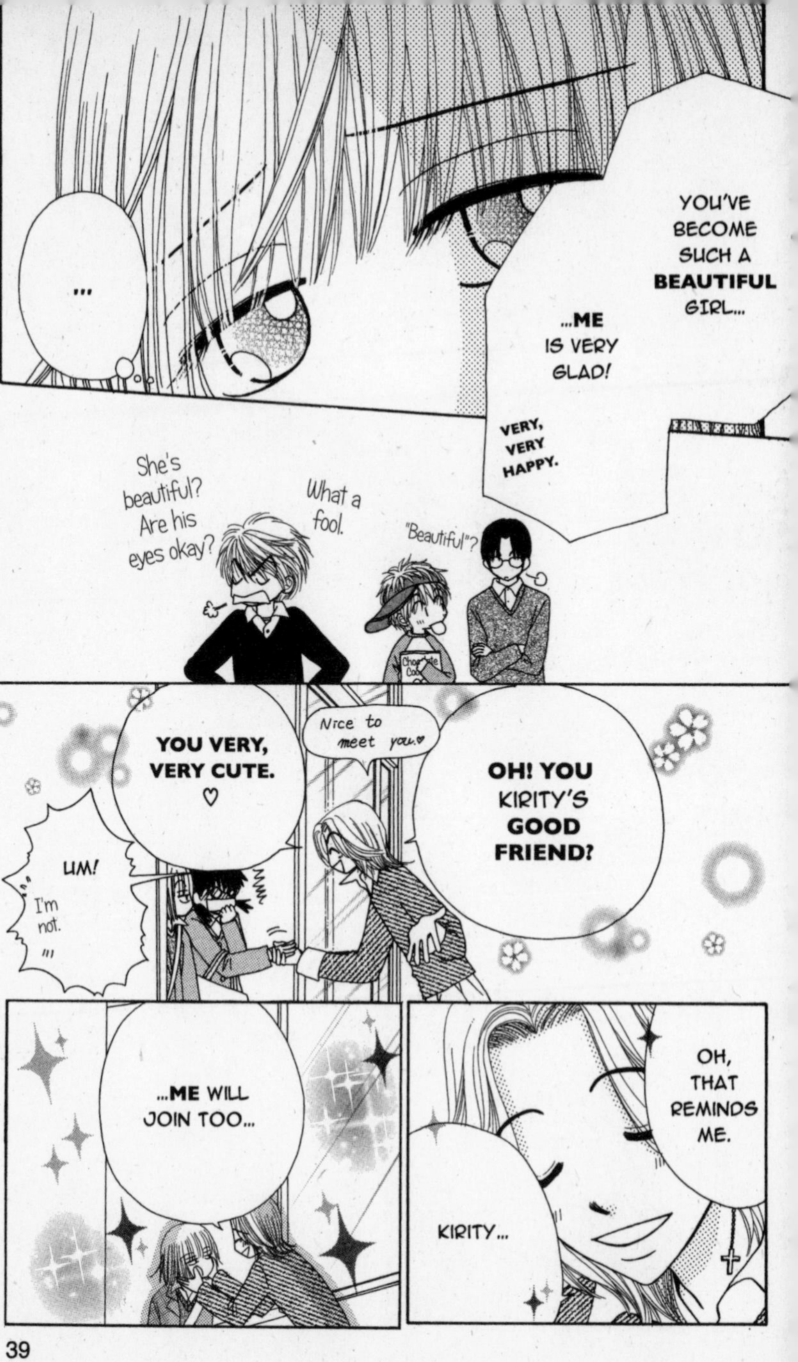
YOU'VE BECOME SUCH A **BEAUTIFUL** GIRL...
...**ME** IS VERY GLAD!
VERY, VERY HAPPY.
...
"Beautiful"?
What a fool.
She's beautiful? Are his eyes okay?
OH! YOU KIRITY'S **GOOD FRIEND?**
Nice to meet you.♥
YOU VERY, VERY CUTE. ♡
UM!
I'm not.
OH, THAT REMINDS ME.
KIRITY...
...**ME** WILL JOIN TOO...

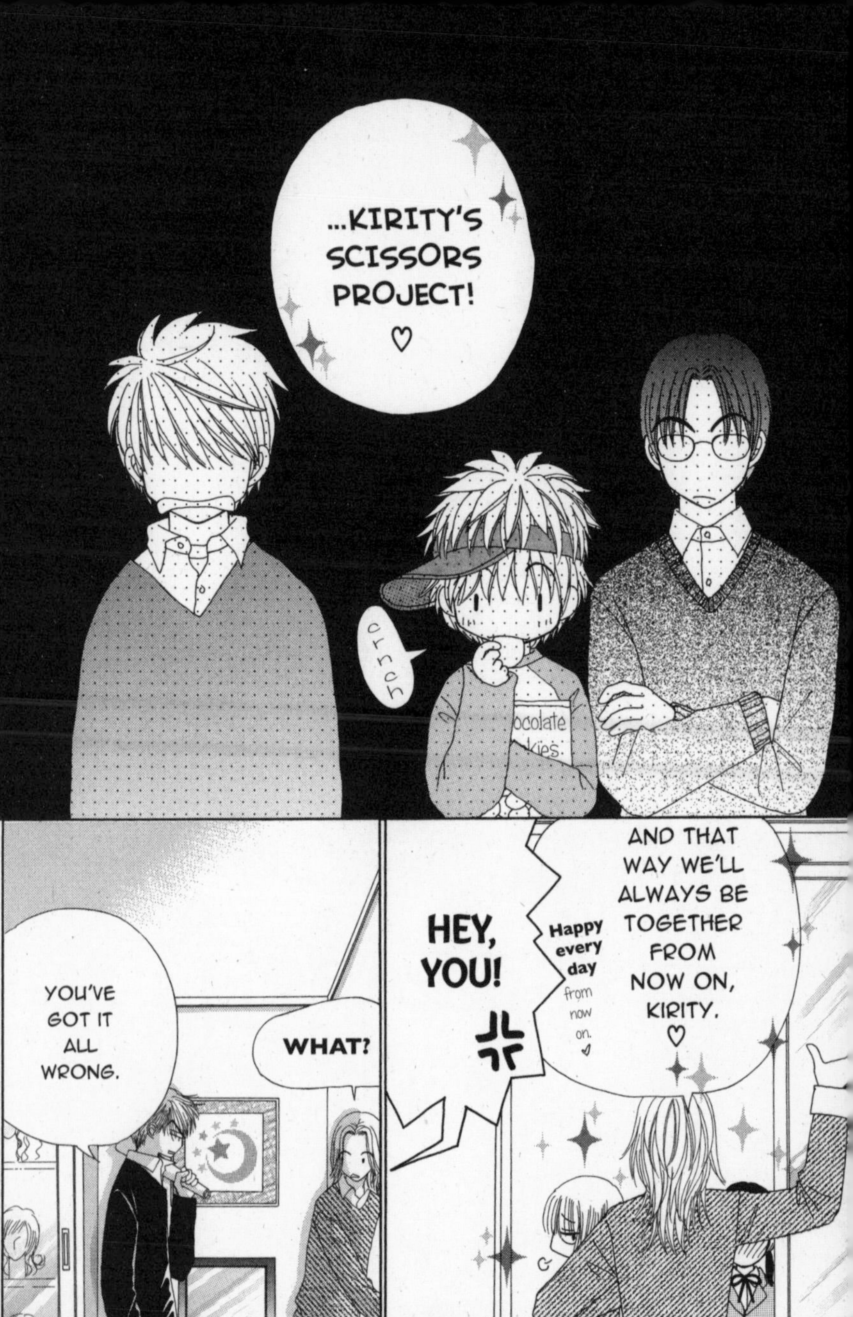
...KIRITY'S SCISSORS PROJECT! ♡
crnch
ocolate kies
AND THAT WAY WE'LL ALWAYS BE TOGETHER FROM NOW ON, KIRITY. ♡
Happy every day from now on. ♡
HEY, YOU!
WHAT?
YOU'VE GOT IT ALL WRONG.

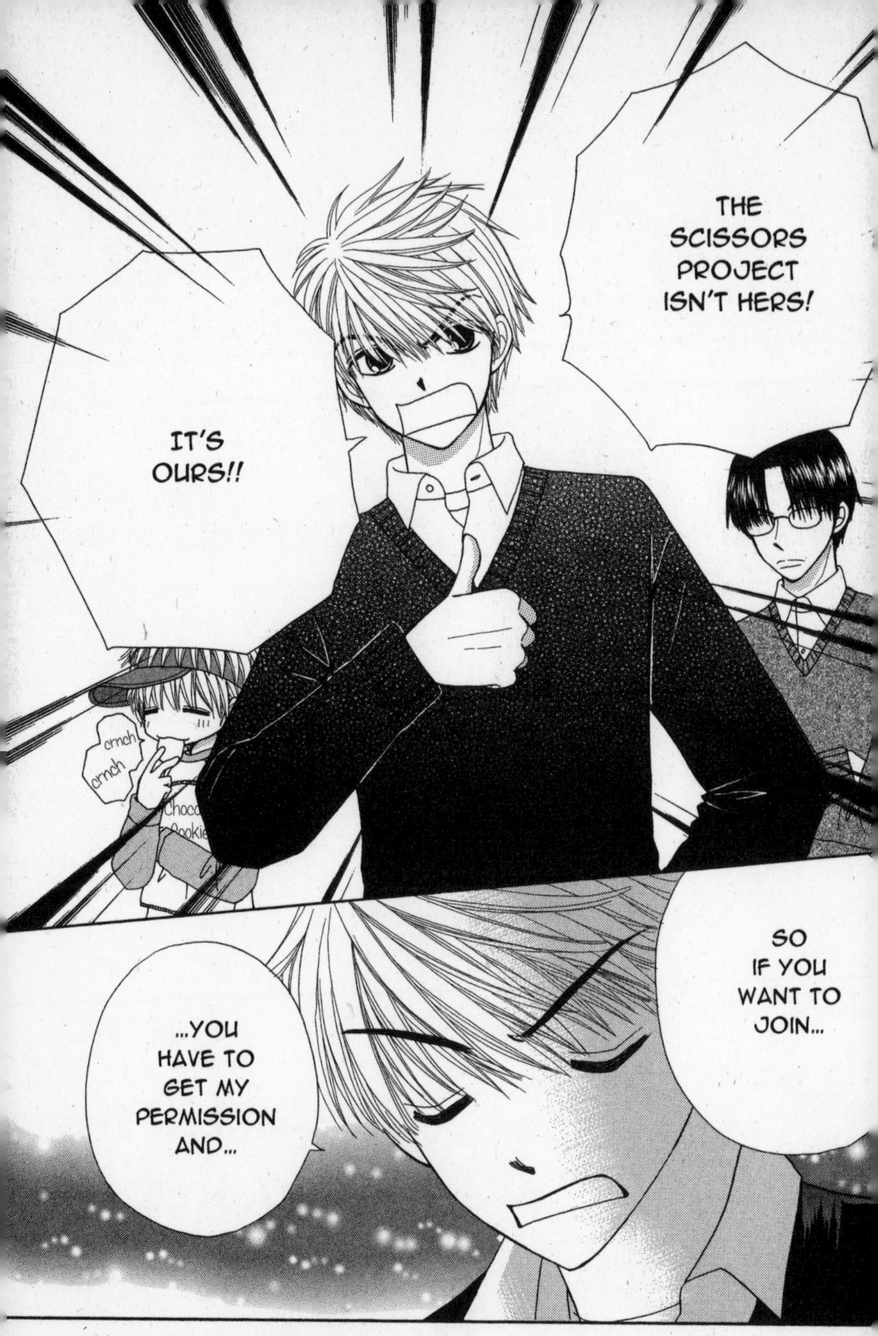
THE SCISSORS PROJECT ISN'T HERS!
IT'S OURS!!
crnch
crnch
SO IF YOU WANT TO JOIN...
...YOU HAVE TO GET MY PERMISSION AND...

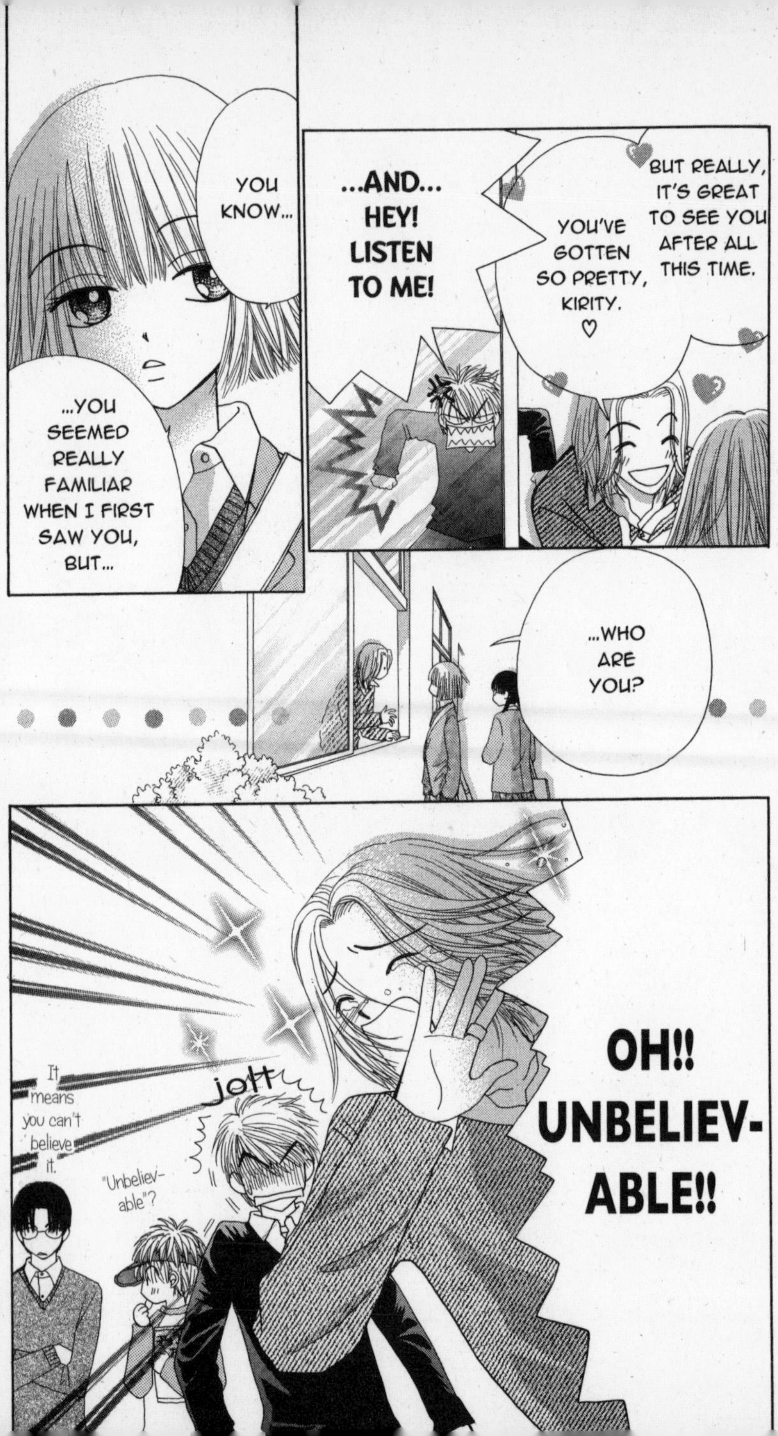
BUT REALLY, IT'S GREAT TO SEE YOU AFTER ALL THIS TIME.
YOU'VE GOTTEN SO PRETTY, KIRITY. ♡
...AND... HEY! LISTEN TO ME!
YOU KNOW...
...YOU SEEMED REALLY FAMILIAR WHEN I FIRST SAW YOU, BUT...
...WHO ARE YOU?
OH!! UNBELIEV-ABLE!!
jolt
"Unbeliev-able"?
It means you can't believe it.

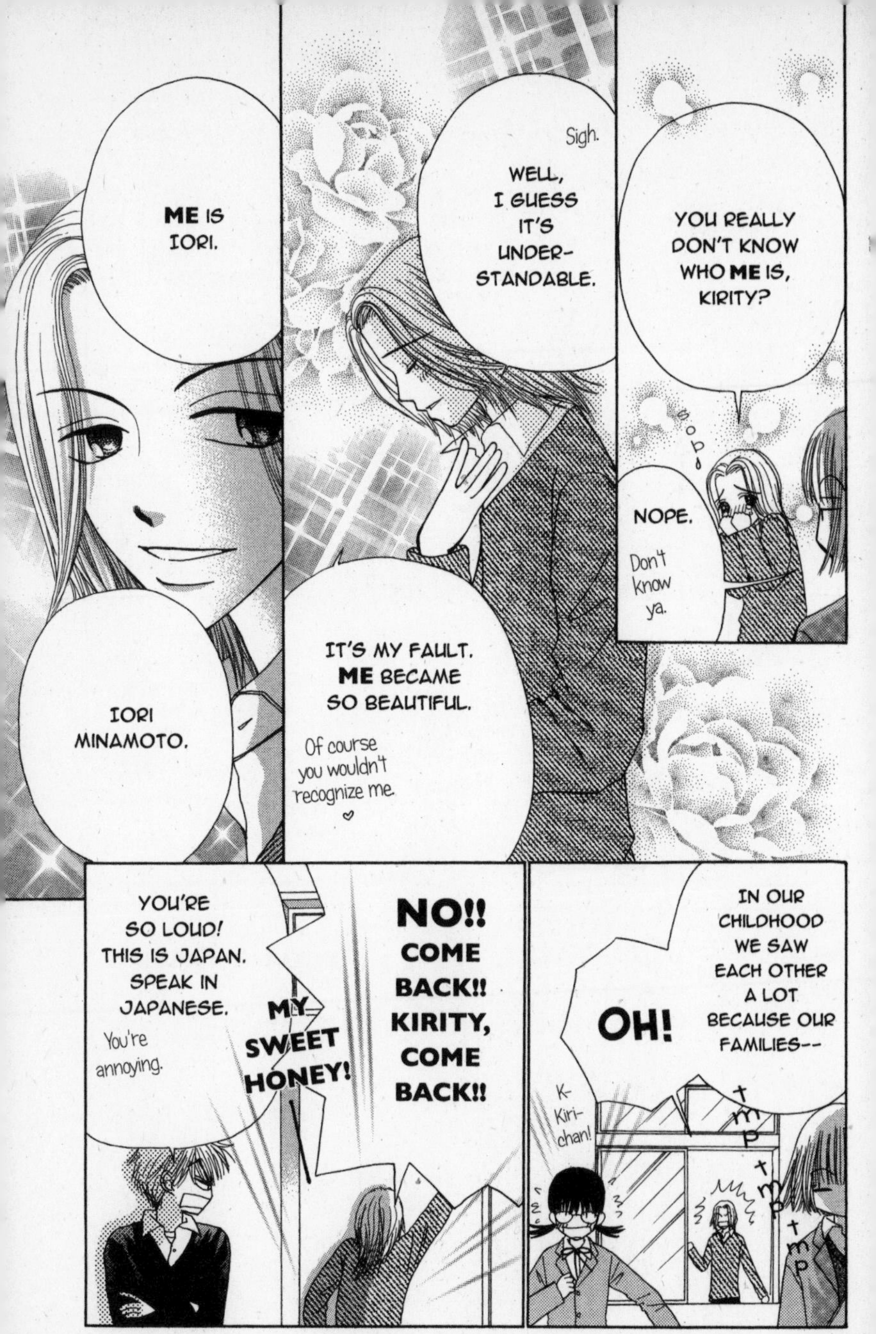

YOU REALLY DON'T KNOW WHO ME IS, KIRITY?
sob
NOPE.
Don't know ya.
Sigh.
WELL, I GUESS IT'S UNDER-STANDABLE.
IT'S MY FAULT. ME BECAME SO BEAUTIFUL.
Of course you wouldn't recognize me.
ME IS IORI.
IORI MINAMOTO.
IN OUR CHILDHOOD WE SAW EACH OTHER A LOT BECAUSE OUR FAMILIES--
OH!
K-Kiri-chan!
tmp tmp tmp
NO!! COME BACK!! KIRITY, COME BACK!!
MY SWEET HONEY!
YOU'RE SO LOUD! THIS IS JAPAN. SPEAK IN JAPANESE.
You're annoying.

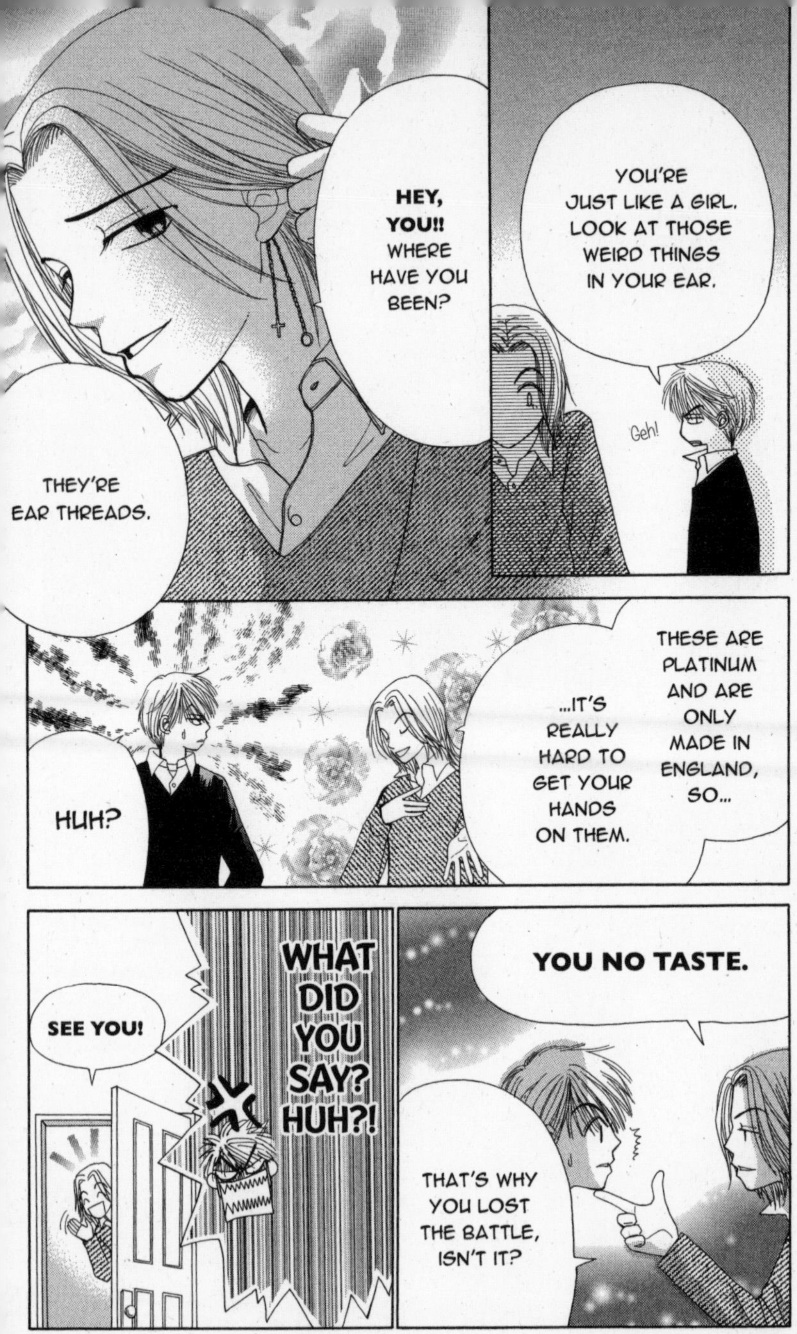
YOU'RE JUST LIKE A GIRL. LOOK AT THOSE WEIRD THINGS IN YOUR EAR.
Geh!
HEY, YOU!! WHERE HAVE YOU BEEN?
THEY'RE EAR THREADS.
THESE ARE PLATINUM AND ARE ONLY MADE IN ENGLAND, SO...
...IT'S REALLY HARD TO GET YOUR HANDS ON THEM.
HUH?
YOU NO TASTE.
THAT'S WHY YOU LOST THE BATTLE, ISN'T IT?
WHAT DID YOU SAY? HUH?!
SEE YOU!

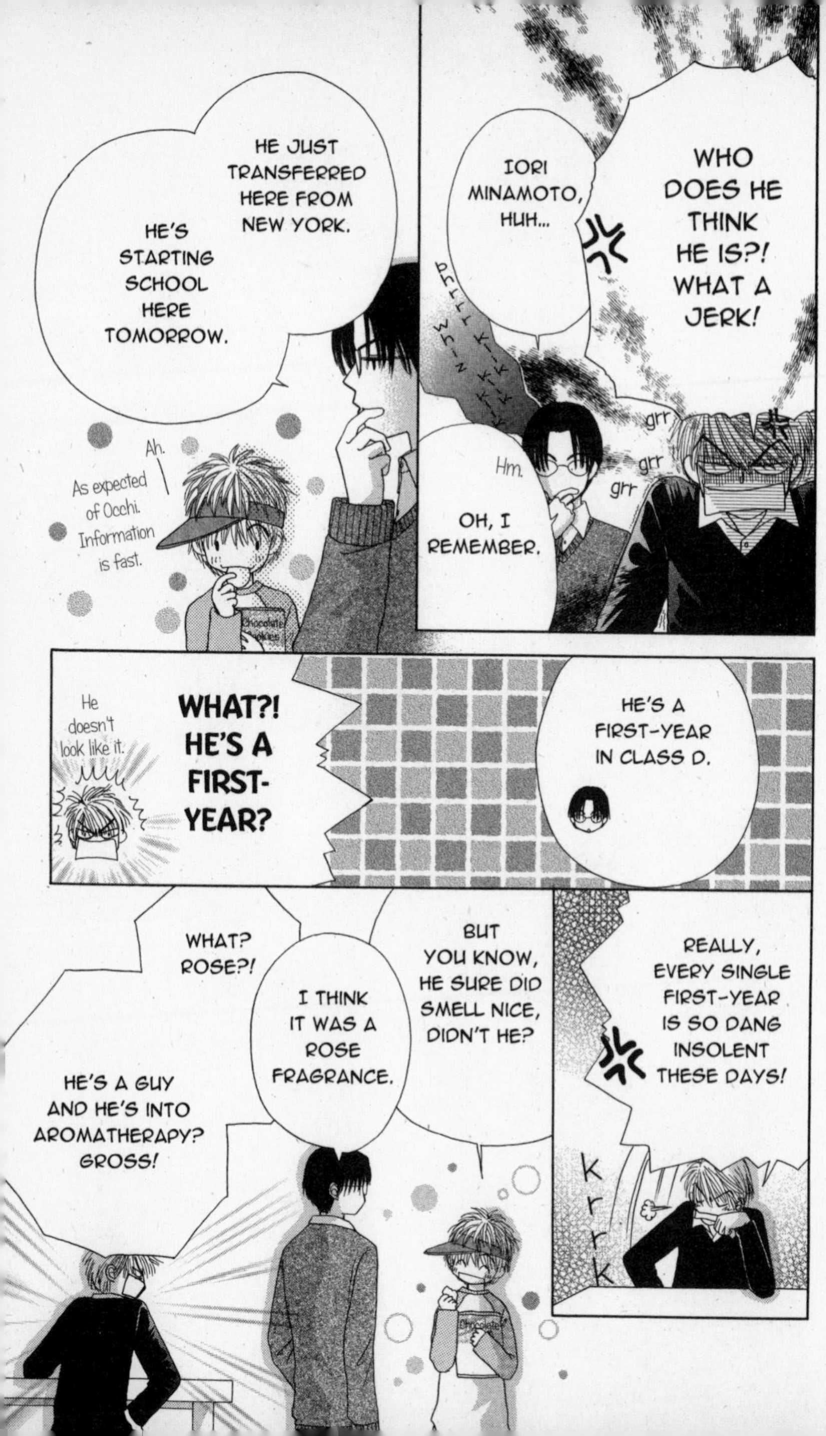
WHO DOES HE THINK HE IS?! WHAT A JERK!
grr
grr
grr
IORI MINAMOTO, HUH...
Hm.
OH, I REMEMBER.
HE JUST TRANSFERRED HERE FROM NEW YORK.
HE'S STARTING SCHOOL HERE TOMORROW.
Ah.
As expected of Occhi. Information is fast.
HE'S A FIRST-YEAR IN CLASS D.
WHAT?! HE'S A FIRST-YEAR?
He doesn't look like it.
REALLY, EVERY SINGLE FIRST-YEAR IS SO DANG INSOLENT THESE DAYS!
Krrk
BUT YOU KNOW, HE SURE DID SMELL NICE, DIDN'T HE?
I THINK IT WAS A ROSE FRAGRANCE.
WHAT? ROSE?!
HE'S A GUY AND HE'S INTO AROMATHERAPY? GROSS!

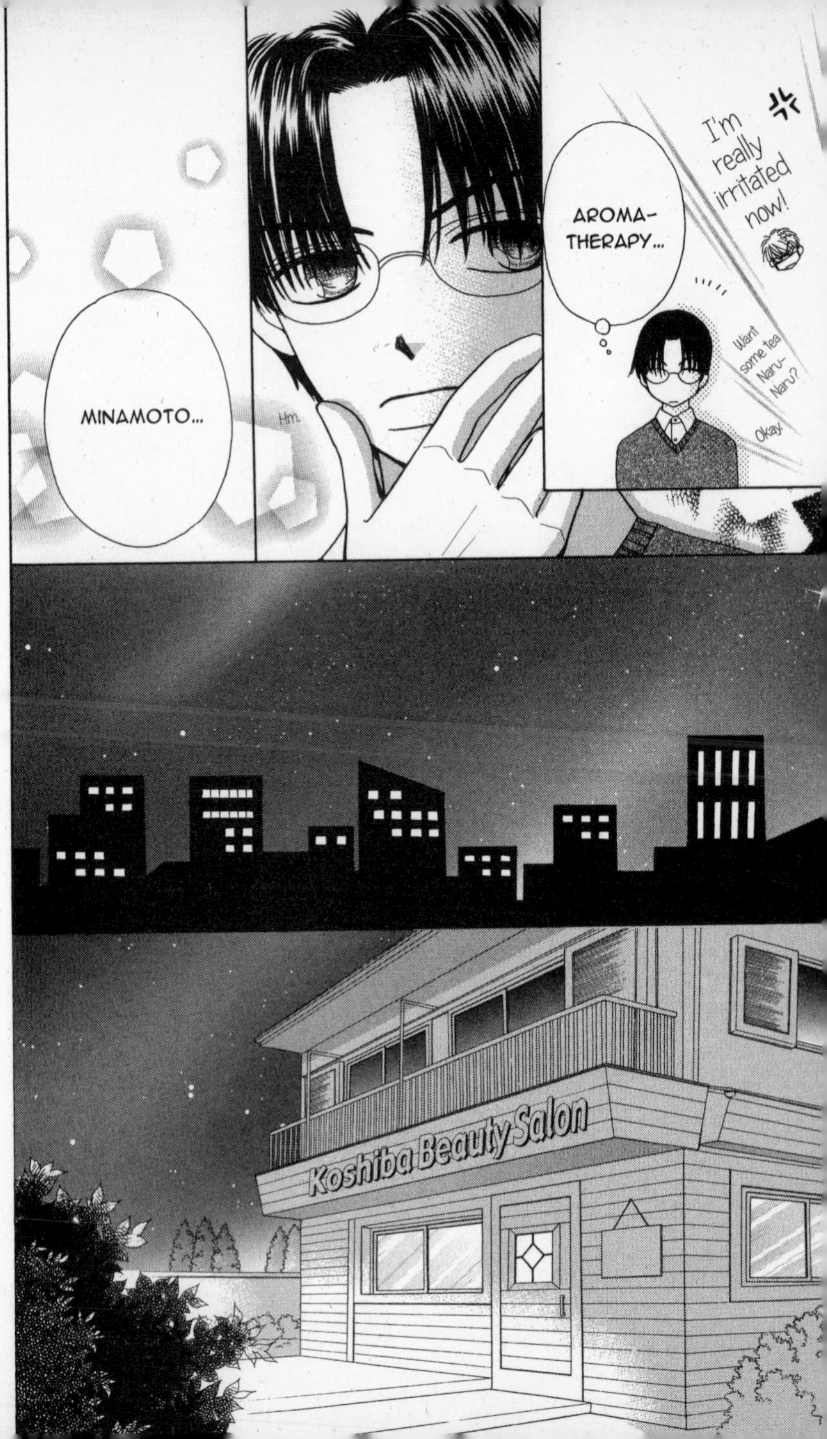

I'm really irritated now!
Want some tea Naru-Naru?
Okay.
AROMA-THERAPY...
Hm.
MINAMOTO...
Koshiba Beauty Salon

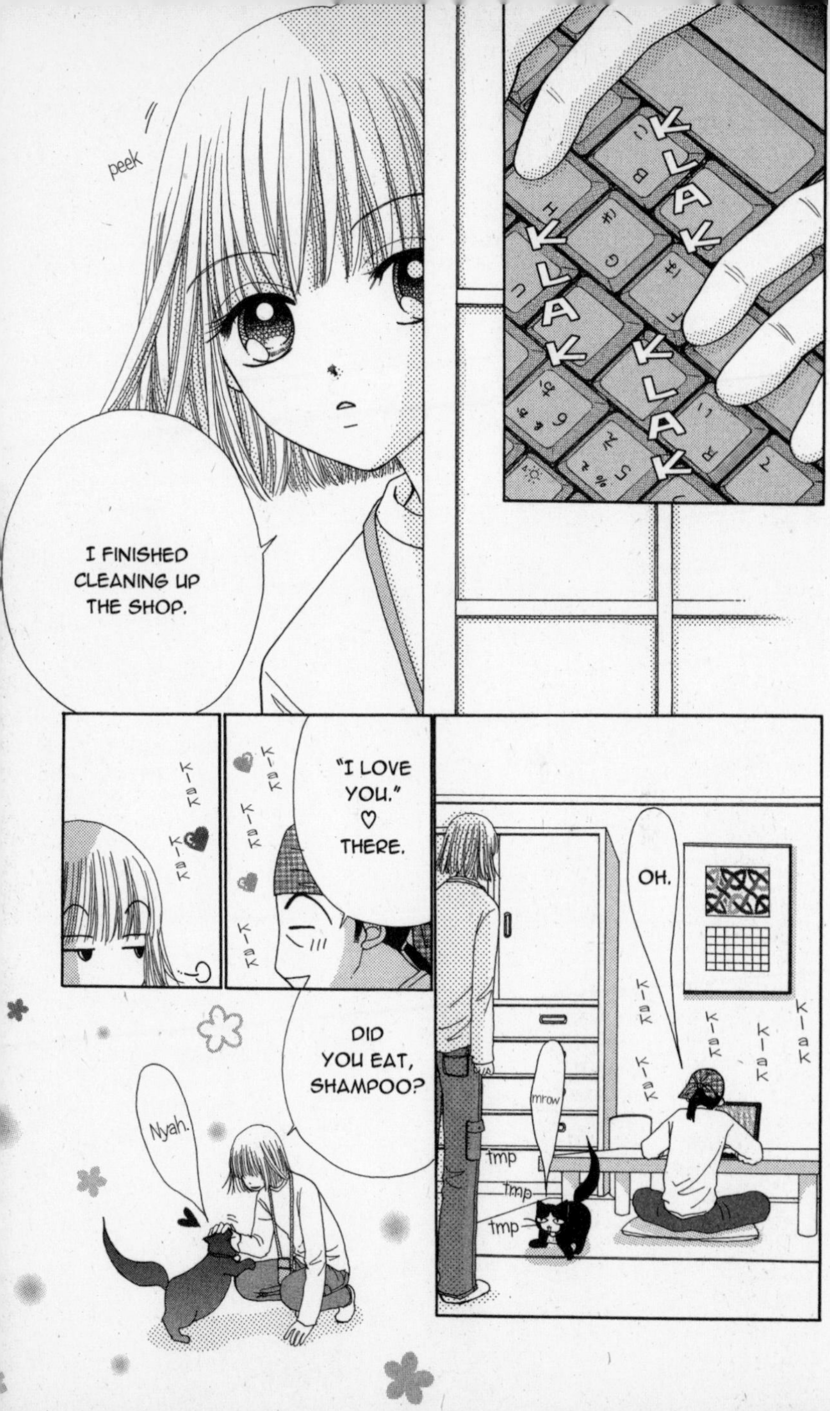
KLAK
KLAK
KLAK
peek
I FINISHED CLEANING UP THE SHOP.
OH.
klak
klak
klak
klak
mrow
tmp
tmp
tmp
"I LOVE YOU." ♡ THERE.
klak
klak
klak
klak
klak
DID YOU EAT, SHAMPOO?
Nyah.

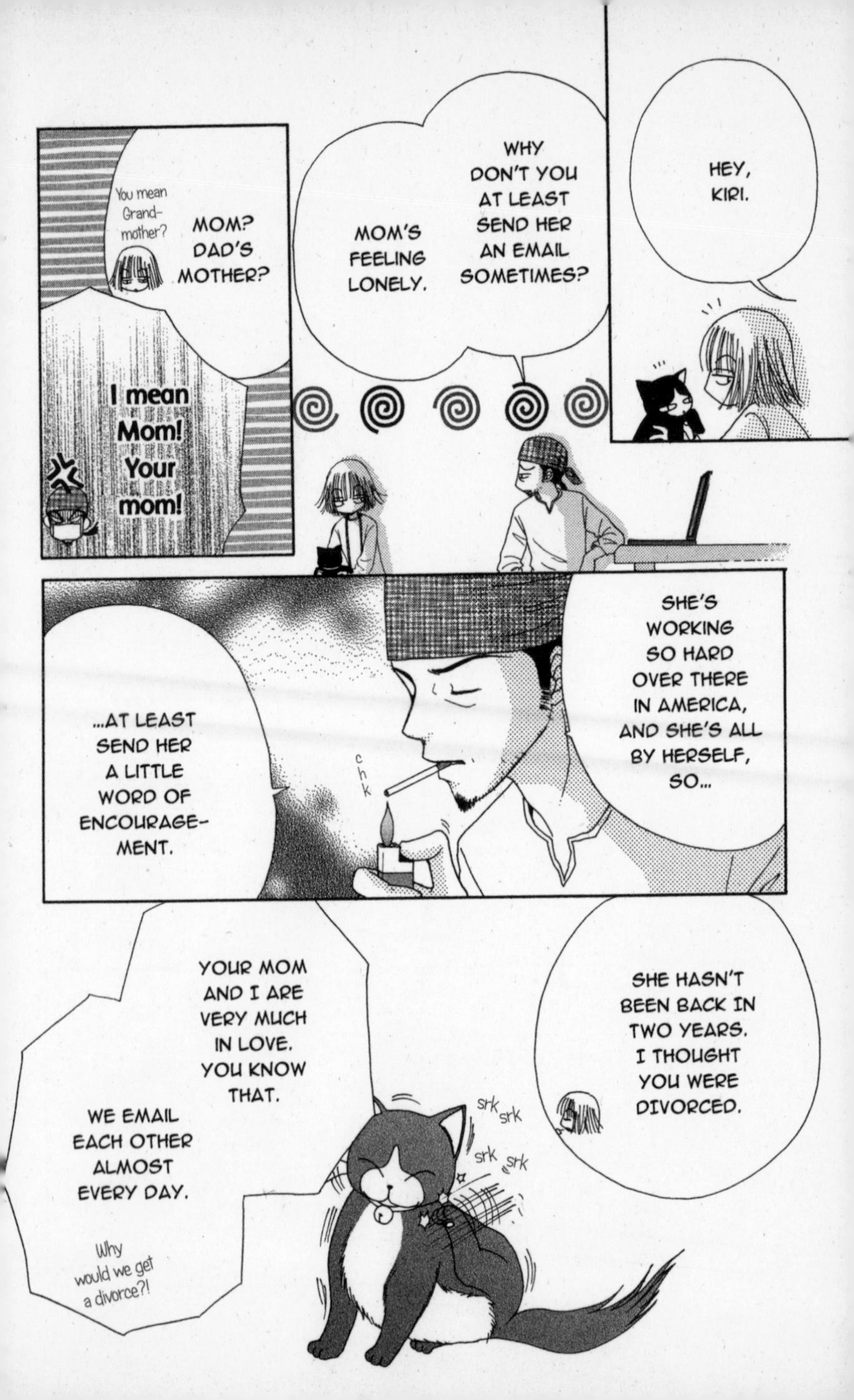
HEY, KIRI.
WHY DON'T YOU AT LEAST SEND HER AN EMAIL SOMETIMES?
MOM'S FEELING LONELY.
MOM? DAD'S MOTHER?
You mean Grand-mother?
I mean Mom! Your mom!
SHE'S WORKING SO HARD OVER THERE IN AMERICA, AND SHE'S ALL BY HERSELF, SO...
chk
...AT LEAST SEND HER A LITTLE WORD OF ENCOURAGE-MENT.
SHE HASN'T BEEN BACK IN TWO YEARS. I THOUGHT YOU WERE DIVORCED.
srk srk
srk srk
YOUR MOM AND I ARE VERY MUCH IN LOVE. YOU KNOW THAT.
WE EMAIL EACH OTHER ALMOST EVERY DAY.
Why would we get a divorce?!

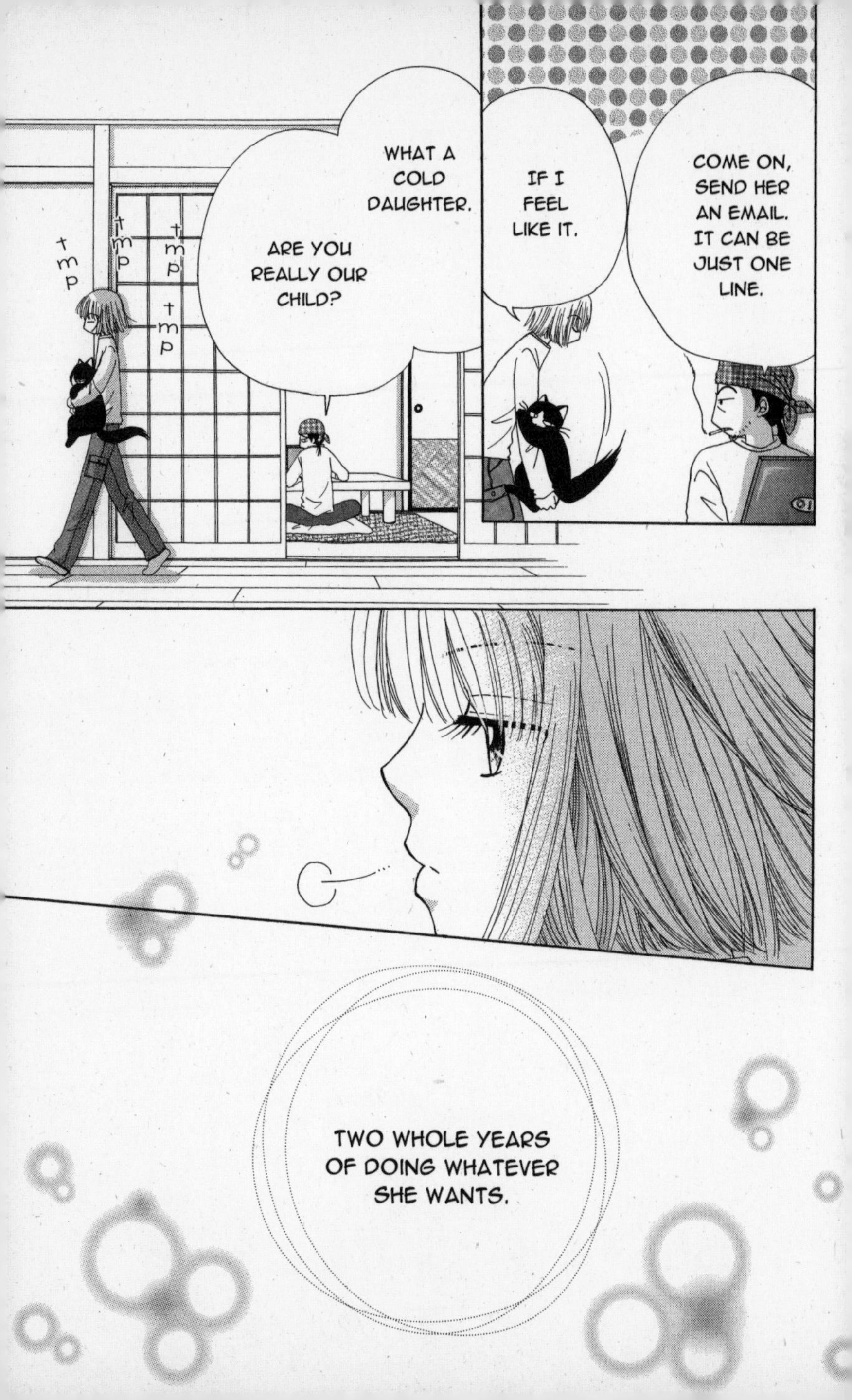
COME ON, SEND HER AN EMAIL. IT CAN BE JUST ONE LINE.
IF I FEEL LIKE IT.
WHAT A COLD DAUGHTER.
ARE YOU REALLY OUR CHILD?
tmp
tmp
tmp
tmp
TWO WHOLE YEARS OF DOING WHATEVER SHE WANTS.

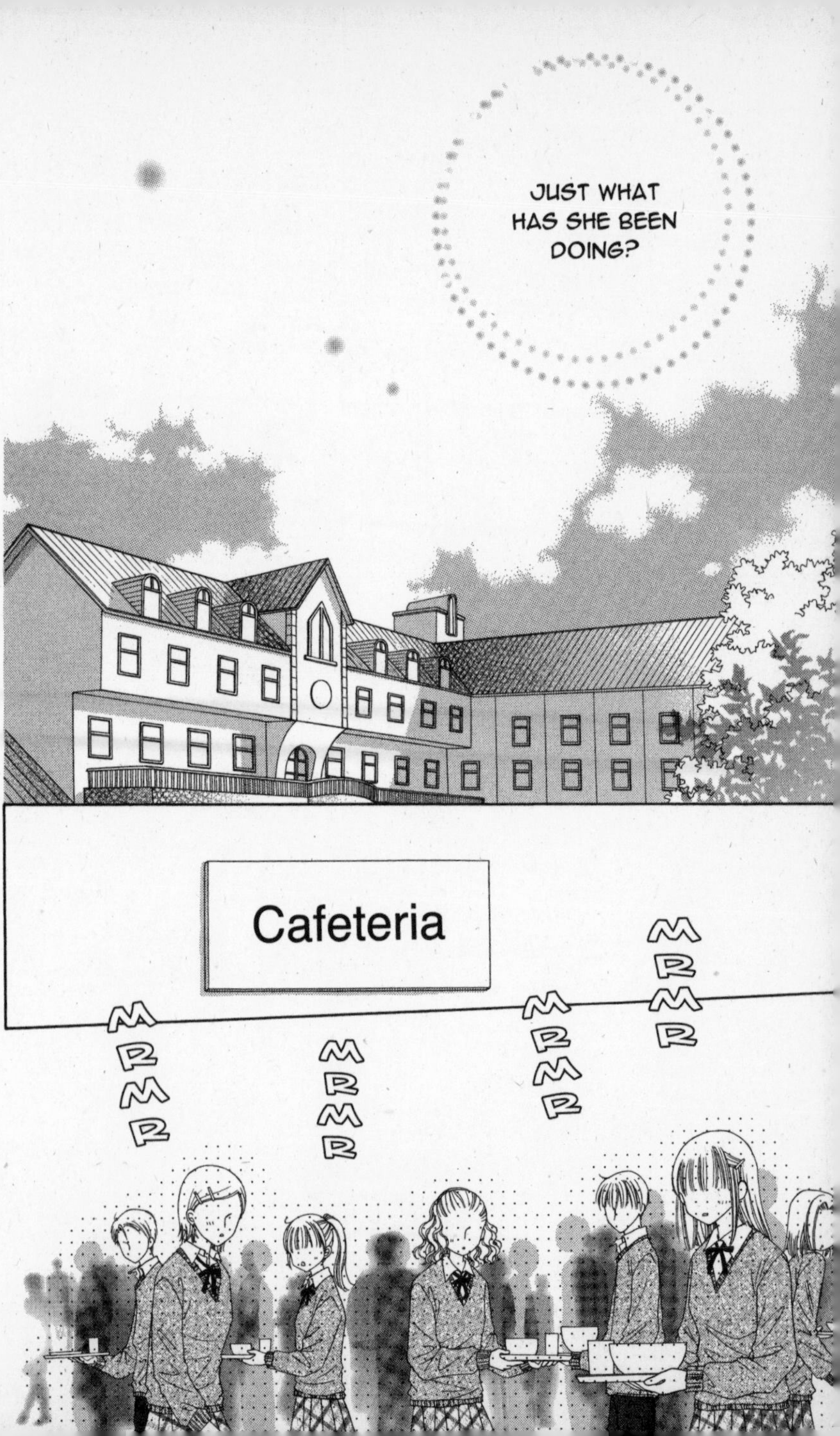
JUST WHAT HAS SHE BEEN DOING?
Cafeteria
MRMR
MRMR
MRMR
MRMR

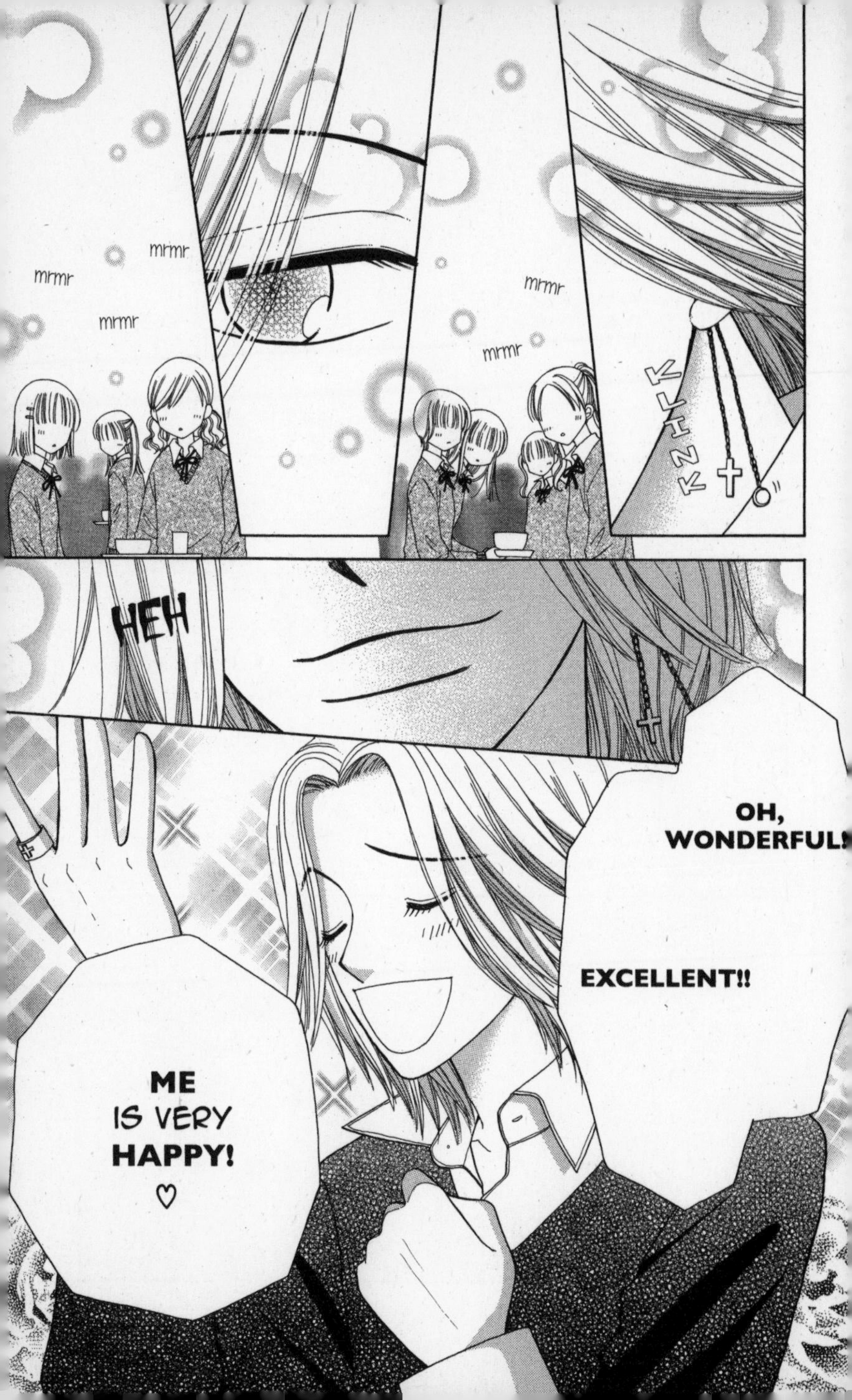
KZHNK
mrmr
mrmr
mrmr
mrmr
mrmr
HEH
OH, WONDERFUL!
EXCELLENT!!
ME IS VERY HAPPY! ♡

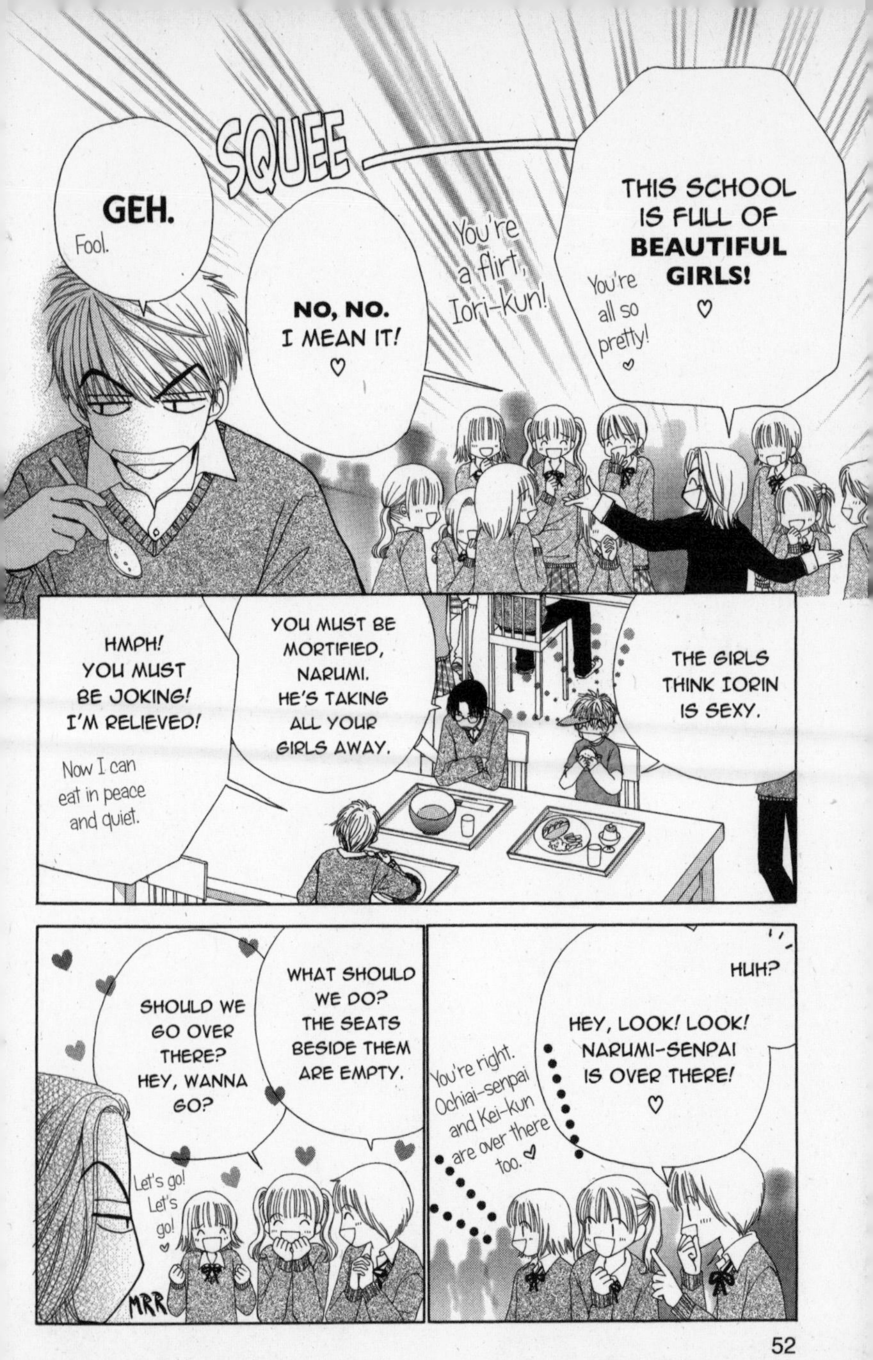
THIS SCHOOL IS FULL OF BEAUTIFUL GIRLS! ♡
You're all so pretty! ♡
You're a flirt, Iori-Kun!
NO, NO. I MEAN IT! ♡
SQUEE
GEH.
Fool.
THE GIRLS THINK IORIN IS SEXY.
YOU MUST BE MORTIFIED, NARUMI. HE'S TAKING ALL YOUR GIRLS AWAY.
HMPH! YOU MUST BE JOKING! I'M RELIEVED!
Now I can eat in peace and quiet.
HUH?
HEY, LOOK! LOOK! NARUMI-SENPAI IS OVER THERE! ♡
You're right. Ochiai-senpai and Kei-Kun are over there too. ♡
WHAT SHOULD WE DO? THE SEATS BESIDE THEM ARE EMPTY.
SHOULD WE GO OVER THERE? HEY, WANNA GO?
Let's go! Let's go! ♡
MRR

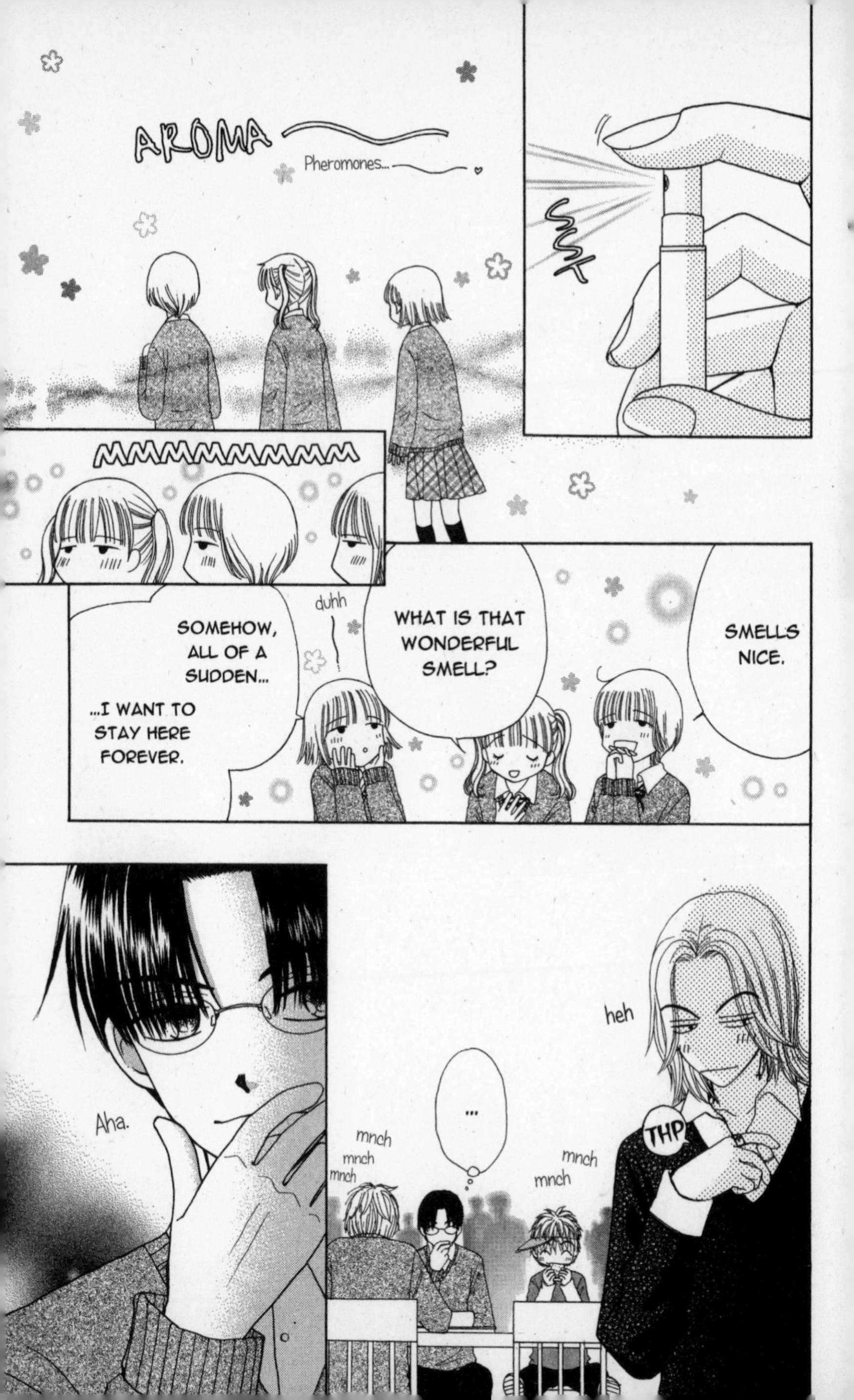
SSST
AROMA
Pheromones...
MMMMMMMMM
SMELLS NICE.
WHAT IS THAT WONDERFUL SMELL?
duhh
SOMEHOW, ALL OF A SUDDEN...
...I WANT TO STAY HERE FOREVER.
heh
THP
mnch mnch
...
mnch mnch mnch
Aha.

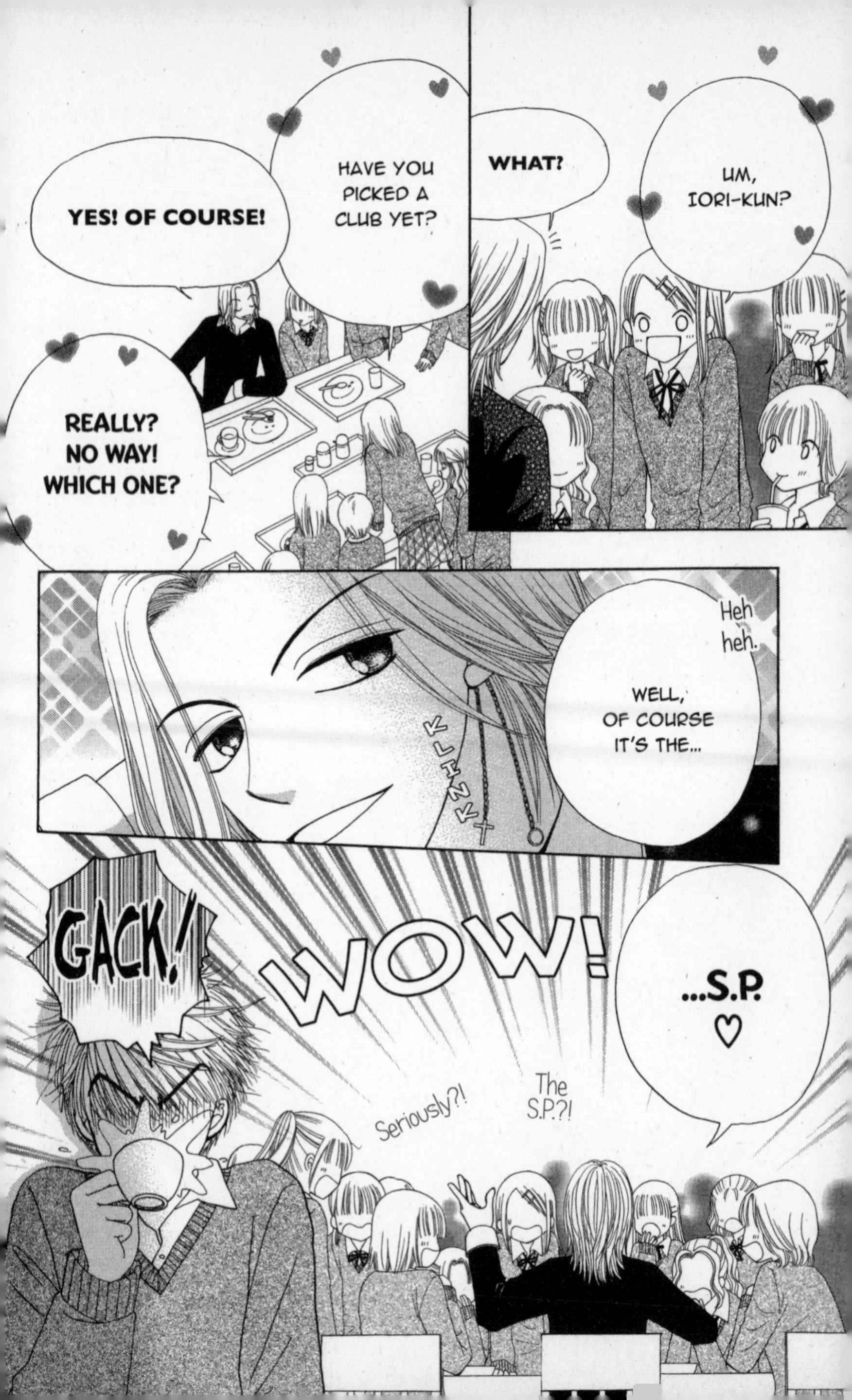
UM, IORI-KUN?
WHAT?
HAVE YOU PICKED A CLUB YET?
YES! OF COURSE!
REALLY? NO WAY! WHICH ONE?
Heh heh.
WELL, OF COURSE IT'S THE...
KLINK
...S.P. ♡
WOW!
The S.P.?!
Seriously?!
GACK!

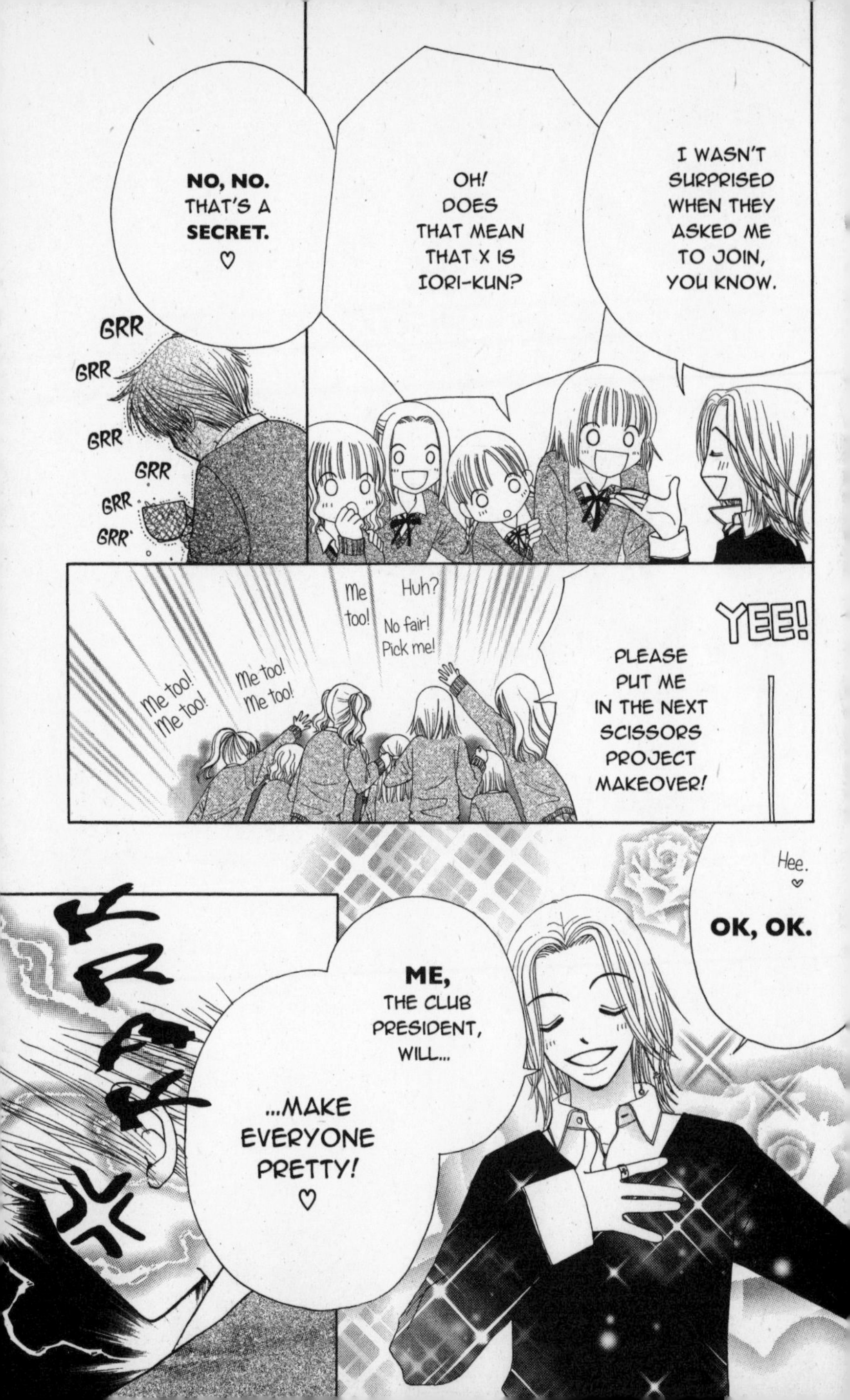
I WASN'T SURPRISED WHEN THEY ASKED ME TO JOIN, YOU KNOW.
OH! DOES THAT MEAN THAT X IS IORI-KUN?
NO, NO. THAT'S A SECRET. ♡
GRR
GRR
GRR
GRR
GRR
GRR
YEE!
PLEASE PUT ME IN THE NEXT SCISSORS PROJECT MAKEOVER!
Huh?
No fair! Pick me!
Me too!
Me too! Me too!
Me too! Me too!
Hee. ♡
OK, OK.
ME, THE CLUB PRESIDENT, WILL...
...MAKE EVERYONE PRETTY! ♡

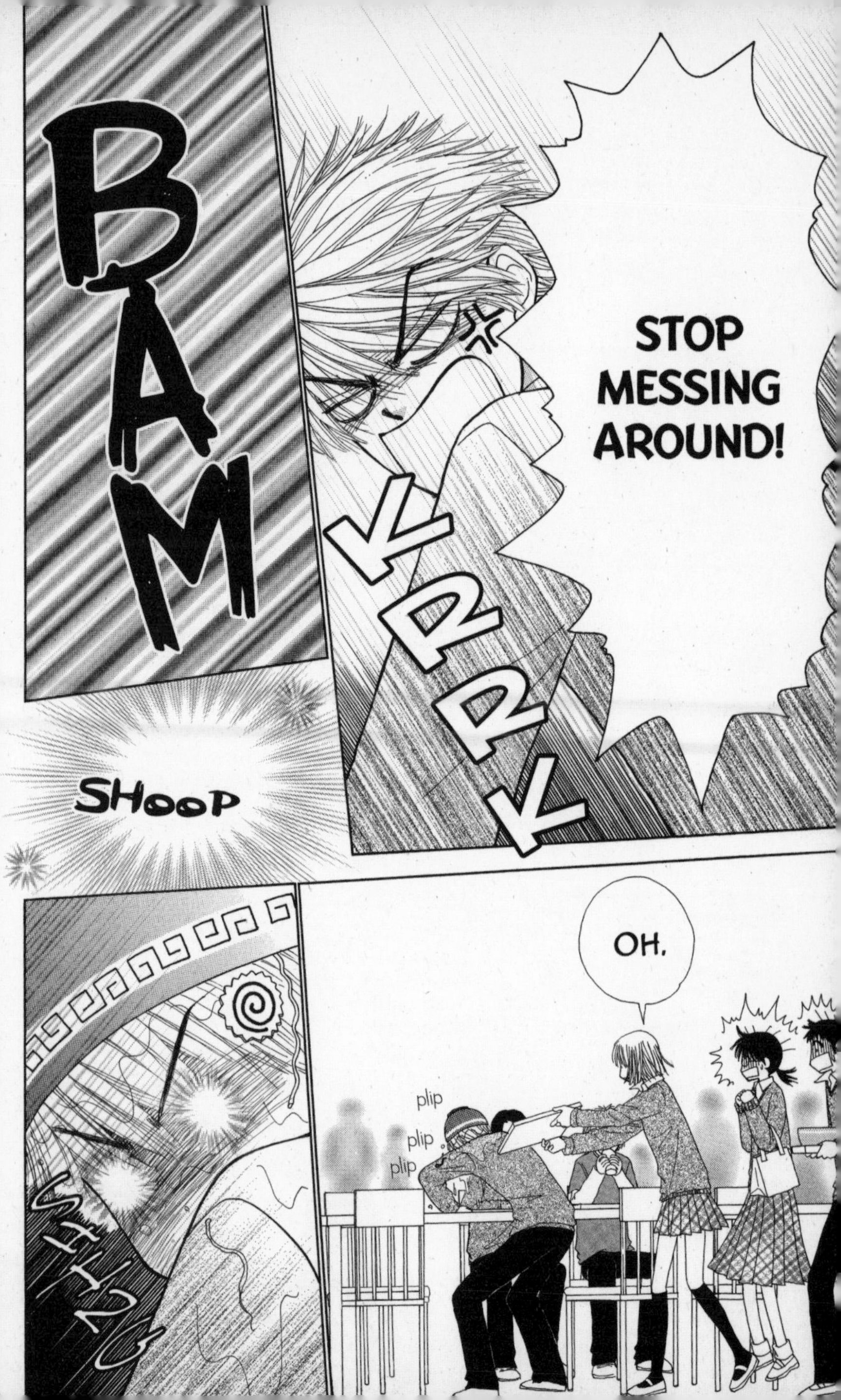
STOP MESSING AROUND!
KRRK
BAM
SHOOP
OH.
plip
plip
plip

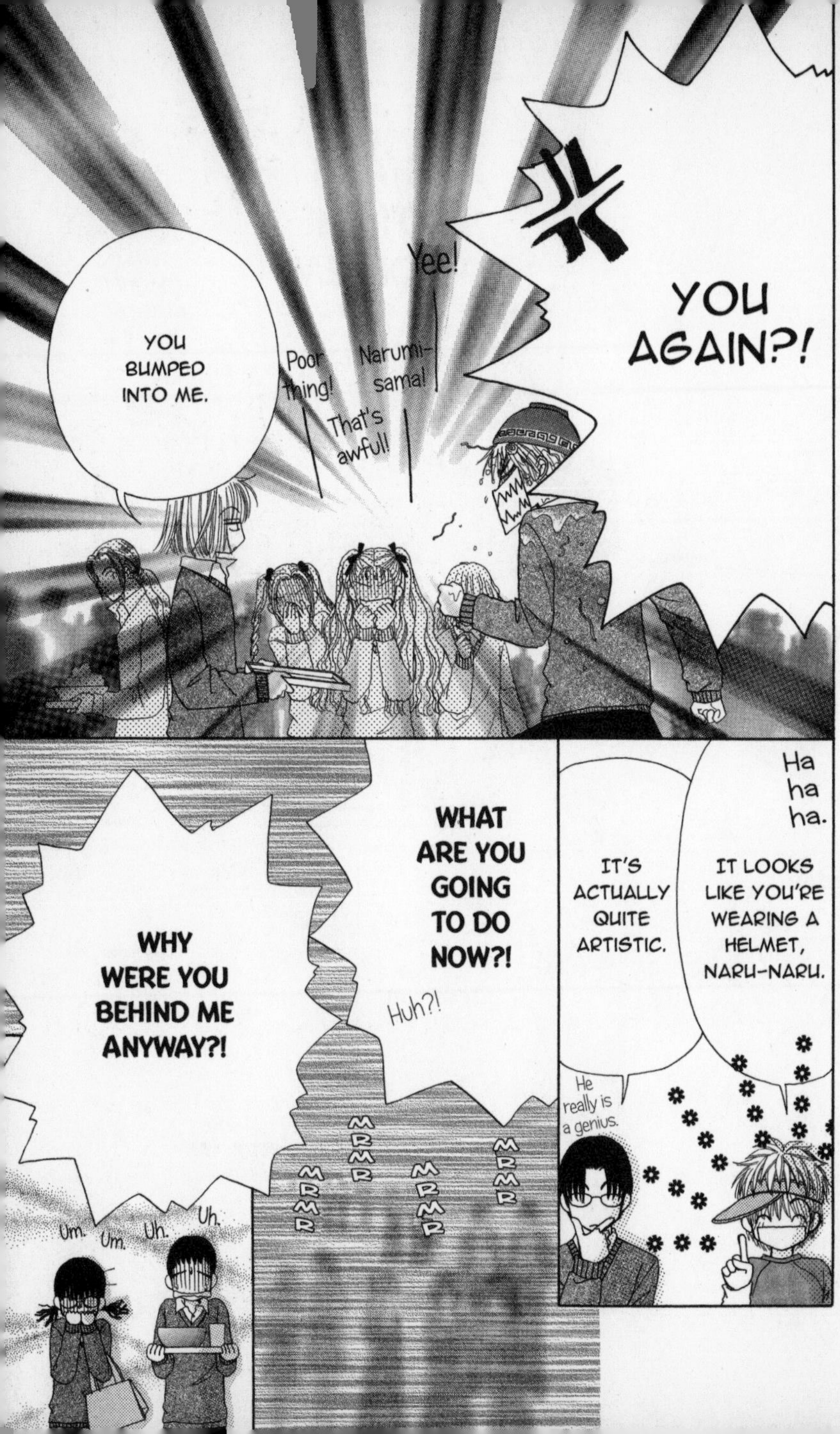

YOU AGAIN?!
Yee!
Narumi-sama!
That's awful!
Poor thing!
YOU BUMPED INTO ME.
Ha ha ha.
IT LOOKS LIKE YOU'RE WEARING A HELMET, NARU-NARU.
IT'S ACTUALLY QUITE ARTISTIC.
He really is a genius.
WHAT ARE YOU GOING TO DO NOW?!
Huh?!
MRMR
MRMR
MRMR
MRMR
WHY WERE YOU BEHIND ME ANYWAY?!
Uh.
Uh.
Um.
Um.

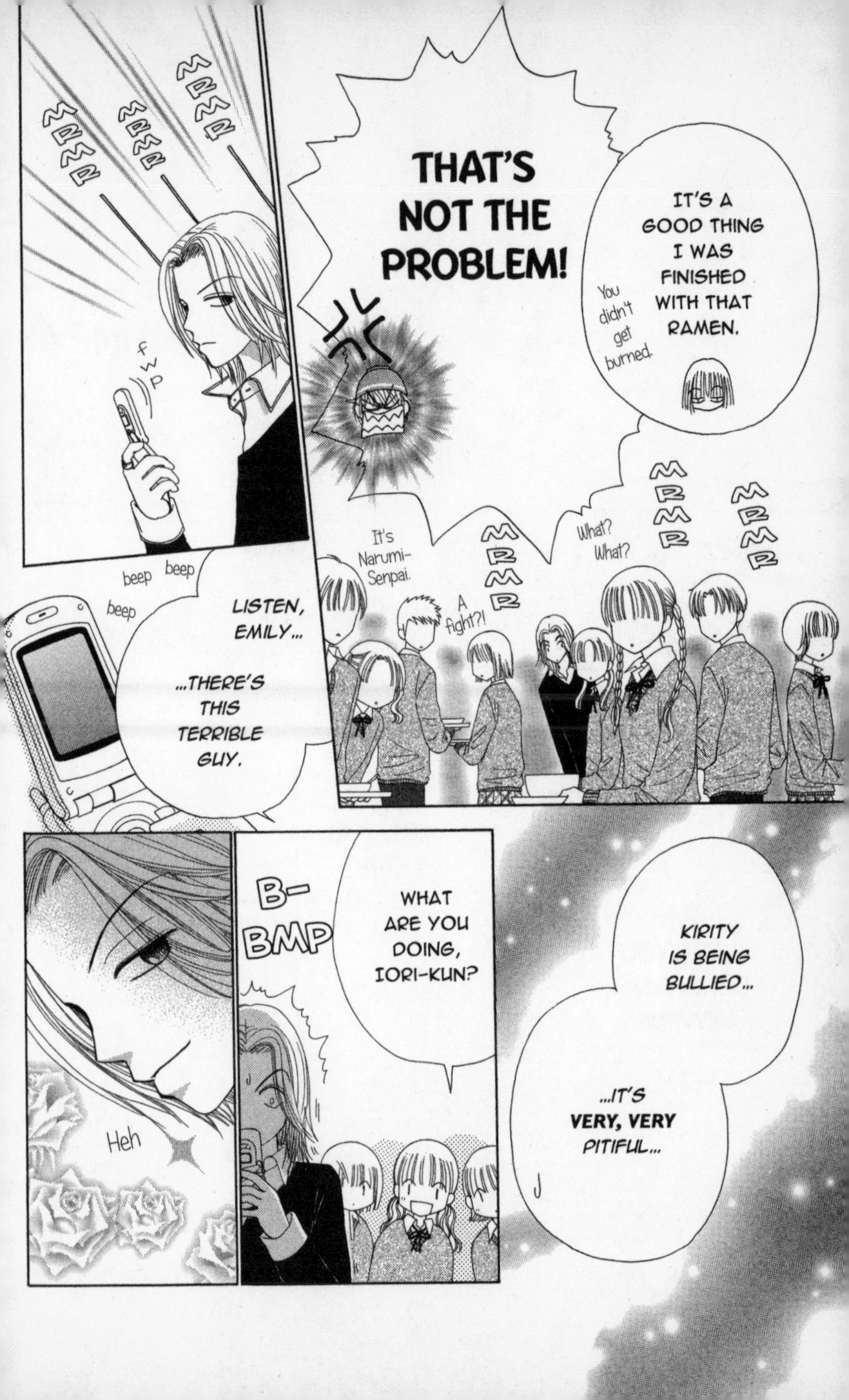
THAT'S NOT THE PROBLEM!
IT'S A GOOD THING I WAS FINISHED WITH THAT RAMEN.
You didn't get burned.
MRMR
MRMR
What? What?
MRMR
A fight?!
It's Narumi-Senpai.
MRMR
MRMR
MRMR
FWP
beep beep
beep
LISTEN, EMILY...
...THERE'S THIS TERRIBLE GUY.
KIRITY IS BEING BULLIED...
...IT'S **VERY, VERY** PITIFUL...
WHAT ARE YOU DOING, IORI-KUN?
B-BMP
Heh

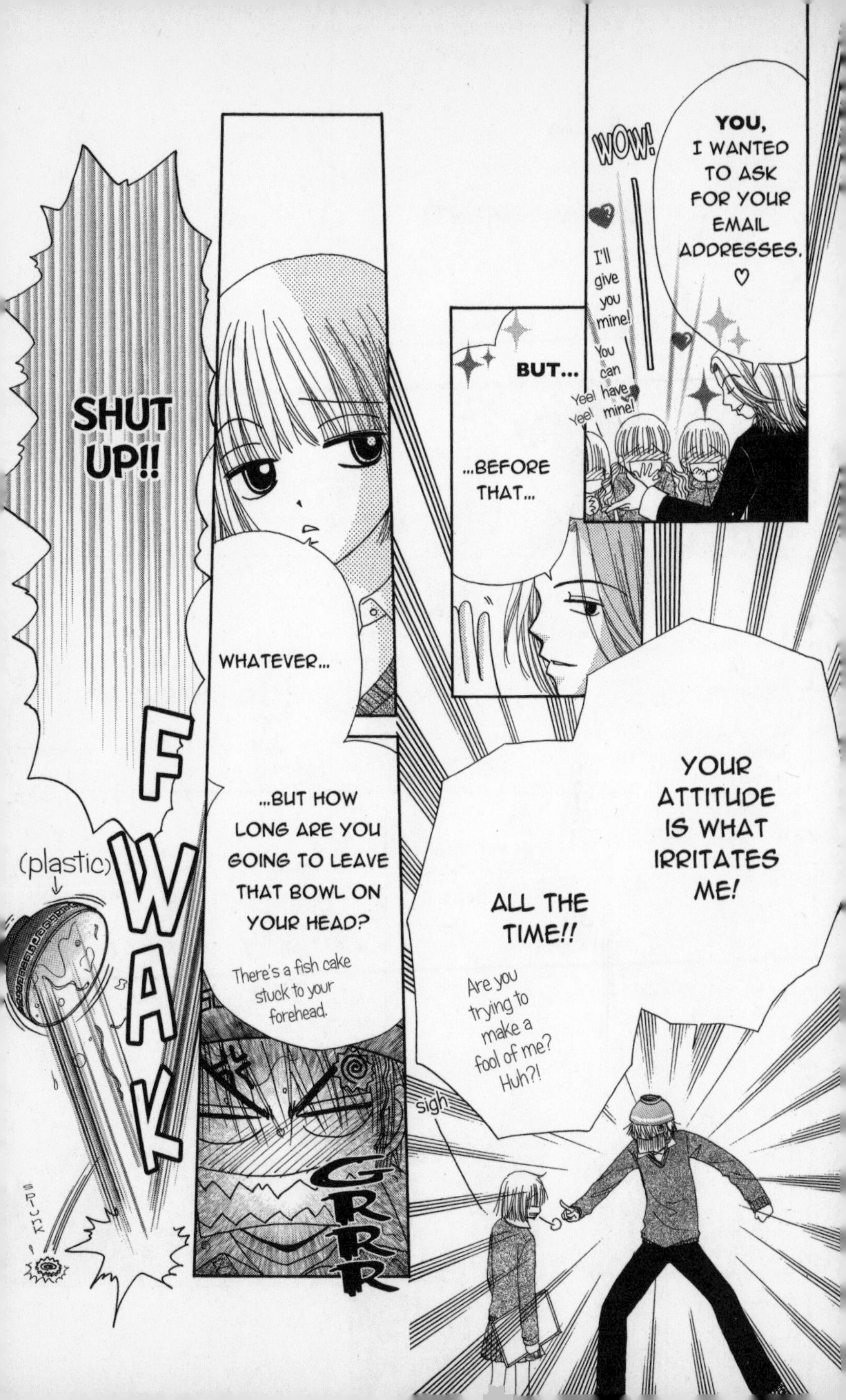

YOU, I WANTED TO ASK FOR YOUR EMAIL ADDRESSES. ♡
WOW!
I'll give you mine!
You can have mine!
Yee! Yee!
BUT...
...BEFORE THAT...
YOUR ATTITUDE IS WHAT IRRITATES ME!
ALL THE TIME!!
Are you trying to make a fool of me? Huh?!
sigh
WHATEVER...
...BUT HOW LONG ARE YOU GOING TO LEAVE THAT BOWL ON YOUR HEAD?
There's a fish cake stuck to your forehead.
GRRR
SHUT UP!!
FWAK
(plastic)

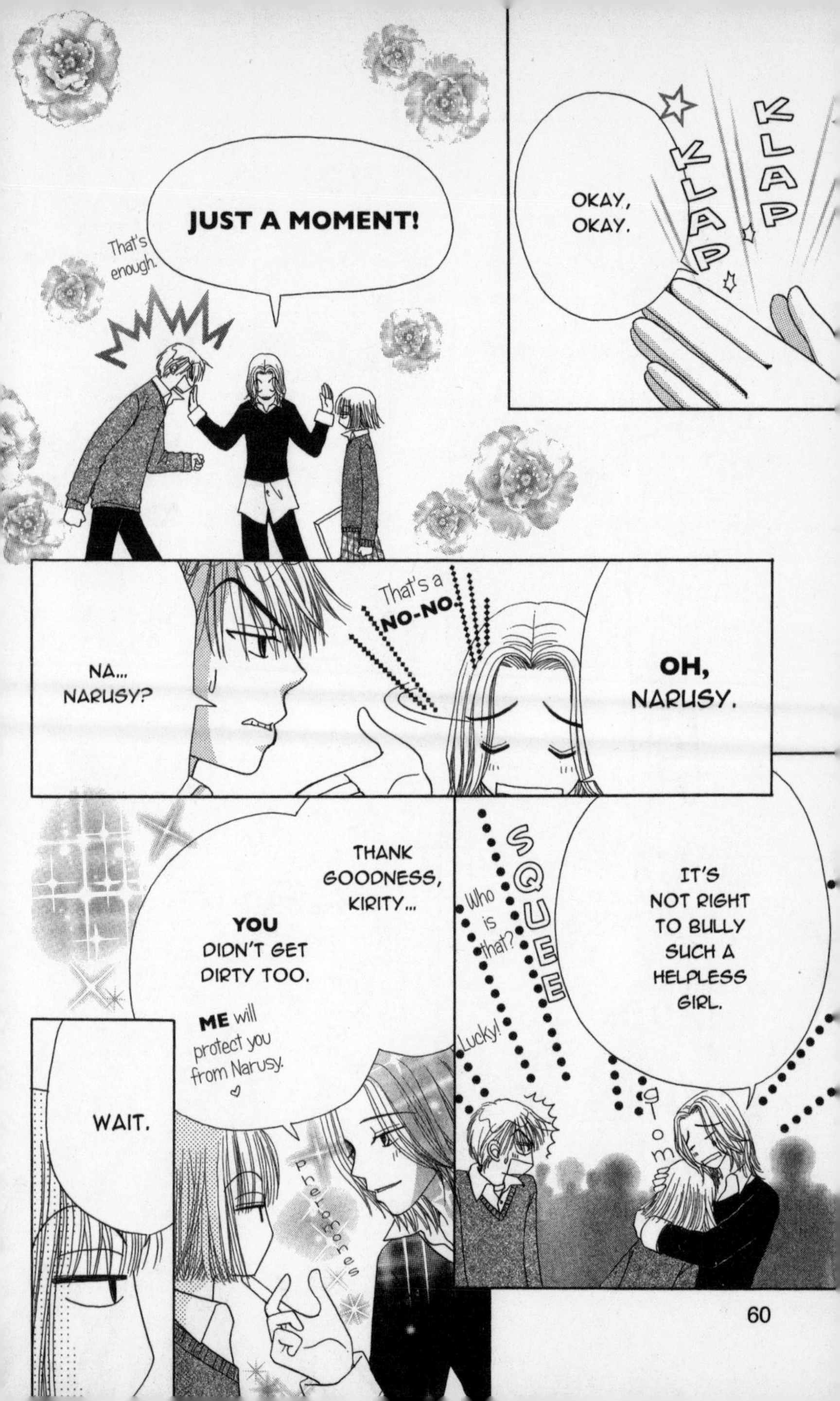

KLAP KLAP
OKAY, OKAY.
JUST A MOMENT!
That's enough.
OH, NARUSY.
That's a NO-NO
NA... NARUSY?
IT'S NOT RIGHT TO BULLY SUCH A HELPLESS GIRL.
SQUEE
Who is that?
Lucky!
glom
THANK GOODNESS, KIRITY...
YOU DIDN'T GET DIRTY TOO.
ME will protect you from Narusy. ♡
Pheromones
WAIT.

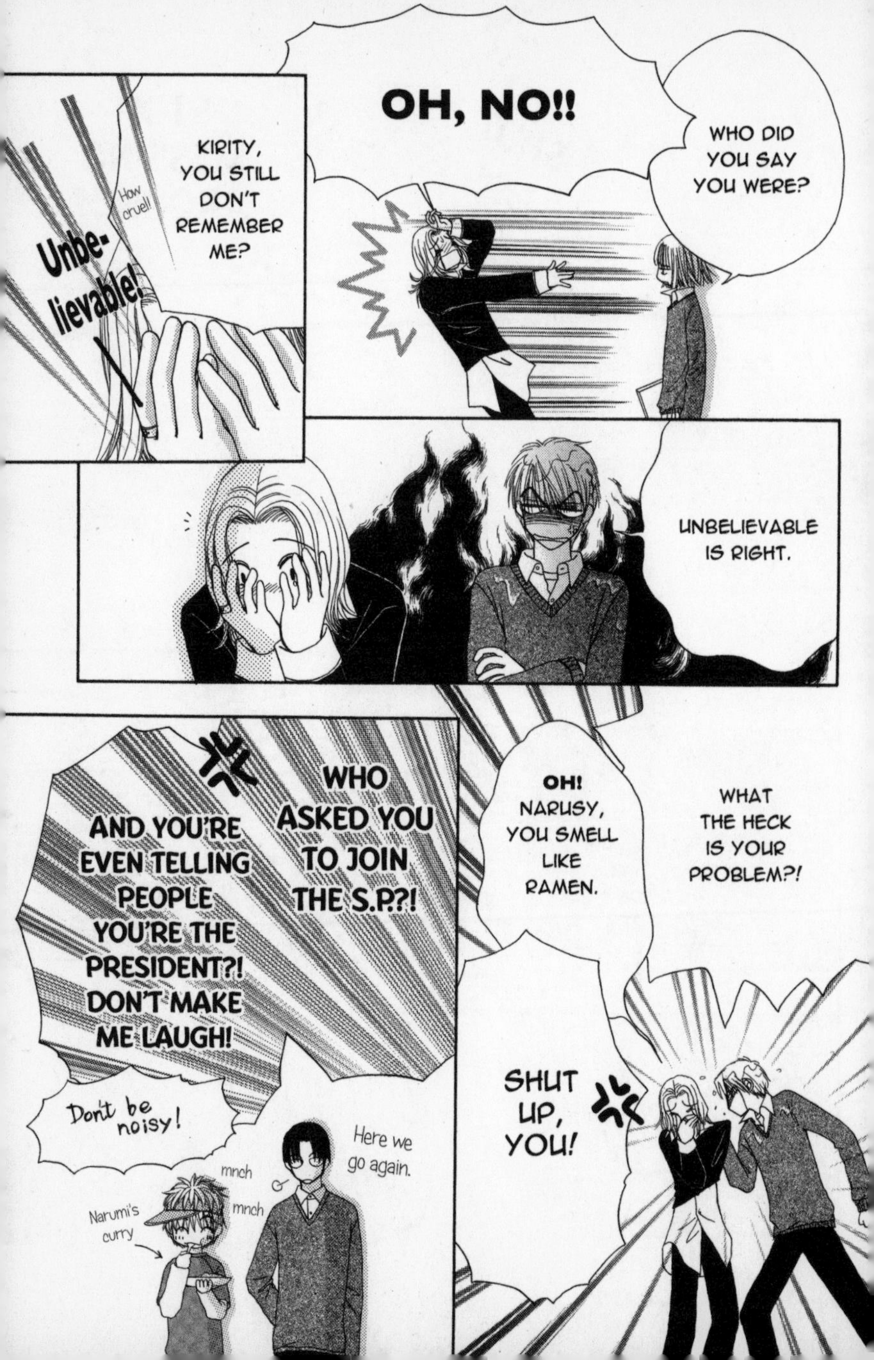
WHO DID YOU SAY YOU WERE?
OH, NO!!
KIRITY, YOU STILL DON'T REMEMBER ME?
How cruel!
Unbe-lievable!
UNBELIEVABLE IS RIGHT.
OH! NARUSY, YOU SMELL LIKE RAMEN.
WHAT THE HECK IS YOUR PROBLEM?!
SHUT UP, YOU!
WHO ASKED YOU TO JOIN THE S.P.?!
AND YOU'RE EVEN TELLING PEOPLE YOU'RE THE PRESIDENT?! DON'T MAKE ME LAUGH!
Don't be noisy!
Here we go again.
mnch
mnch
Narumi's curry

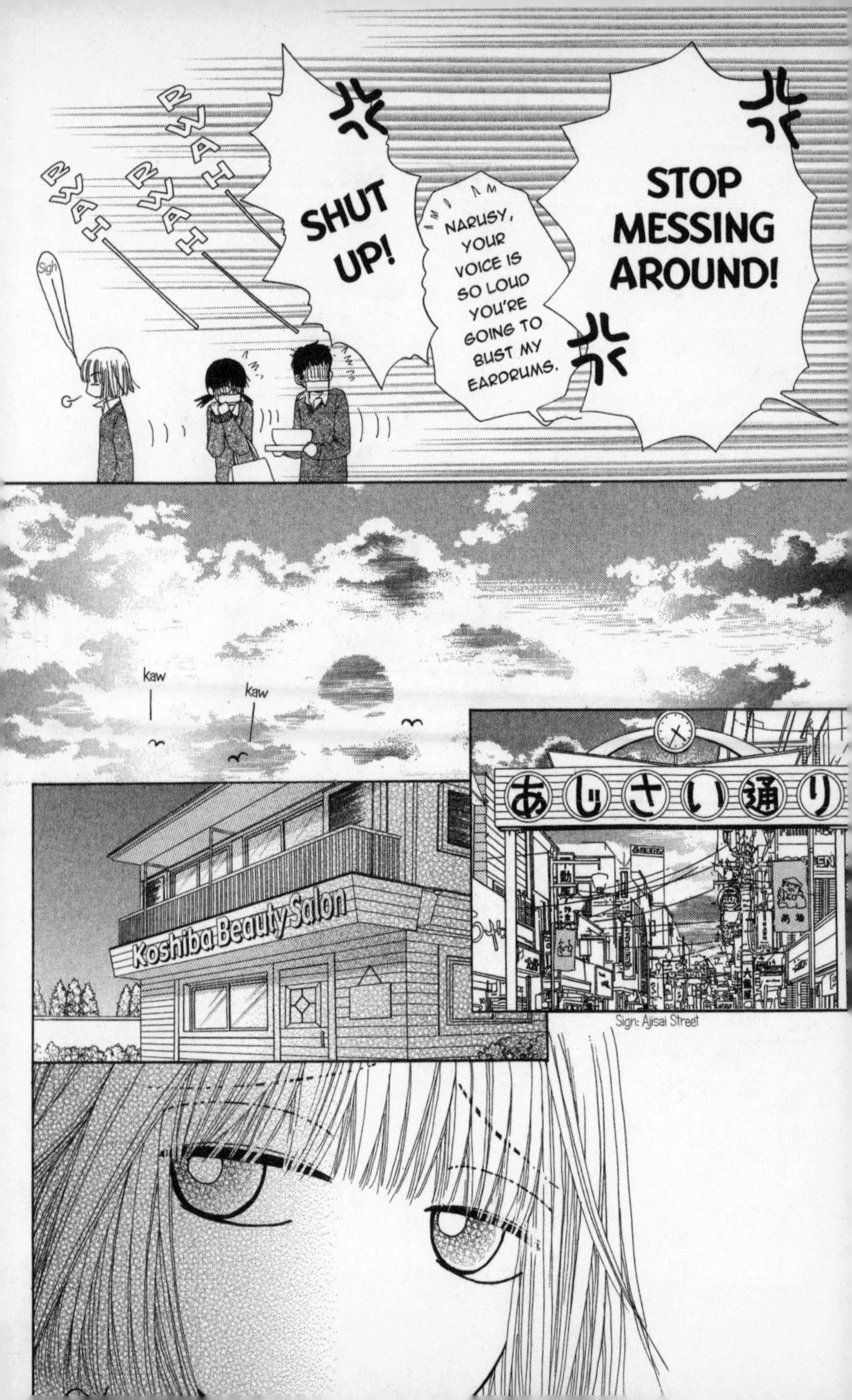
STOP MESSING AROUND!
NARUSY, YOUR VOICE IS SO LOUD YOU'RE GOING TO BUST MY EARDRUMS.
SHUT UP!
Sigh
kaw
kaw
Sign: Ajisai Street
Koshiba Beauty Salon

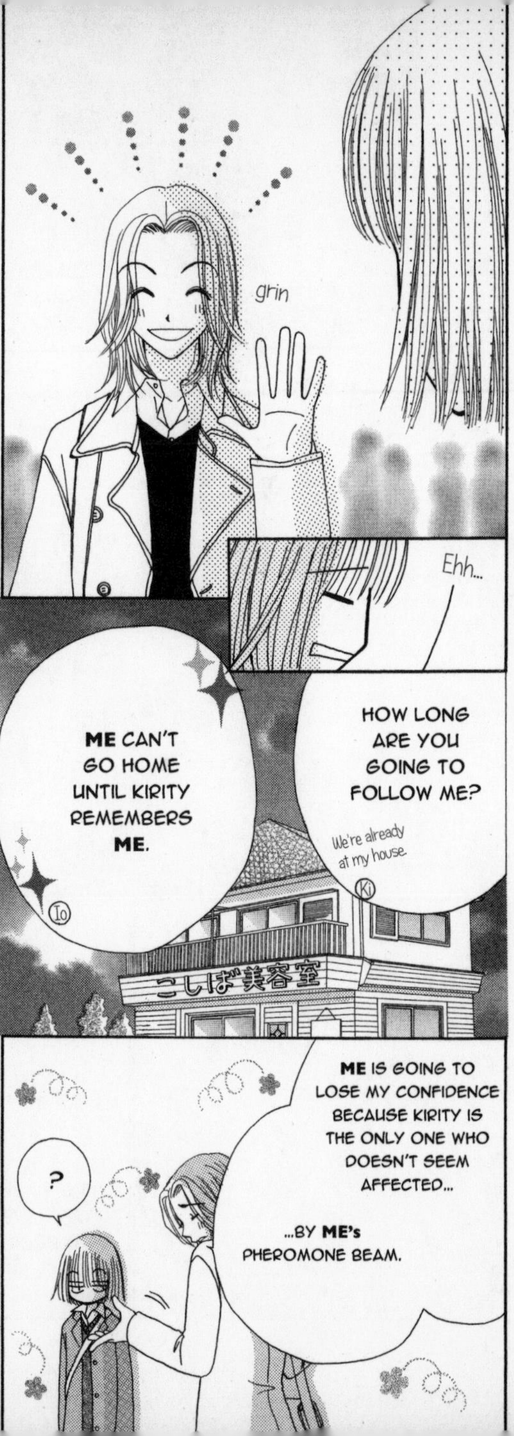
grin
Ehh...
HOW LONG ARE YOU GOING TO FOLLOW ME?
We're already at my house.
ME CAN'T GO HOME UNTIL KIRITY REMEMBERS ME.
こしば美容室
ME IS GOING TO LOSE MY CONFIDENCE BECAUSE KIRITY IS THE ONLY ONE WHO DOESN'T SEEM AFFECTED...
...BY ME's PHEROMONE BEAM.
?

K's Club Talk

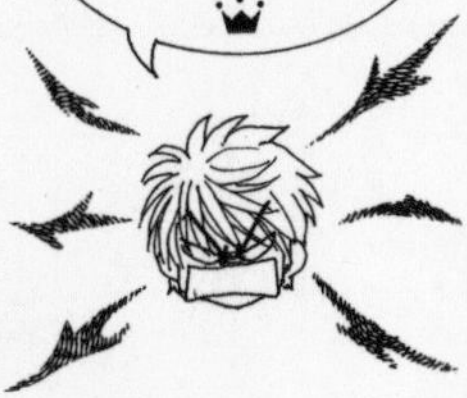

- There are lots of different characters in BP, but Naru-Naru is the one who is always angry.~~~ ♪♪♪ I realized that as I read back through the first volume. He might pop a blood vessel before long!

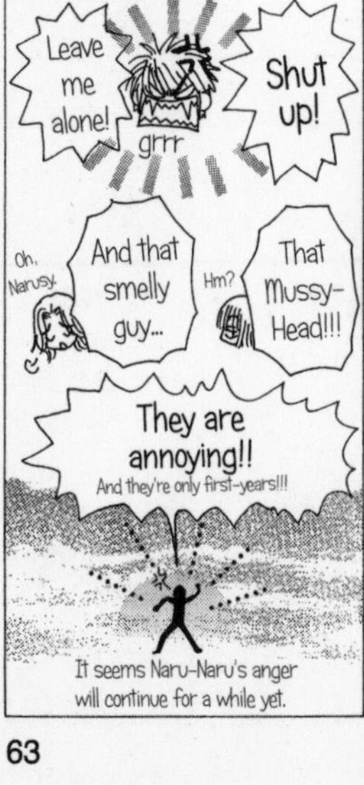
Leave me alone!
grrr
Shut up!
Oh, Narusy.
And that smelly guy...
Hm?
That Mussy-Head!!!
They are annoying!!
And they're only first-years!!!

It seems Naru-Naru's anger will continue for a while yet.

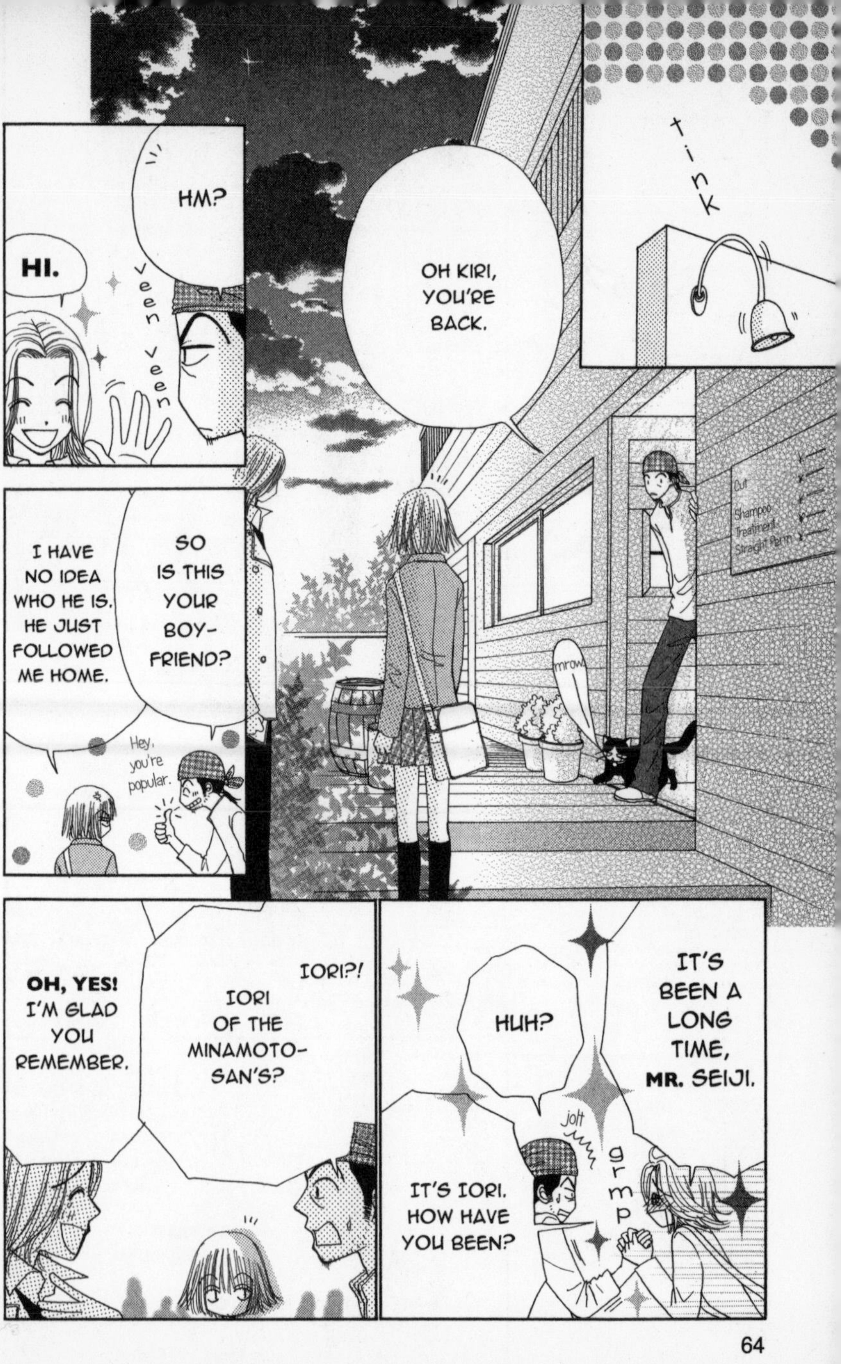

tink
OH KIRI, YOU'RE BACK.
mrow
Cut
Shampoo
Treatment
Straight Perm
HM?
veen veen
HI.
SO IS THIS YOUR BOY-FRIEND?
I HAVE NO IDEA WHO HE IS. HE JUST FOLLOWED ME HOME.
Hey, you're popular.
IT'S BEEN A LONG TIME, MR. SEIJI.
HUH?
jolt
grmp
IT'S IORI. HOW HAVE YOU BEEN?
IORI?!
IORI OF THE MINAMOTO-SAN'S?
OH, YES! I'M GLAD YOU REMEMBER.

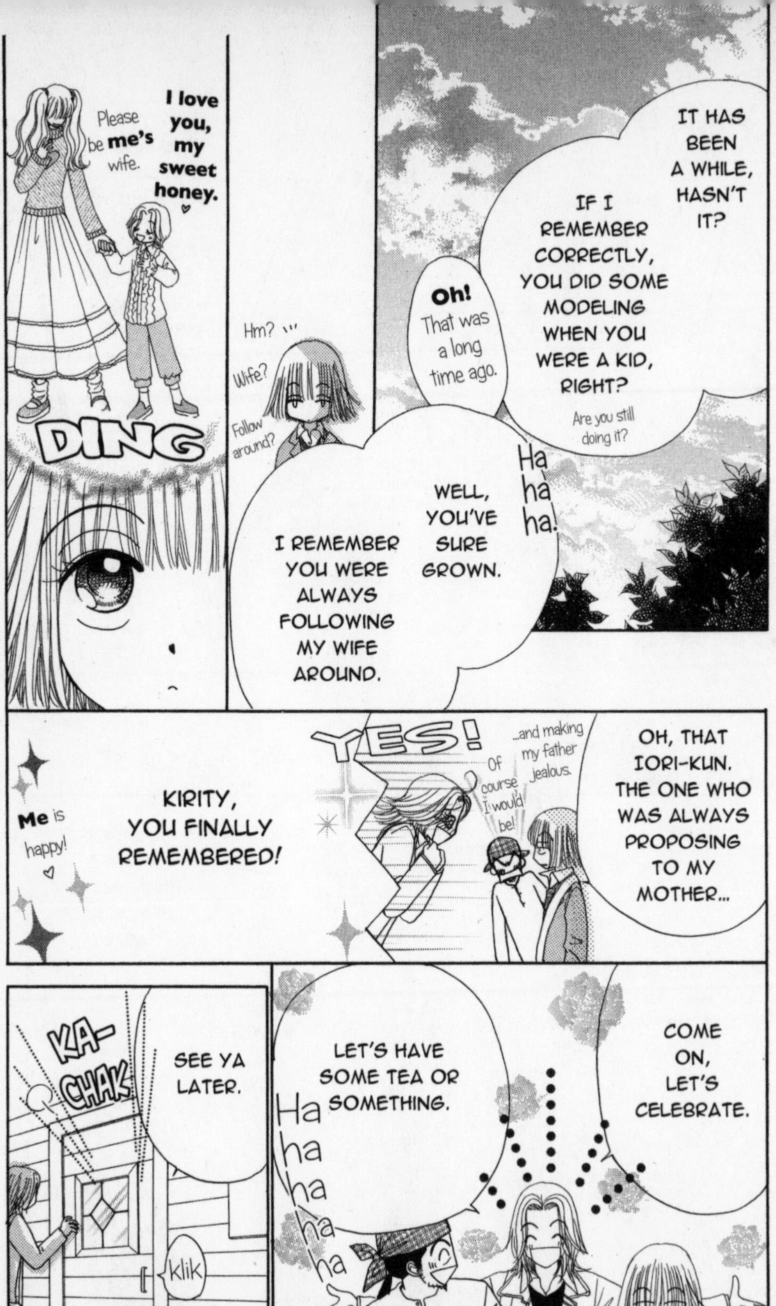
IT HAS BEEN A WHILE, HASN'T IT?
IF I REMEMBER CORRECTLY, YOU DID SOME MODELING WHEN YOU WERE A KID, RIGHT?
Are you still doing it?
Oh! That was a long time ago.
Ha ha ha!
WELL, YOU'VE SURE GROWN.
I REMEMBER YOU WERE ALWAYS FOLLOWING MY WIFE AROUND.
Hm?
Wife?
Follow around?
I love you, my sweet honey.
Please be me's wife.
DING
OH, THAT IORI-KUN. THE ONE WHO WAS ALWAYS PROPOSING TO MY MOTHER...
...and making my father jealous.
Of course I would be!
YES!
KIRITY, YOU FINALLY REMEMBERED!
Me is happy!
COME ON, LET'S CELEBRATE.
LET'S HAVE SOME TEA OR SOMETHING.
Ha ha ha ha ha
SEE YA LATER.
KA-CHAK
klik

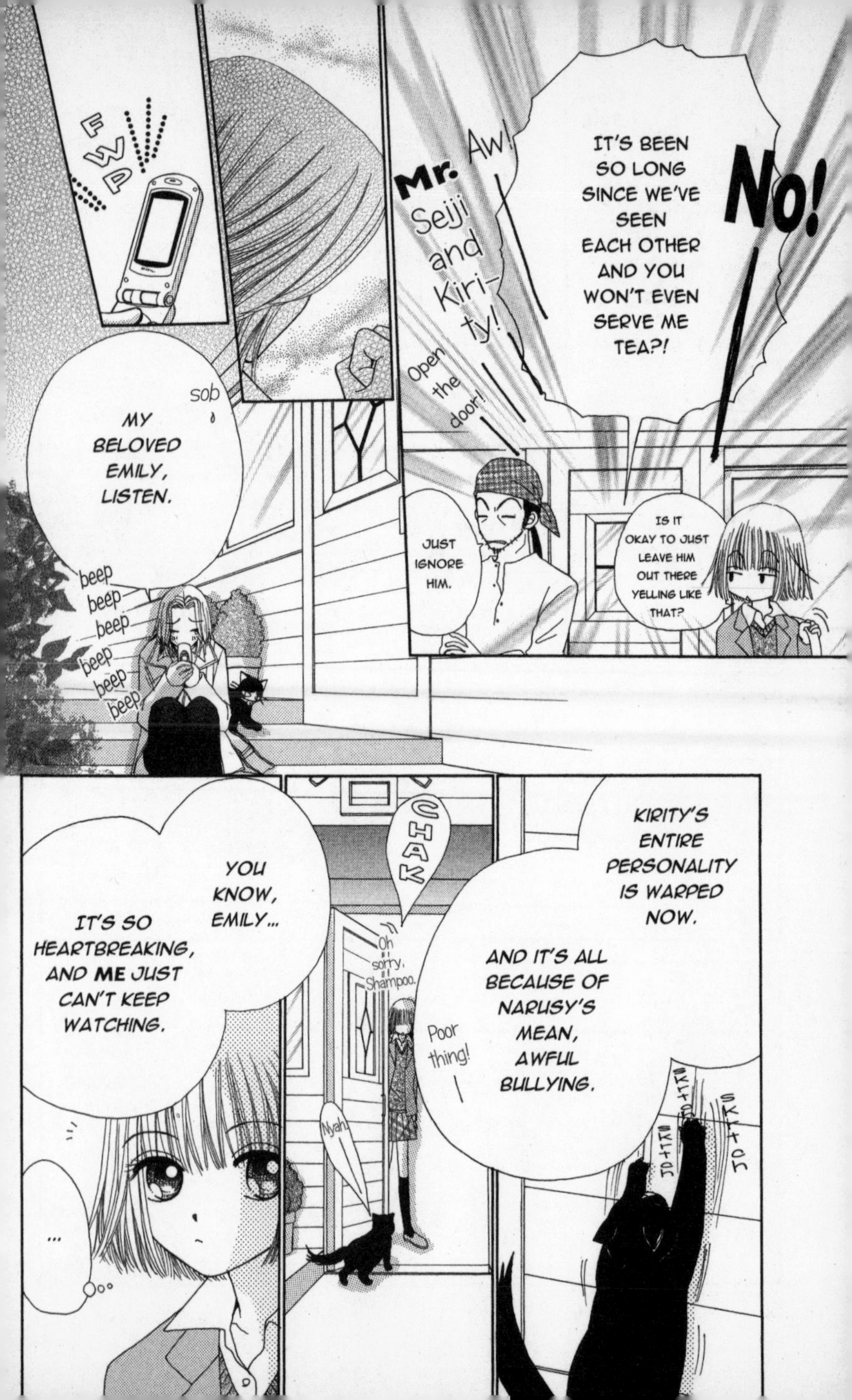
Mr. Seiji and Kirity!
Aw!
Open the door!
IT'S BEEN SO LONG SINCE WE'VE SEEN EACH OTHER AND YOU WON'T EVEN SERVE ME TEA?!
No!
IS IT OKAY TO JUST LEAVE HIM OUT THERE YELLING LIKE THAT?
JUST IGNORE HIM.
FWP
sob
MY BELOVED EMILY, LISTEN.
beep beep beep beep beep beep
KIRITY'S ENTIRE PERSONALITY IS WARPED NOW.
AND IT'S ALL BECAUSE OF NARUSY'S MEAN, AWFUL BULLYING.
SKITCH
SKITCH
CHAK
Oh sorry, Shampoo.
Poor thing!
Nyah.
YOU KNOW, EMILY...
IT'S SO HEARTBREAKING, AND ME JUST CAN'T KEEP WATCHING.
...

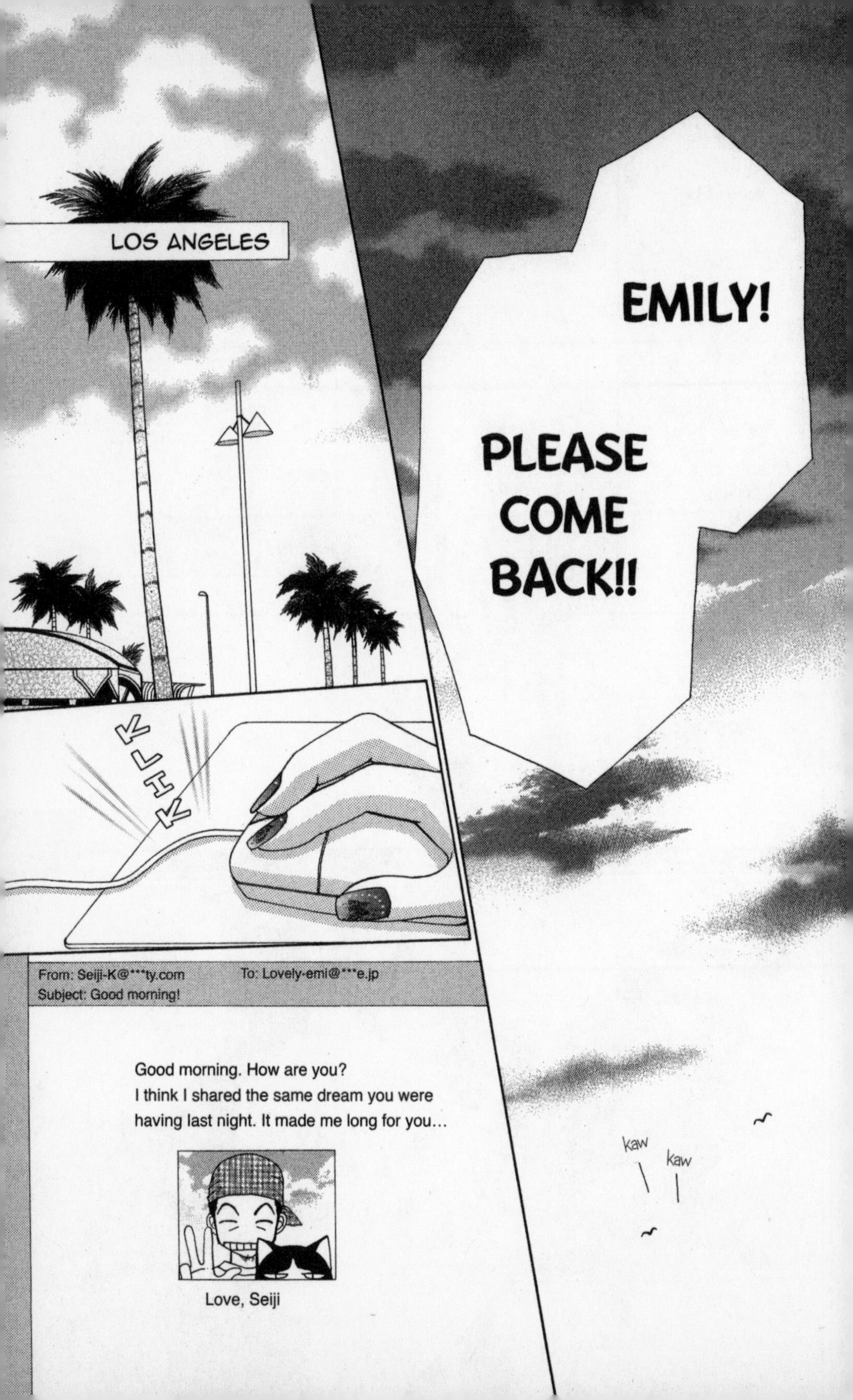
EMILY!
PLEASE COME BACK!!
kaw
kaw
LOS ANGELES
KLIK
From: Seiji-K@***ty.com
To: Lovely-emi@***e.jp
Subject: Good morning!
Good morning. How are you?
I think I shared the same dream you were having last night. It made me long for you…
Love, Seiji

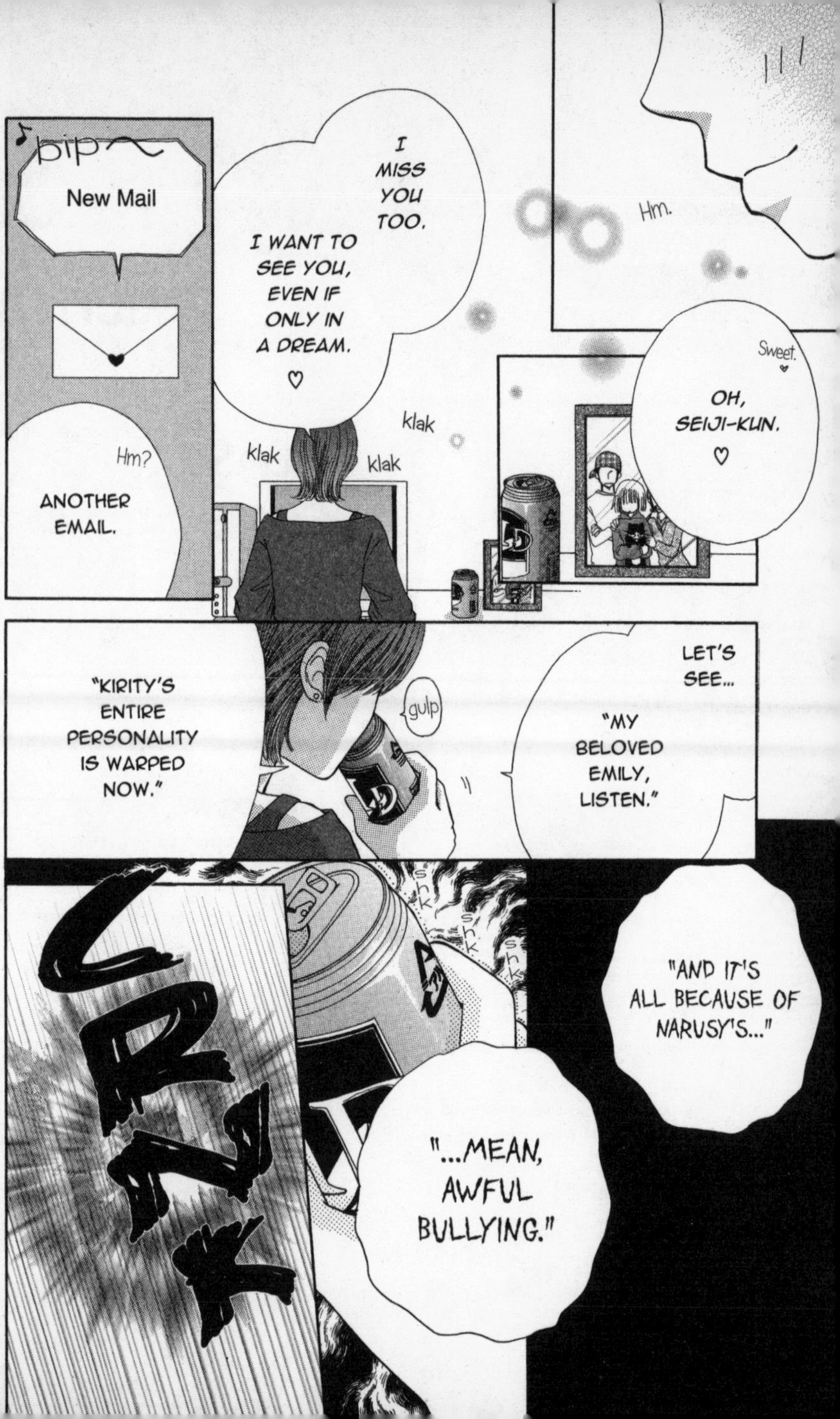
Hm.
Sweet.
OH, SEIJI-KUN. ♡
I MISS YOU TOO.
I WANT TO SEE YOU, EVEN IF ONLY IN A DREAM. ♡
klak
klak
klak
bip
New Mail
Hm?
ANOTHER EMAIL.
LET'S SEE...
"MY BELOVED EMILY, LISTEN."
gulp
"KIRITY'S ENTIRE PERSONALITY IS WARPED NOW."
"AND IT'S ALL BECAUSE OF NARUSY'S..."
"...MEAN, AWFUL BULLYING."
shk
shk
shk

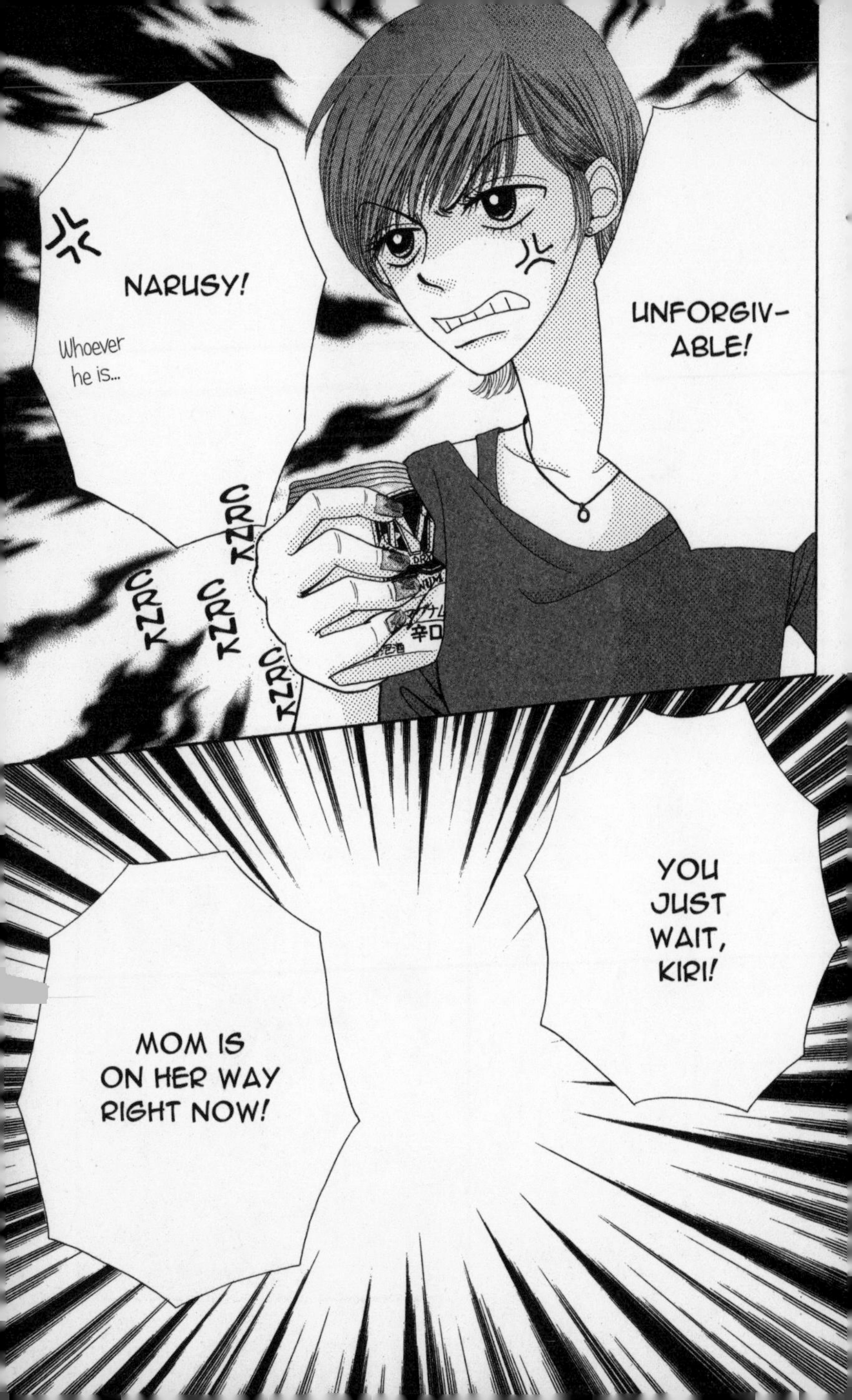
UNFORGIV-
ABLE!
NARUSY!
Whoever he is...
CRNK KZRK
CRNK KZRK
CRNK KZRK
CRNK KZRK
YOU JUST WAIT, KIRI!
MOM IS ON HER WAY RIGHT NOW!

Beauty Pop

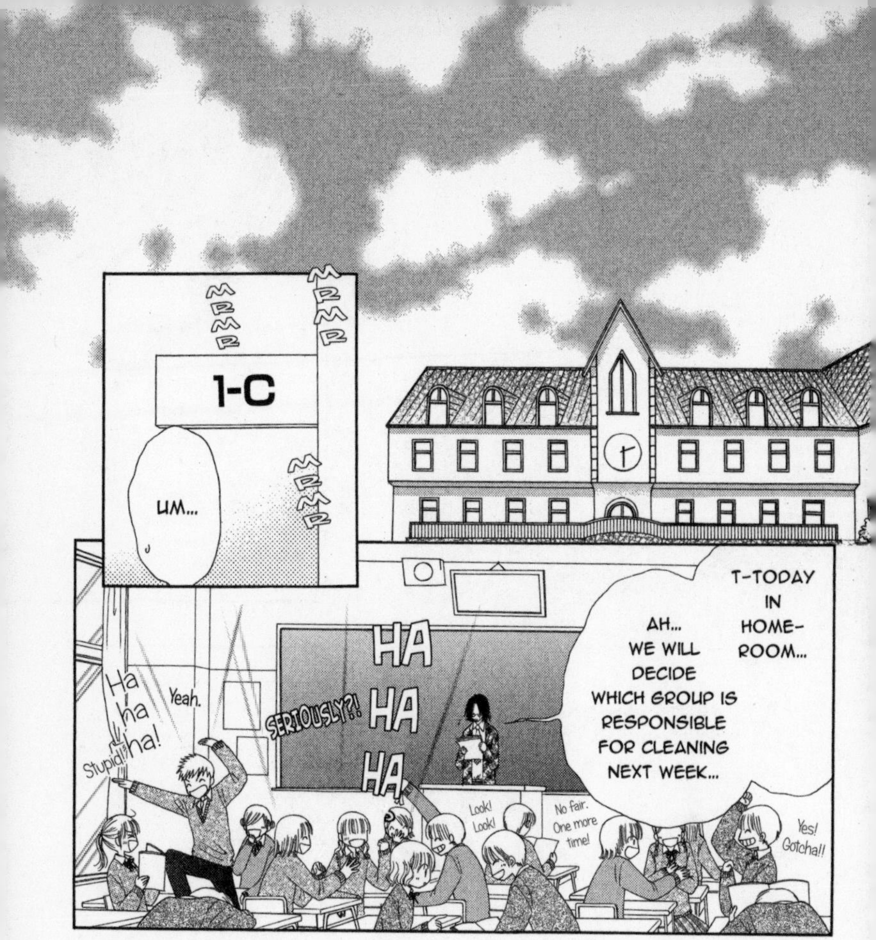
MRMR
MRMR
1-C
MRMR
UM...
T-TODAY IN HOMEROOM...
AH... WE WILL DECIDE WHICH GROUP IS RESPONSIBLE FOR CLEANING NEXT WEEK...
Yes! Gotcha!!
No fair. One more time!
Look! Look!
HA HA HA
SERIOUSLY?!
Yeah.
Ha ha ha!
Stupid!!
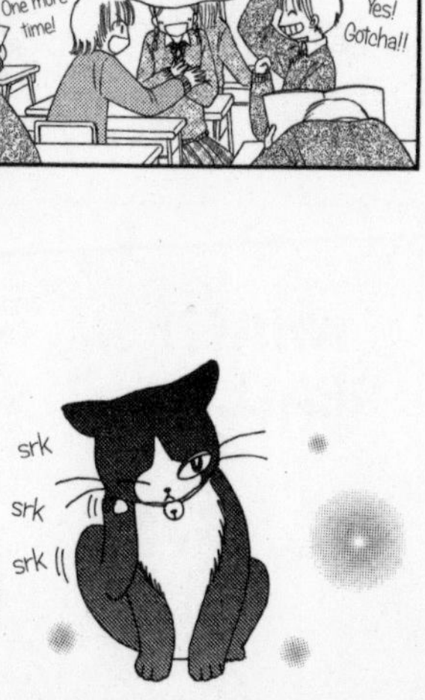
srk
srk
srk

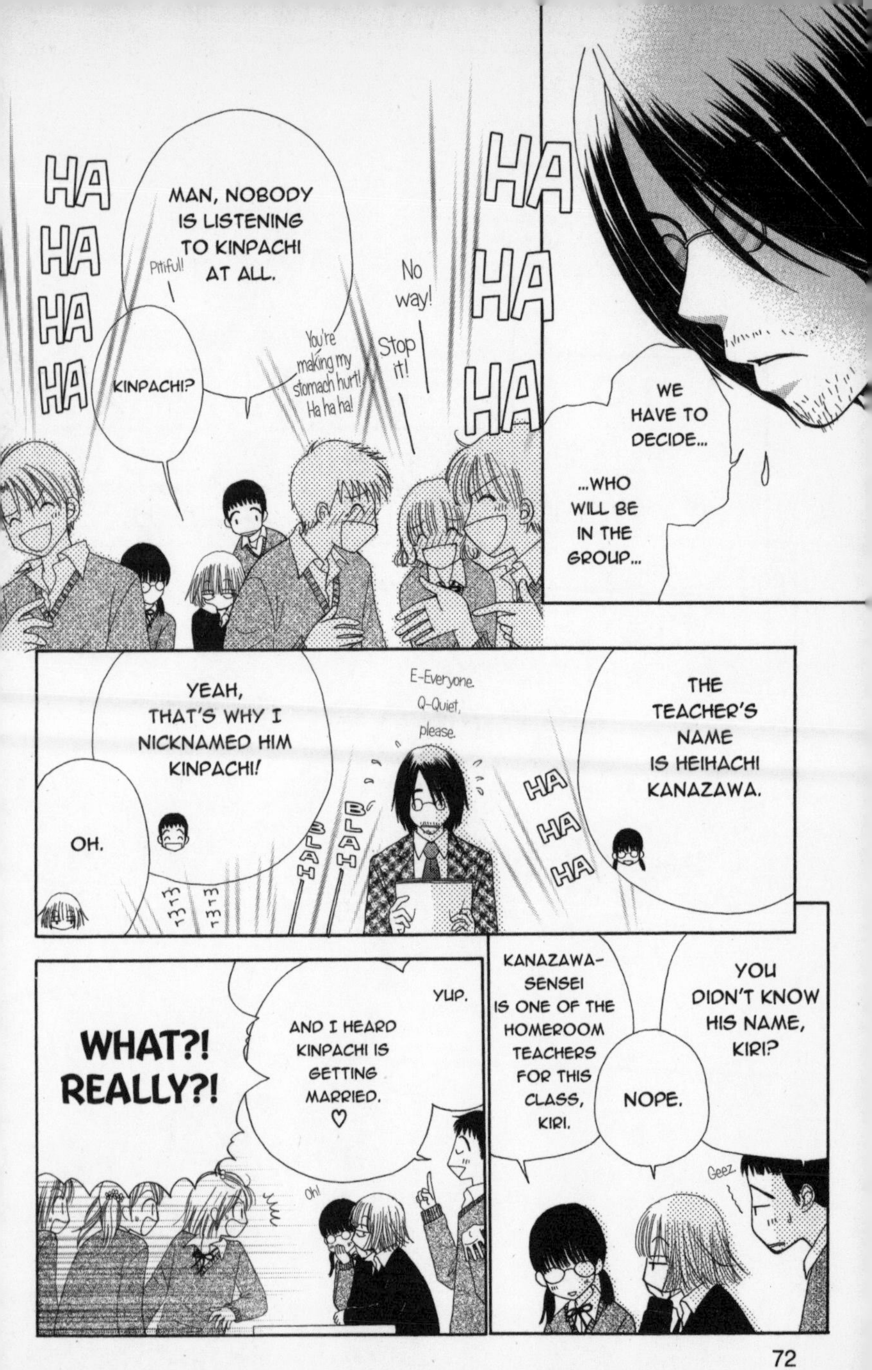
HA
HA
HA
HA
WE HAVE TO DECIDE...
...WHO WILL BE IN THE GROUP...
HA
HA
HA
HA
MAN, NOBODY IS LISTENING TO KINPACHI AT ALL.
Pitiful!
No way!
Stop it!
You're making my stomach hurt! Ha ha ha!
KINPACHI?
THE TEACHER'S NAME IS HEIHACHI KANAZAWA.
HA
HA
HA
E-Everyone. Q-Quiet, please.
BLAH
BLAH
YEAH, THAT'S WHY I NICKNAMED HIM KINPACHI!
OH.
YOU DIDN'T KNOW HIS NAME, KIRI?
KANAZAWA-SENSEI IS ONE OF THE HOMEROOM TEACHERS FOR THIS CLASS, KIRI.
NOPE.
Geez.
YUP.
AND I HEARD KINPACHI IS GETTING MARRIED. ♡
Oh!
WHAT?! REALLY?!

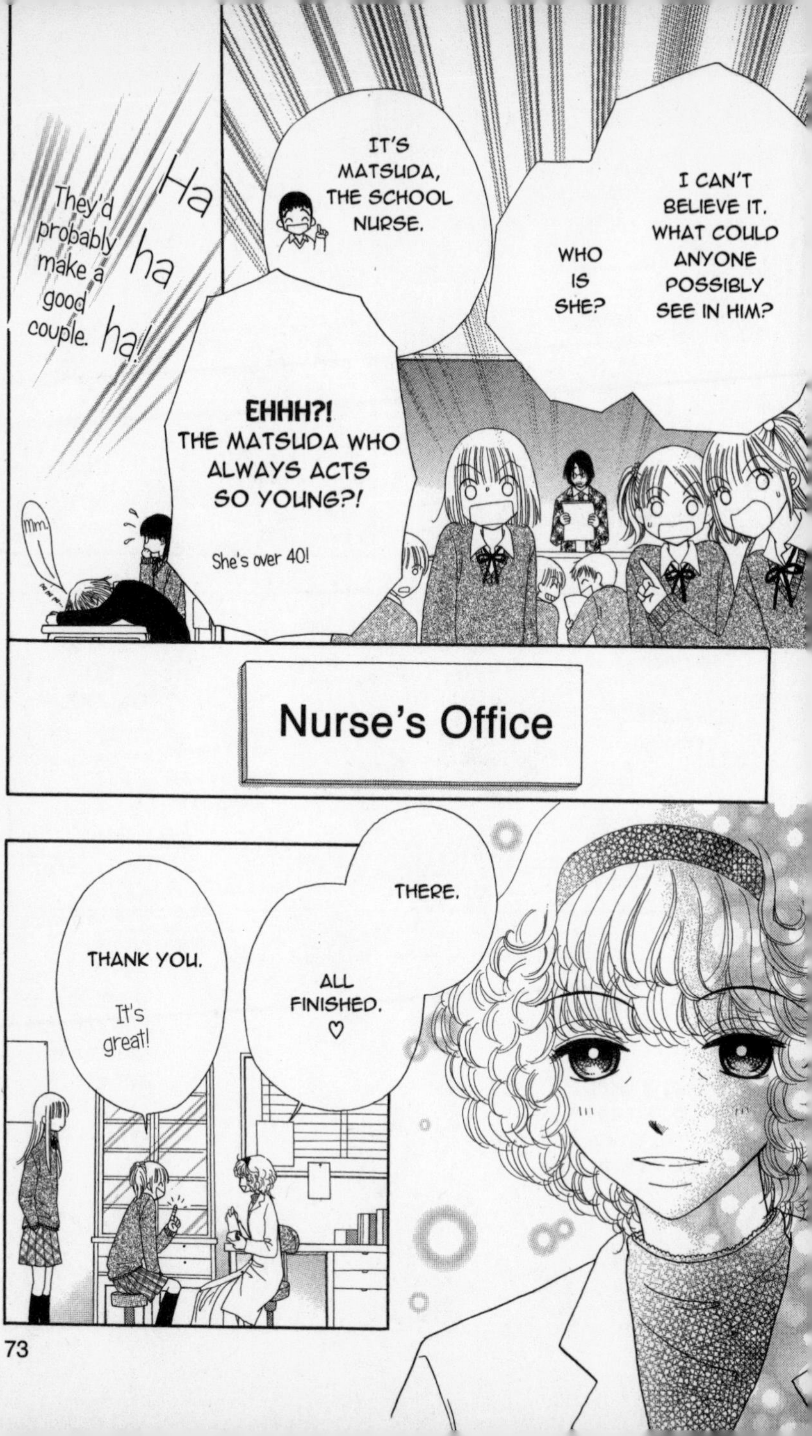

I CAN'T BELIEVE IT. WHAT COULD ANYONE POSSIBLY SEE IN HIM?
WHO IS SHE?
IT'S MATSUDA, THE SCHOOL NURSE.
EHHH?! THE MATSUDA WHO ALWAYS ACTS SO YOUNG?!
She's over 40!
Ha ha ha!
They'd probably make a good couple.
Mm.
Nurse's Office
THERE.
ALL FINISHED. ♡
THANK YOU.
It's great!

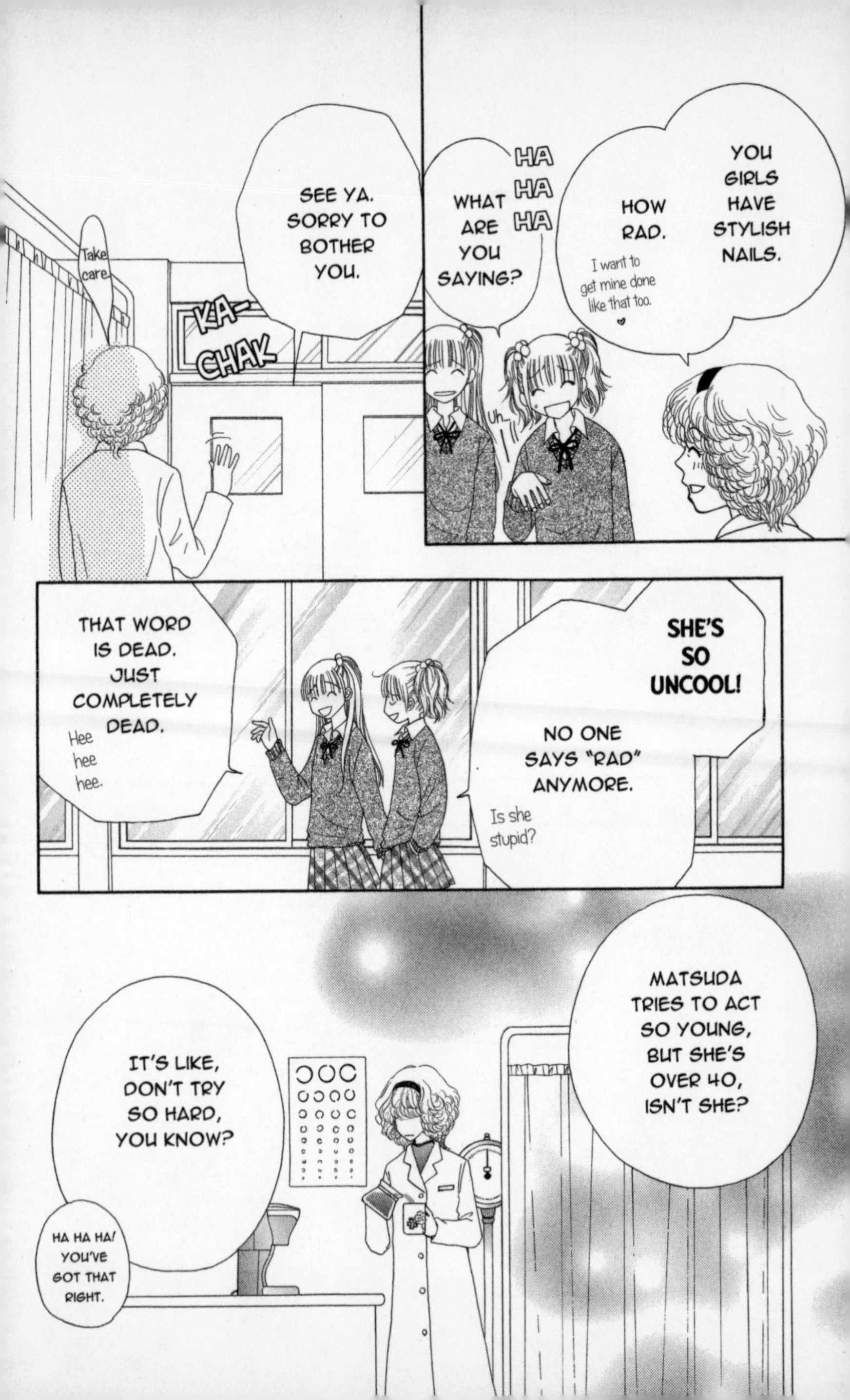
YOU GIRLS HAVE STYLISH NAILS.
HOW RAD.
I want to get mine done like that too. ♥
HA HA HA
WHAT ARE YOU SAYING?
Uh...
SEE YA. SORRY TO BOTHER YOU.
KA-CHAK
Take care.
SHE'S SO UNCOOL!
NO ONE SAYS "RAD" ANYMORE.
Is she stupid?
THAT WORD IS DEAD. JUST COMPLETELY DEAD.
Hee hee hee.
MATSUDA TRIES TO ACT SO YOUNG, BUT SHE'S OVER 40, ISN'T SHE?
IT'S LIKE, DON'T TRY SO HARD, YOU KNOW?
HA HA HA! YOU'VE GOT THAT RIGHT.

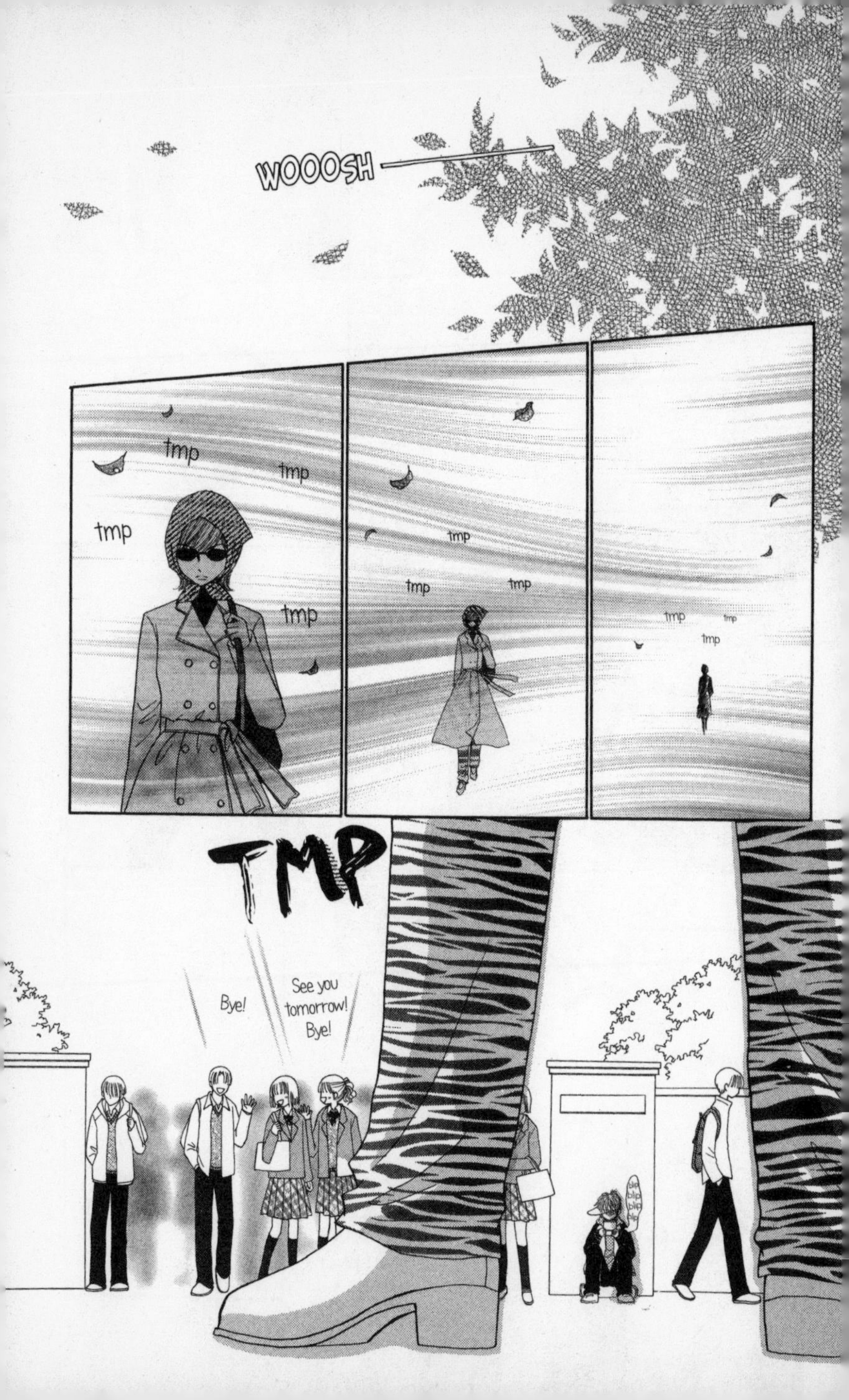
WOOOSH
tmp
tmp
tmp
tmp
tmp
tmp
tmp
tmp
tmp
tmp
tmp
TMP
blip blip blip blip
See you tomorrow! Bye!
Bye!

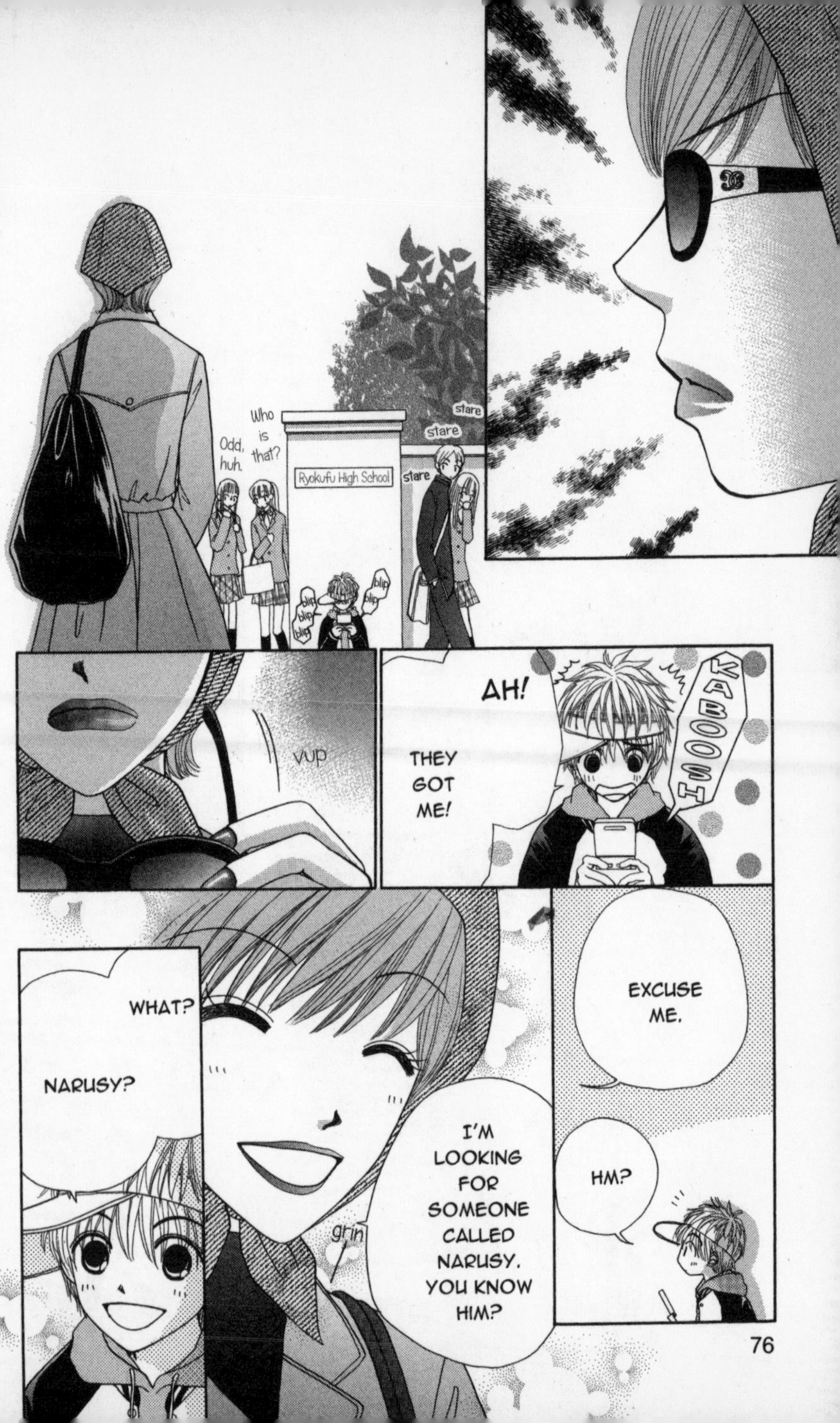
stare
stare
stare
Ryokufu High School
Who is that?
Odd, huh.
blip blip
blip blip blip
KABOOSH
AH!
THEY GOT ME!
VUP
EXCUSE ME.
HM?
I'M LOOKING FOR SOMEONE CALLED NARUSY. YOU KNOW HIM?
grin
WHAT?
NARUSY?

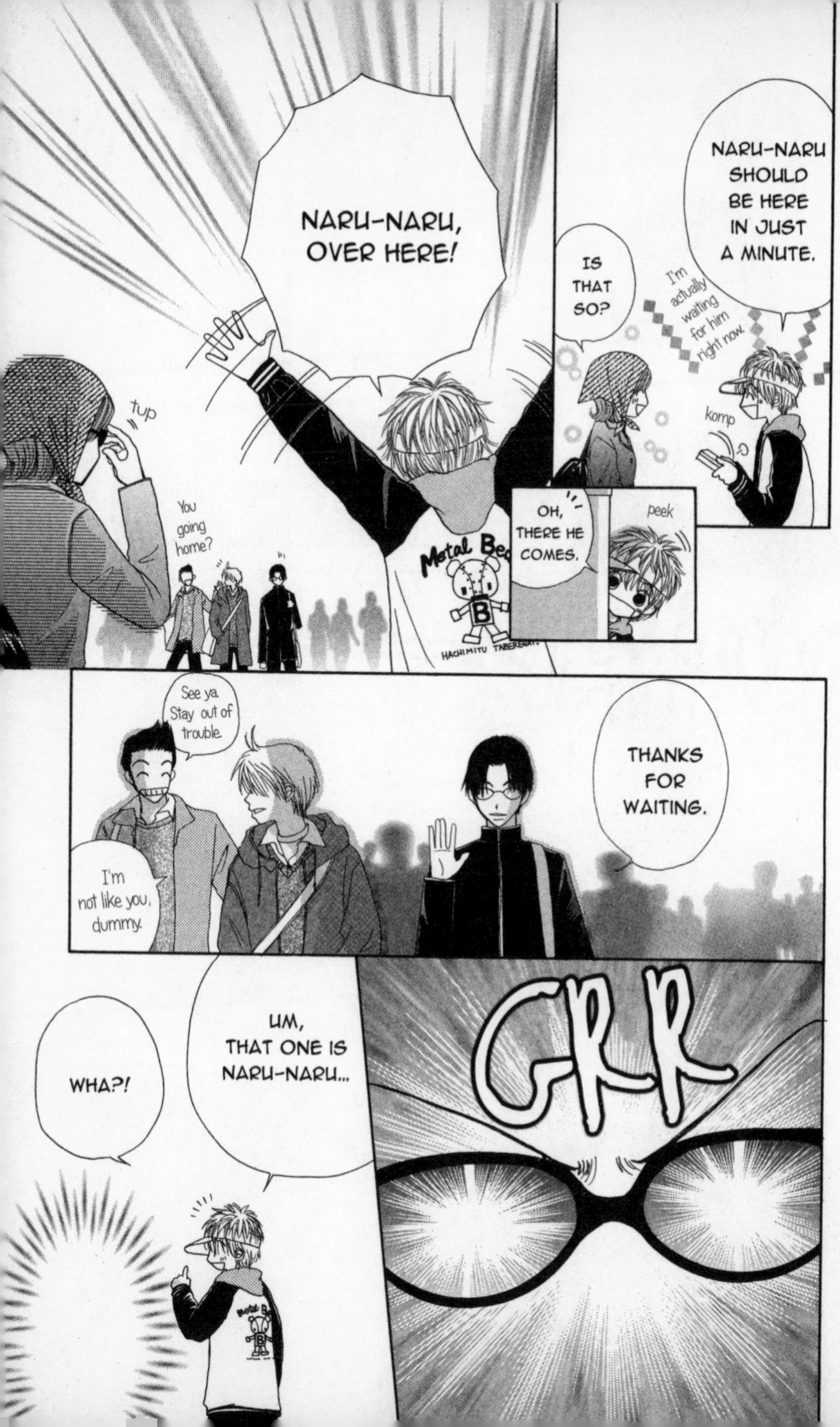
NARU-NARU SHOULD BE HERE IN JUST A MINUTE.
I'm actually waiting for him right now.
komp
IS THAT SO?
peek
OH, THERE HE COMES.
NARU-NARU, OVER HERE!
HACHIMITU TABERENAI.
tup
You going home?
THANKS FOR WAITING.
See ya. Stay out of trouble.
I'm not like you, dummy.
GRR
UM, THAT ONE IS NARU-NARU...
WHA?!

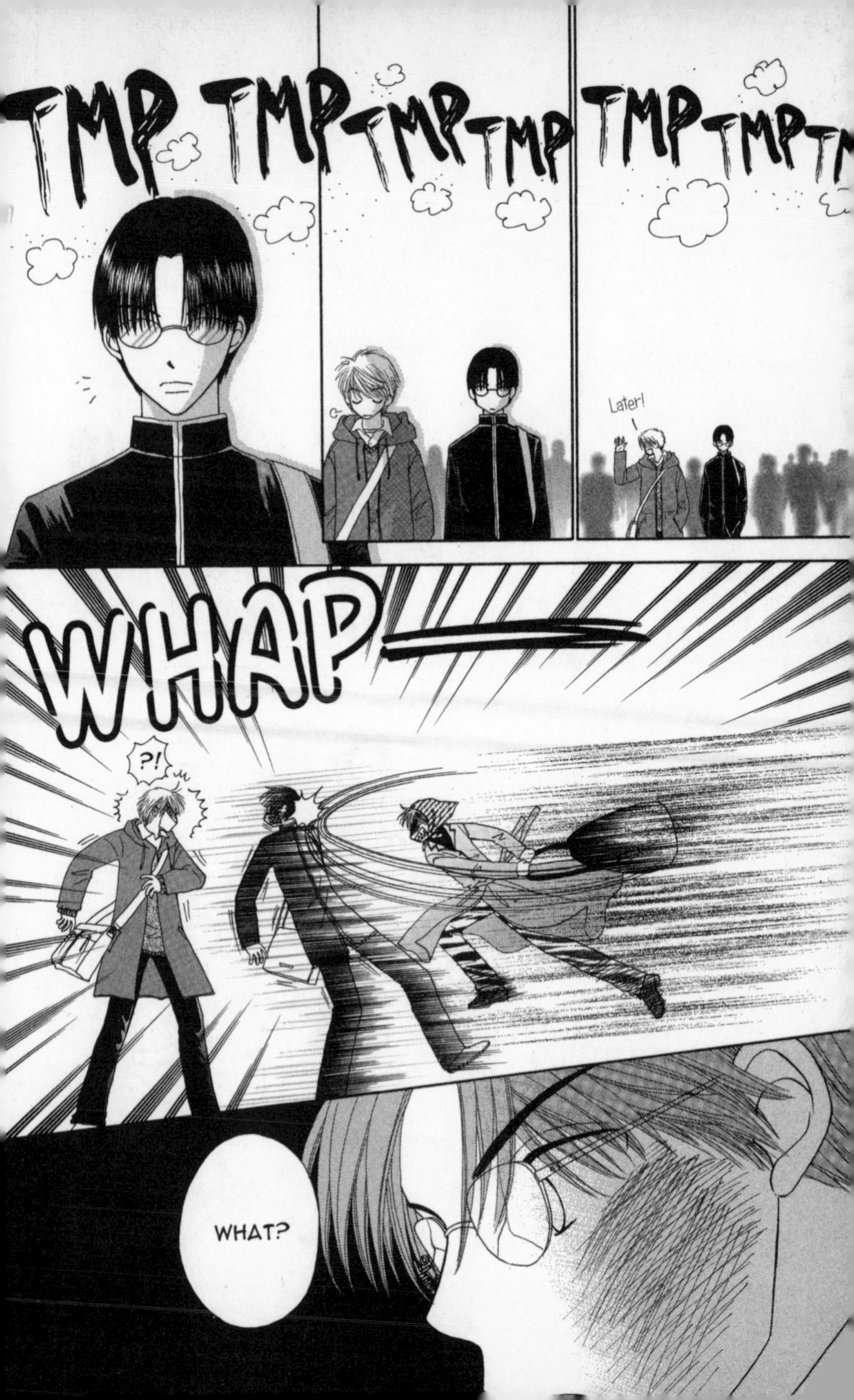
TMP TMP TM
Later!
TMP TMP
TMP TMP
WHAP
?!
WHAT?

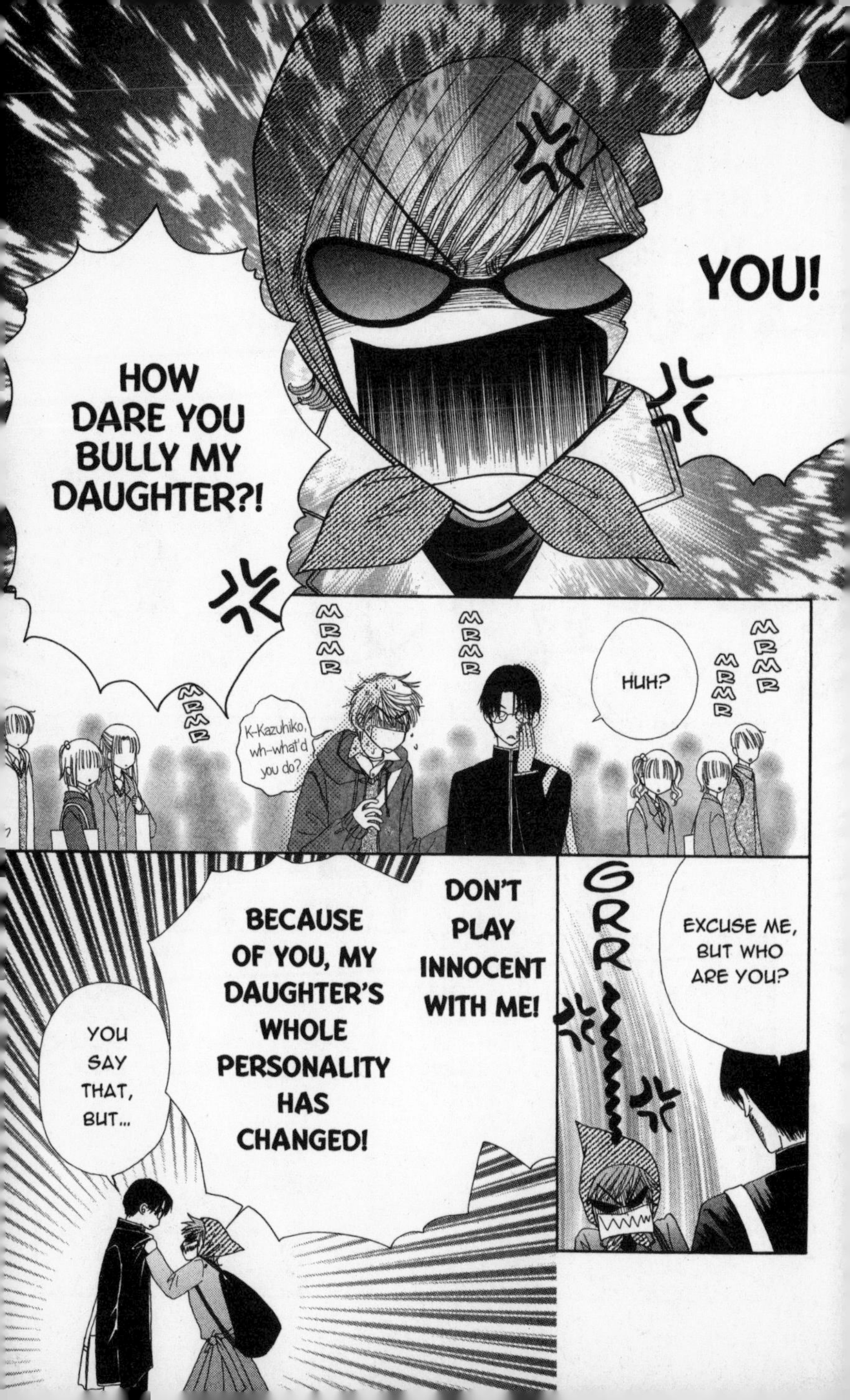
YOU!
HOW DARE YOU BULLY MY DAUGHTER?!
MRMR
MRMR
HUH?
MRMR
MRMR
K-Kazuhiko, wh-what'd you do?
MRMR
EXCUSE ME, BUT WHO ARE YOU?
GRR
DON'T PLAY INNOCENT WITH ME!
BECAUSE OF YOU, MY DAUGHTER'S WHOLE PERSONALITY HAS CHANGED!
YOU SAY THAT, BUT...

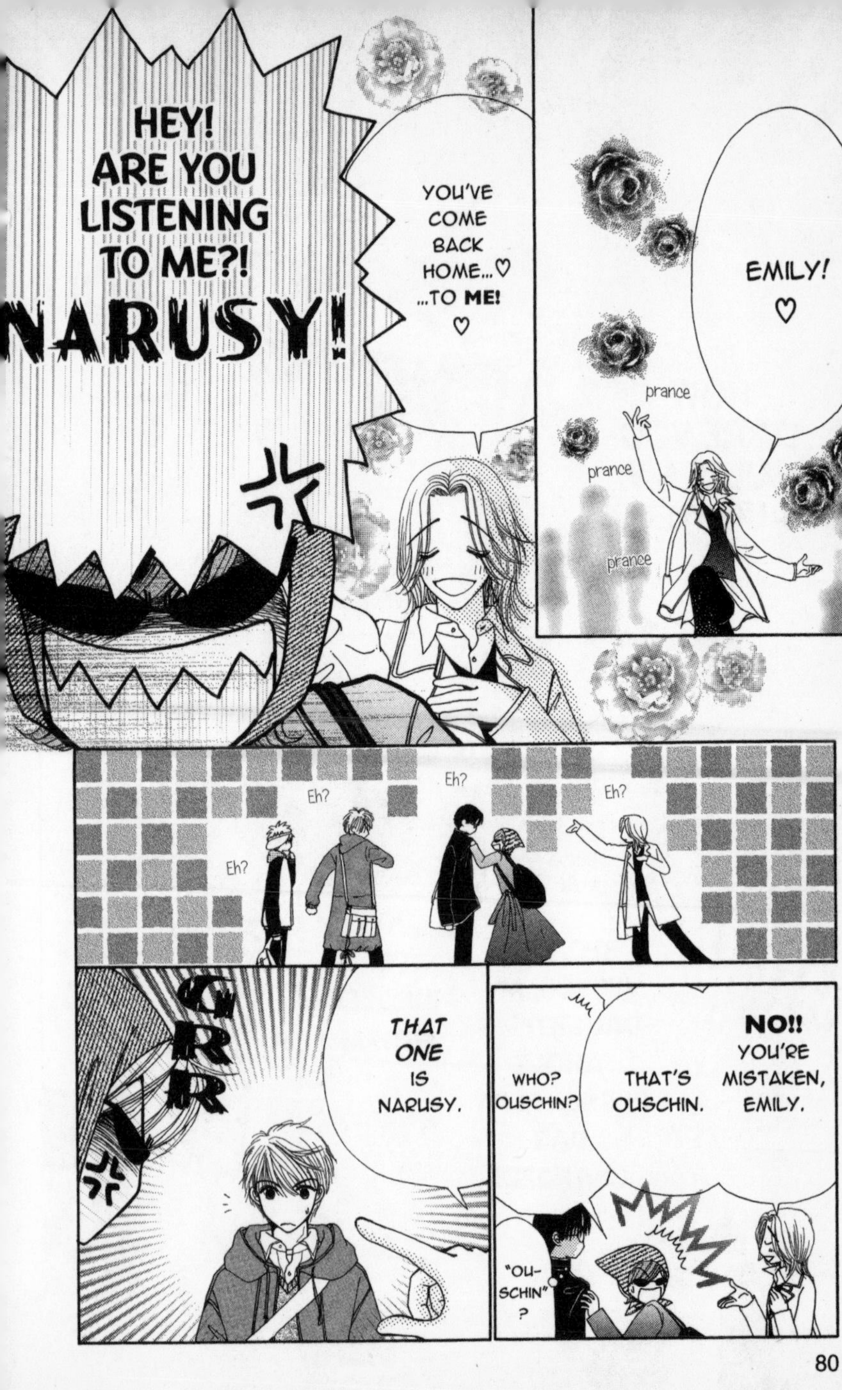
EMILY! ♡
prance
prance
prance
YOU'VE COME BACK HOME...♡ ...TO **ME!** ♡
HEY! ARE YOU LISTENING TO ME?! NARUSY!
Eh?
Eh?
Eh?
Eh?
NO!! YOU'RE MISTAKEN, EMILY.
THAT'S OUSCHIN.
WHO? OUSCHIN?
"OU-SCHIN"?
THAT ONE IS NARUSY.
GRR

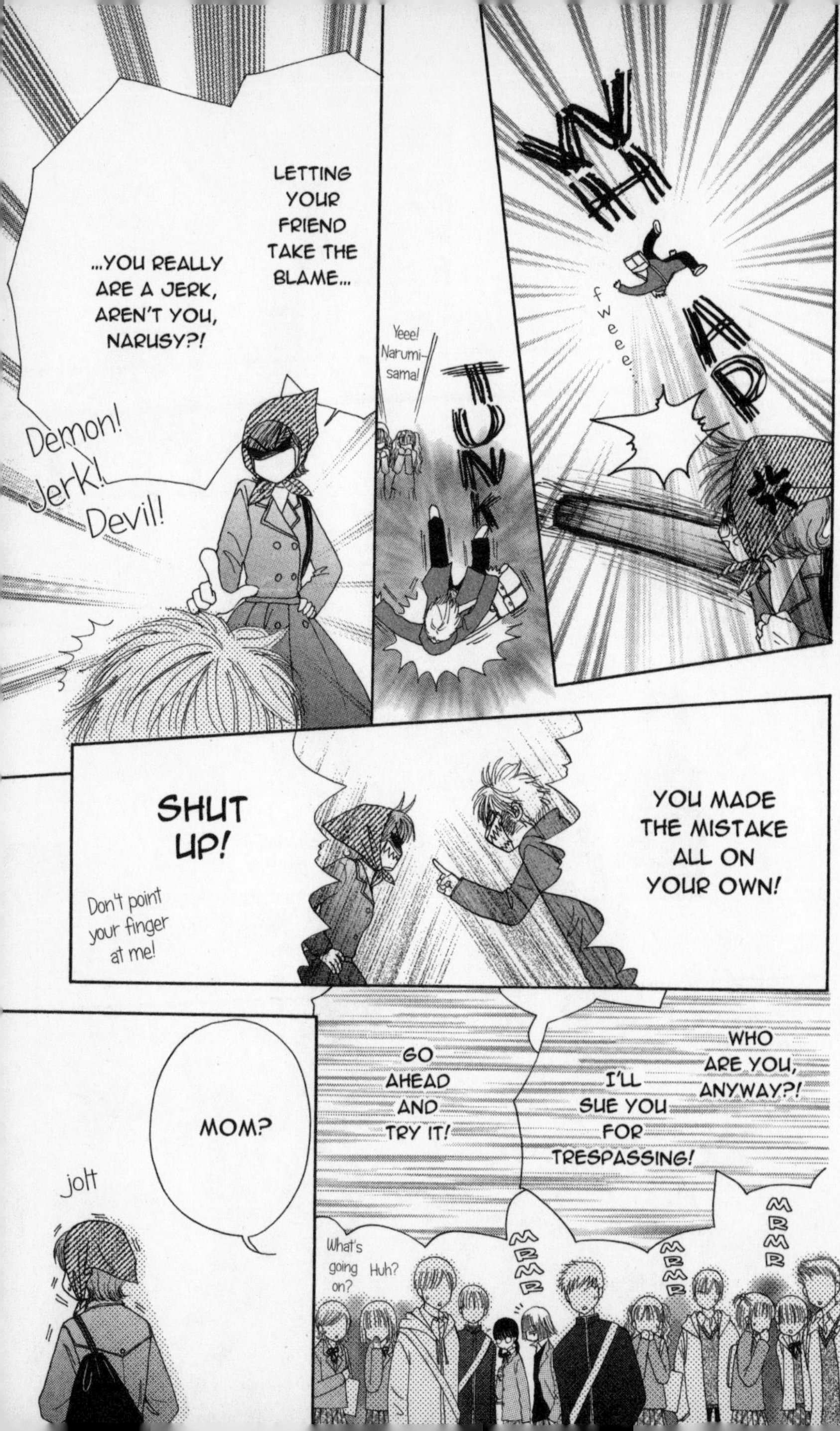
WHAP
fweee...
Yeee! Narumi-sama!
THUNK
LETTING YOUR FRIEND TAKE THE BLAME...
...YOU REALLY ARE A JERK, AREN'T YOU, NARUSY?!
Demon! Jerk! Devil!
YOU MADE THE MISTAKE ALL ON YOUR OWN!
SHUT UP!
Don't point your finger at me!
WHO ARE YOU, ANYWAY?!
I'LL SUE YOU FOR TRESPASSING!
GO AHEAD AND TRY IT!
MRMR
MRMR
MRMR
What's going on?
Huh?
MOM?
jolt

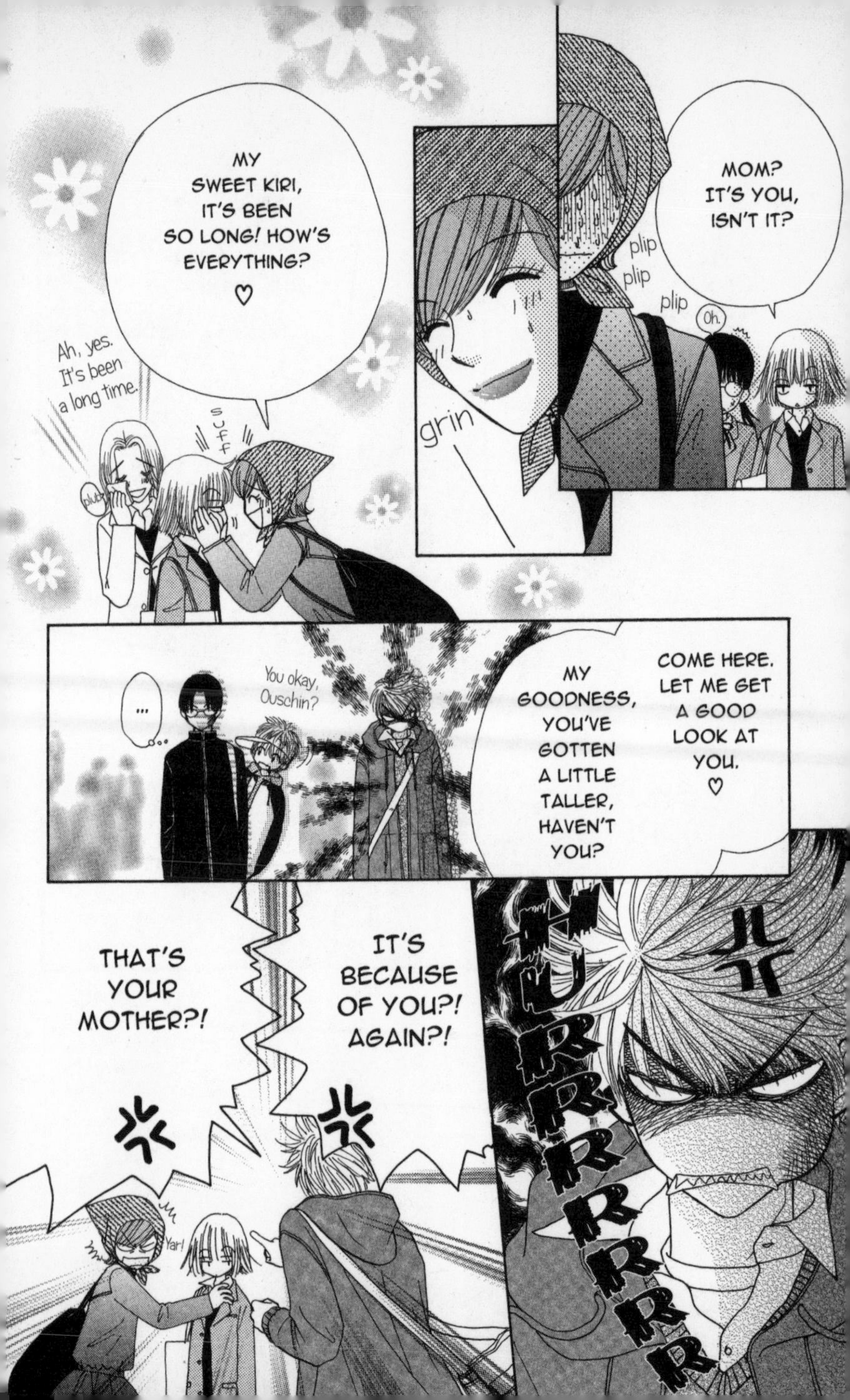
MOM? IT'S YOU, ISN'T IT?
plip
plip
plip
Oh.
grin
MY SWEET KIRI, IT'S BEEN SO LONG! HOW'S EVERYTHING? ♡
Ah, yes. It's been a long time.
suff
plub
COME HERE. LET ME GET A GOOD LOOK AT YOU. ♡
MY GOODNESS, YOU'VE GOTTEN A LITTLE TALLER, HAVEN'T YOU?
You okay, Ouschin?
...
HURRRRRRR
IT'S BECAUSE OF YOU?! AGAIN?!
THAT'S YOUR MOTHER?!
Yar!

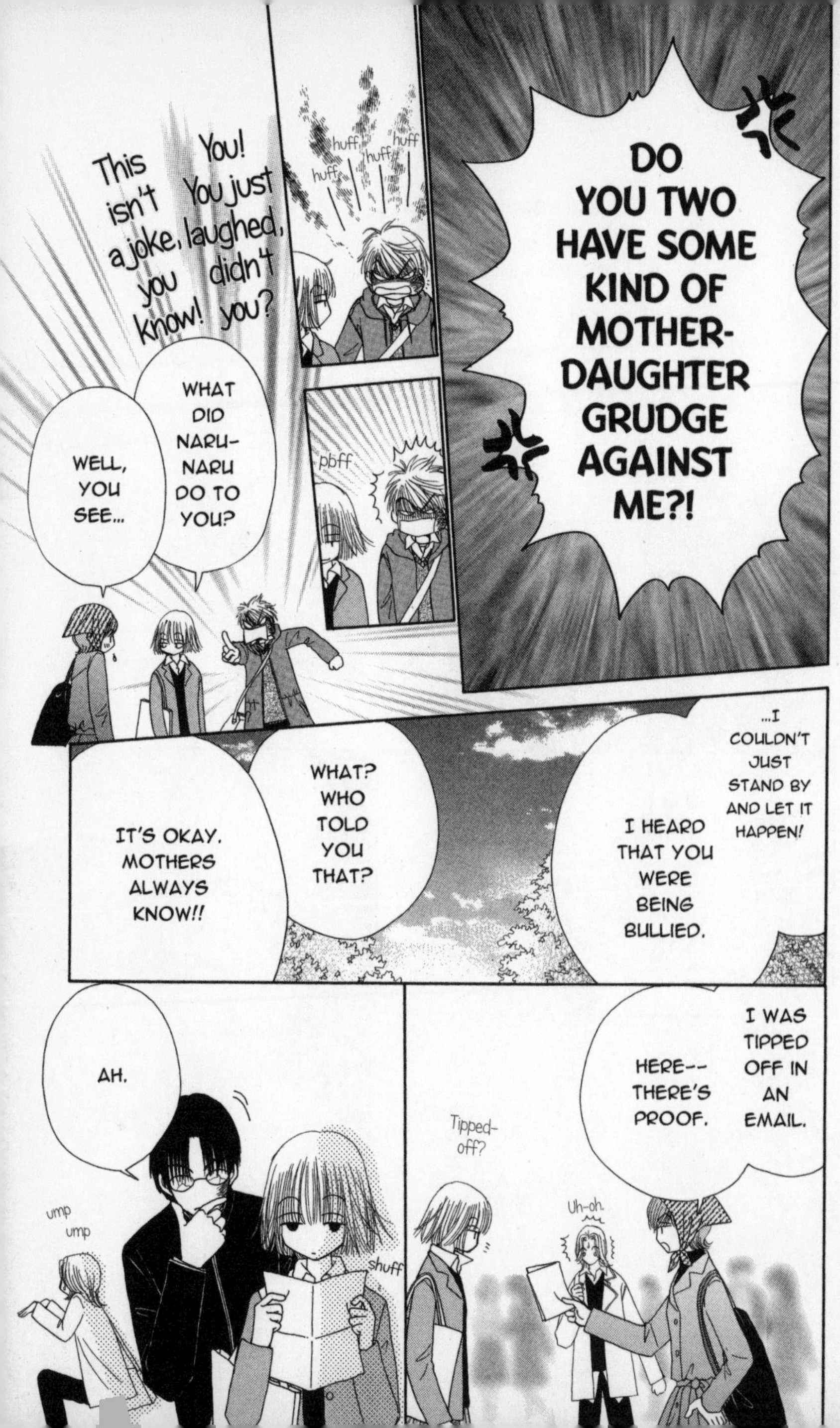
DO YOU TWO HAVE SOME KIND OF MOTHER-DAUGHTER GRUDGE AGAINST ME?!
huff huff huff huff
pbff
You! You just laughed, didn't you?
This isn't a joke, you know!
WHAT DID NARU-NARU DO TO YOU?
WELL, YOU SEE...
...I COULDN'T JUST STAND BY AND LET IT HAPPEN!
I HEARD THAT YOU WERE BEING BULLIED.
WHAT? WHO TOLD YOU THAT?
IT'S OKAY. MOTHERS ALWAYS KNOW!!
I WAS TIPPED OFF IN AN EMAIL.
HERE-- THERE'S PROOF.
Uh-oh.
Tipped-off?
AH.
shuff
ump ump

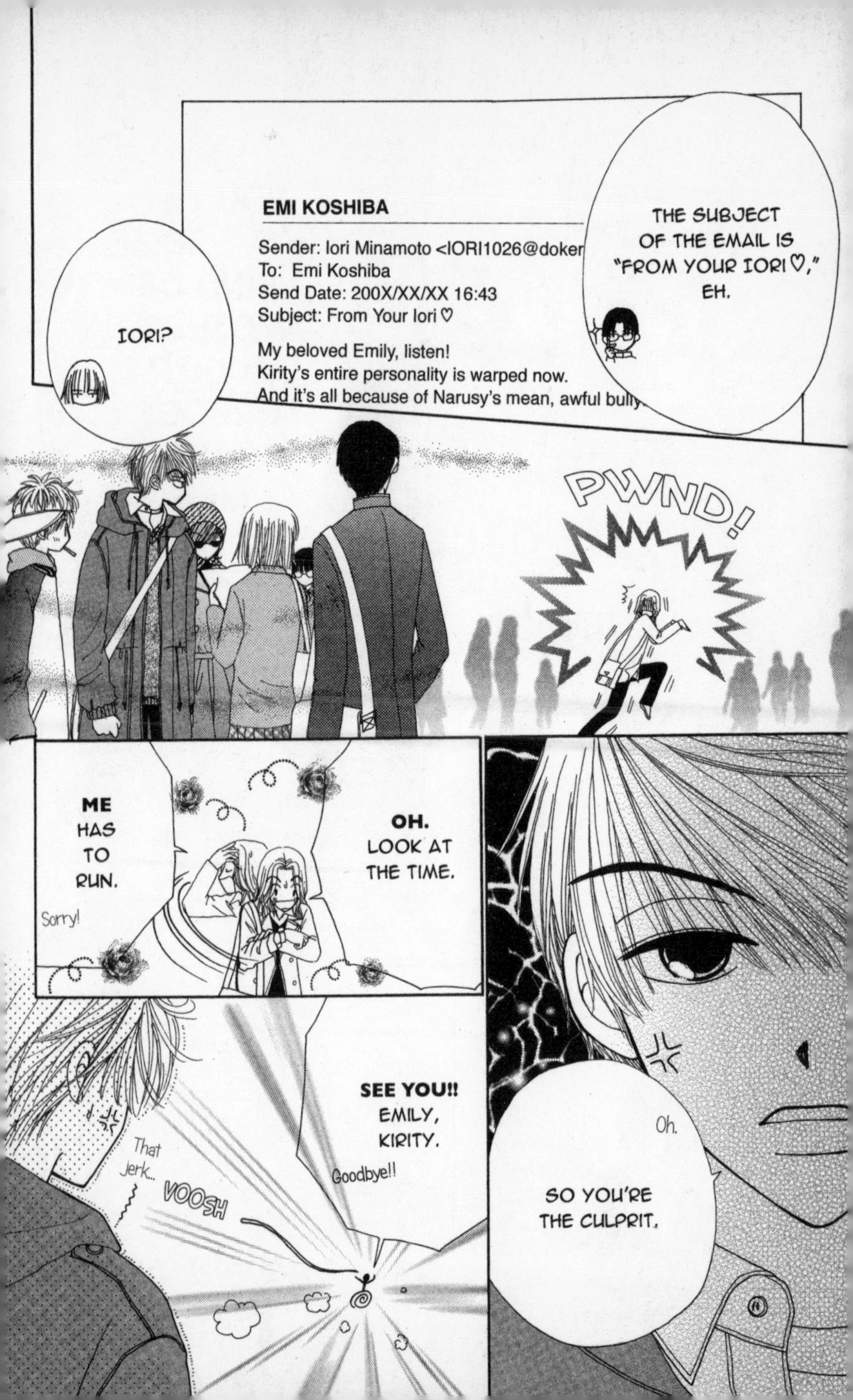
THE SUBJECT OF THE EMAIL IS "FROM YOUR IORI♡," EH.
EMI KOSHIBA
Sender: Iori Minamoto <IORI1026@doker
To: Emi Koshiba
Send Date: 200X/XX/XX 16:43
Subject: From Your Iori ♡
My beloved Emily, listen!
Kirity's entire personality is warped now.
And it's all because of Narusy's mean, awful bully
IORI?
PWND!
Oh.
SO YOU'RE THE CULPRIT.
OH. LOOK AT THE TIME.
ME HAS TO RUN.
Sorry!
SEE YOU!! EMILY, KIRITY.
Goodbye!!
VOOSH
That jerk...

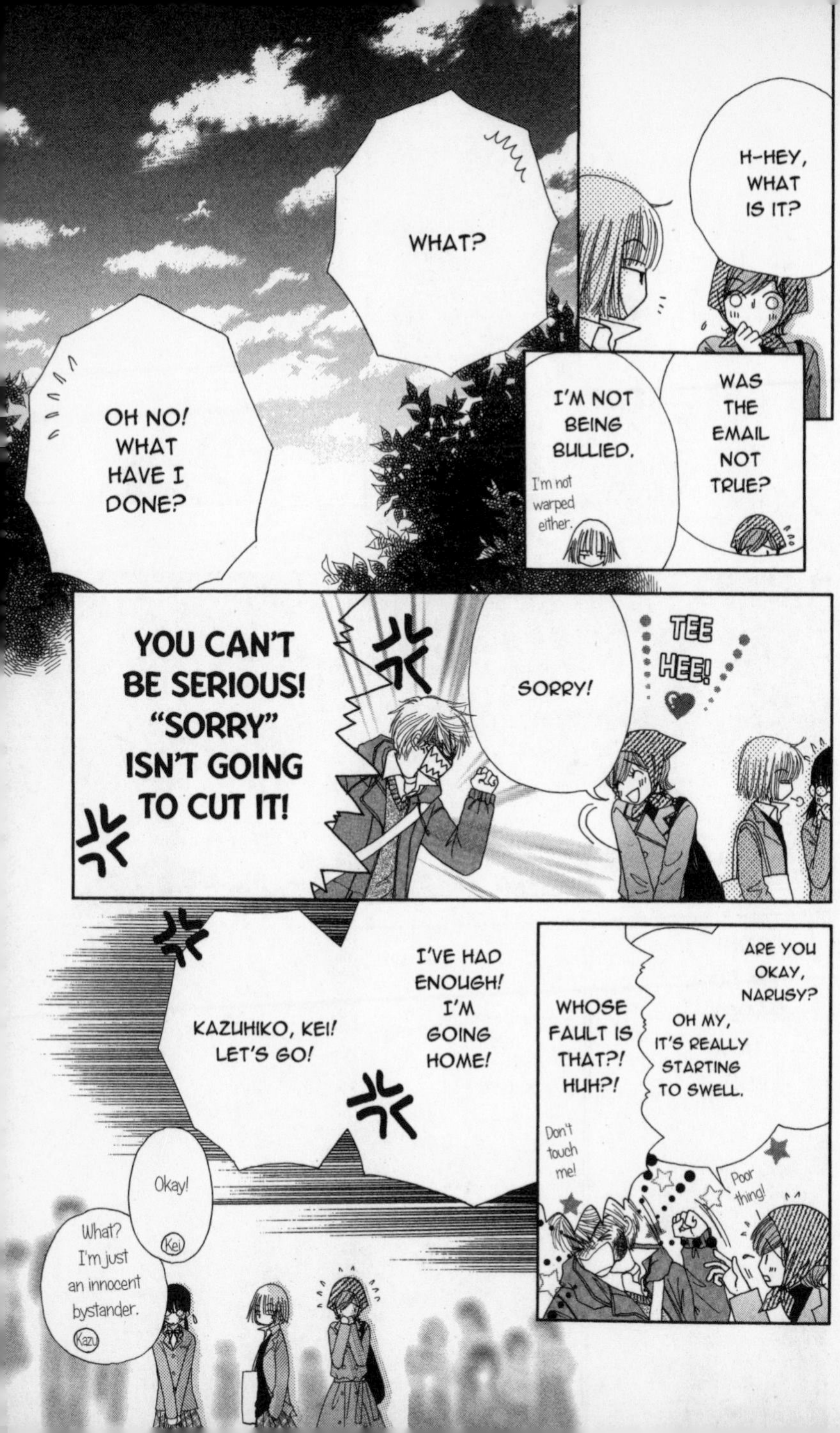
H-HEY, WHAT IS IT?
WAS THE EMAIL NOT TRUE?
I'M NOT BEING BULLIED.
I'm not warped either.
WHAT?
OH NO! WHAT HAVE I DONE?
TEE HEE!
SORRY!
YOU CAN'T BE SERIOUS! "SORRY" ISN'T GOING TO CUT IT!
ARE YOU OKAY, NARUSY?
OH MY, IT'S REALLY STARTING TO SWELL.
WHOSE FAULT IS THAT?! HUH?!
Poor thing!
Don't touch me!
I'VE HAD ENOUGH! I'M GOING HOME!
KAZUHIKO, KEI! LET'S GO!
Okay!
Kei
What? I'm just an innocent bystander.
Kazu

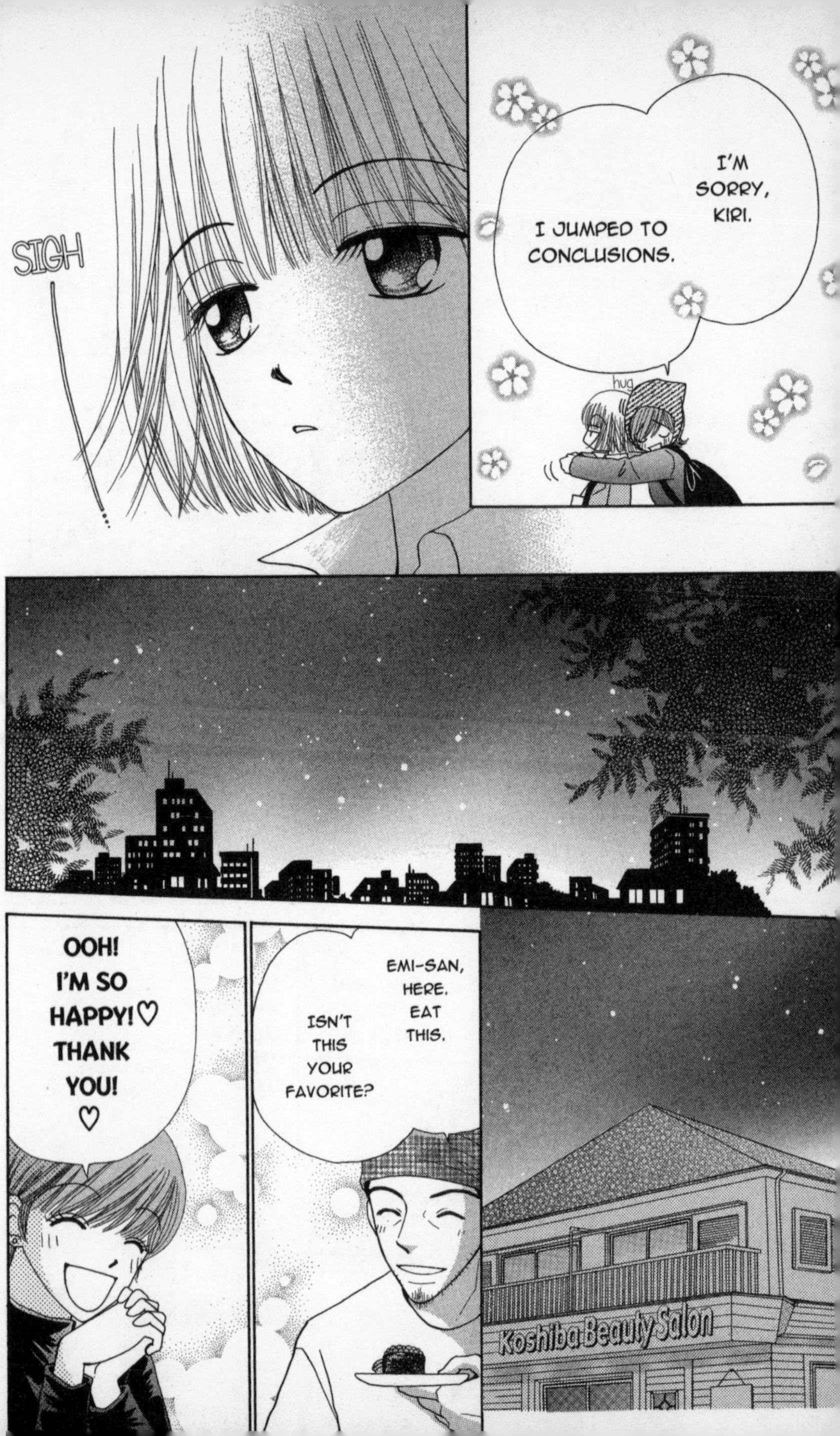
I'M SORRY, KIRI.
I JUMPED TO CONCLUSIONS.
hug
SIGH
Koshiba Beauty Salon
EMI-SAN, HERE. EAT THIS.
ISN'T THIS YOUR FAVORITE?
OOH! I'M SO HAPPY! ♡ THANK YOU! ♡

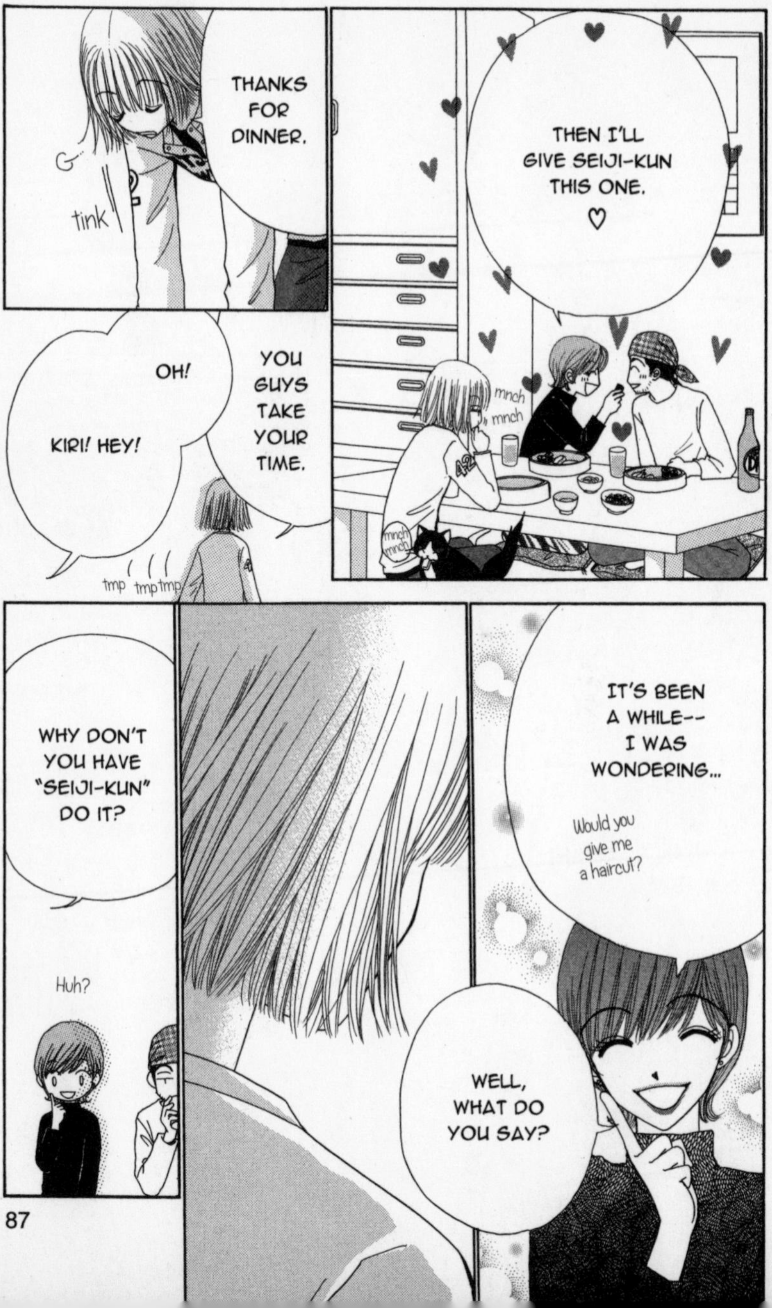
THEN I'LL GIVE SEIJI-KUN THIS ONE. ♡
mnch mnch
mnch mnch
THANKS FOR DINNER.
G-
tink
YOU GUYS TAKE YOUR TIME.
OH!
KIRI! HEY!
tmp tmp tmp
IT'S BEEN A WHILE-- I WAS WONDERING...
Would you give me a haircut?
WELL, WHAT DO YOU SAY?
WHY DON'T YOU HAVE "SEIJI-KUN" DO IT?
Huh?

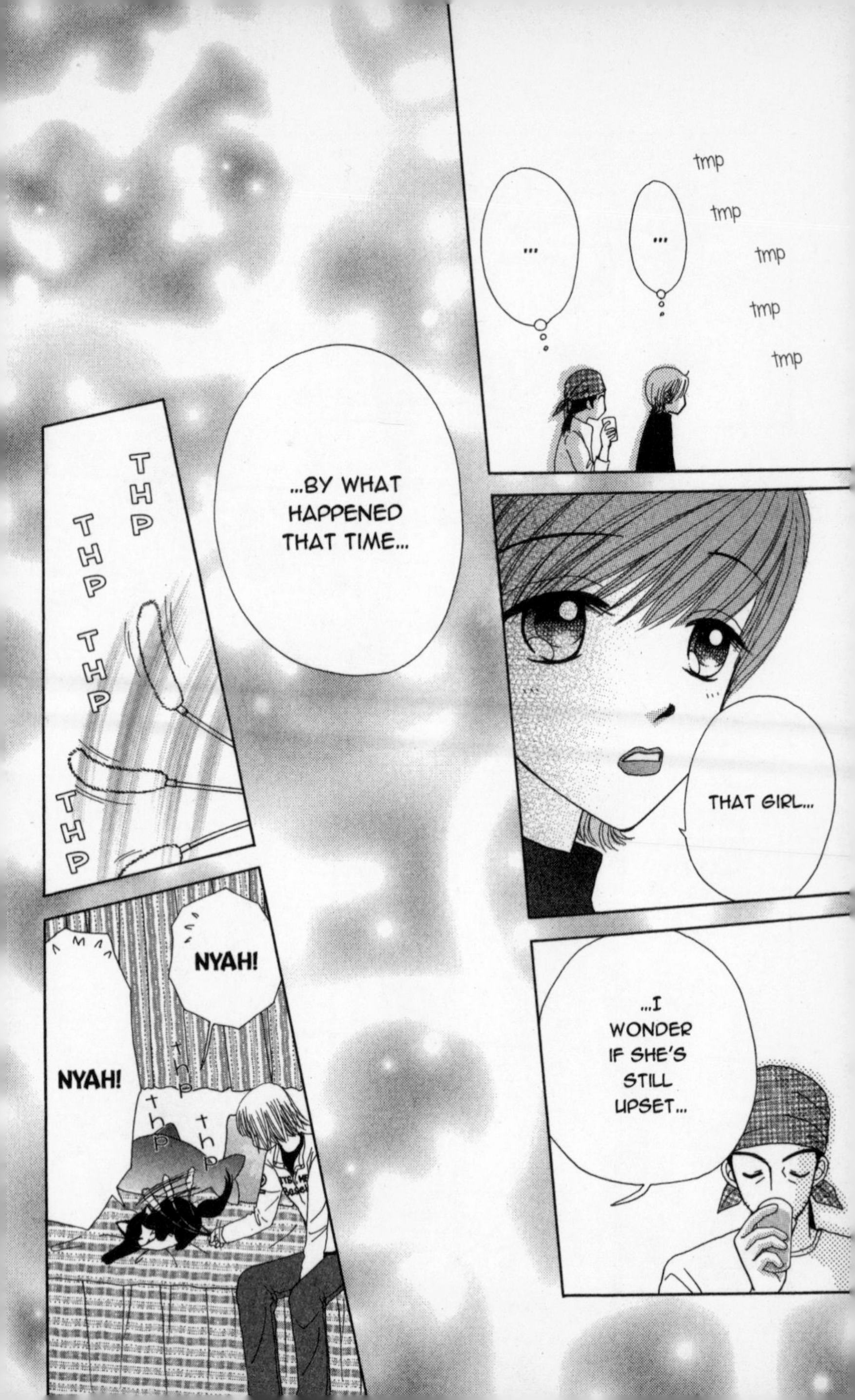
tmp
tmp
tmp
tmp
tmp
...
...
THAT GIRL...
...I WONDER IF SHE'S STILL UPSET...
...BY WHAT HAPPENED THAT TIME...
THP
THP
THP
THP
NYAH!
NYAH!
thp
thp
thp

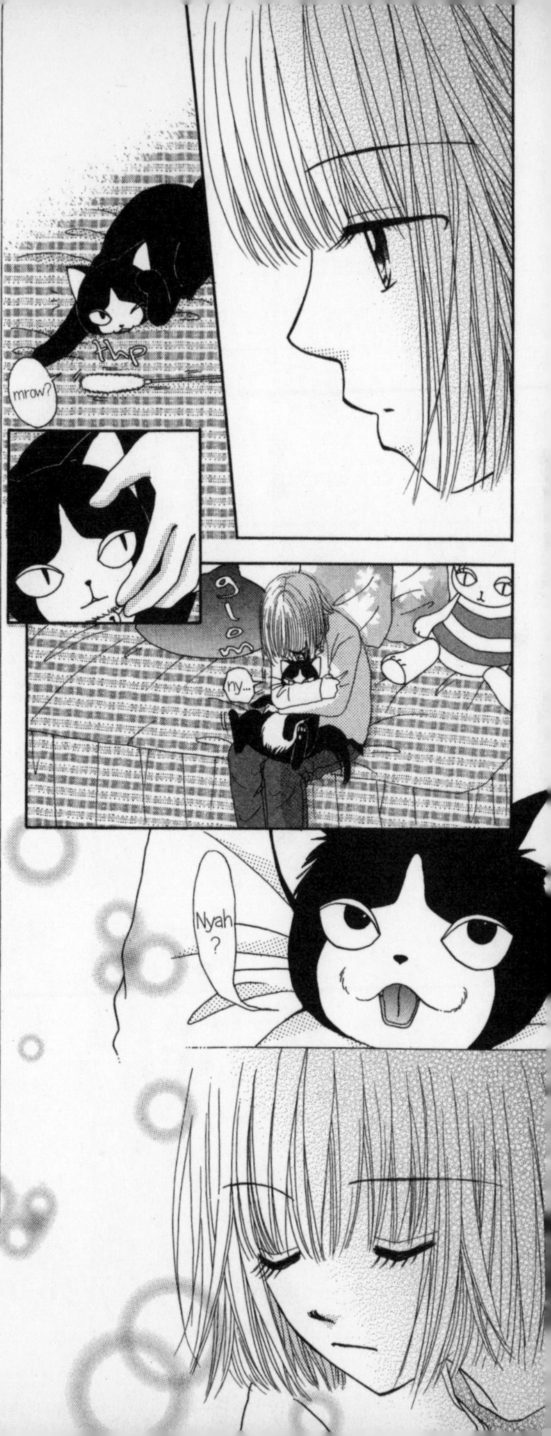

thp
mrow?
glom
ny...
Nyah?

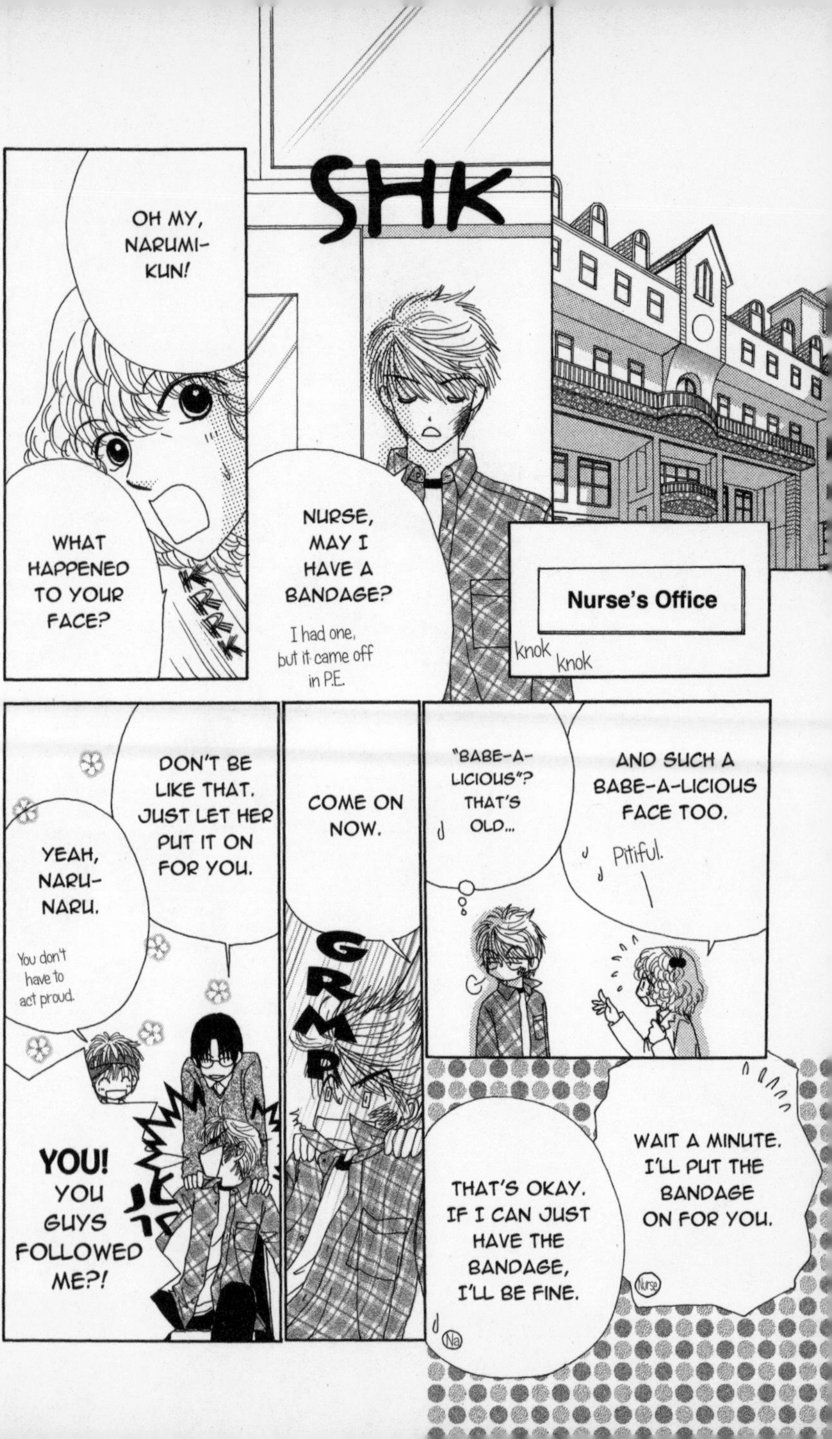
Nurse's Office
knok knok
SHK
NURSE, MAY I HAVE A BANDAGE?
I had one, but it came off in P.E.
OH MY, NARUMI-KUN!
WHAT HAPPENED TO YOUR FACE?
KRRK
AND SUCH A BABE-A-LICIOUS FACE TOO.
Pitiful.
"BABE-A-LICIOUS"? THAT'S OLD...
WAIT A MINUTE. I'LL PUT THE BANDAGE ON FOR YOU.
Nurse
THAT'S OKAY. IF I CAN JUST HAVE THE BANDAGE, I'LL BE FINE.
Na
COME ON NOW.
GRMP
DON'T BE LIKE THAT. JUST LET HER PUT IT ON FOR YOU.
YEAH, NARU-NARU.
You don't have to act proud.
YOU! YOU GUYS FOLLOWED ME?!

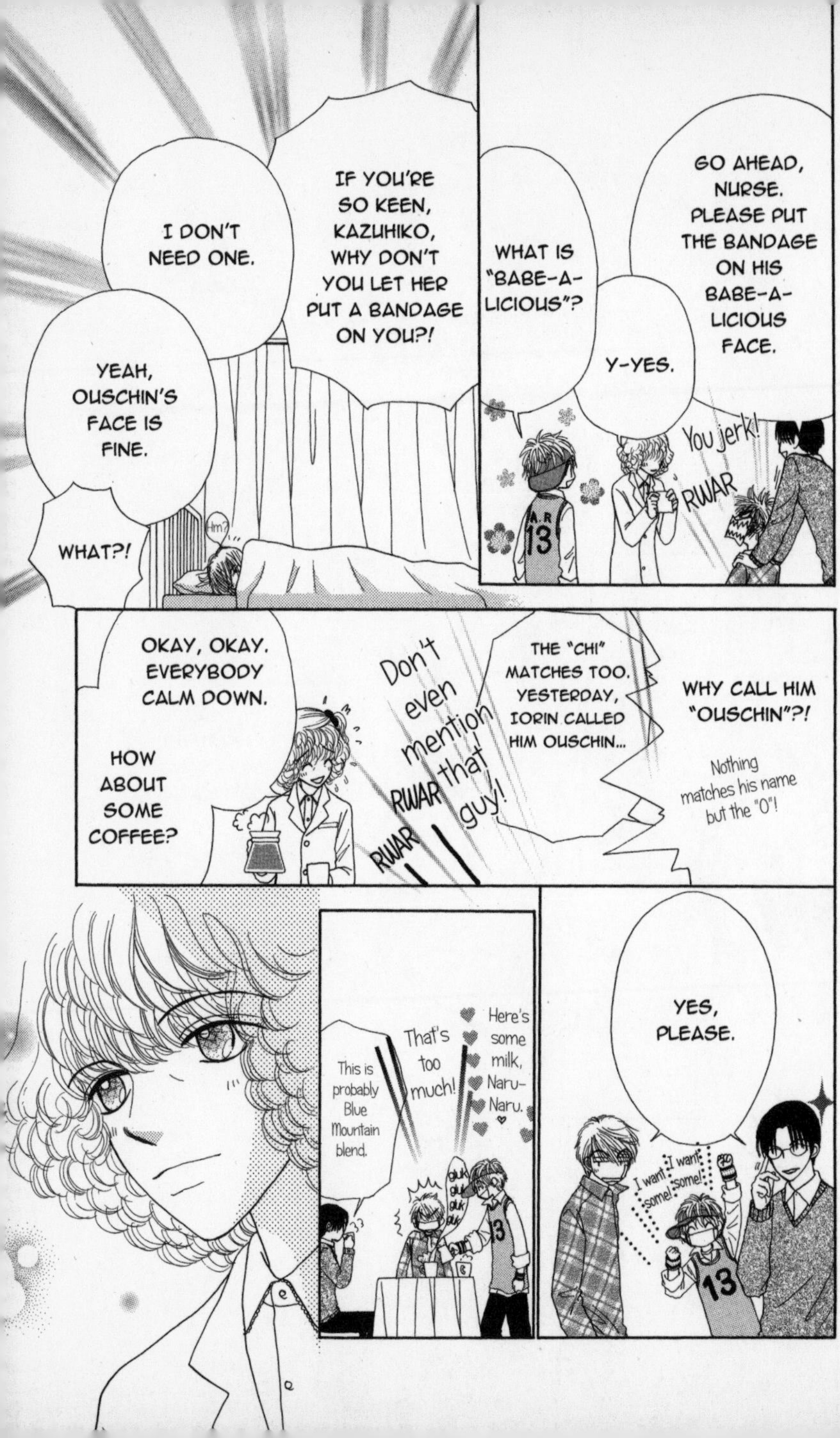
GO AHEAD, NURSE. PLEASE PUT THE BANDAGE ON HIS BABE-A-LICIOUS FACE.
Y-YES.
WHAT IS "BABE-A-LICIOUS"?
You jerk!
RWAR
IF YOU'RE SO KEEN, KAZUHIKO, WHY DON'T YOU LET HER PUT A BANDAGE ON YOU?!
I DON'T NEED ONE.
YEAH, OUSCHIN'S FACE IS FINE.
Hm?
WHAT?!
WHY CALL HIM "OUSCHIN"?!
Nothing matches his name but the "O"!
THE "CHI" MATCHES TOO. YESTERDAY, IORIN CALLED HIM OUSCHIN...
Don't even mention that guy!
RWAR
RWAR
OKAY, OKAY. EVERYBODY CALM DOWN.
HOW ABOUT SOME COFFEE?
YES, PLEASE.
I want some!
I want some!
Here's some milk, Naru-Naru.
That's too much!
glug glug glug glug
This is probably Blue Mountain blend.

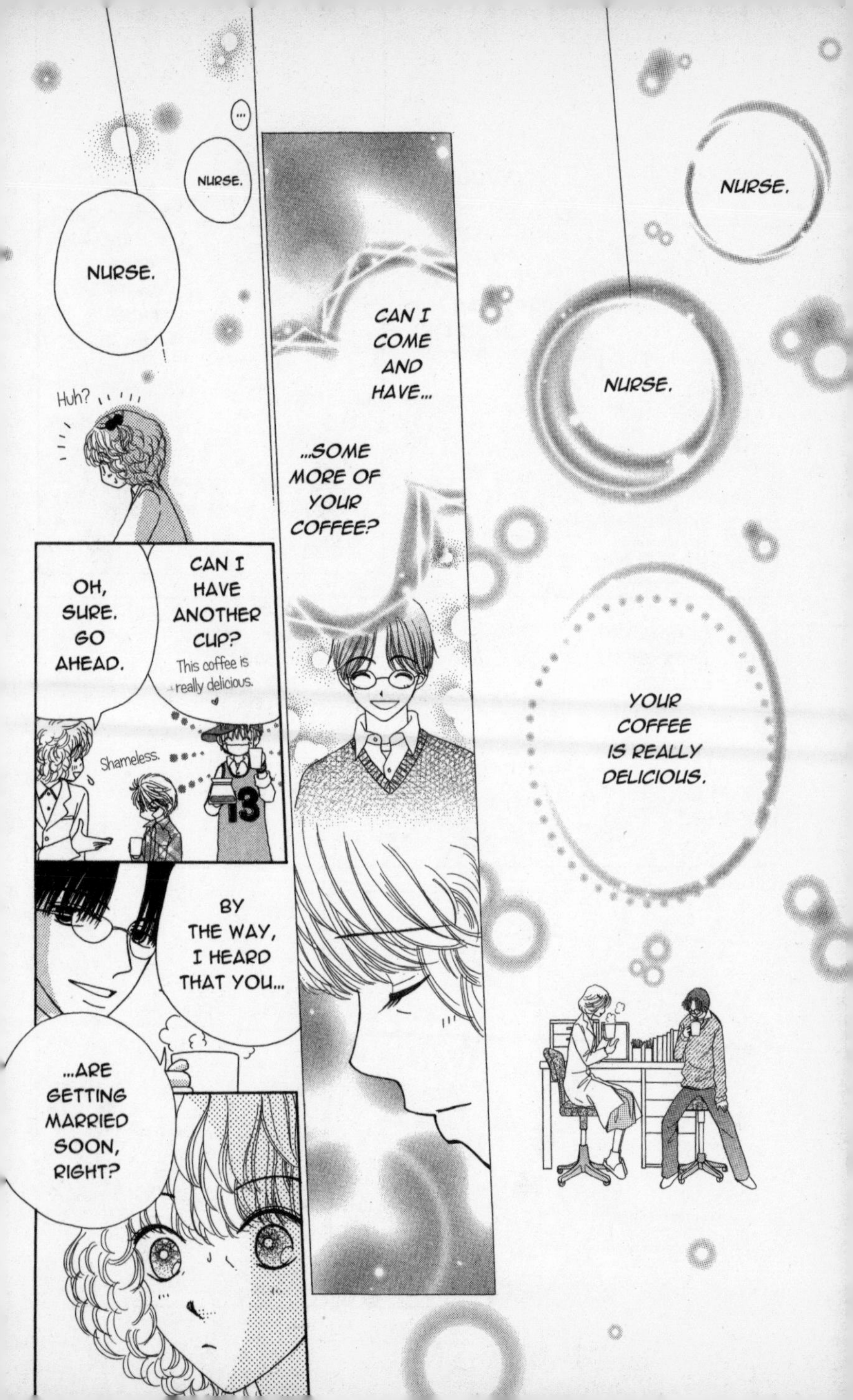
NURSE.
NURSE.
YOUR COFFEE IS REALLY DELICIOUS.
CAN I COME AND HAVE...
...SOME MORE OF YOUR COFFEE?
...
NURSE.
NURSE.
Huh?
CAN I HAVE ANOTHER CUP?
This coffee is really delicious.
OH, SURE. GO AHEAD.
Shameless.
13
BY THE WAY, I HEARD THAT YOU...
...ARE GETTING MARRIED SOON, RIGHT?

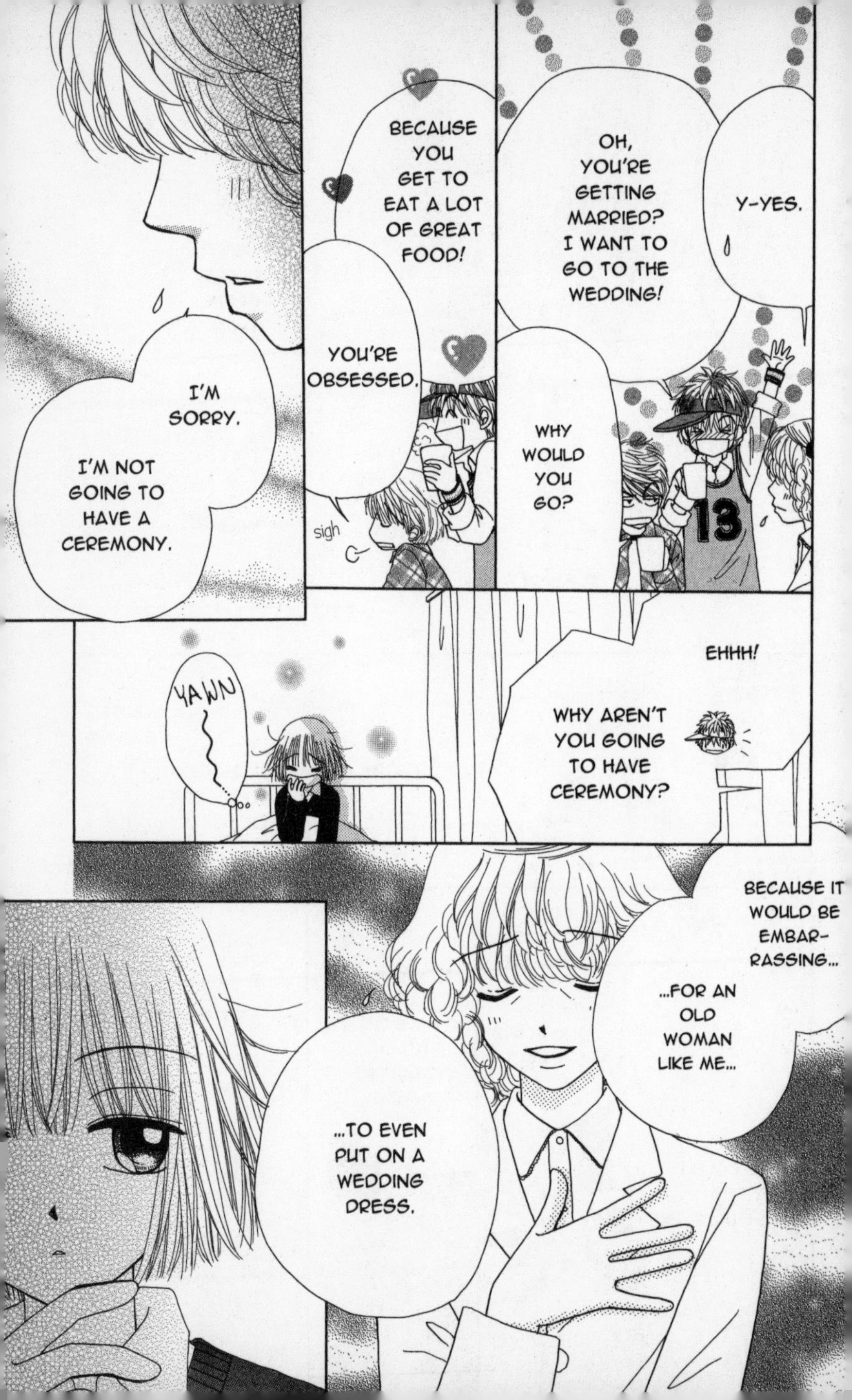
Y-YES.
OH, YOU'RE GETTING MARRIED? I WANT TO GO TO THE WEDDING!
WHY WOULD YOU GO?
BECAUSE YOU GET TO EAT A LOT OF GREAT FOOD!
YOU'RE OBSESSED.
sigh
I'M SORRY.
I'M NOT GOING TO HAVE A CEREMONY.
EHHH!
WHY AREN'T YOU GOING TO HAVE CEREMONY?
YAWN
BECAUSE IT WOULD BE EMBAR-RASSING...
...FOR AN OLD WOMAN LIKE ME...
...TO EVEN PUT ON A WEDDING DRESS.

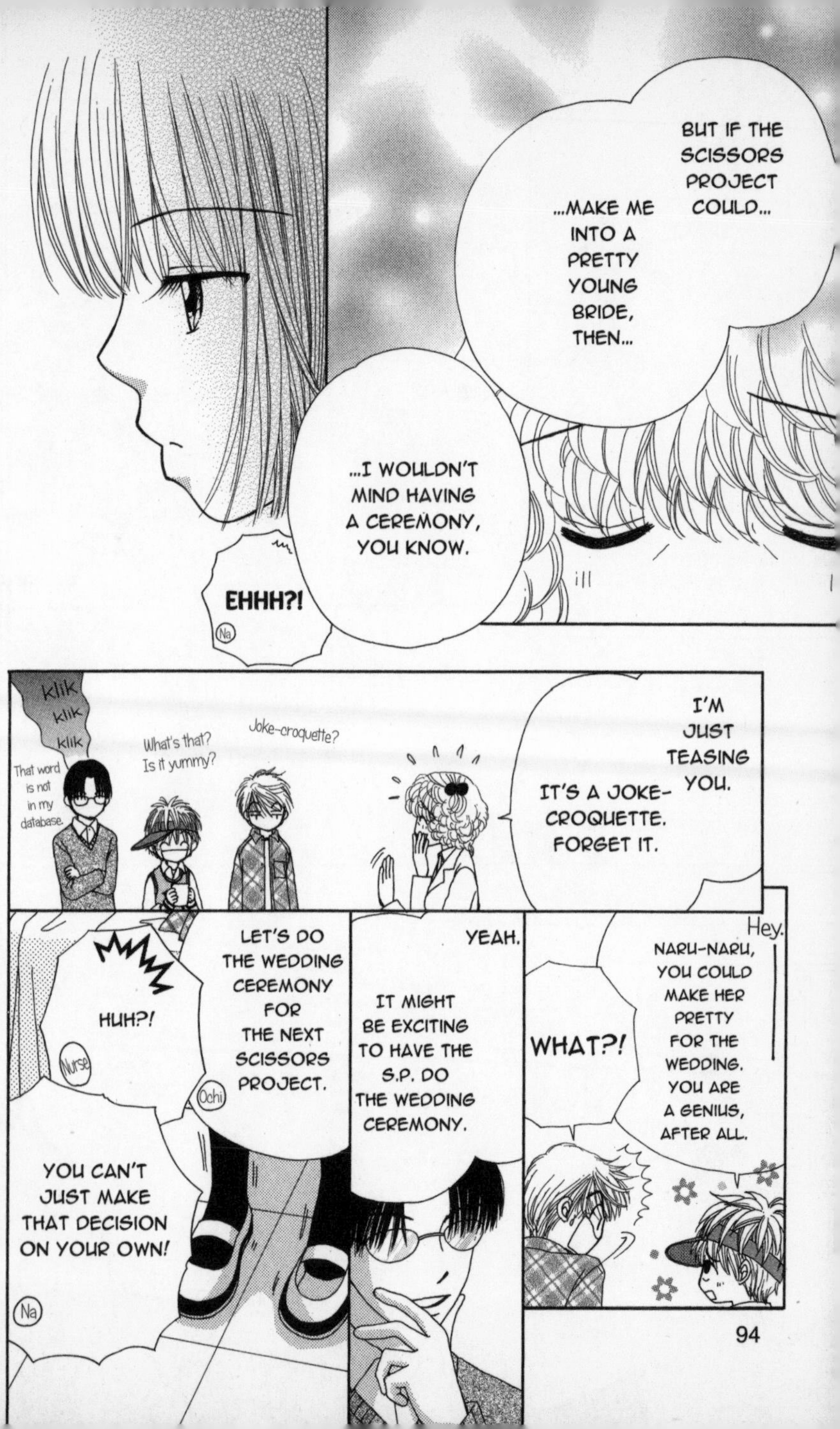
BUT IF THE SCISSORS PROJECT COULD...
...MAKE ME INTO A PRETTY YOUNG BRIDE, THEN...
...I WOULDN'T MIND HAVING A CEREMONY, YOU KNOW.
EHHH?!
Na
I'M JUST TEASING YOU.
IT'S A JOKE-CROQUETTE. FORGET IT.
Joke-croquette?
What's that? Is it yummy?
klik klik klik
That word is not in my database.
Hey.
NARU-NARU, YOU COULD MAKE HER PRETTY FOR THE WEDDING. YOU ARE A GENIUS, AFTER ALL.
WHAT?!
YEAH.
IT MIGHT BE EXCITING TO HAVE THE S.P. DO THE WEDDING CEREMONY.
LET'S DO THE WEDDING CEREMONY FOR THE NEXT SCISSORS PROJECT.
Ochi
HUH?!
Nurse
YOU CAN'T JUST MAKE THAT DECISION ON YOUR OWN!
Na

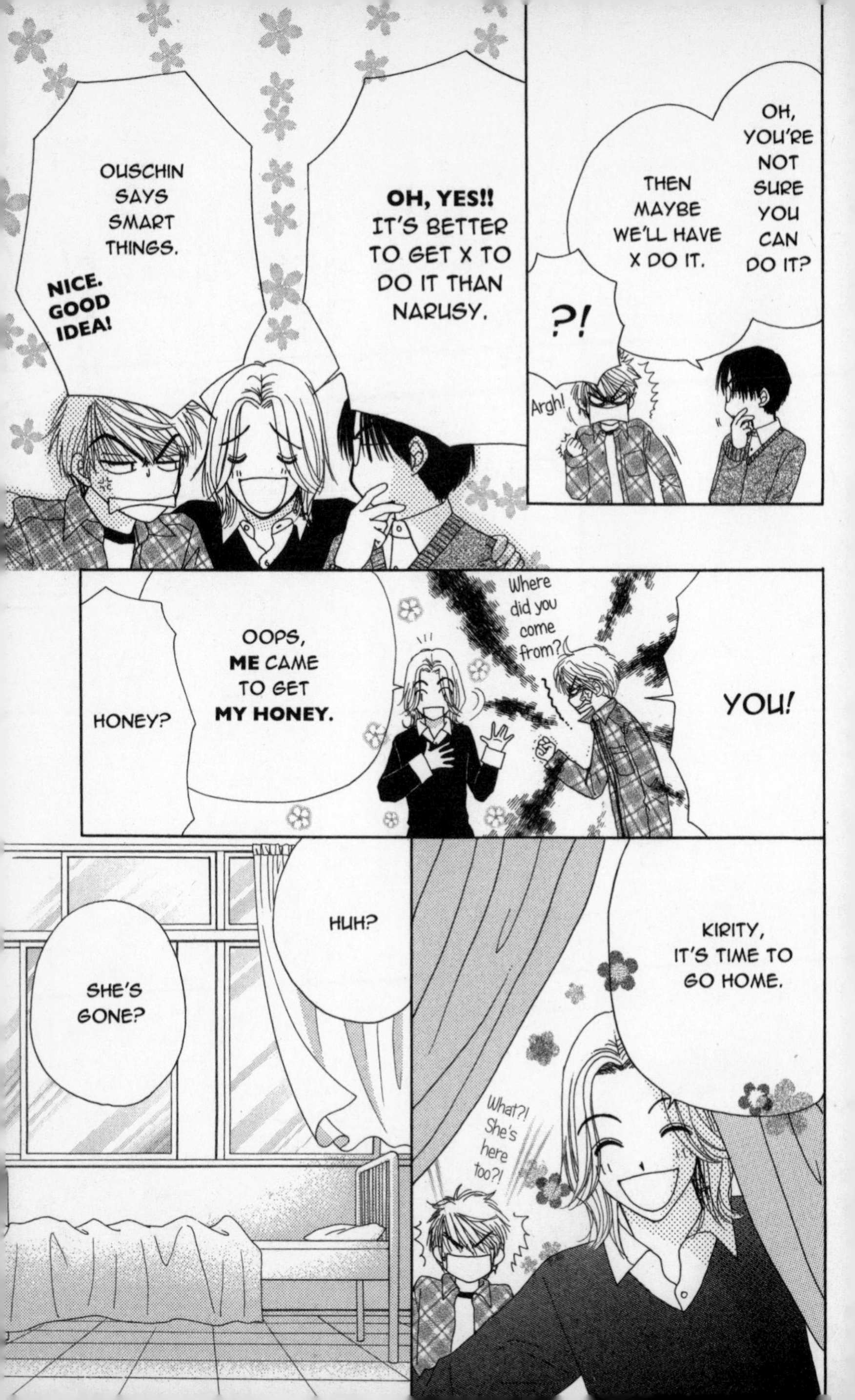
OH, YOU'RE NOT SURE YOU CAN DO IT?
THEN MAYBE WE'LL HAVE X DO IT.
?!
Argh!
OH, YES!! IT'S BETTER TO GET X TO DO IT THAN NARUSY.
OUSCHIN SAYS SMART THINGS.
NICE. GOOD IDEA!
YOU!
Where did you come from?
OOPS, **ME** CAME TO GET **MY HONEY.**
HONEY?
KIRITY, IT'S TIME TO GO HOME.
What?! She's here too?!
HUH?
SHE'S GONE?

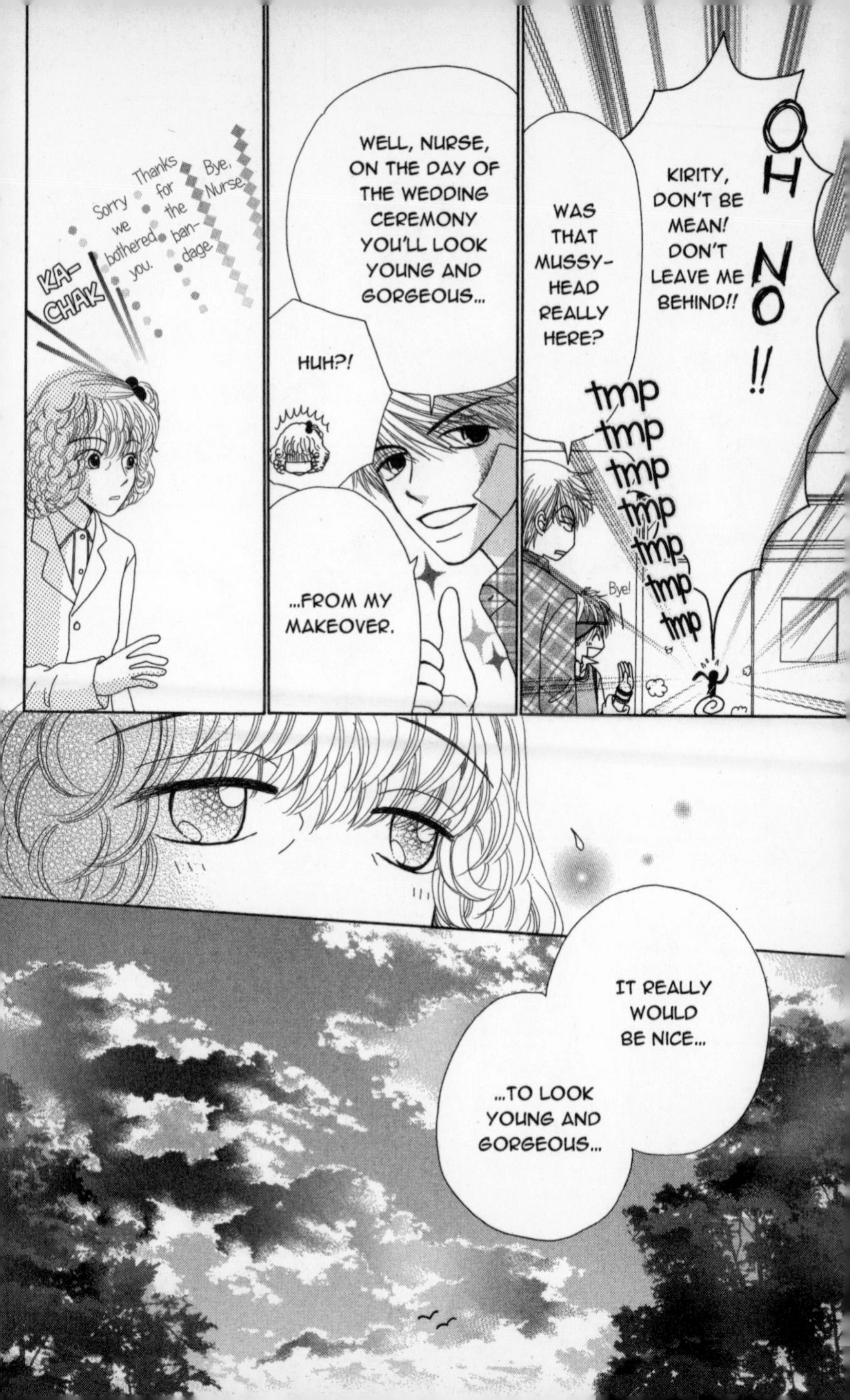
OH NO!!
KIRITY, DON'T BE MEAN! DON'T LEAVE ME BEHIND!!
WAS THAT MUSSY-HEAD REALLY HERE?
tmp tmp tmp tmp tmp tmp tmp
Bye!
WELL, NURSE, ON THE DAY OF THE WEDDING CEREMONY YOU'LL LOOK YOUNG AND GORGEOUS...
HUH?!
...FROM MY MAKEOVER.
Bye, Nurse.
Thanks for the ban-dage.
Sorry we bothered you.
KA-CHAK
IT REALLY WOULD BE NICE...
...TO LOOK YOUNG AND GORGEOUS...

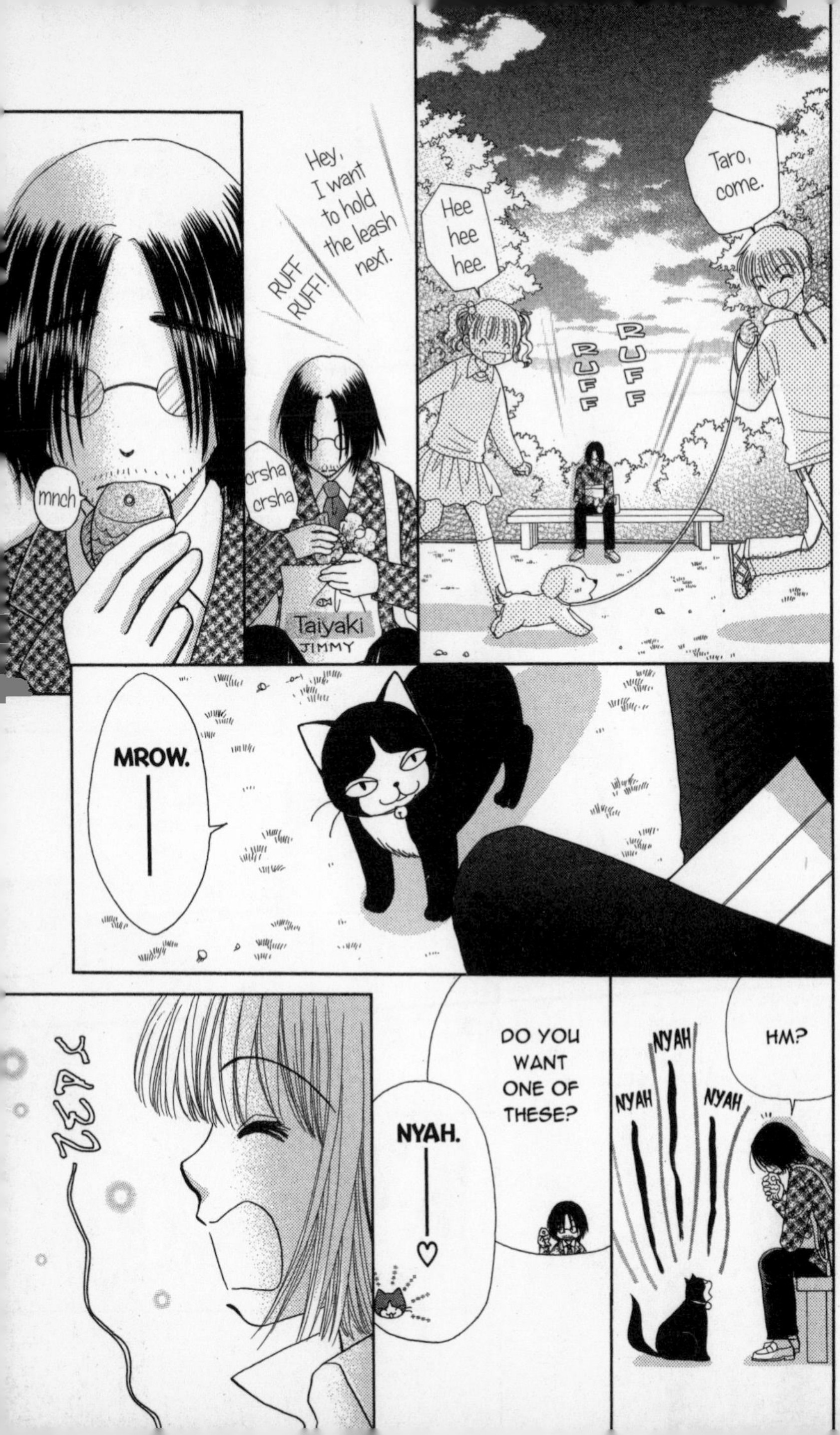
Taro, come.
Hee hee hee.
RUFF RUFF
Hey, I want to hold the leash next.
RUFF RUFF!
crsha crsha
Taiyaki JIMMY
mnch
MROW.
HM?
NYAH NYAH NYAH
DO YOU WANT ONE OF THESE?
NYAH.
YAY

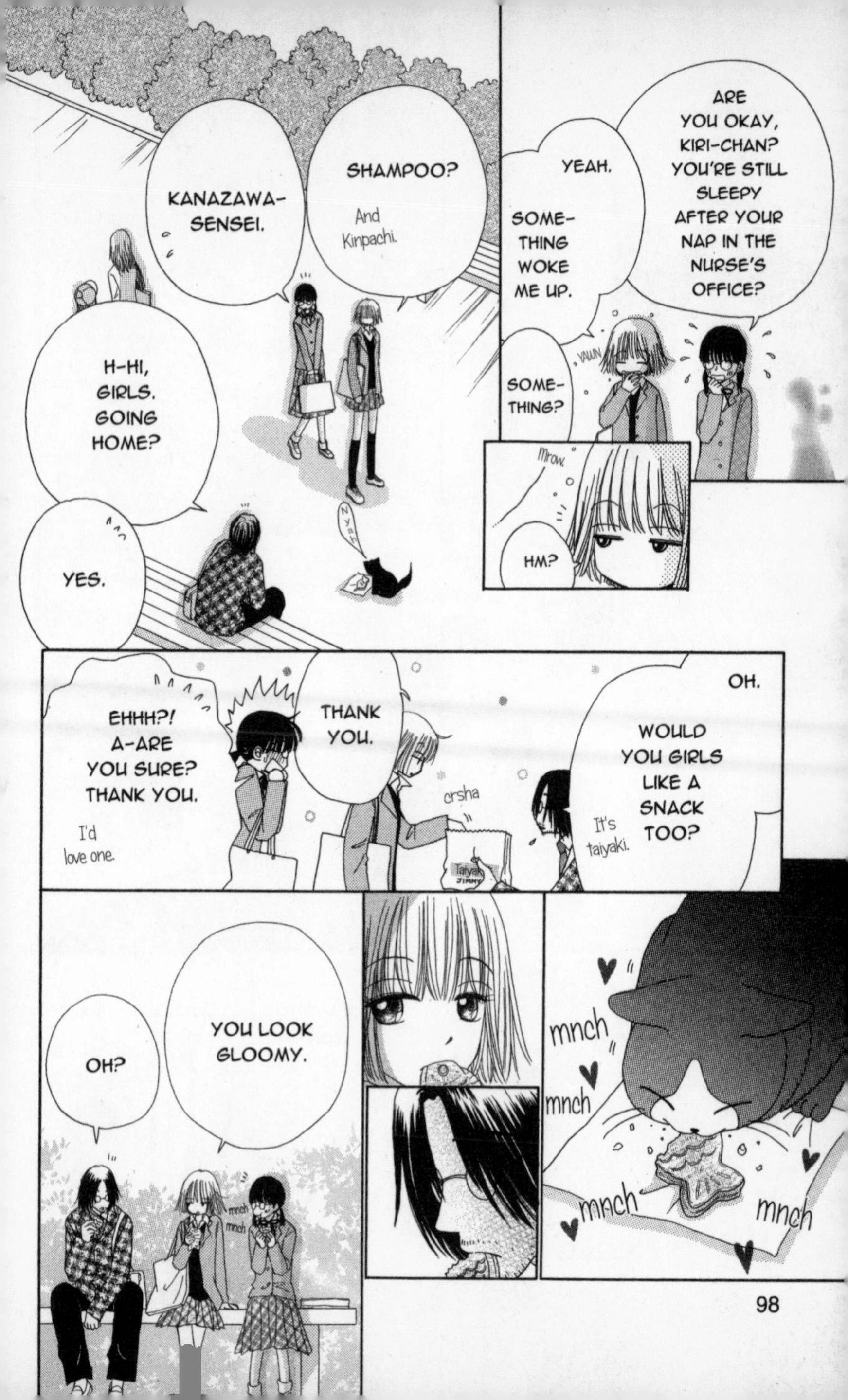

ARE YOU OKAY, KIRI-CHAN? YOU'RE STILL SLEEPY AFTER YOUR NAP IN THE NURSE'S OFFICE?
YEAH.
SOME-THING WOKE ME UP.
YAWN
SOME-THING?
Mrow.
HM?
SHAMPOO?
And Kinpachi.
KANAZAWA-SENSEI.
Nyah
H-HI, GIRLS. GOING HOME?
YES.
OH.
WOULD YOU GIRLS LIKE A SNACK TOO?
It's taiyaki.
crsha
THANK YOU.
EHHH?! A-ARE YOU SURE? THANK YOU.
I'd love one.
mnch
mnch
mnch
mnch
YOU LOOK GLOOMY.
OH?
mnch
mnch

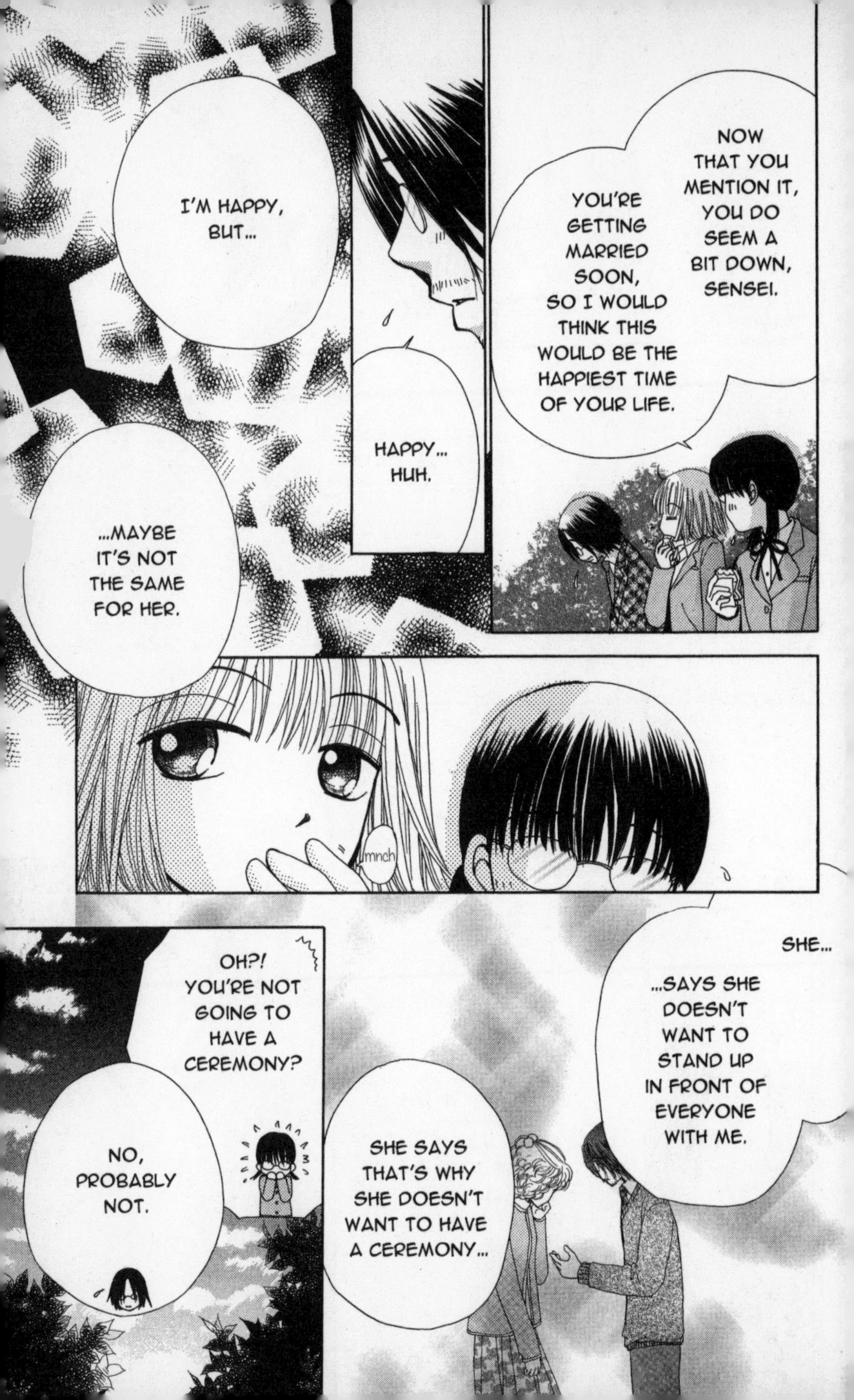
NOW THAT YOU MENTION IT, YOU DO SEEM A BIT DOWN, SENSEI.
YOU'RE GETTING MARRIED SOON, SO I WOULD THINK THIS WOULD BE THE HAPPIEST TIME OF YOUR LIFE.
HAPPY... HUH.
I'M HAPPY, BUT...
...MAYBE IT'S NOT THE SAME FOR HER.
mnch
SHE...
...SAYS SHE DOESN'T WANT TO STAND UP IN FRONT OF EVERYONE WITH ME.
SHE SAYS THAT'S WHY SHE DOESN'T WANT TO HAVE A CEREMONY...
OH?! YOU'RE NOT GOING TO HAVE A CEREMONY?
NO, PROBABLY NOT.

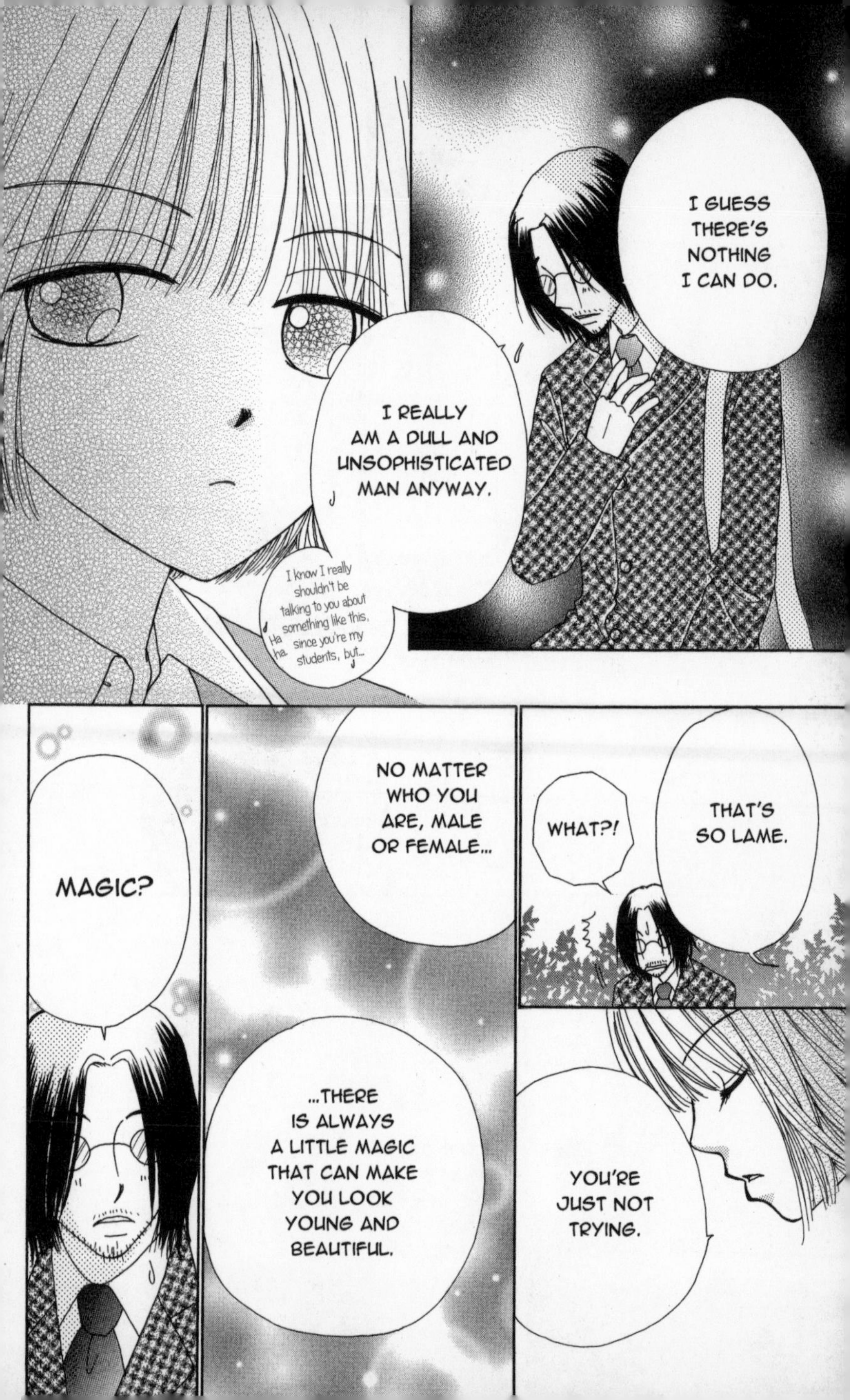
I GUESS THERE'S NOTHING I CAN DO.
I REALLY AM A DULL AND UNSOPHISTICATED MAN ANYWAY.
I know I really shouldn't be talking to you about something like this, since you're my students, but...
Ha ha.
THAT'S SO LAME.
WHAT?!
YOU'RE JUST NOT TRYING.
NO MATTER WHO YOU ARE, MALE OR FEMALE...
...THERE IS ALWAYS A LITTLE MAGIC THAT CAN MAKE YOU LOOK YOUNG AND BEAUTIFUL.
MAGIC?

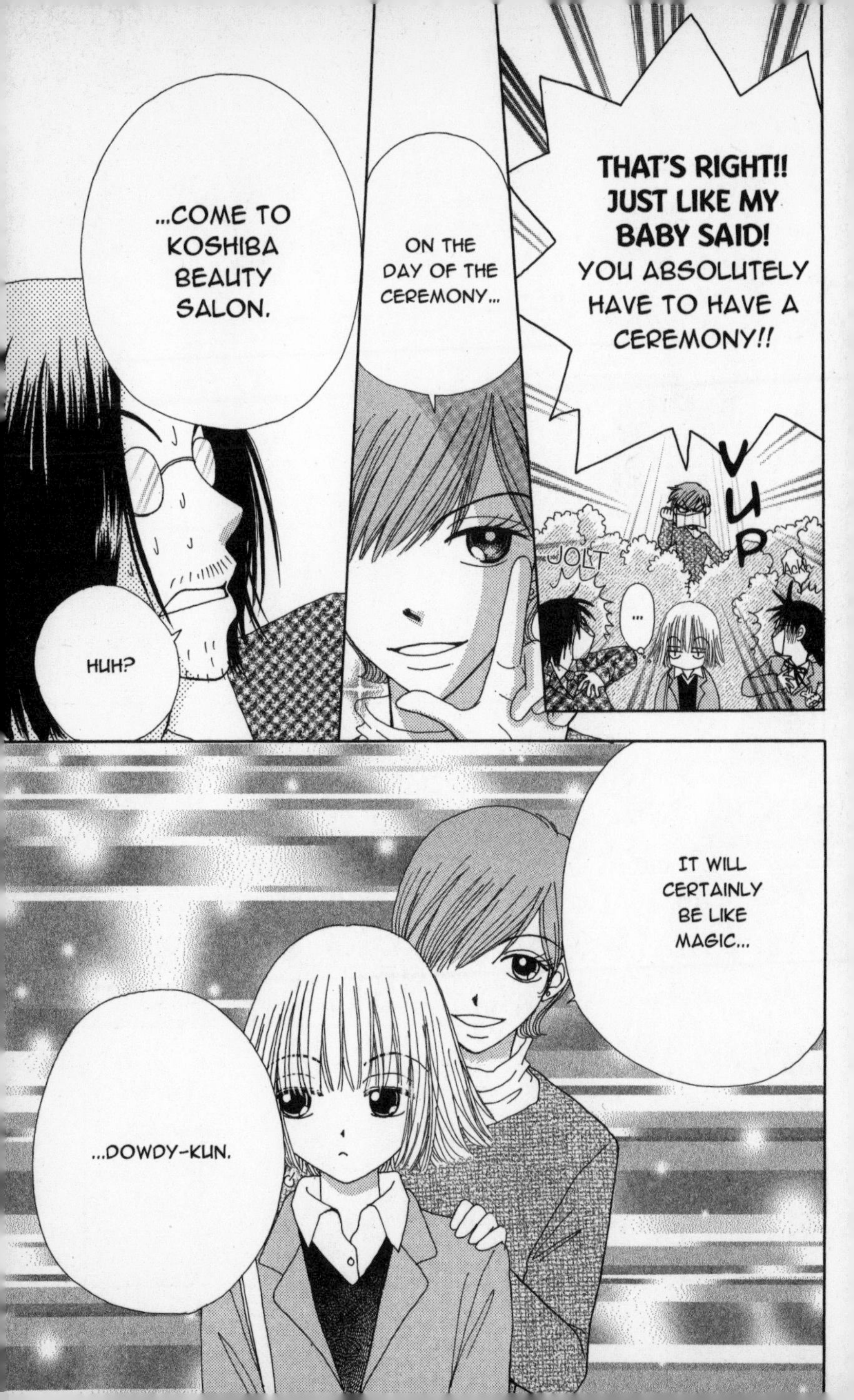
THAT'S RIGHT!! JUST LIKE MY BABY SAID! YOU ABSOLUTELY HAVE TO HAVE A CEREMONY!!
VUP
JOLT
...
ACK
ON THE DAY OF THE CEREMONY...
...COME TO KOSHIBA BEAUTY SALON.
HUH?
IT WILL CERTAINLY BE LIKE MAGIC...
...DOWDY-KUN.

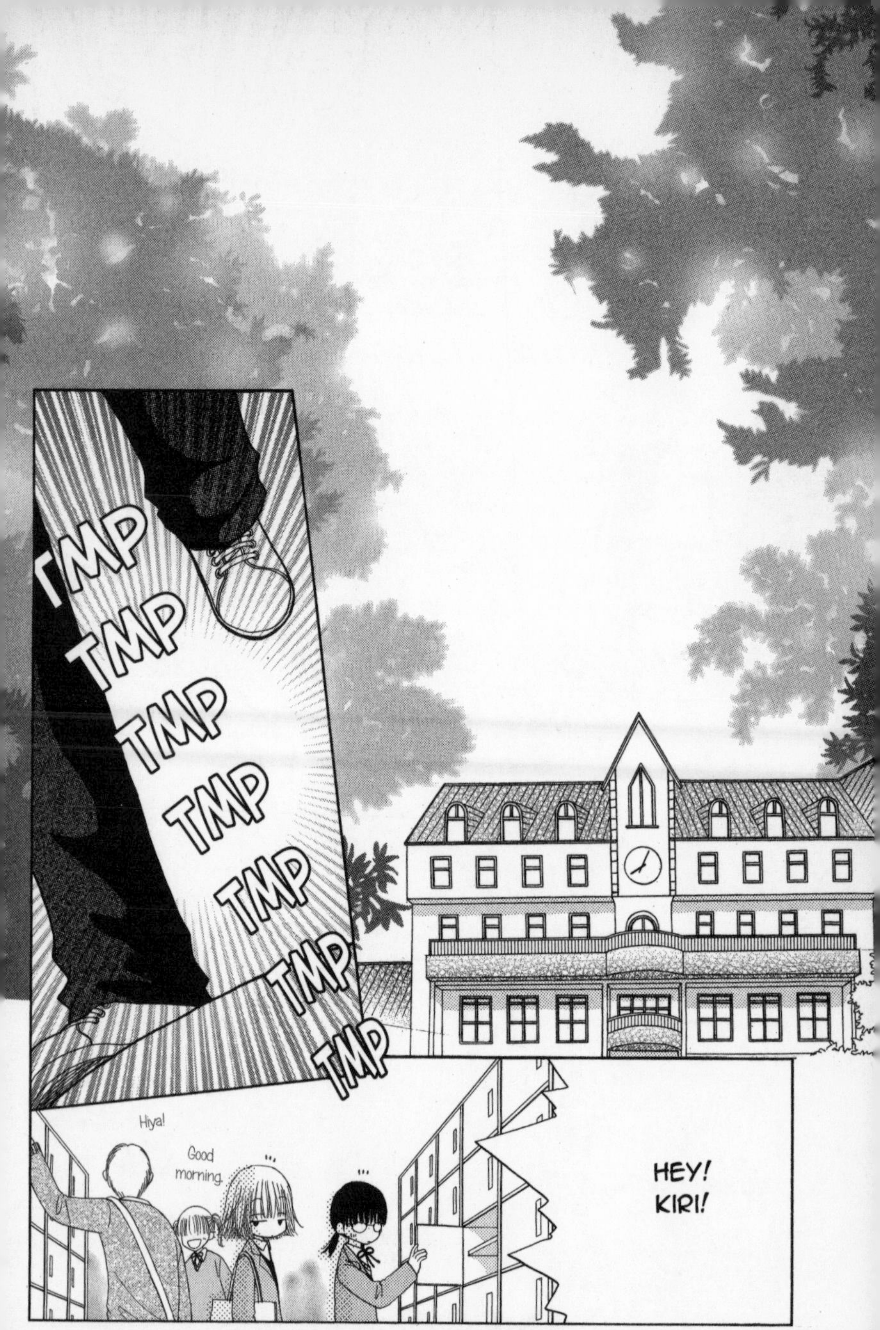
TMP TMP TMP TMP TMP TMP TMP
HEY! KIRI!
Good morning.
Hiya!

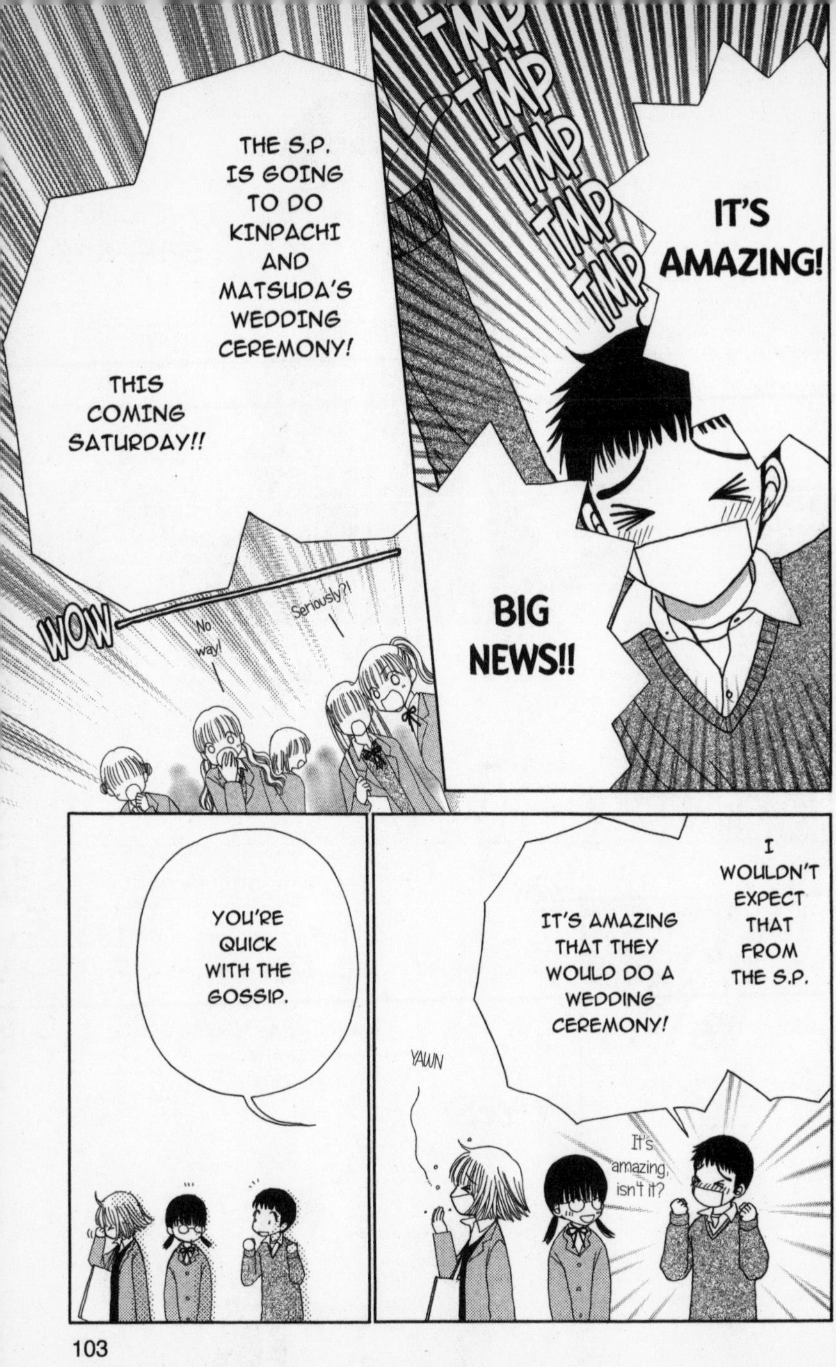
TMP TMP TMP TMP TMP TMP
IT'S AMAZING!
BIG NEWS!!
THE S.P. IS GOING TO DO KINPACHI AND MATSUDA'S WEDDING CEREMONY!
THIS COMING SATURDAY!!
WOW
Seriously?!
No way!
I WOULDN'T EXPECT THAT FROM THE S.P.
IT'S AMAZING THAT THEY WOULD DO A WEDDING CEREMONY!
YAWN
It's amazing, isn't it?
YOU'RE QUICK WITH THE GOSSIP.

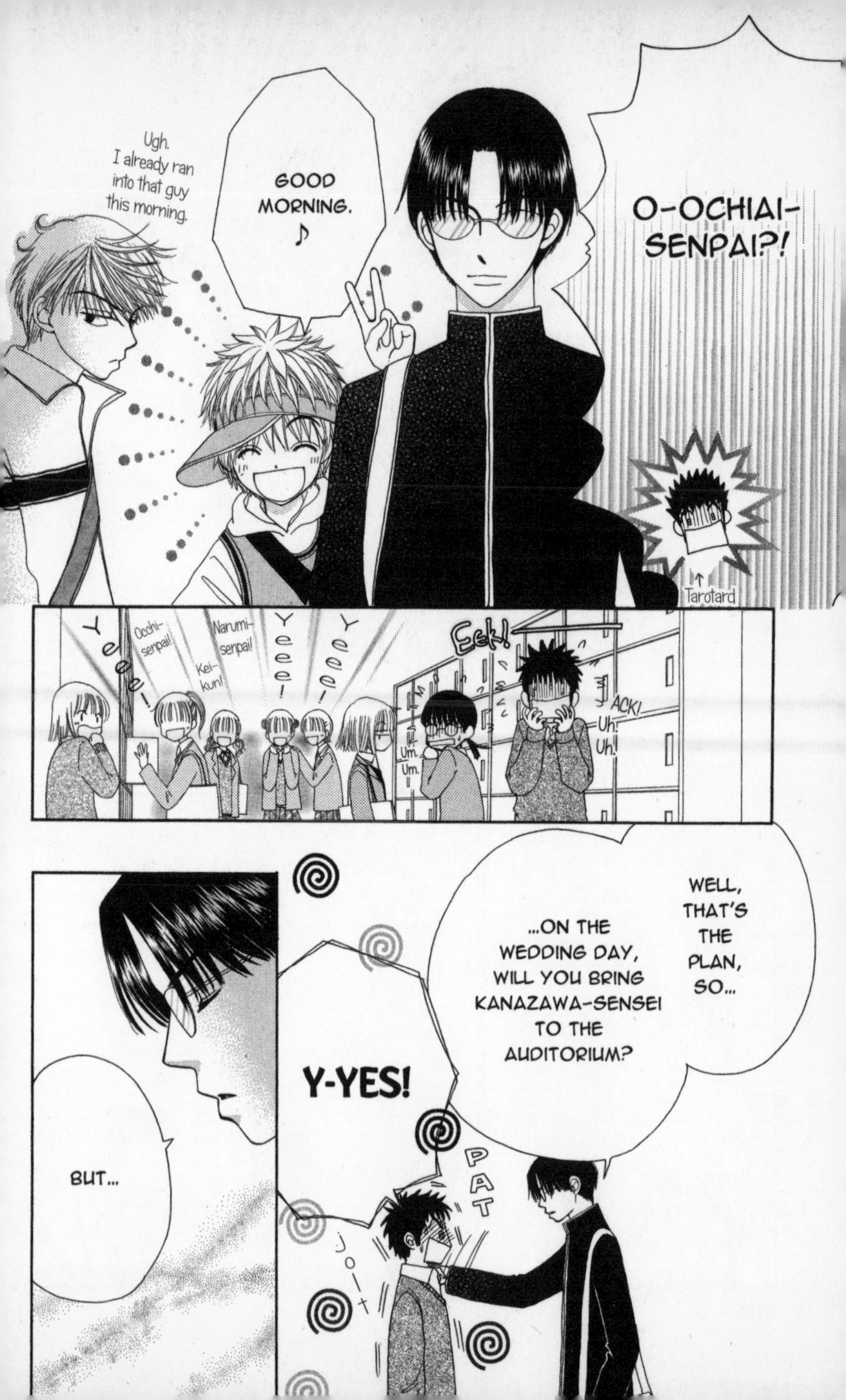
O-OCHIAI-SENPAI?!
GOOD MORNING. ♪
Ugh. I already ran into that guy this morning.
Tarotard
ACK! Uh. Uh.
Eek!
Um. Um.
Yeee!
Yeee!
Narumi-senpai!
Kei-kun!
Occhi-senpai!
Yeee!
WELL, THAT'S THE PLAN, SO...
...ON THE WEDDING DAY, WILL YOU BRING KANAZAWA-SENSEI TO THE AUDITORIUM?
Y-YES!
PAT
jolt
BUT...

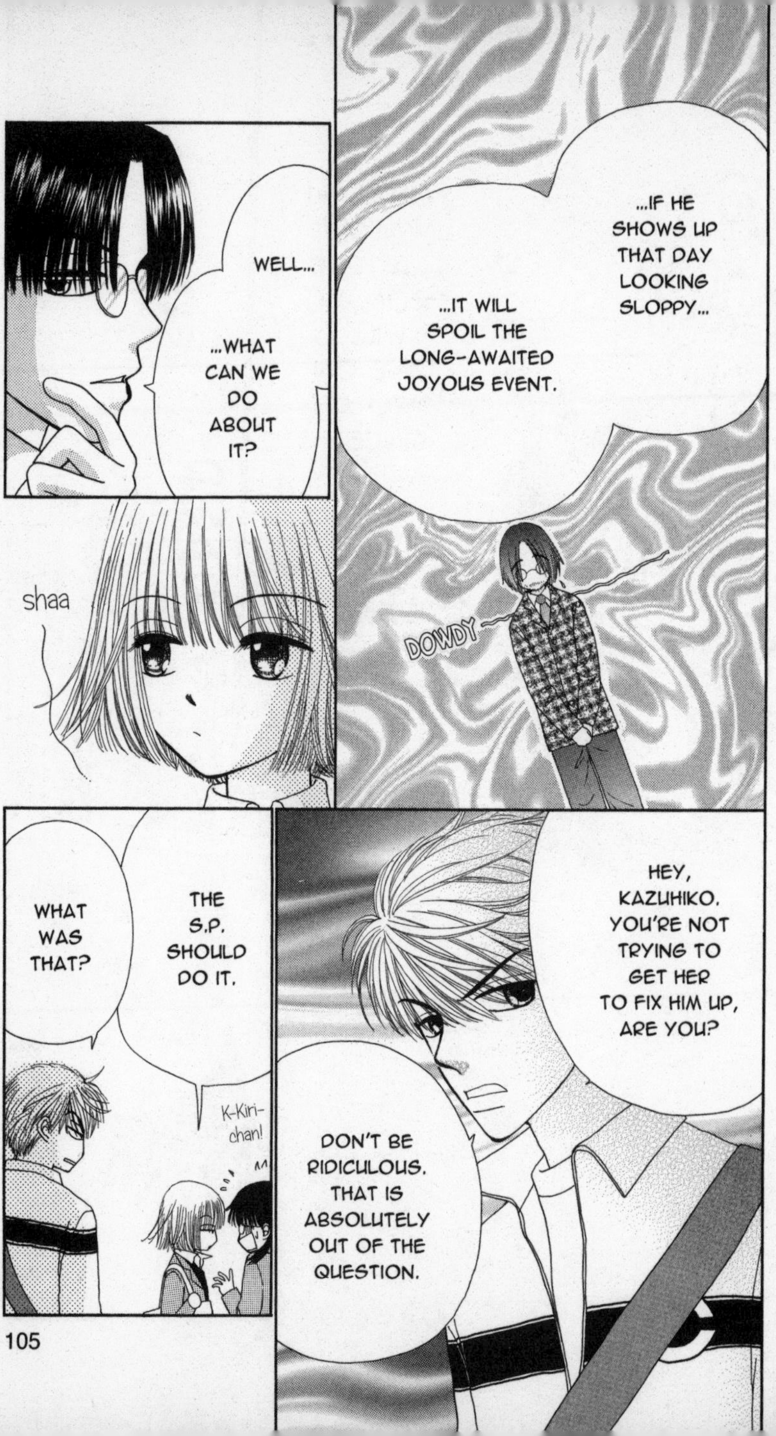
...IF HE SHOWS UP THAT DAY LOOKING SLOPPY...
...IT WILL SPOIL THE LONG-AWAITED JOYOUS EVENT.
DOWDY
WELL...
...WHAT CAN WE DO ABOUT IT?
shaa
HEY, KAZUHIKO. YOU'RE NOT TRYING TO GET HER TO FIX HIM UP, ARE YOU?
DON'T BE RIDICULOUS. THAT IS ABSOLUTELY OUT OF THE QUESTION.
THE S.P. SHOULD DO IT.
WHAT WAS THAT?
K-Kiri-chan!

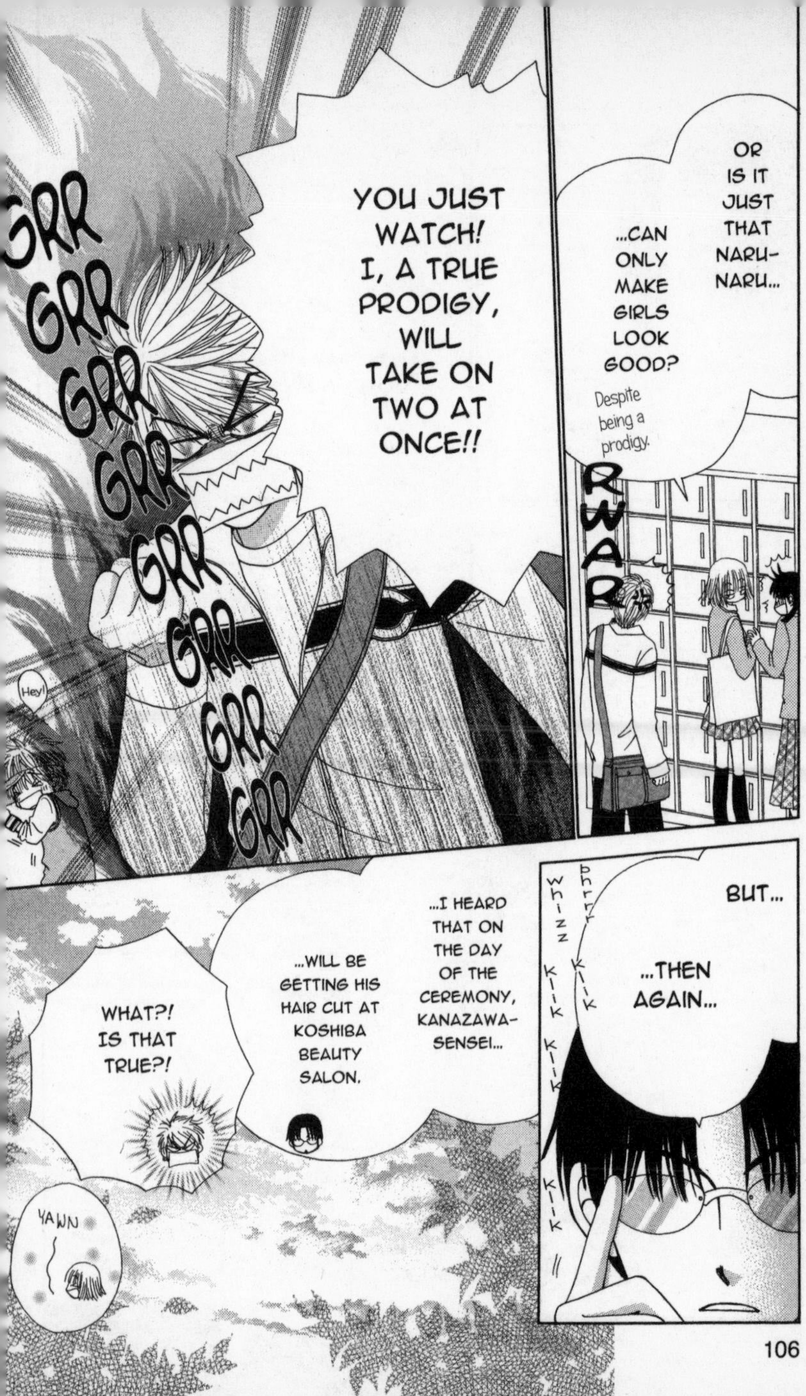
OR IS IT JUST THAT NARU-NARU...
...CAN ONLY MAKE GIRLS LOOK GOOD?
Despite being a prodigy.
RWAR
YOU JUST WATCH! I, A TRUE PRODIGY, WILL TAKE ON TWO AT ONCE!!
GRR GRR GRR GRR GRR GRR GRR GRR
Hey!
bhrrr
whizz
klik klik
klik klik klik
BUT...
...THEN AGAIN...
...I HEARD THAT ON THE DAY OF THE CEREMONY, KANAZAWA-SENSEI...
...WILL BE GETTING HIS HAIR CUT AT KOSHIBA BEAUTY SALON.
WHAT?! IS THAT TRUE?!
YAWN

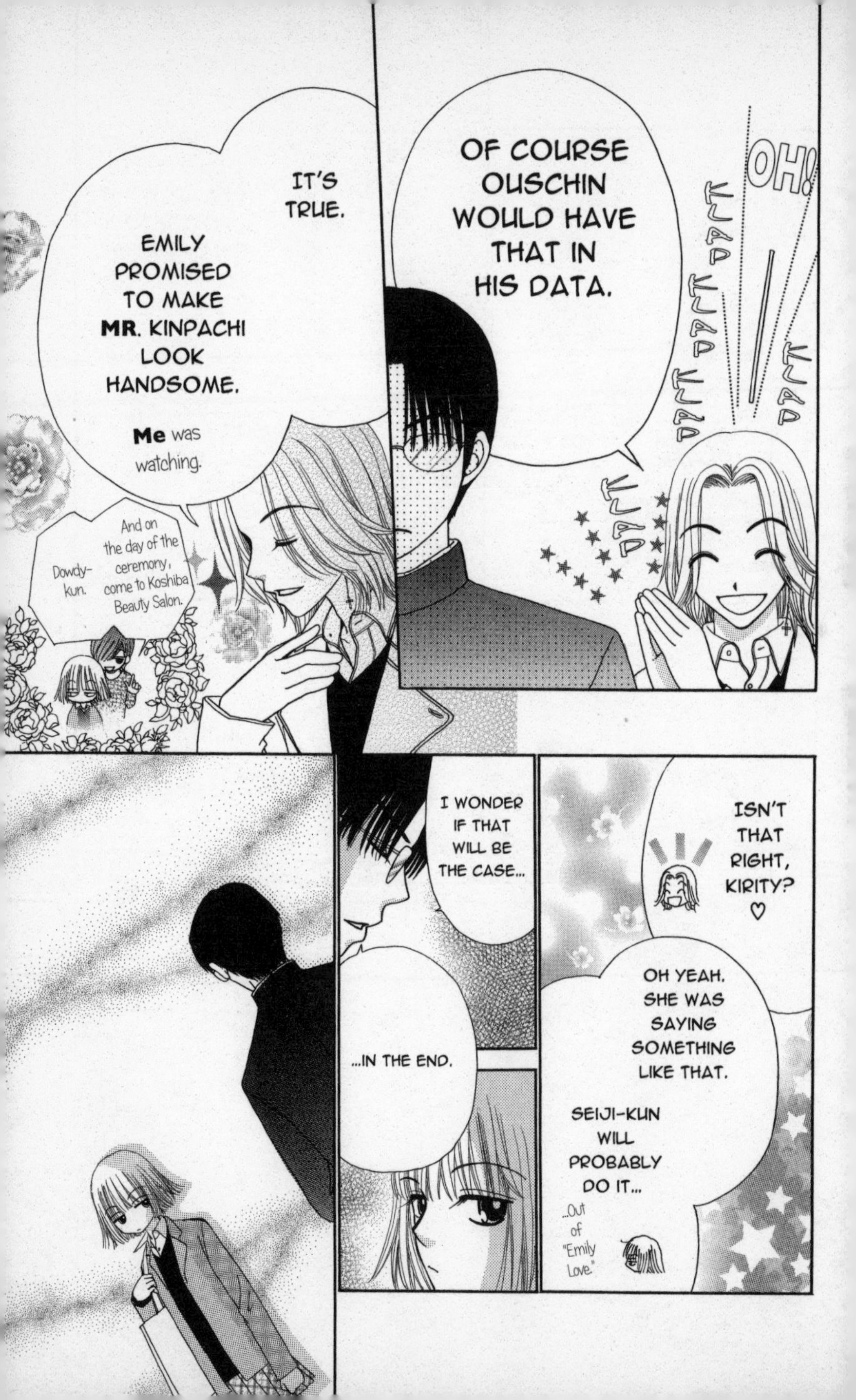
OH!
KLAP KLAP KLAP KLAP
KLAP
KLAP
OF COURSE OUSCHIN WOULD HAVE THAT IN HIS DATA.
IT'S TRUE.
EMILY PROMISED TO MAKE MR. KINPACHI LOOK HANDSOME.
Me was watching.
And on the day of the ceremony, come to Koshiba Beauty Salon.
Dowdy-kun.
ISN'T THAT RIGHT, KIRITY? ♡
OH YEAH. SHE WAS SAYING SOMETHING LIKE THAT.
SEIJI-KUN WILL PROBABLY DO IT...
...Out of "Emily Love."
I WONDER IF THAT WILL BE THE CASE...
...IN THE END.

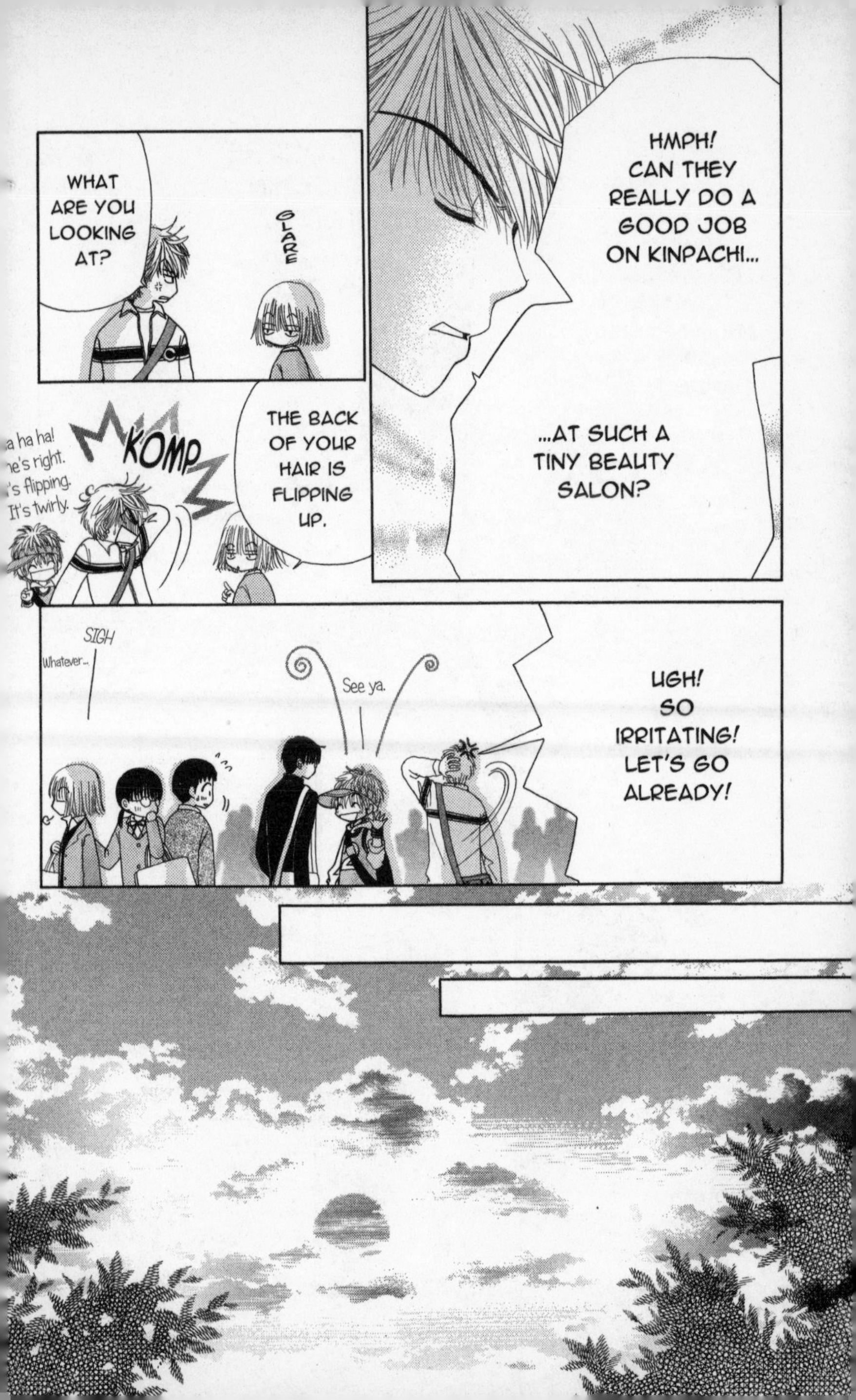
HMPH! CAN THEY REALLY DO A GOOD JOB ON KINPACHI...
...AT SUCH A TINY BEAUTY SALON?
WHAT ARE YOU LOOKING AT?
GLARE
THE BACK OF YOUR HAIR IS FLIPPING UP.
KOMP
a ha ha! ne's right. 's flipping. It's twirly.
UGH! SO IRRITATING! LET'S GO ALREADY!
See ya.
SIGH
Whatever...

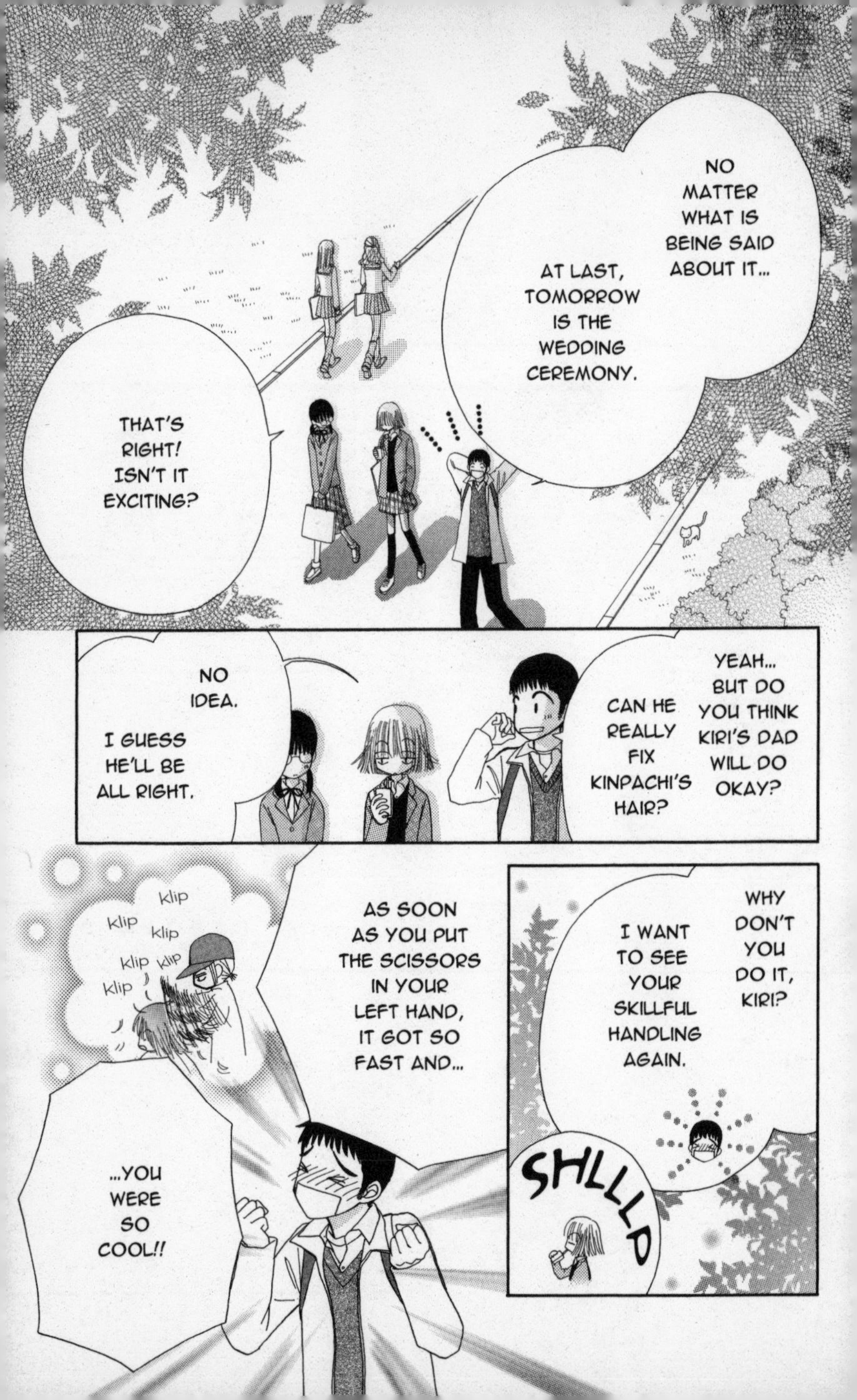
NO MATTER WHAT IS BEING SAID ABOUT IT...
AT LAST, TOMORROW IS THE WEDDING CEREMONY.
THAT'S RIGHT! ISN'T IT EXCITING?
YEAH... BUT DO YOU THINK KIRI'S DAD WILL DO OKAY?
CAN HE REALLY FIX KINPACHI'S HAIR?
NO IDEA.
I GUESS HE'LL BE ALL RIGHT.
WHY DON'T YOU DO IT, KIRI?
I WANT TO SEE YOUR SKILLFUL HANDLING AGAIN.
SHLLLP
AS SOON AS YOU PUT THE SCISSORS IN YOUR LEFT HAND, IT GOT SO FAST AND...
klip
klip
klip
klip
klip
klip
...YOU WERE SO COOL!!

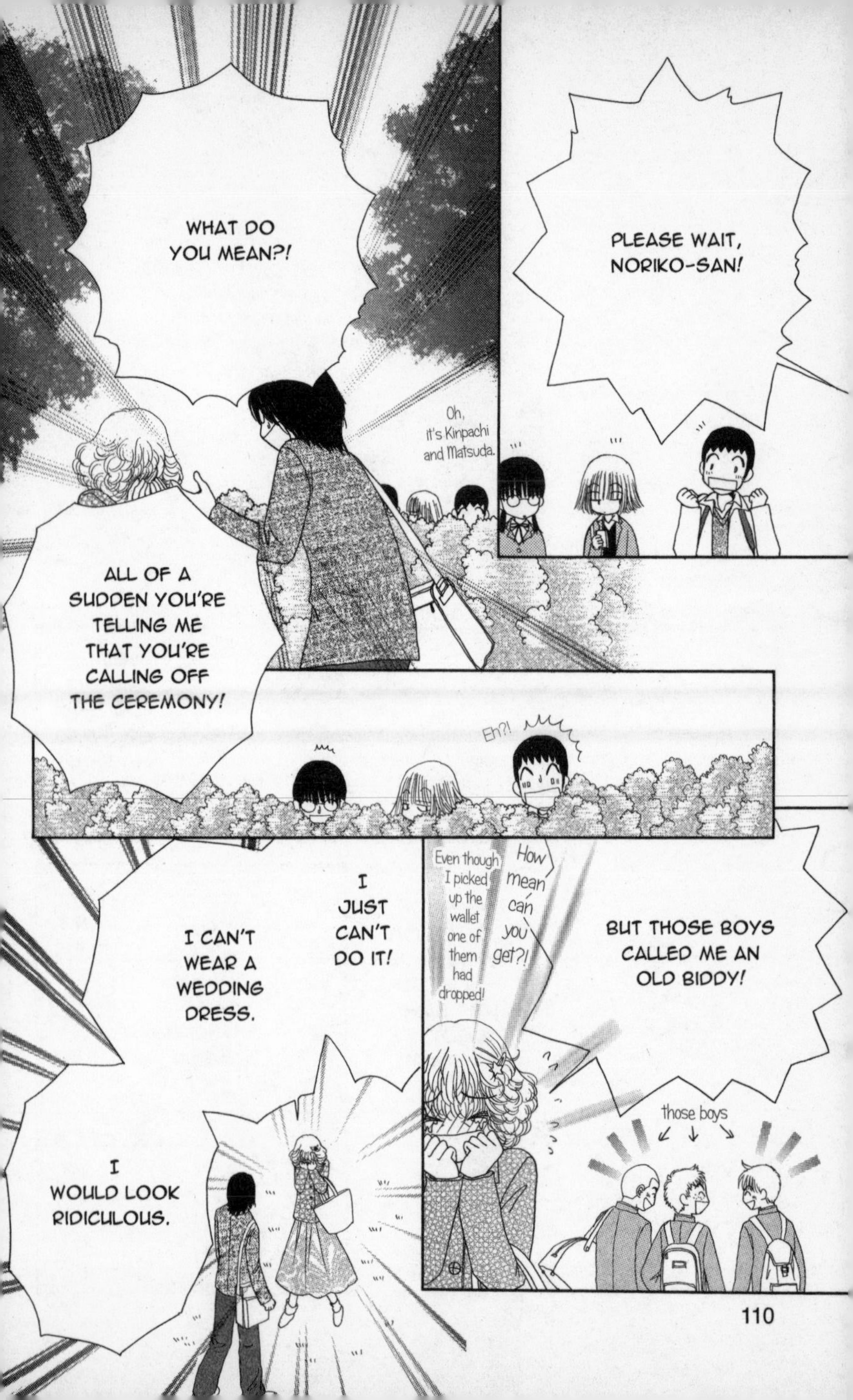
PLEASE WAIT, NORIKO-SAN!
Oh, it's Kinpachi and Matsuda.
WHAT DO YOU MEAN?!
ALL OF A SUDDEN YOU'RE TELLING ME THAT YOU'RE CALLING OFF THE CEREMONY!
Eh?!
BUT THOSE BOYS CALLED ME AN OLD BIDDY!
How mean can you get?!
Even though I picked up the wallet one of them had dropped!
those boys
I JUST CAN'T DO IT!
I CAN'T WEAR A WEDDING DRESS.
I WOULD LOOK RIDICULOUS.

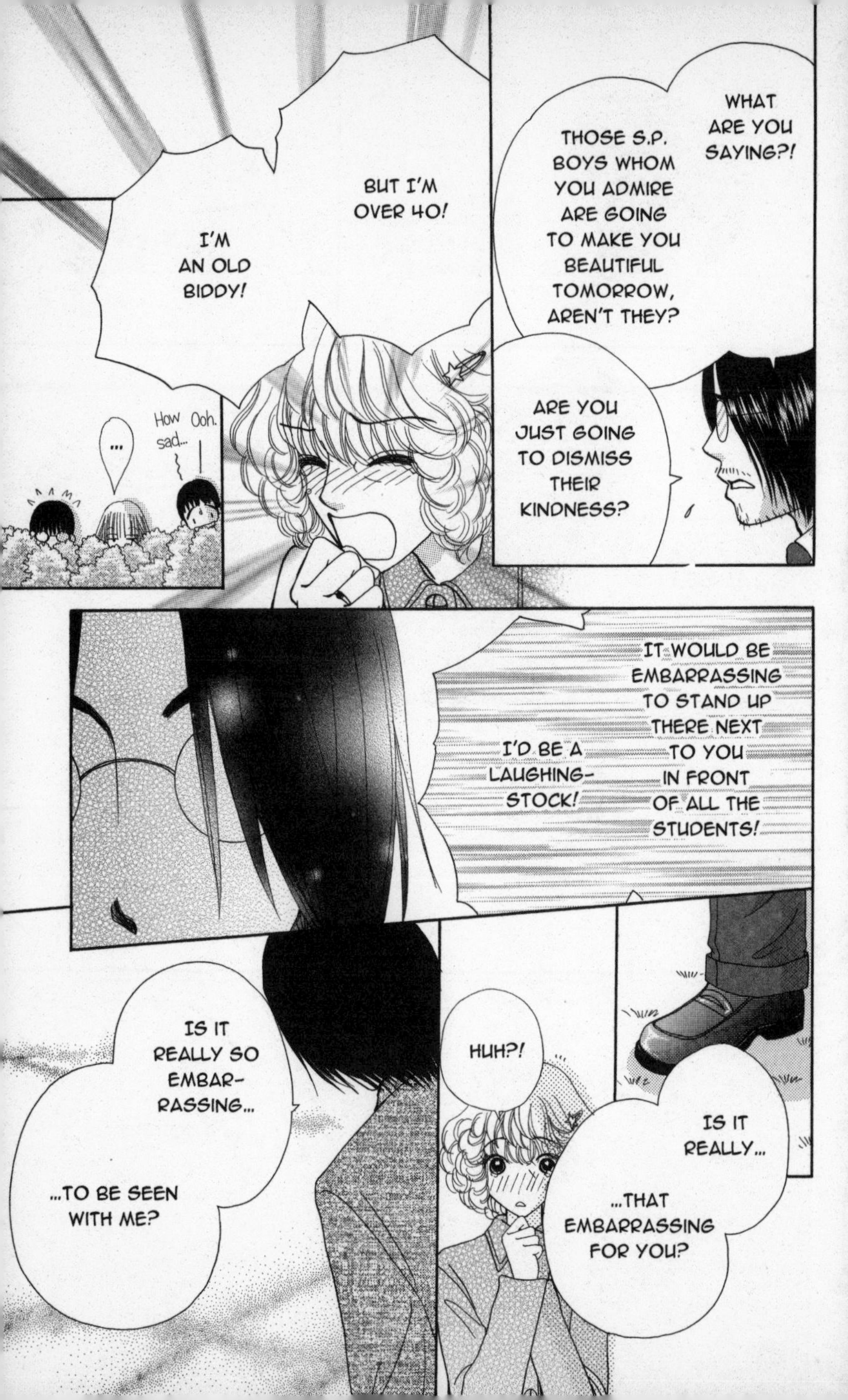
WHAT ARE YOU SAYING?!
THOSE S.P. BOYS WHOM YOU ADMIRE ARE GOING TO MAKE YOU BEAUTIFUL TOMORROW, AREN'T THEY?
ARE YOU JUST GOING TO DISMISS THEIR KINDNESS?
BUT I'M OVER 40!
I'M AN OLD BIDDY!
Ooh.
How sad...
...
IT WOULD BE EMBARRASSING TO STAND UP THERE NEXT TO YOU IN FRONT OF ALL THE STUDENTS!
I'D BE A LAUGHING-STOCK!
IS IT REALLY...
...THAT EMBARRASSING FOR YOU?
HUH?!
IS IT REALLY SO EMBAR-RASSING...
...TO BE SEEN WITH ME?

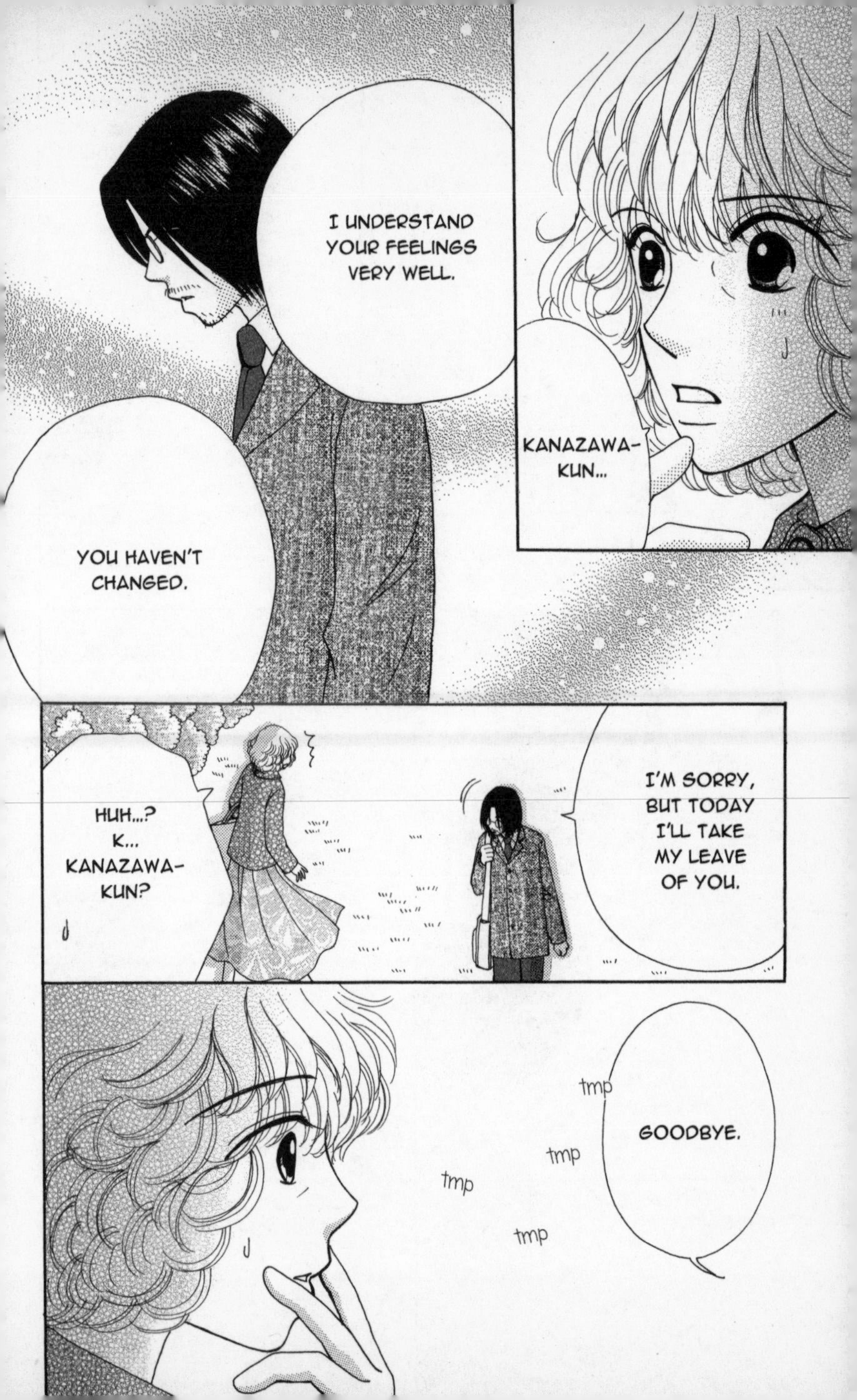
KANAZAWA-KUN...
I UNDERSTAND YOUR FEELINGS VERY WELL.
YOU HAVEN'T CHANGED.
I'M SORRY, BUT TODAY I'LL TAKE MY LEAVE OF YOU.
HUH...? K... KANAZAWA-KUN?
GOODBYE.
tmp
tmp
tmp
tmp

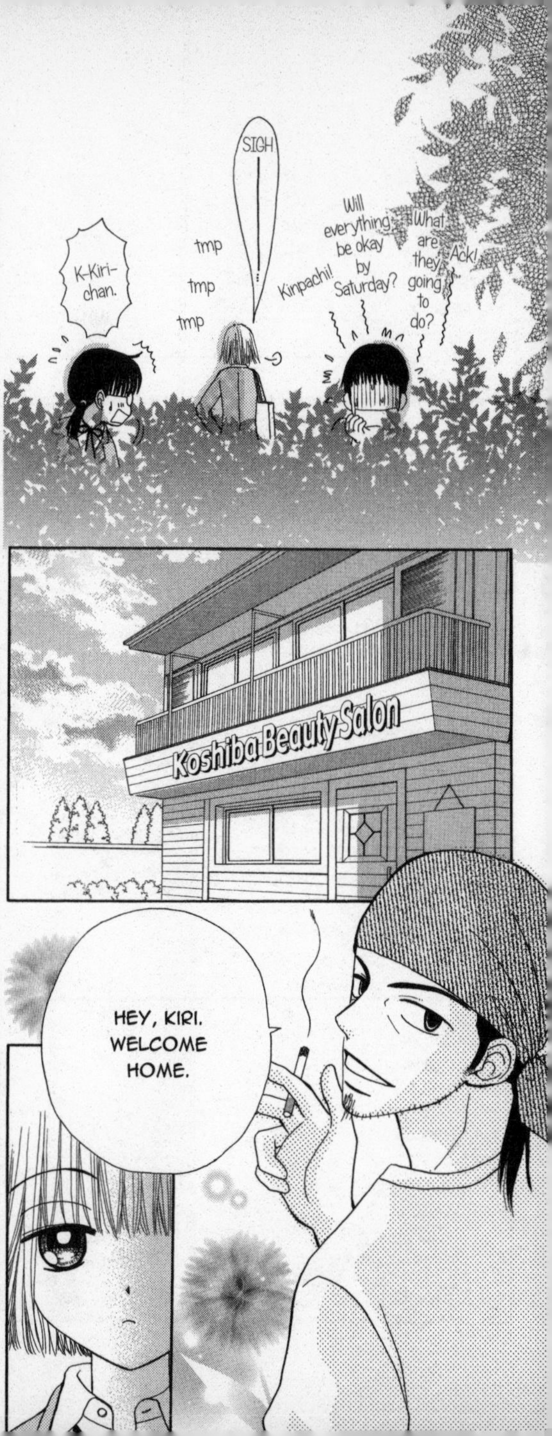
Ack!
What are they going to do?
Will everything be okay by Saturday?
Kinpachi!
SIGH
tmp
tmp
tmp
K-Kiri-chan.
Koshiba Beauty Salon
HEY, KIRI. WELCOME HOME.

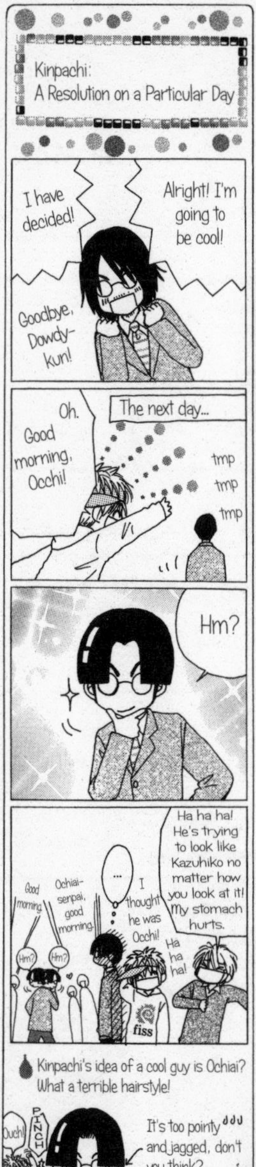
Kinpachi: A Resolution on a Particular Day
Alright! I'm going to be cool!
I have decided!
Goodbye, Dowdy-kun!
The next day...
Oh. Good morning, Occhi!
tmp
tmp
tmp
Hm?
Ha ha ha! He's trying to look like Kazuhiko no matter how you look at it! My stomach hurts.
Ha ha ha!
I thought he was Occhi!
...
Ochiai-senpai, good morning.
Good morning.
Hm?
Hm?
Kinpachi's idea of a cool guy is Ochiai? What a terrible hairstyle!
It's too pointy and jagged, don't you think?
PINCH
Ouch!

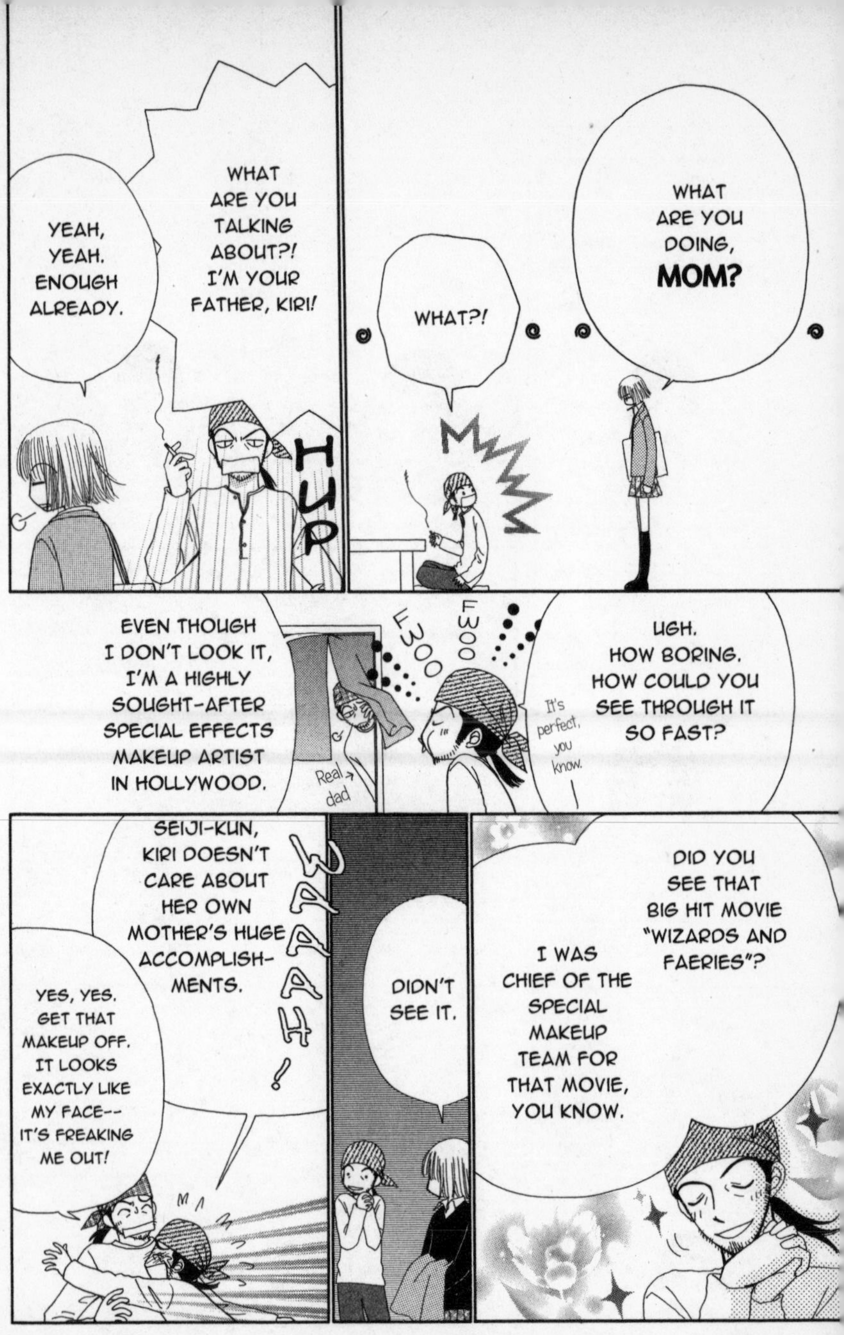
WHAT ARE YOU DOING, **MOM?**
WHAT?!
WHAT ARE YOU TALKING ABOUT?! I'M YOUR FATHER, KIRI!
HUP
YEAH, YEAH. ENOUGH ALREADY.
UGH. HOW BORING. HOW COULD YOU SEE THROUGH IT SO FAST?
It's perfect, you know.
FWOO
FWOO
Real dad
EVEN THOUGH I DON'T LOOK IT, I'M A HIGHLY SOUGHT-AFTER SPECIAL EFFECTS MAKEUP ARTIST IN HOLLYWOOD.
DID YOU SEE THAT BIG HIT MOVIE "WIZARDS AND FAERIES"?
I WAS CHIEF OF THE SPECIAL MAKEUP TEAM FOR THAT MOVIE, YOU KNOW.
DIDN'T SEE IT.
WAAAH!
SEIJI-KUN, KIRI DOESN'T CARE ABOUT HER OWN MOTHER'S HUGE ACCOMPLISH-MENTS.
YES, YES. GET THAT MAKEUP OFF. IT LOOKS EXACTLY LIKE MY FACE-- IT'S FREAKING ME OUT!

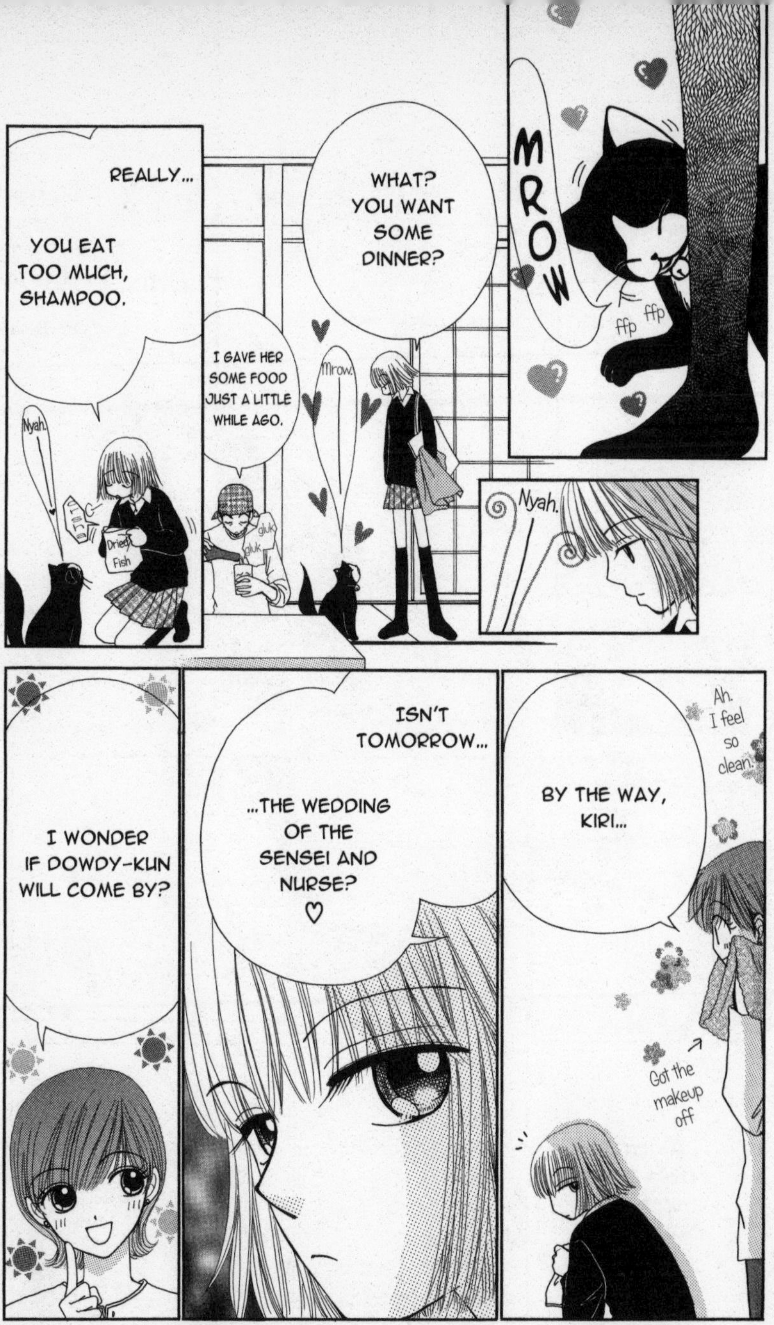
MROW
ffp ffp
Nyah.
WHAT? YOU WANT SOME DINNER?
Mrow.
I GAVE HER SOME FOOD JUST A LITTLE WHILE AGO.
gluk gluk
REALLY...
YOU EAT TOO MUCH, SHAMPOO.
Nyah.
Dried Fish
Ah. I feel so clean.
BY THE WAY, KIRI...
Got the makeup off
ISN'T TOMORROW...
...THE WEDDING OF THE SENSEI AND NURSE? ♡
I WONDER IF DOWDY-KUN WILL COME BY?

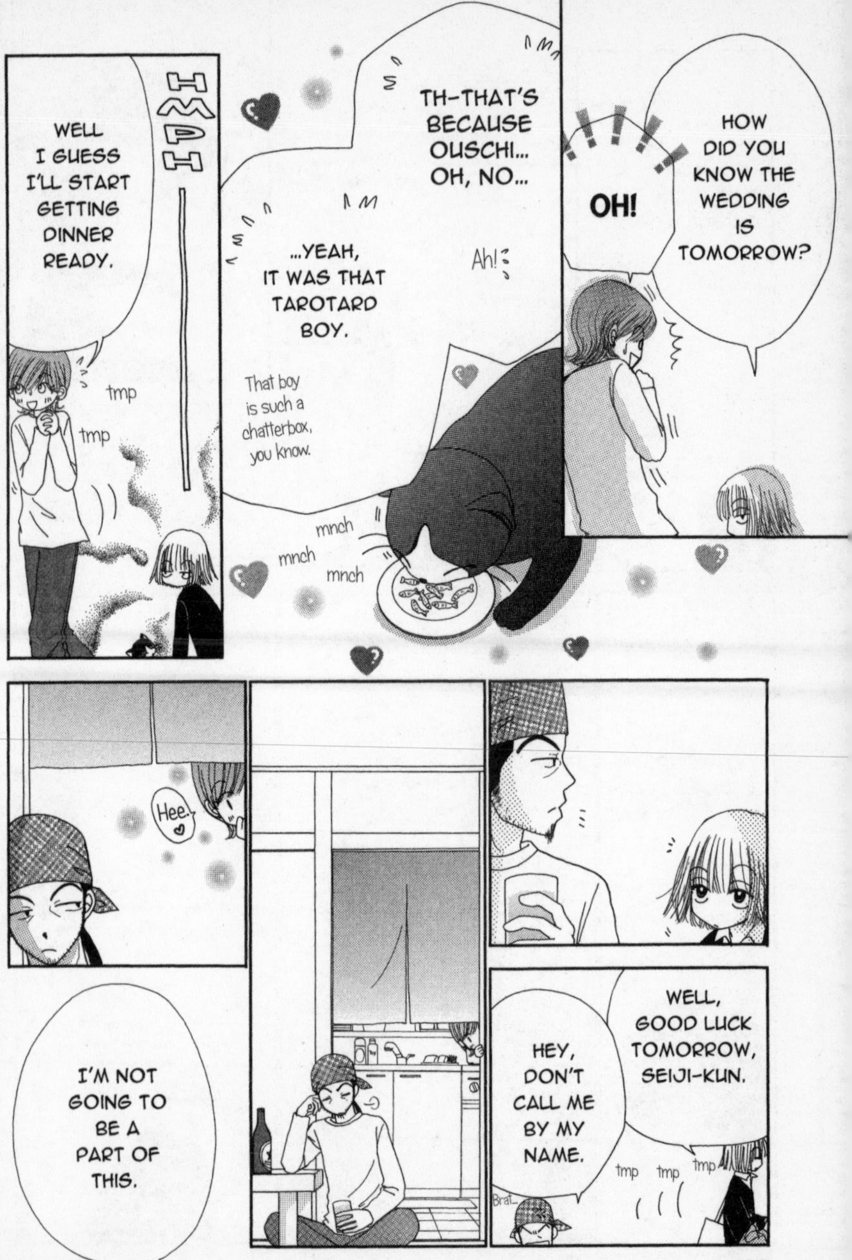
HOW DID YOU KNOW THE WEDDING IS TOMORROW?
OH!
TH-THAT'S BECAUSE OUSCHI... OH, NO...
Ah!
...YEAH, IT WAS THAT TAROTARD BOY.
That boy is such a chatterbox, you know.
mnch
mnch
mnch
HMPH
WELL I GUESS I'LL START GETTING DINNER READY.
tmp
tmp
WELL, GOOD LUCK TOMORROW, SEIJI-KUN.
HEY, DON'T CALL ME BY MY NAME.
tmp
tmp
tmp
Brat...
Hee.
I'M NOT GOING TO BE A PART OF THIS.

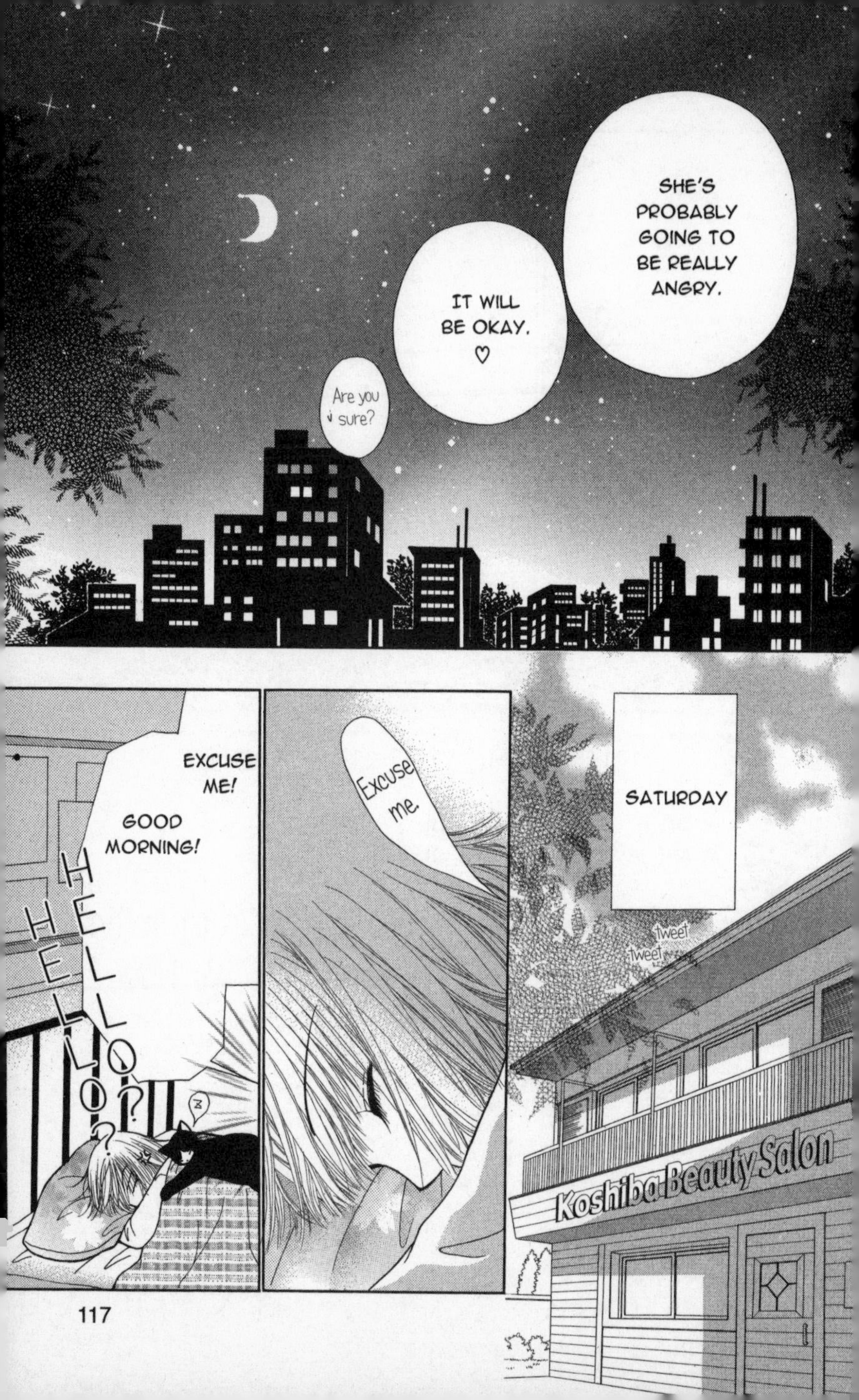
SHE'S PROBABLY GOING TO BE REALLY ANGRY.
IT WILL BE OKAY. ♡
Are you sure?
SATURDAY
tweet
tweet
Koshiba Beauty Salon
Excuse me.
EXCUSE ME!
GOOD MORNING!
HELLO?
HELLO?

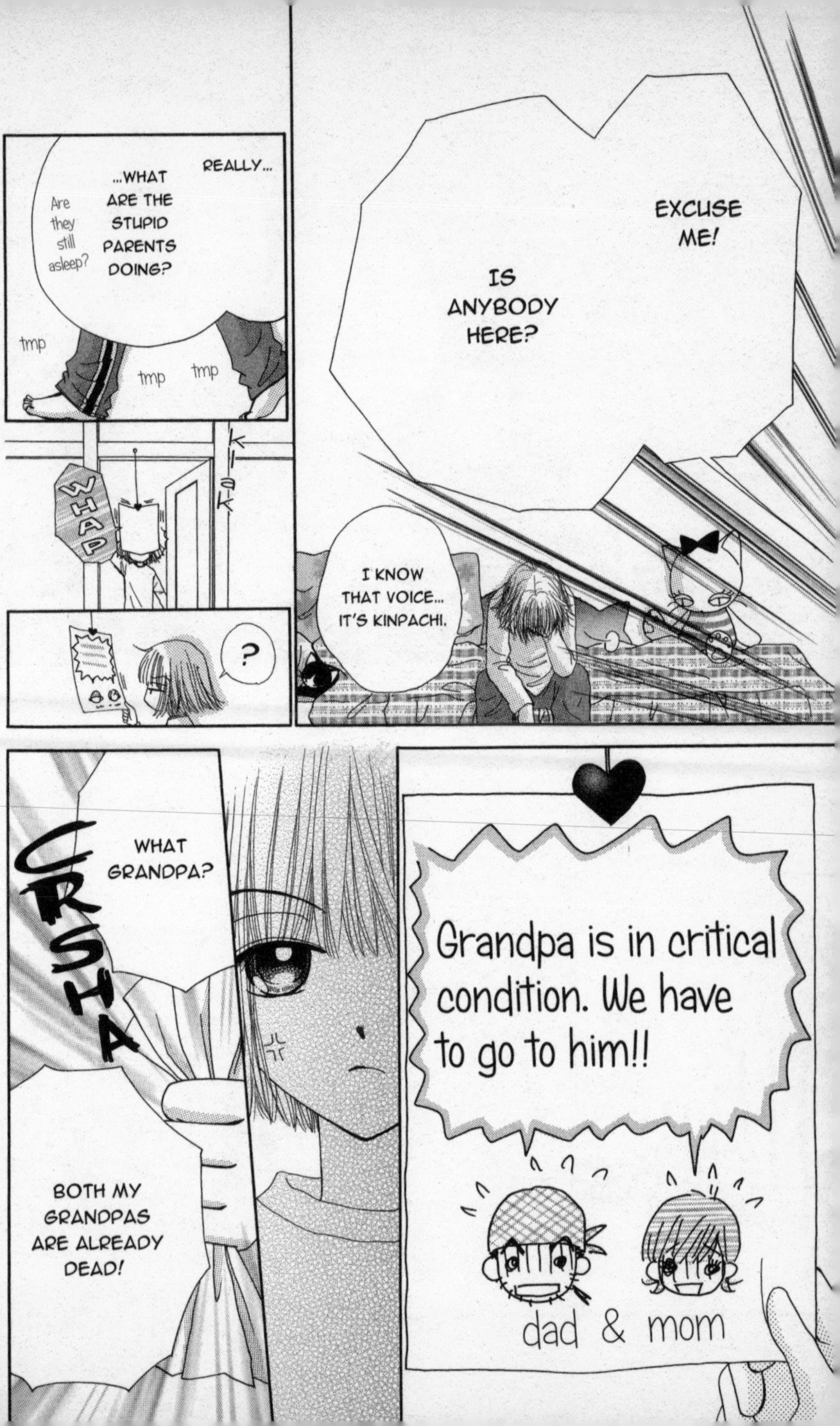
EXCUSE ME!
IS ANYBODY HERE?
I KNOW THAT VOICE... IT'S KINPACHI.
REALLY...
...WHAT ARE THE STUPID PARENTS DOING?
Are they still asleep?
tmp
tmp
tmp
klak
WHAP
?
Grandpa is in critical condition. We have to go to him!!
dad & mom
CRSHA
WHAT GRANDPA?
BOTH MY GRANDPAS ARE ALREADY DEAD!

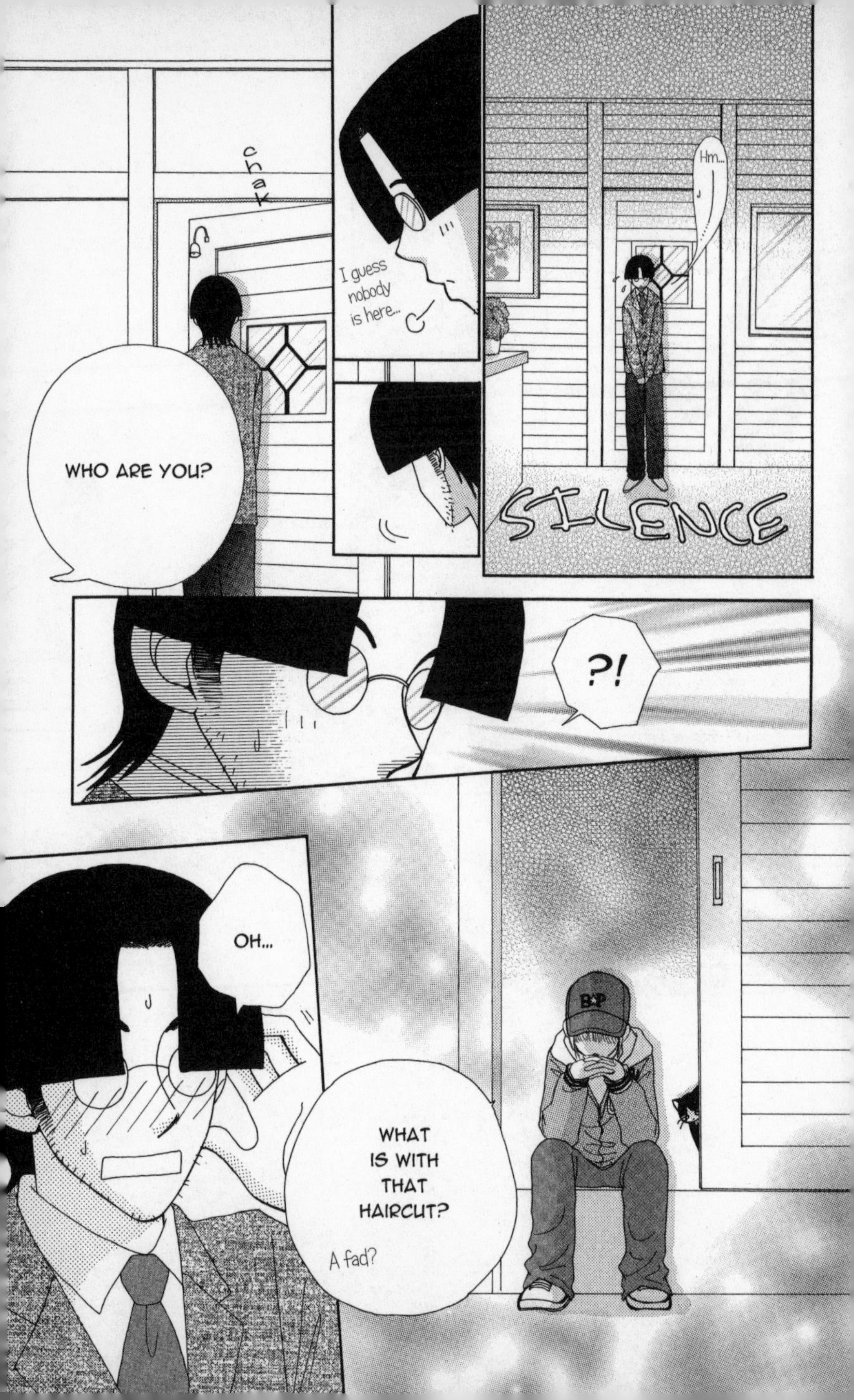
Hm...
SILENCE
I guess nobody is here..
chak
WHO ARE YOU?
?!
OH...
WHAT IS WITH THAT HAIRCUT?
A fad?

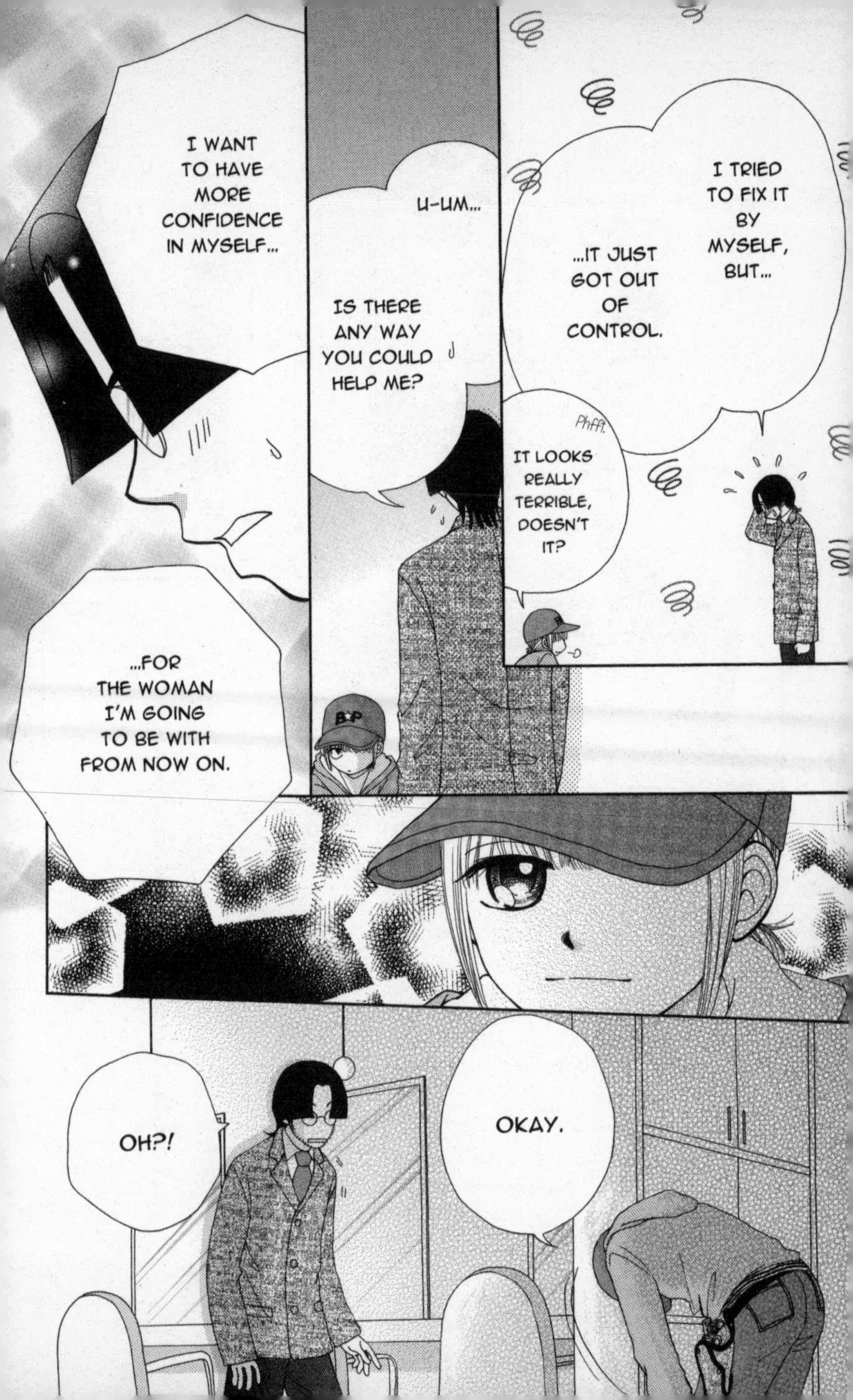
I TRIED TO FIX IT BY MYSELF, BUT...
...IT JUST GOT OUT OF CONTROL.
Phfft.
IT LOOKS REALLY TERRIBLE, DOESN'T IT?
U-UM...
IS THERE ANY WAY YOU COULD HELP ME?
I WANT TO HAVE MORE CONFIDENCE IN MYSELF...
...FOR THE WOMAN I'M GOING TO BE WITH FROM NOW ON.
OKAY.
OH?!

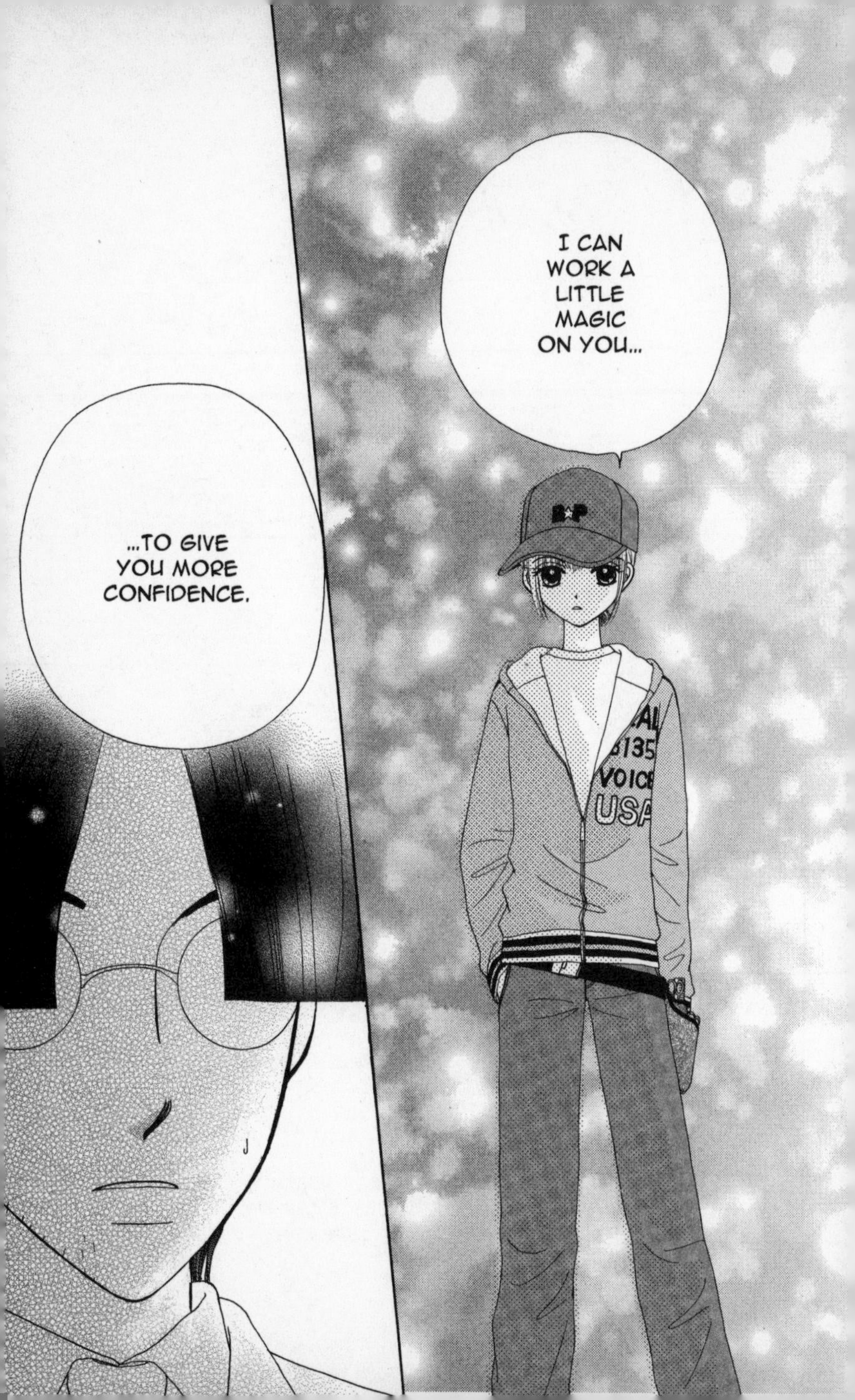
I CAN WORK A LITTLE MAGIC ON YOU...
...TO GIVE YOU MORE CONFIDENCE.
B★P
CAL 3135 VOICE USA

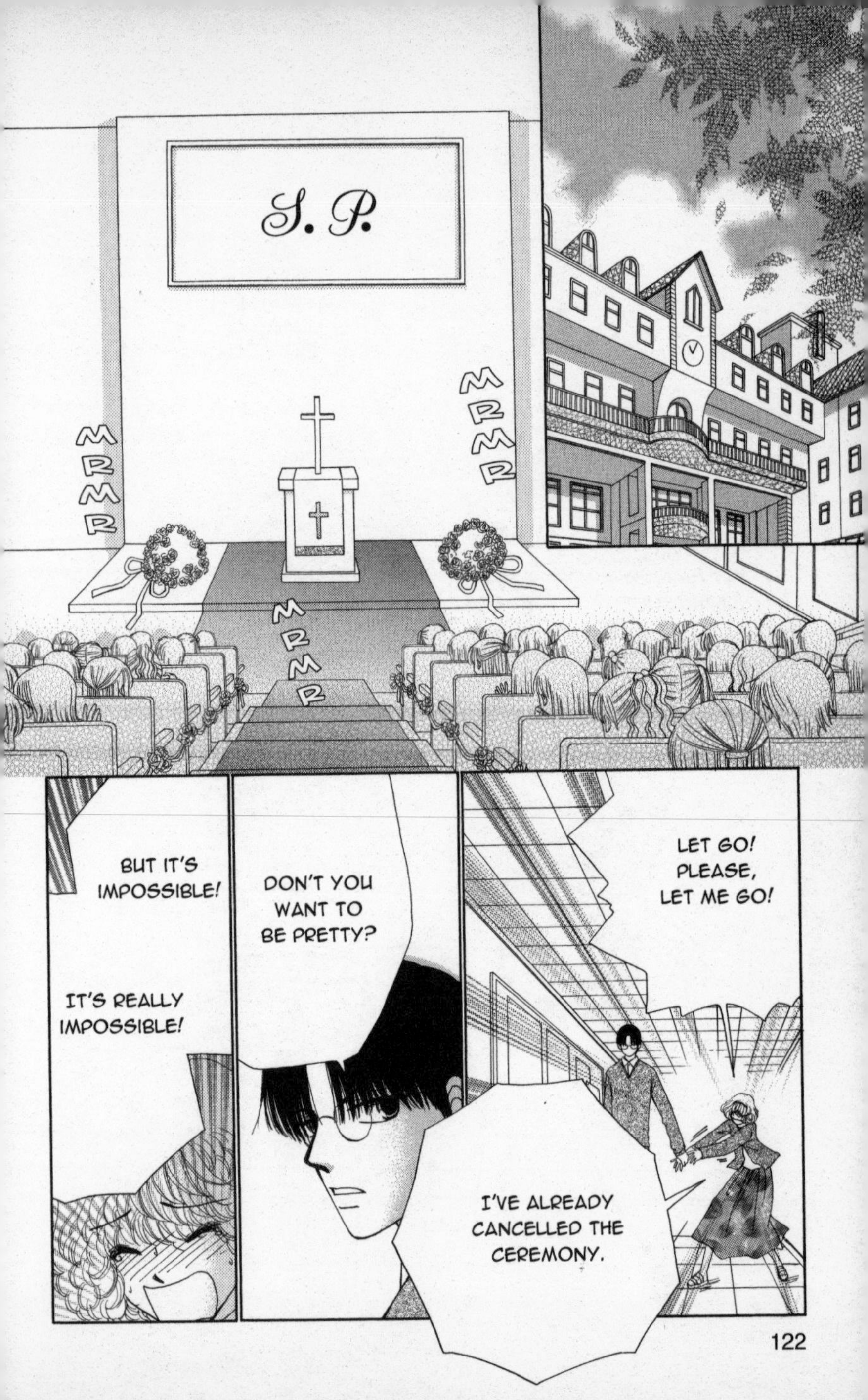
S. P.
MRMR
MRMR
MRMR
LET GO! PLEASE, LET ME GO!
I'VE ALREADY CANCELLED THE CEREMONY.
DON'T YOU WANT TO BE PRETTY?
BUT IT'S IMPOSSIBLE!
IT'S REALLY IMPOSSIBLE!

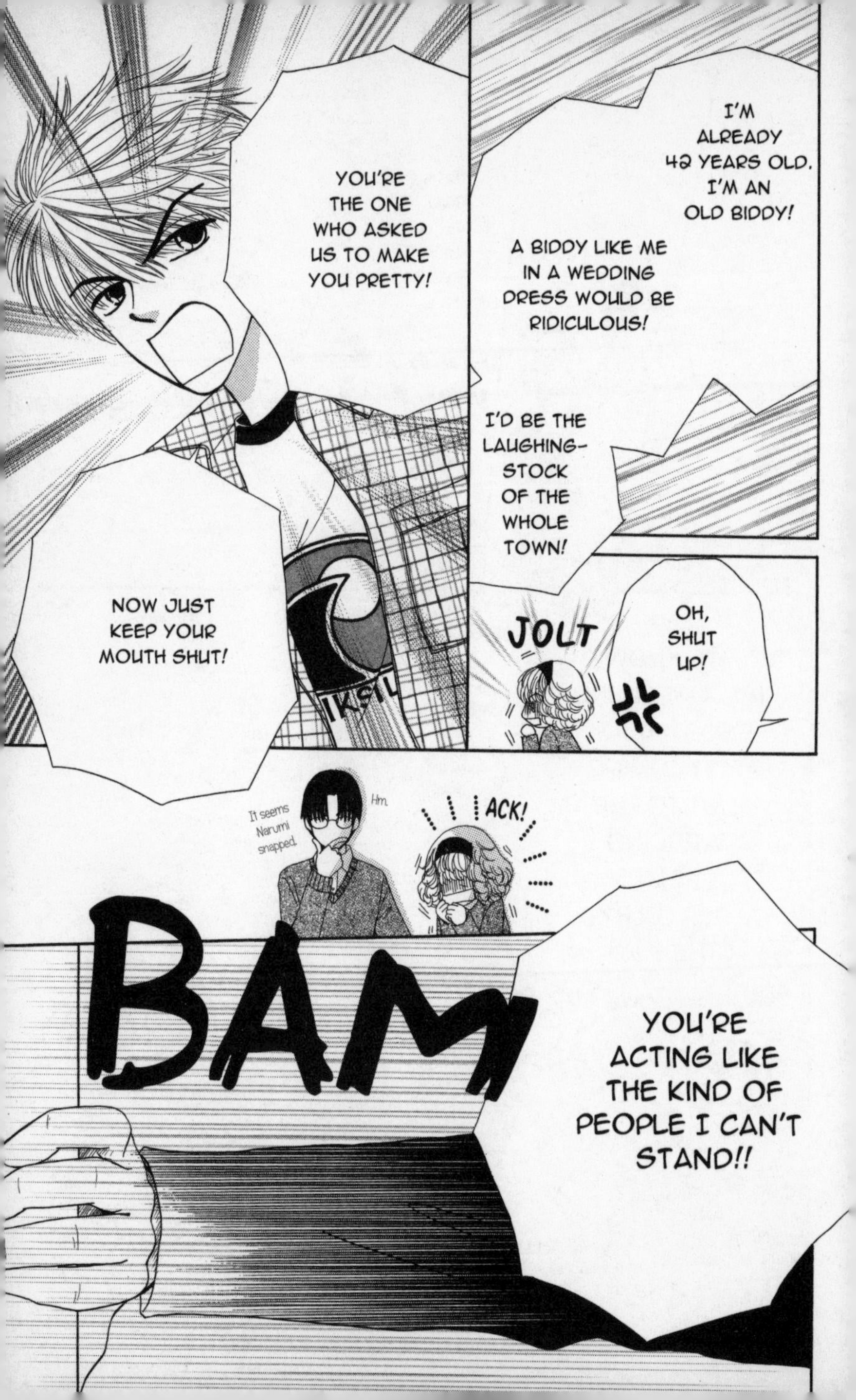
I'M ALREADY 42 YEARS OLD. I'M AN OLD BIDDY!
A BIDDY LIKE ME IN A WEDDING DRESS WOULD BE RIDICULOUS!
I'D BE THE LAUGHING-STOCK OF THE WHOLE TOWN!
JOLT
OH, SHUT UP!
YOU'RE THE ONE WHO ASKED US TO MAKE YOU PRETTY!
NOW JUST KEEP YOUR MOUTH SHUT!
IKSIL
ACK!
Hm.
It seems Narumi snapped.
BAM
YOU'RE ACTING LIKE THE KIND OF PEOPLE I CAN'T STAND!!

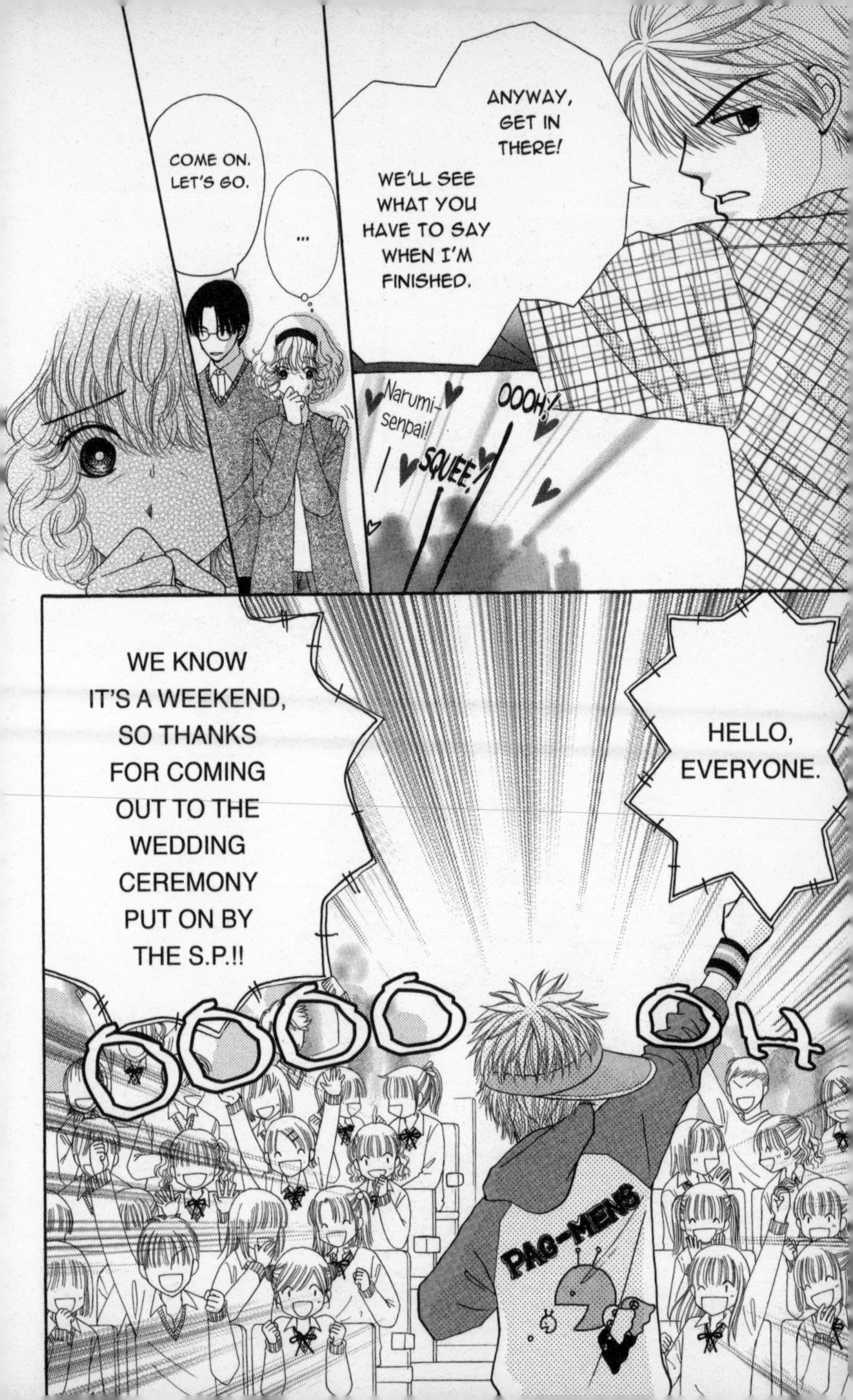
ANYWAY, GET IN THERE!
WE'LL SEE WHAT YOU HAVE TO SAY WHEN I'M FINISHED.
Narumi-senpai!
OOOH!
SQUEE!
COME ON. LET'S GO.
...
HELLO, EVERYONE.
WE KNOW IT'S A WEEKEND, SO THANKS FOR COMING OUT TO THE WEDDING CEREMONY PUT ON BY THE S.P.!!
OOOOO OH
PAG-MENS

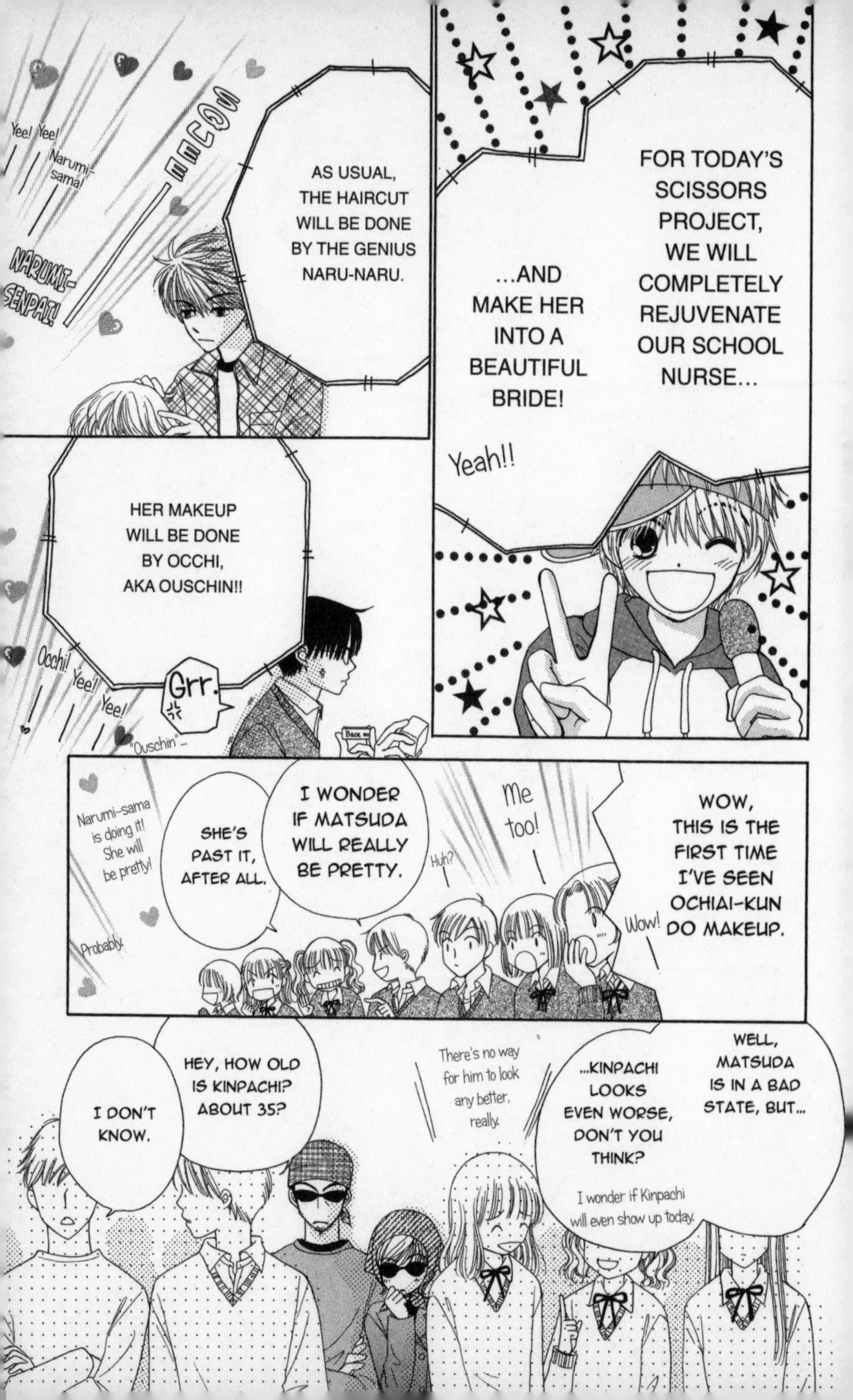
FOR TODAY'S SCISSORS PROJECT, WE WILL COMPLETELY REJUVENATE OUR SCHOOL NURSE...
...AND MAKE HER INTO A BEAUTIFUL BRIDE!
AS USUAL, THE HAIRCUT WILL BE DONE BY THE GENIUS NARU-NARU.
Yee! Yee!
Narumi-sama!
NARUMI-SENPAI!
Yeah!!
HER MAKEUP WILL BE DONE BY OCCHI, AKA OUSCHIN!!
Grr.
Occhi!
Yee!
Yee!
"Ouschin"...
WOW, THIS IS THE FIRST TIME I'VE SEEN OCHIAI-KUN DO MAKEUP.
Wow!
Me too!
Huh?
I WONDER IF MATSUDA WILL REALLY BE PRETTY.
SHE'S PAST IT, AFTER ALL.
Narumi-sama is doing it! She will be pretty!
Probably.
WELL, MATSUDA IS IN A BAD STATE, BUT...
...KINPACHI LOOKS EVEN WORSE, DON'T YOU THINK?
I wonder if Kinpachi will even show up today.
There's no way for him to look any better, really.
HEY, HOW OLD IS KINPACHI? ABOUT 35?
I DON'T KNOW.

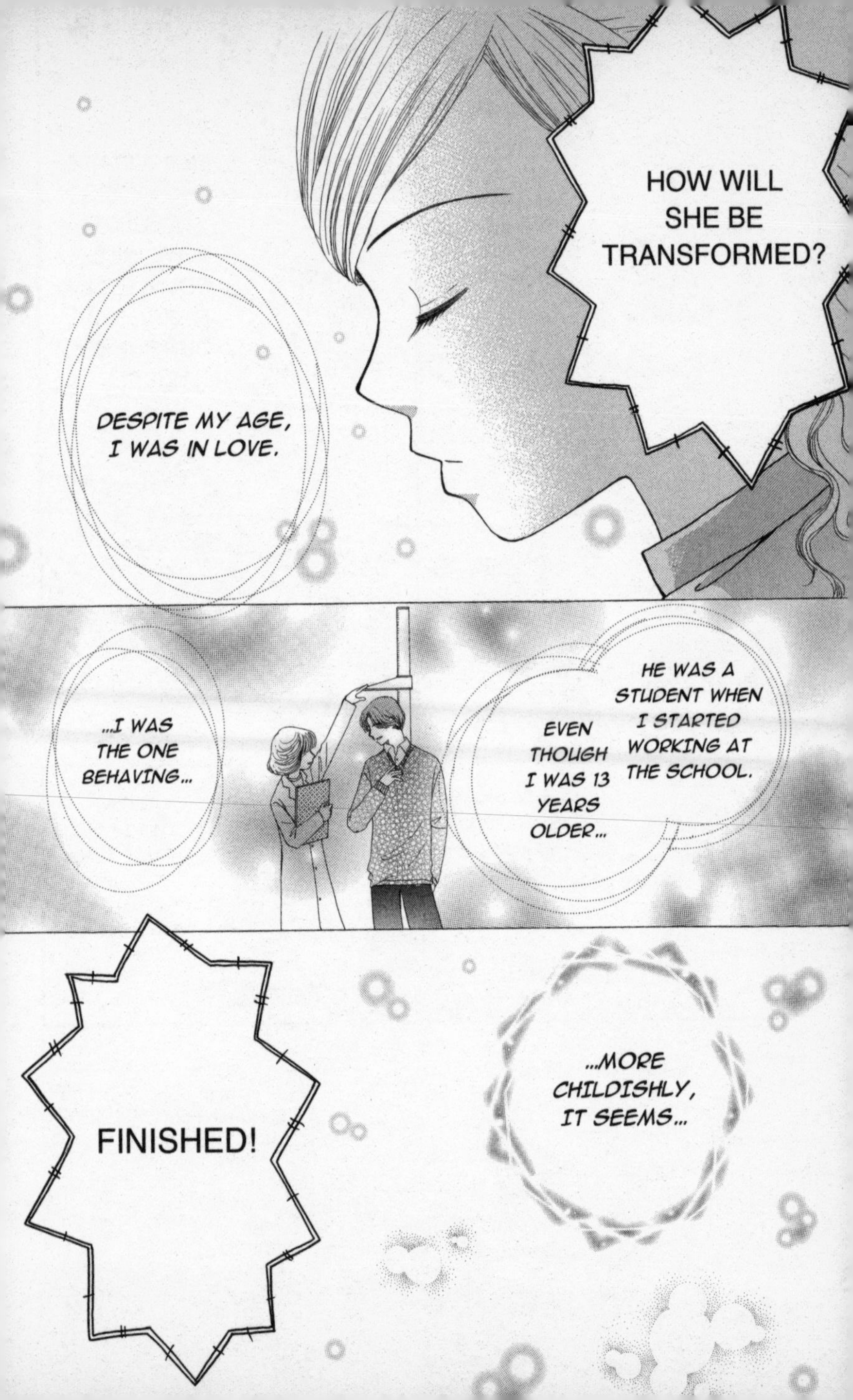
HOW WILL SHE BE TRANSFORMED?
DESPITE MY AGE, I WAS IN LOVE.
HE WAS A STUDENT WHEN I STARTED WORKING AT THE SCHOOL.
EVEN THOUGH I WAS 13 YEARS OLDER...
...I WAS THE ONE BEHAVING...
...MORE CHILDISHLY, IT SEEMS...
FINISHED!

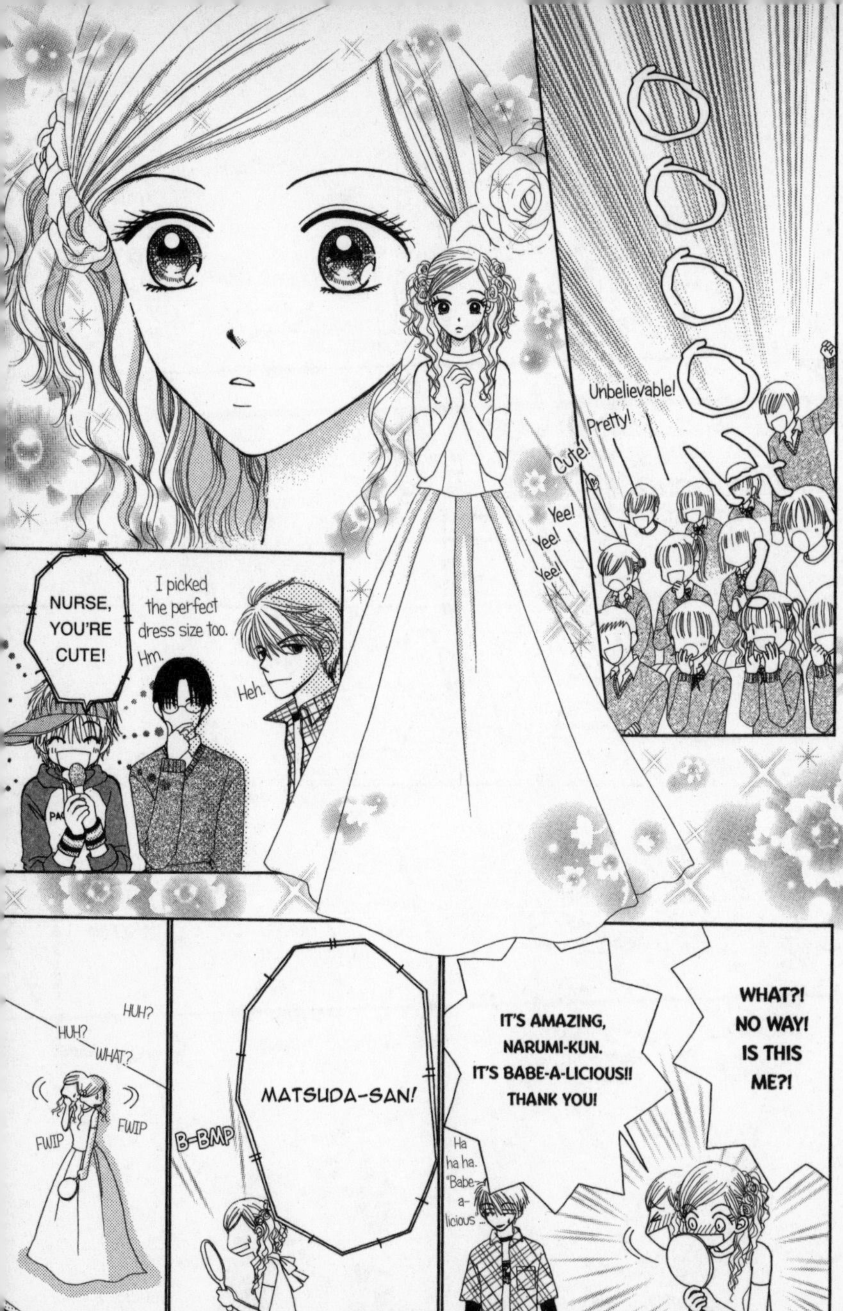

OOOOH
Unbelievable!
Pretty!
Cute!
Yee!
Yee!
Yee!
I picked the perfect dress size too.
Hm.
Heh.
NURSE, YOU'RE CUTE!
WHAT?! NO WAY! IS THIS ME?!
IT'S AMAZING, NARUMI-KUN. IT'S BABE-A-LICIOUS!! THANK YOU!
Ha ha ha. "Babe-a-licious"...
MATSUDA-SAN!
B-BMP
HUH?
HUH?
WHAT?
FWIP
FWIP

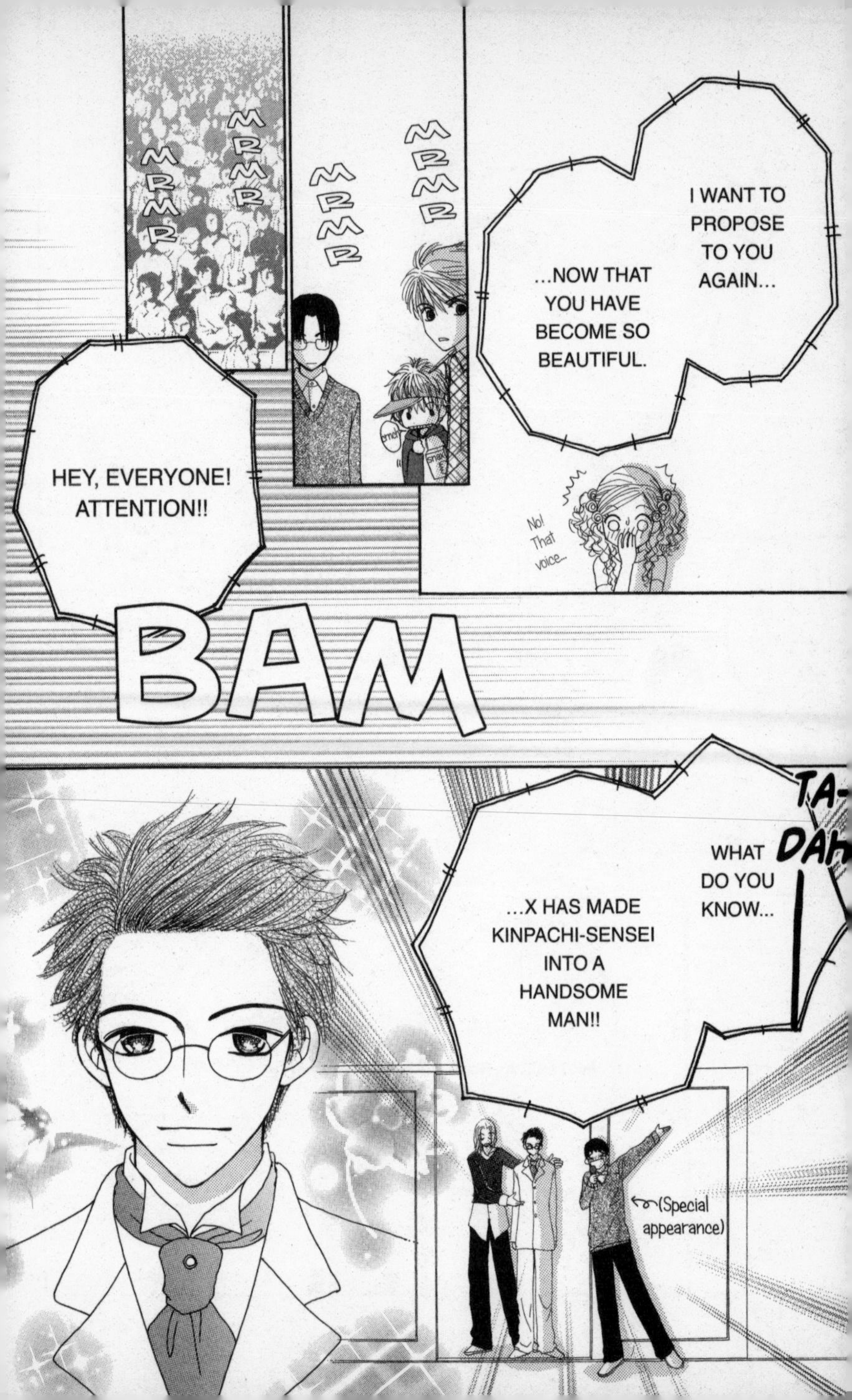
I WANT TO PROPOSE TO YOU AGAIN...
...NOW THAT YOU HAVE BECOME SO BEAUTIFUL.
No! That voice...
MRMR
MRMR
MRMR
MRMR
HEY, EVERYONE! ATTENTION!!
BAM
TA-DAH
WHAT DO YOU KNOW...
...X HAS MADE KINPACHI-SENSEI INTO A HANDSOME MAN!!
(Special appearance)

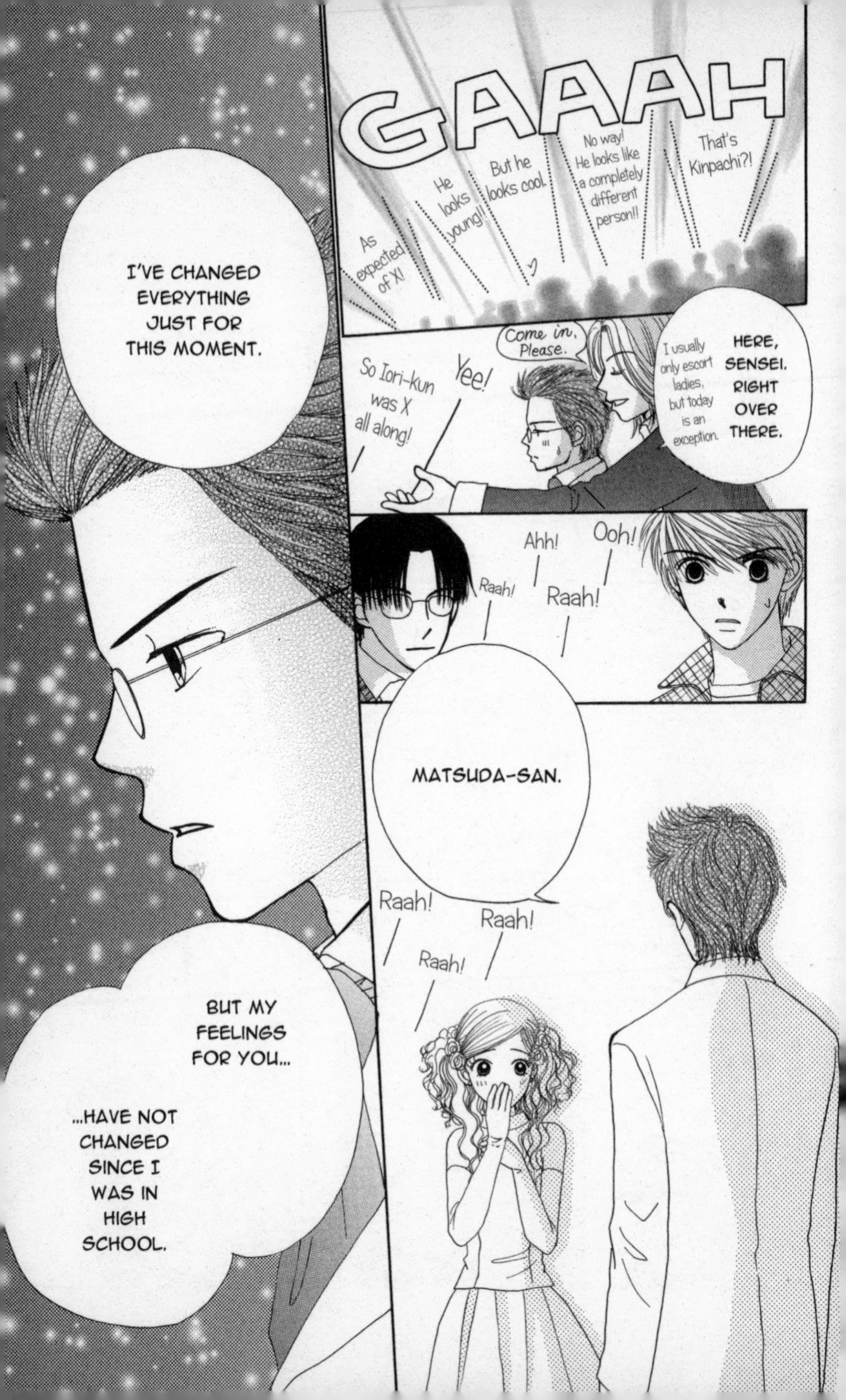
GAAAH
That's Kinpachi?!
No way! He looks like a completely different person!!
But he looks cool.
He looks young!!
As expected of X!
HERE, SENSEI. RIGHT OVER THERE.
I usually only escort ladies, but today is an exception.
Come in, Please.
Yee!
So Iori-kun was X all along!
Ooh!
Raah!
Ahh!
Raah!
MATSUDA-SAN.
Raah!
Raah!
Raah!
I'VE CHANGED EVERYTHING JUST FOR THIS MOMENT.
BUT MY FEELINGS FOR YOU...
...HAVE NOT CHANGED SINCE I WAS IN HIGH SCHOOL.

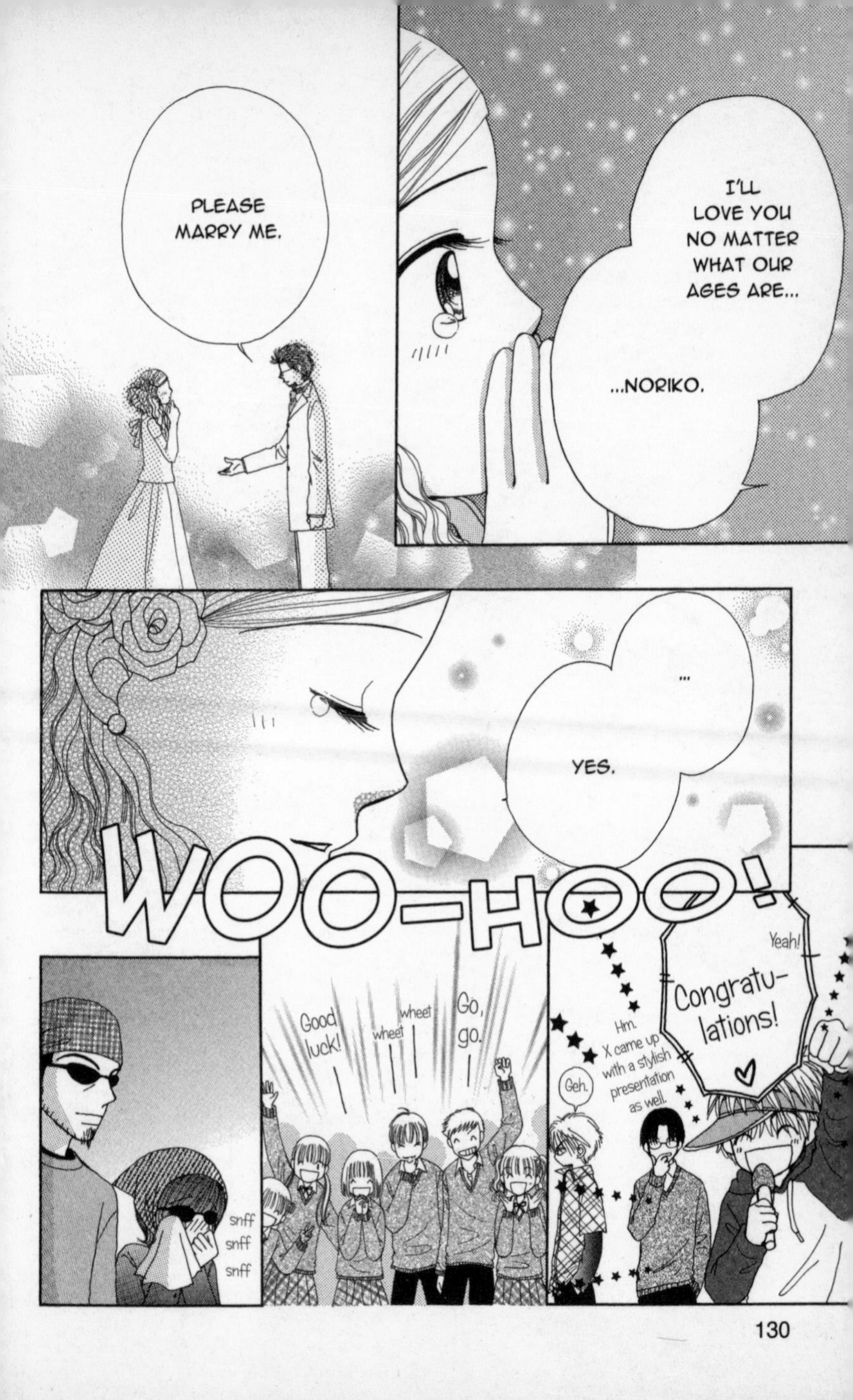
I'LL LOVE YOU NO MATTER WHAT OUR AGES ARE...
...NORIKO.
PLEASE MARRY ME.
...
YES.
WOO-HOO!
Yeah!
Congratu-lations!
Hm. X came up with a stylish presentation as well.
Geh.
Go, go.
wheet
wheet
Good luck!
snff
snff
snff

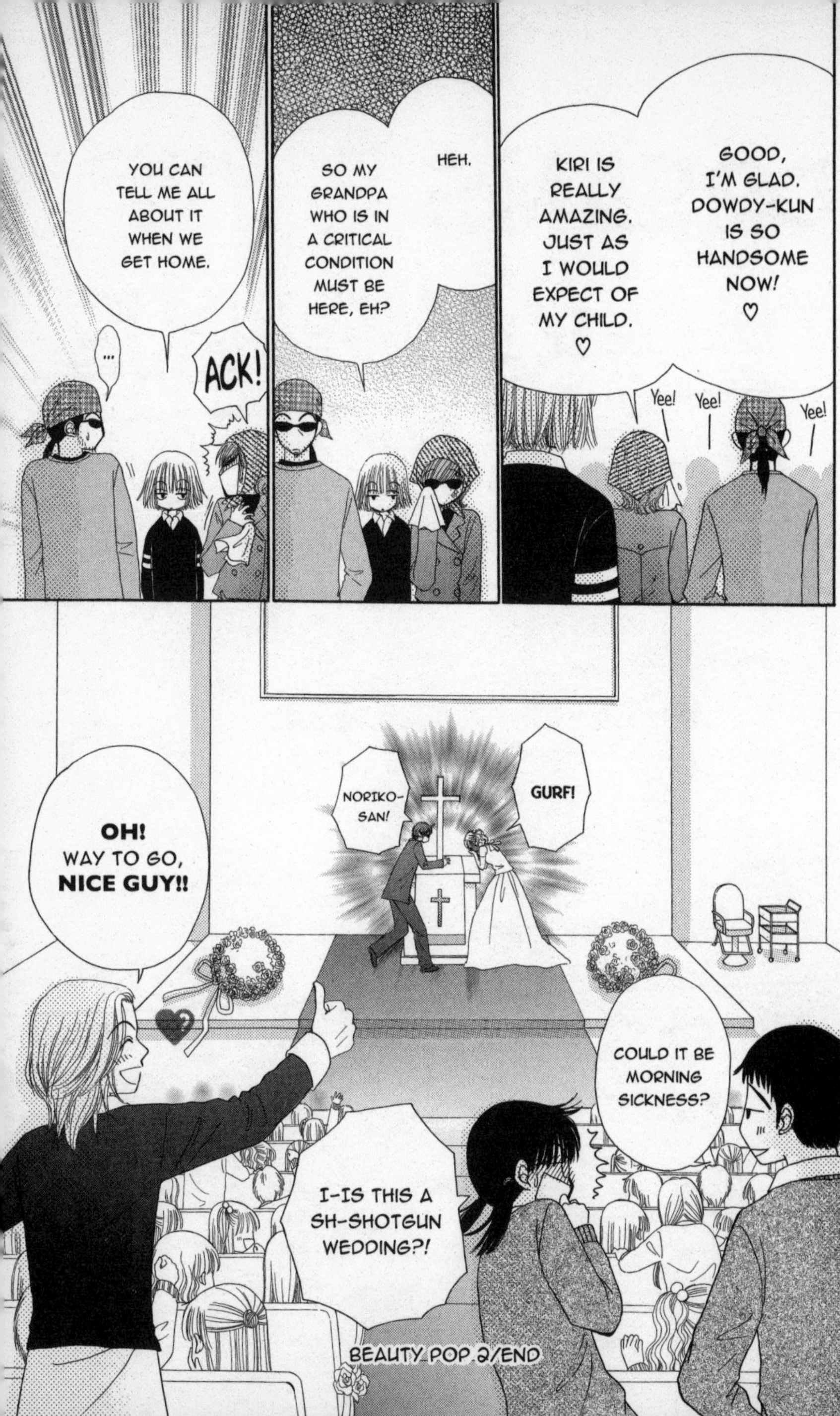
GOOD, I'M GLAD. DOWDY-KUN IS SO HANDSOME NOW! ♡
KIRI IS REALLY AMAZING. JUST AS I WOULD EXPECT OF MY CHILD. ♡
Yee!
Yee!
Yee!
HEH.
SO MY GRANDPA WHO IS IN A CRITICAL CONDITION MUST BE HERE, EH?
YOU CAN TELL ME ALL ABOUT IT WHEN WE GET HOME.
ACK!
...
GURF!
NORIKO-SAN!
OH! WAY TO GO, NICE GUY!!
COULD IT BE MORNING SICKNESS?
I-IS THIS A SH-SHOTGUN WEDDING?!
BEAUTY POP 2/END

Beauty Pop

BONUS STORY:

DREAMS COME TRUE

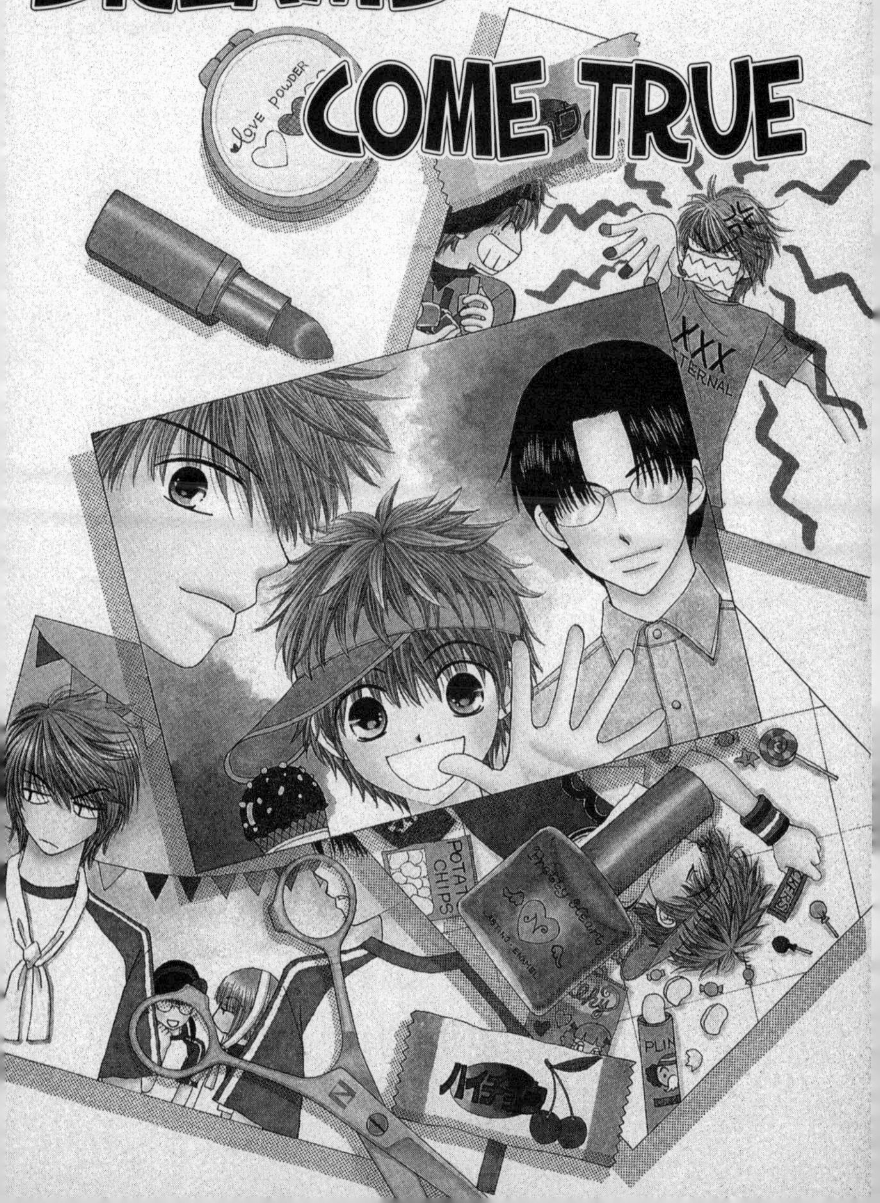
LOVE POWDER
XXX

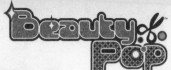

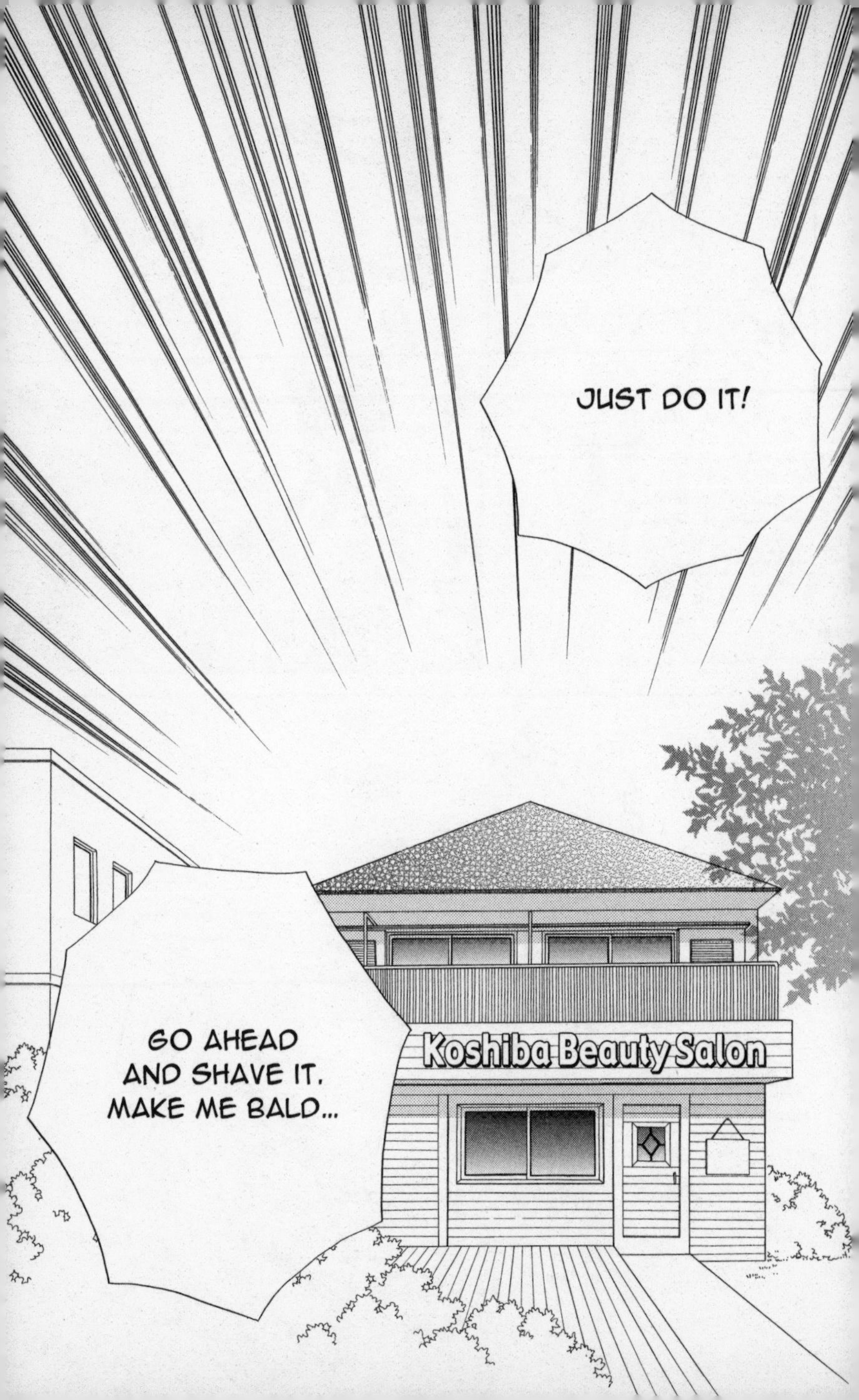
JUST DO IT!
Koshiba Beauty Salon
GO AHEAD AND SHAVE IT. MAKE ME BALD...

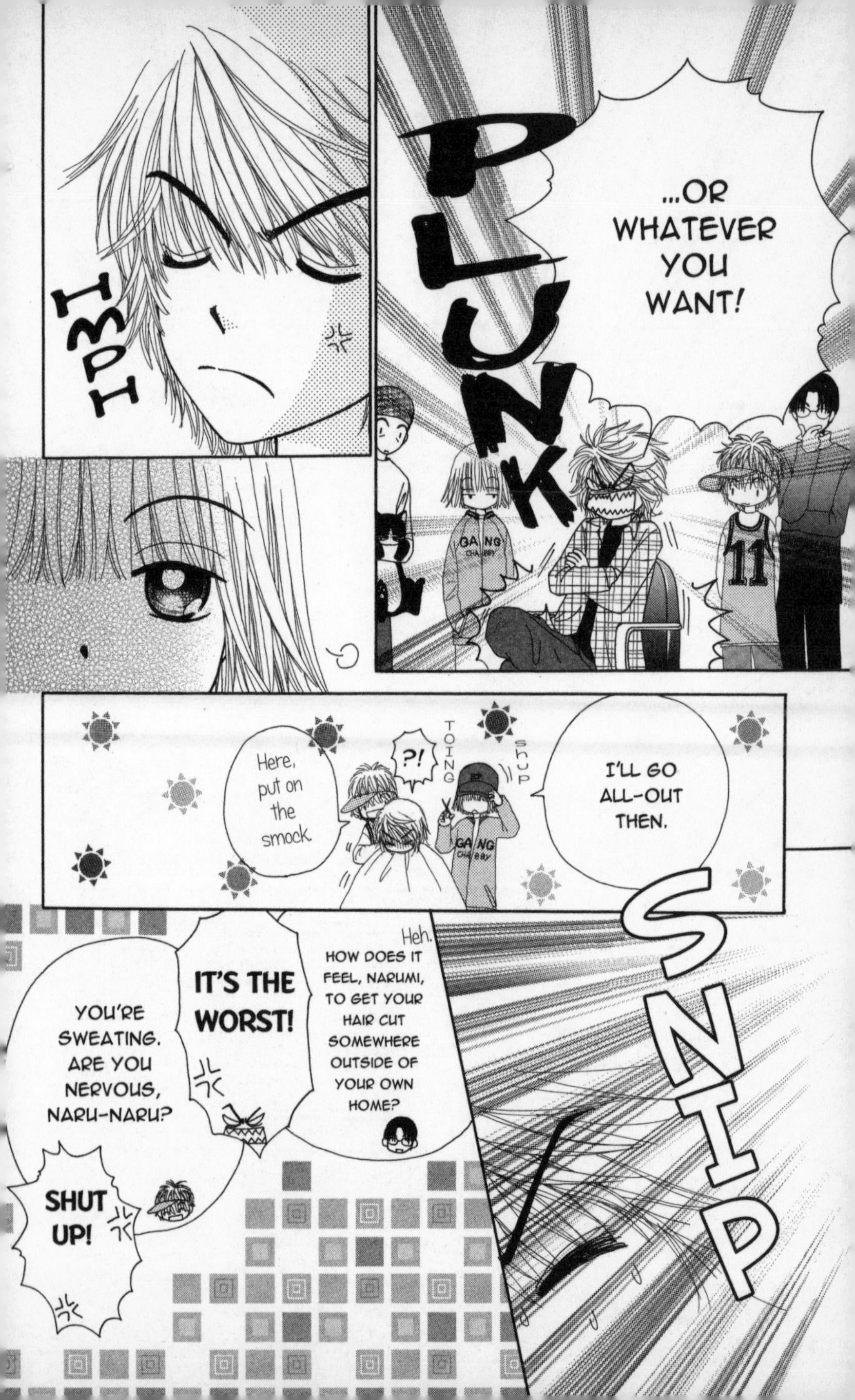
PLUNK
...OR WHATEVER YOU WANT!
HMPH
I'LL GO ALL-OUT THEN.
SHUP
TOING
?!
Here, put on the smock.
SNIP
Heh.
HOW DOES IT FEEL, NARUMI, TO GET YOUR HAIR CUT SOMEWHERE OUTSIDE OF YOUR OWN HOME?
IT'S THE WORST!
YOU'RE SWEATING. ARE YOU NERVOUS, NARU-NARU?
SHUT UP!

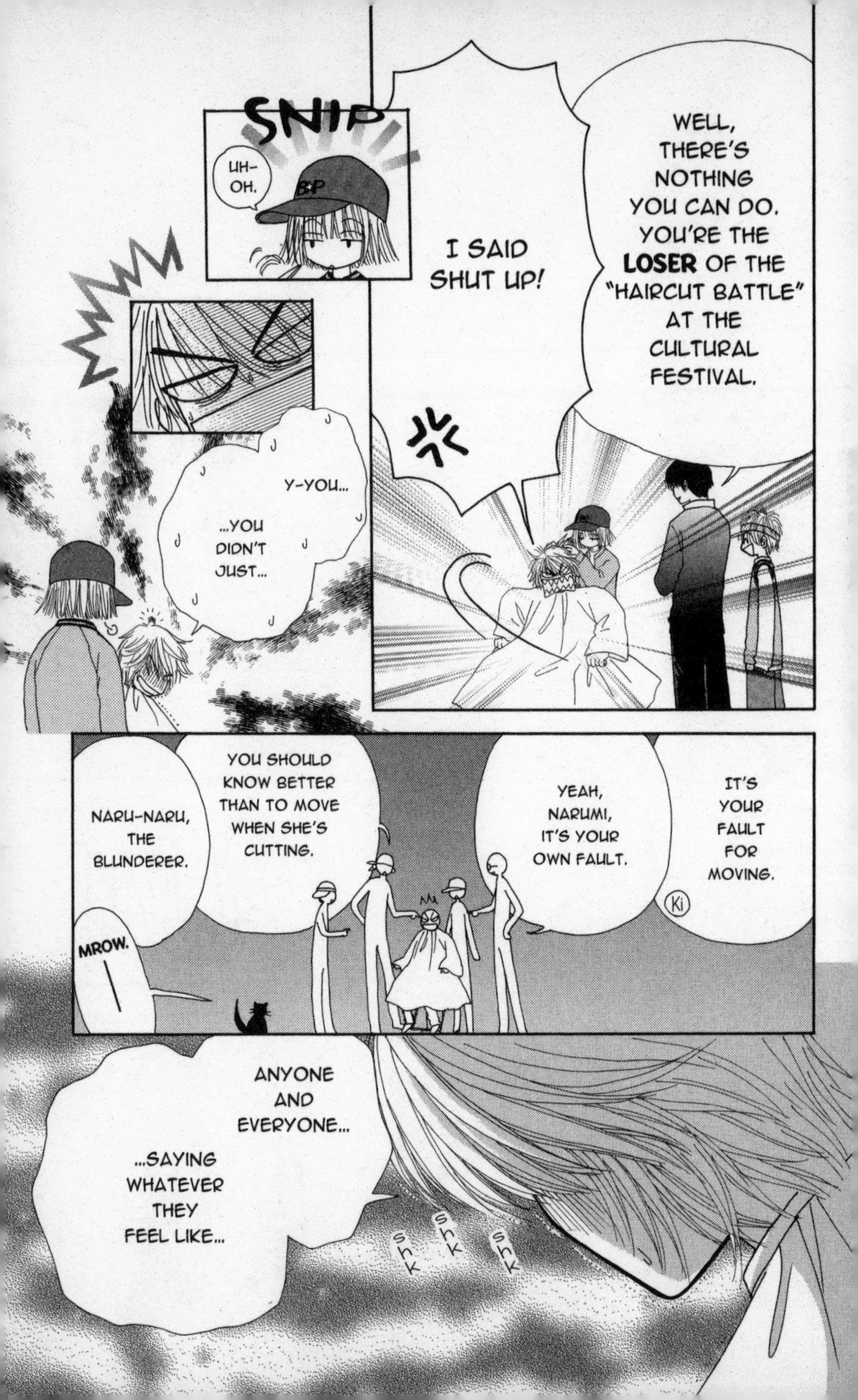
WELL, THERE'S NOTHING YOU CAN DO. YOU'RE THE **LOSER** OF THE "HAIRCUT BATTLE" AT THE CULTURAL FESTIVAL.
I SAID SHUT UP!
SNIP
UH-OH.
Y-YOU...
...YOU DIDN'T JUST...
IT'S YOUR FAULT FOR MOVING.
YEAH, NARUMI, IT'S YOUR OWN FAULT.
YOU SHOULD KNOW BETTER THAN TO MOVE WHEN SHE'S CUTTING.
NARU-NARU, THE BLUNDERER.
MROW.
ANYONE AND EVERYONE...
...SAYING WHATEVER THEY FEEL LIKE...
shk shk shk

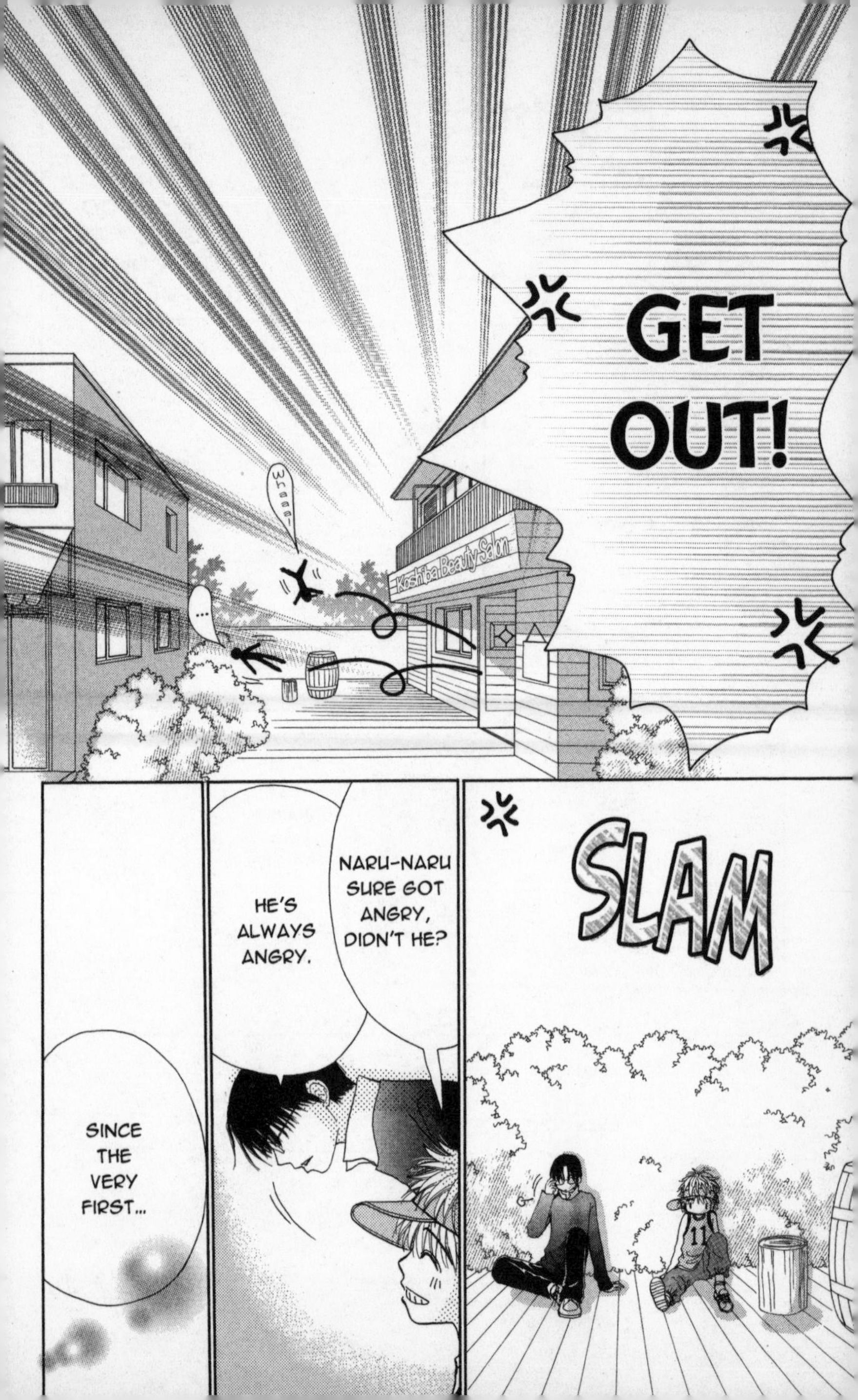
GET OUT!
Koshiba Beauty Salon
Whaaa!
...
SLAM
NARU-NARU SURE GOT ANGRY, DIDN'T HE?
HE'S ALWAYS ANGRY.
SINCE THE VERY FIRST...

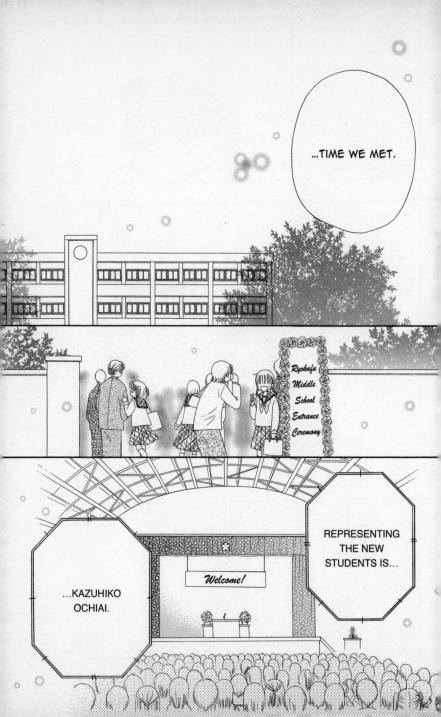

...TIME WE MET.

Ryokufu Middle School Entrance Ceremony

REPRESENTING THE NEW STUDENTS IS...

Welcome!

...KAZUHIKO OCHIAI.

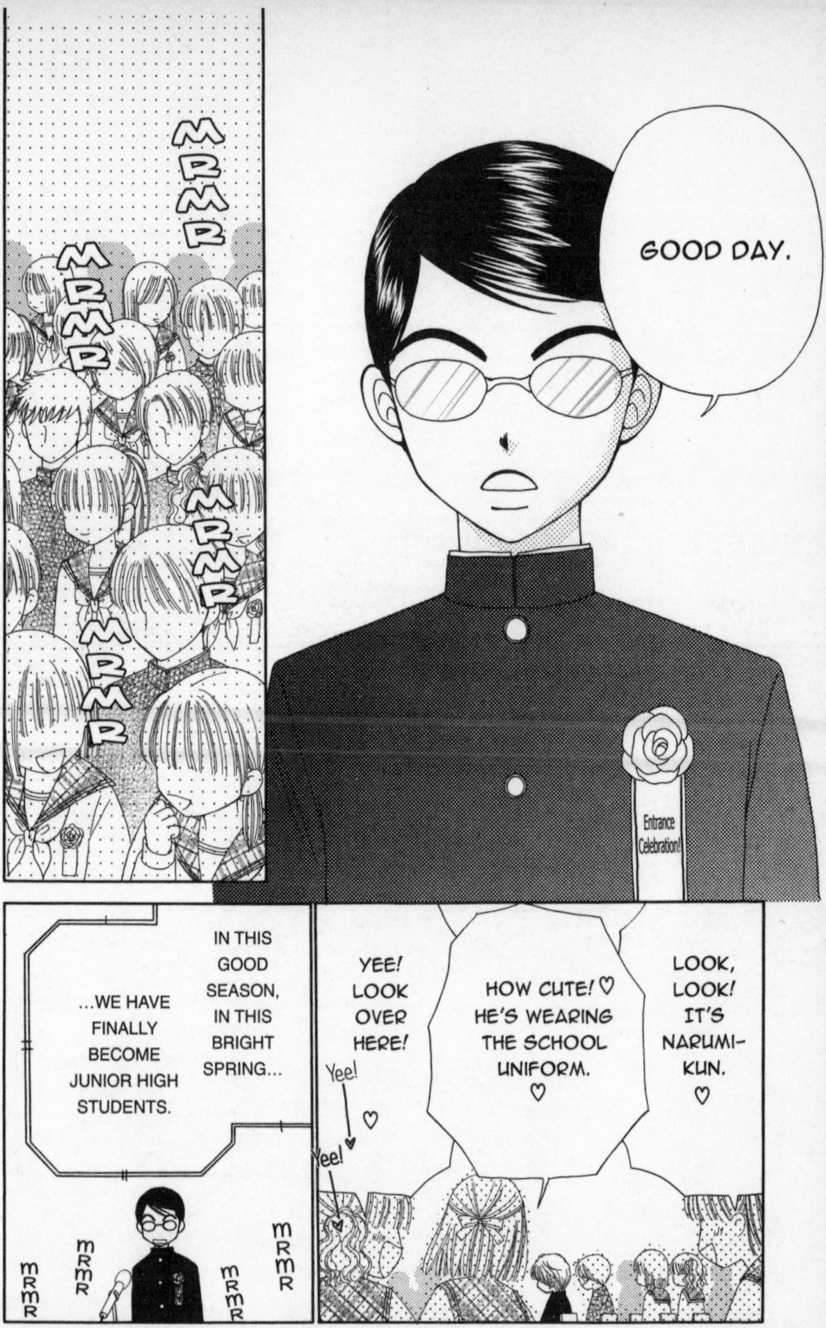
GOOD DAY.
Entrance Celebration!
MRMR
MRMR
MRMR
MRMR
LOOK, LOOK! IT'S NARUMI-KUN. ♡
HOW CUTE! ♡ HE'S WEARING THE SCHOOL UNIFORM. ♡
YEE! LOOK OVER HERE!
Yee!
Yee!
IN THIS GOOD SEASON, IN THIS BRIGHT SPRING...
...WE HAVE FINALLY BECOME JUNIOR HIGH STUDENTS.
MRMR
MRMR
MRMR
MRMR

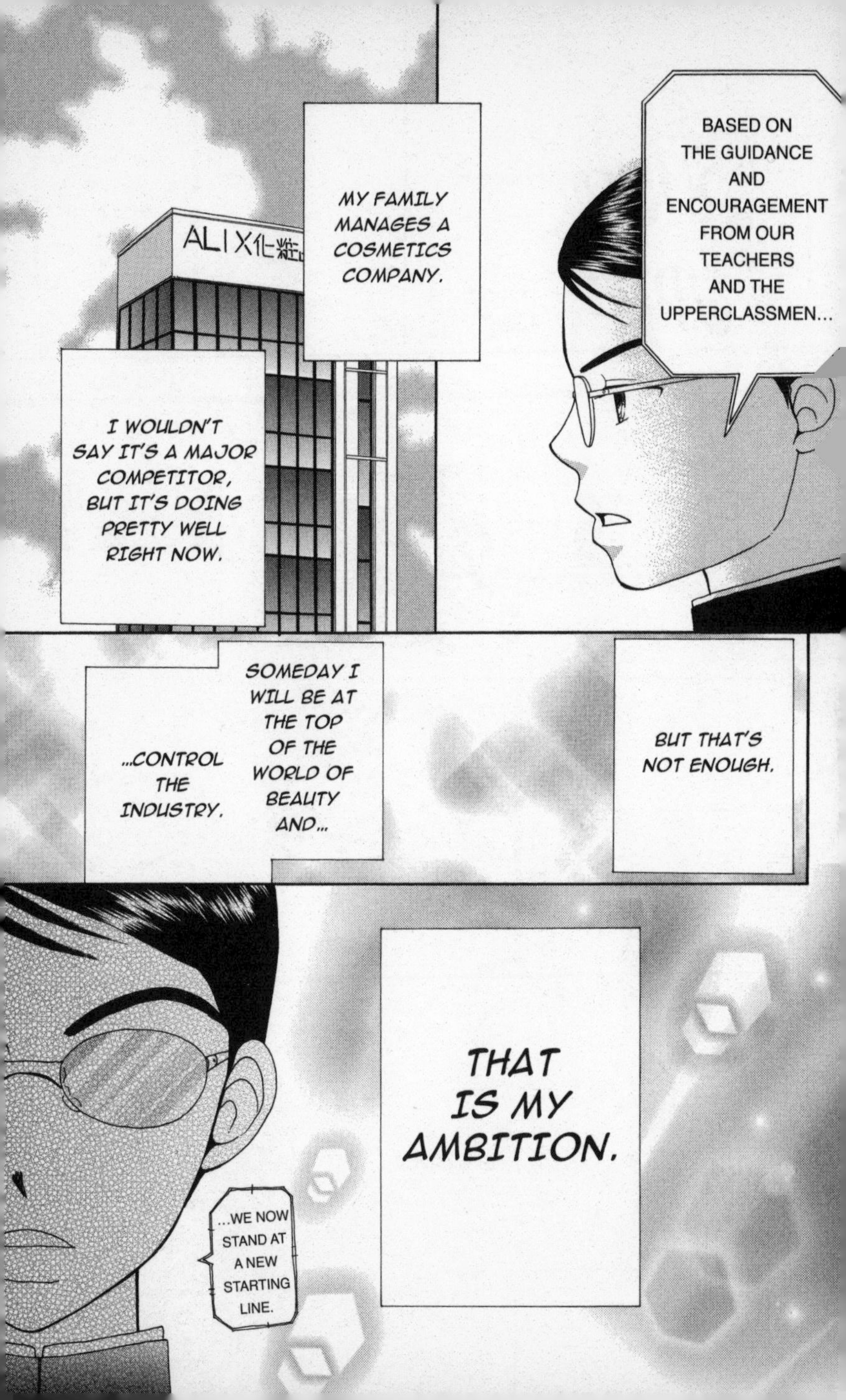
BASED ON THE GUIDANCE AND ENCOURAGEMENT FROM OUR TEACHERS AND THE UPPERCLASSMEN...
ALIX化粧
MY FAMILY MANAGES A COSMETICS COMPANY.
I WOULDN'T SAY IT'S A MAJOR COMPETITOR, BUT IT'S DOING PRETTY WELL RIGHT NOW.
BUT THAT'S NOT ENOUGH.
SOMEDAY I WILL BE AT THE TOP OF THE WORLD OF BEAUTY AND...
...CONTROL THE INDUSTRY.
THAT IS MY AMBITION.
...WE NOW STAND AT A NEW STARTING LINE.

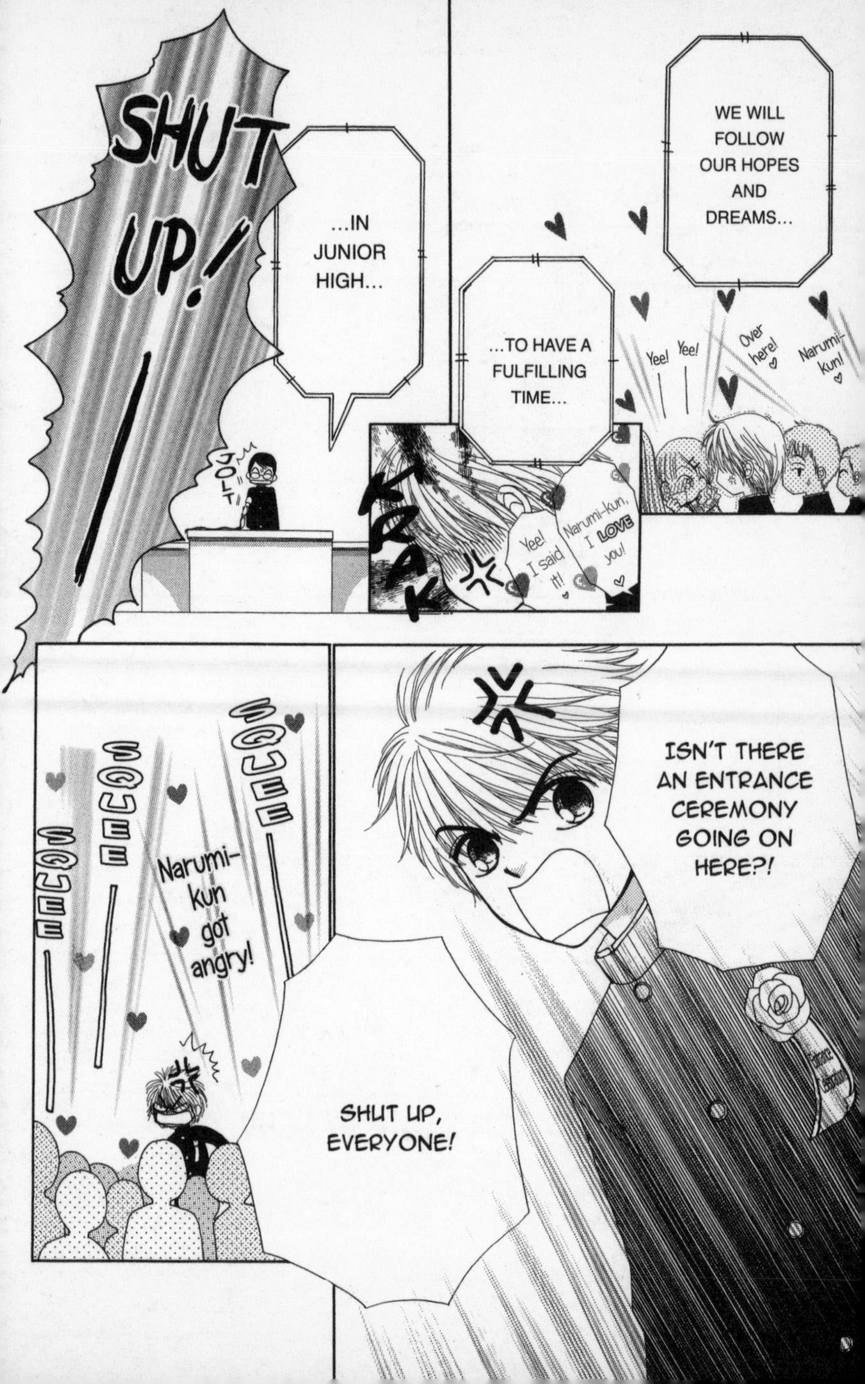
WE WILL FOLLOW OUR HOPES AND DREAMS...
Yee! Yee!
Over here!
Narumi-kun!
...TO HAVE A FULFILLING TIME...
Narumi-kun, I LOVE you!
Yee! I said it!
KRAK
...IN JUNIOR HIGH...
JOLT
SHUT UP!
ISN'T THERE AN ENTRANCE CEREMONY GOING ON HERE?!
SHUT UP, EVERYONE!
SQUEE
SQUEE
SQUEE
Narumi-kun got angry!

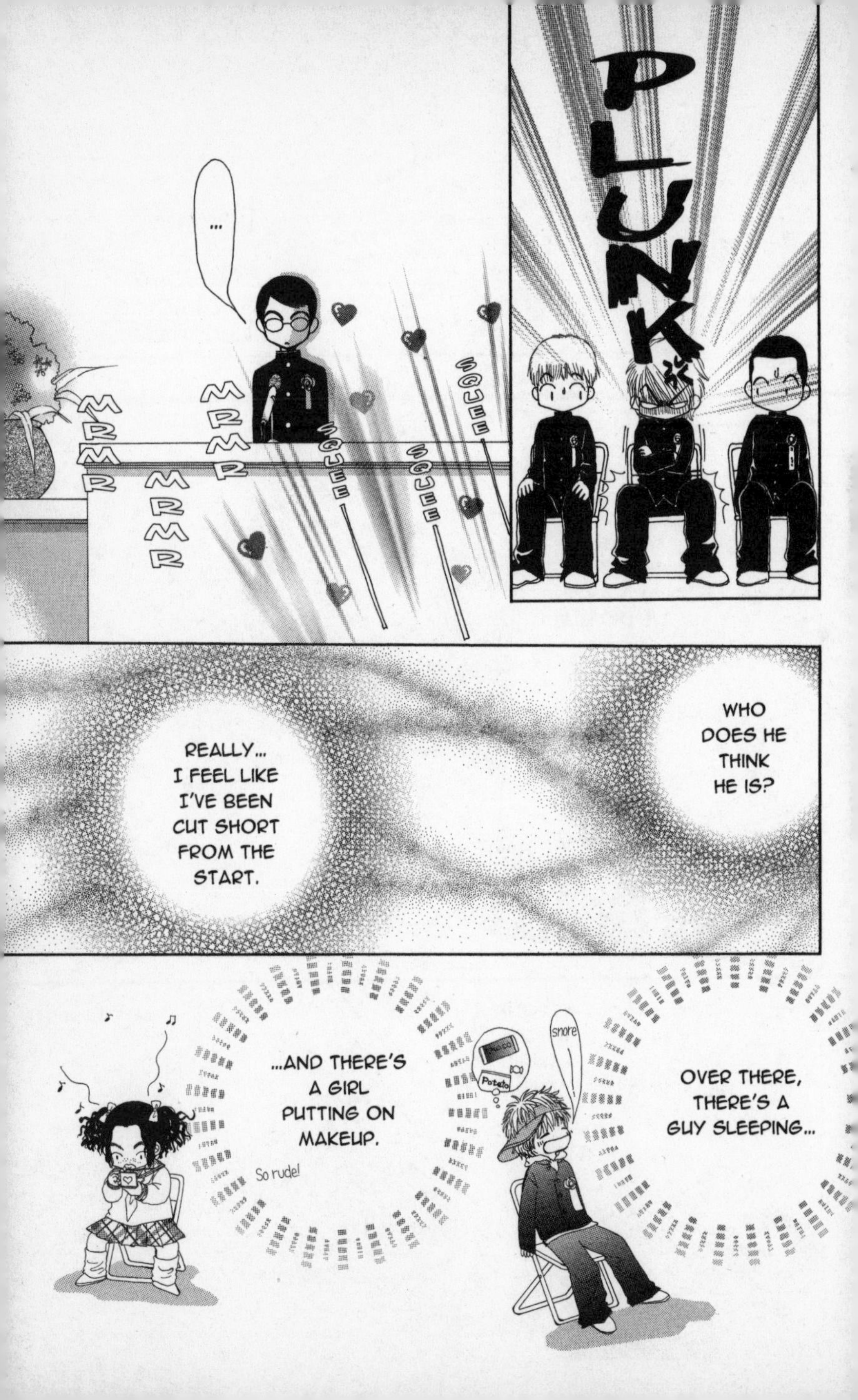
PLUNK
SQUEE
SQUEE
SQUEE
...
MRMR
MRMR
MRMR
WHO DOES HE THINK HE IS?
REALLY... I FEEL LIKE I'VE BEEN CUT SHORT FROM THE START.
OVER THERE, THERE'S A GUY SLEEPING...
snore
Potato
...AND THERE'S A GIRL PUTTING ON MAKEUP.
So rude!

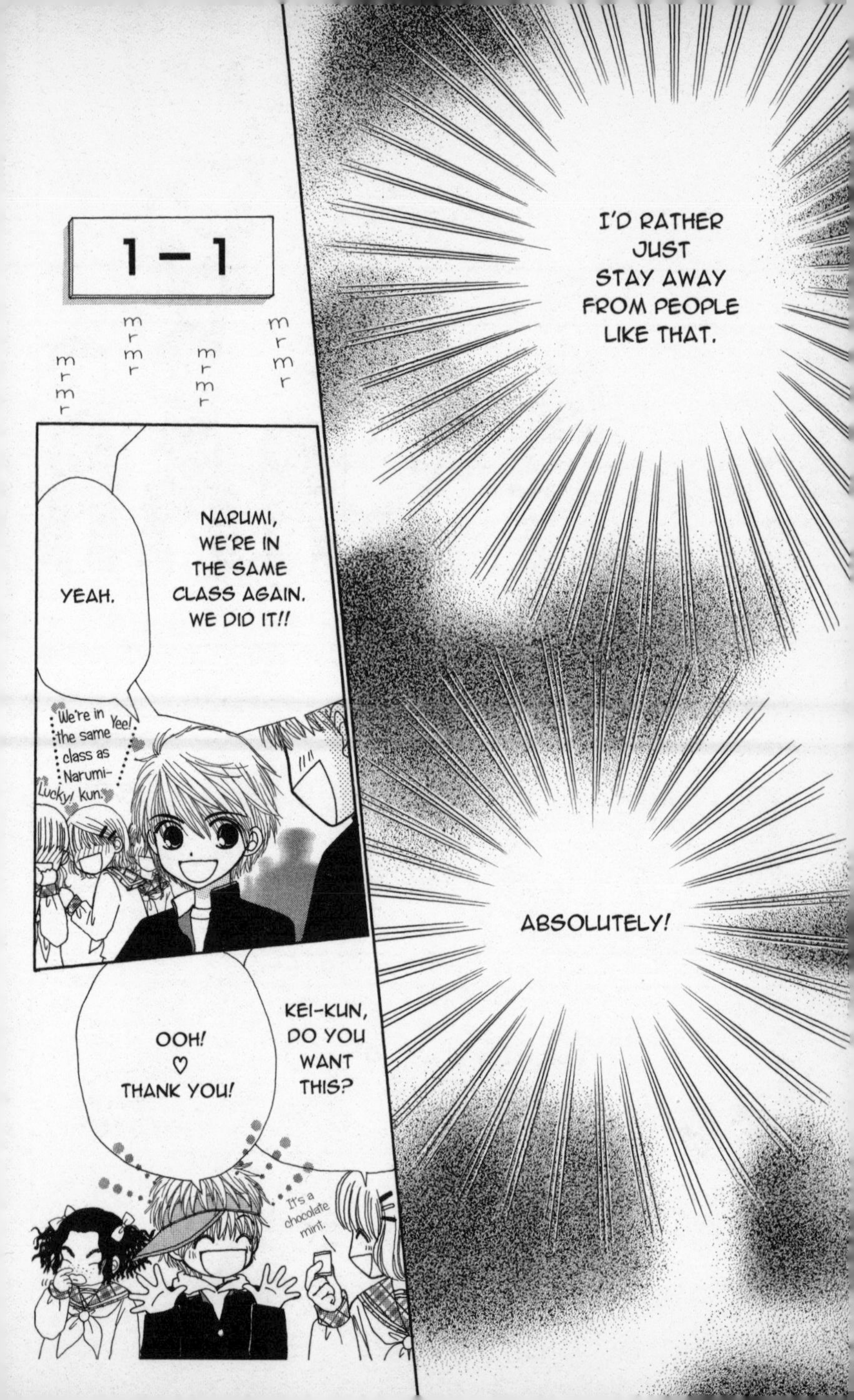
I'D RATHER JUST STAY AWAY FROM PEOPLE LIKE THAT.
ABSOLUTELY!
1-1
mrmr
mrmr
mrmr
mrmr
NARUMI, WE'RE IN THE SAME CLASS AGAIN. WE DID IT!!
YEAH.
Yee!
We're in the same class as Narumi-kun.
Lucky!
KEI-KUN, DO YOU WANT THIS?
OOH! ♡ THANK YOU!
It's a chocolate mint.

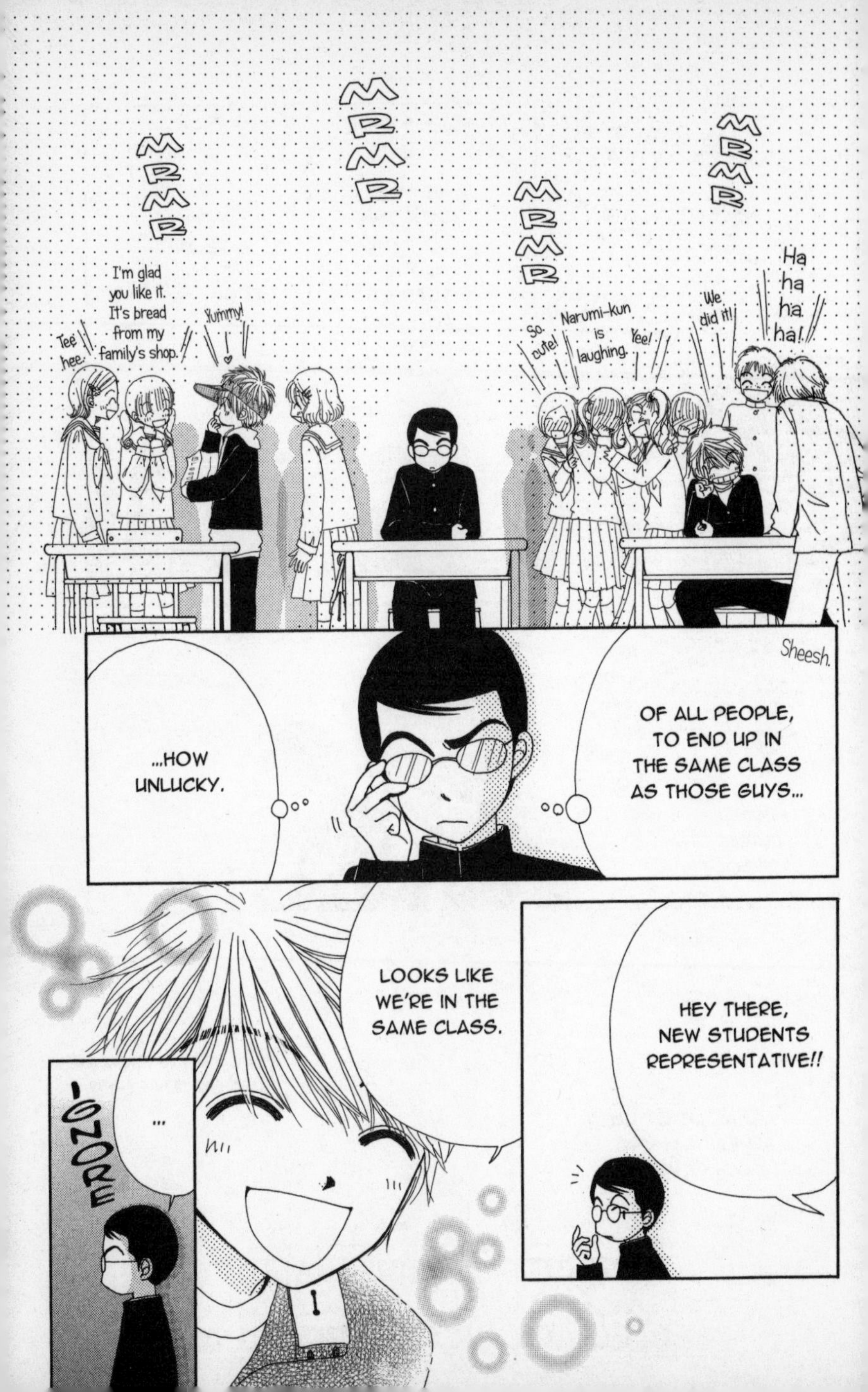
MRMR
Ha ha ha ha!
We did it!
Yee!
Narumi-kun is laughing.
So cute!
MRMR
MRMR
MRMR
Yummy!
I'm glad you like it. It's bread from my family's shop.
Tee hee.
Sheesh.
OF ALL PEOPLE, TO END UP IN THE SAME CLASS AS THOSE GUYS...
...HOW UNLUCKY.
HEY THERE, NEW STUDENTS REPRESENTATIVE!!
LOOKS LIKE WE'RE IN THE SAME CLASS.
IGNORE
...

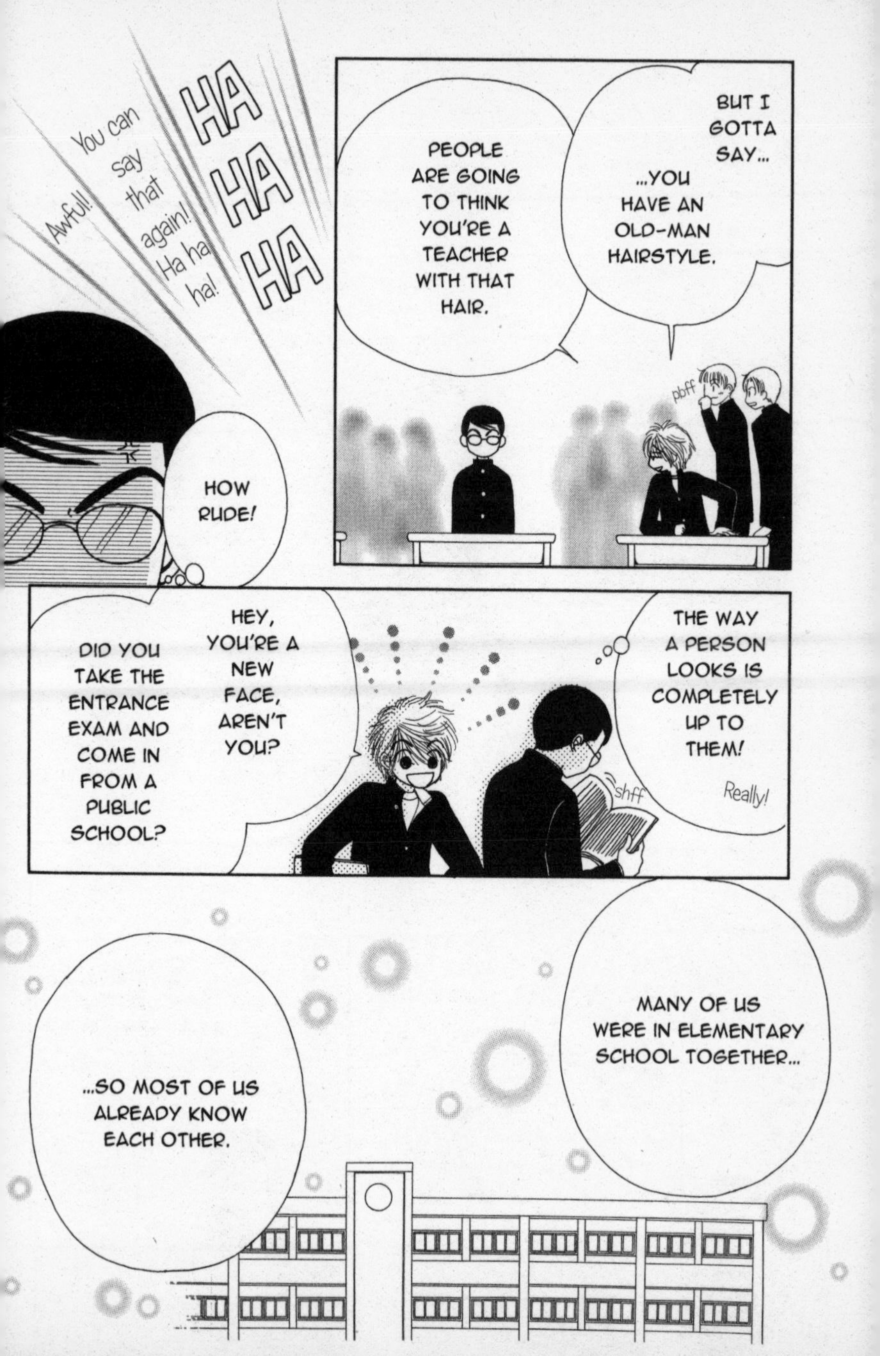
BUT I GOTTA SAY... ...YOU HAVE AN OLD-MAN HAIRSTYLE.
PEOPLE ARE GOING TO THINK YOU'RE A TEACHER WITH THAT HAIR.
pbff
HA HA HA
You can say that again! Ha ha ha!
Awful!
HOW RUDE!
THE WAY A PERSON LOOKS IS COMPLETELY UP TO THEM!
Really!
shff
HEY, YOU'RE A NEW FACE, AREN'T YOU?
DID YOU TAKE THE ENTRANCE EXAM AND COME IN FROM A PUBLIC SCHOOL?
MANY OF US WERE IN ELEMENTARY SCHOOL TOGETHER...
...SO MOST OF US ALREADY KNOW EACH OTHER.

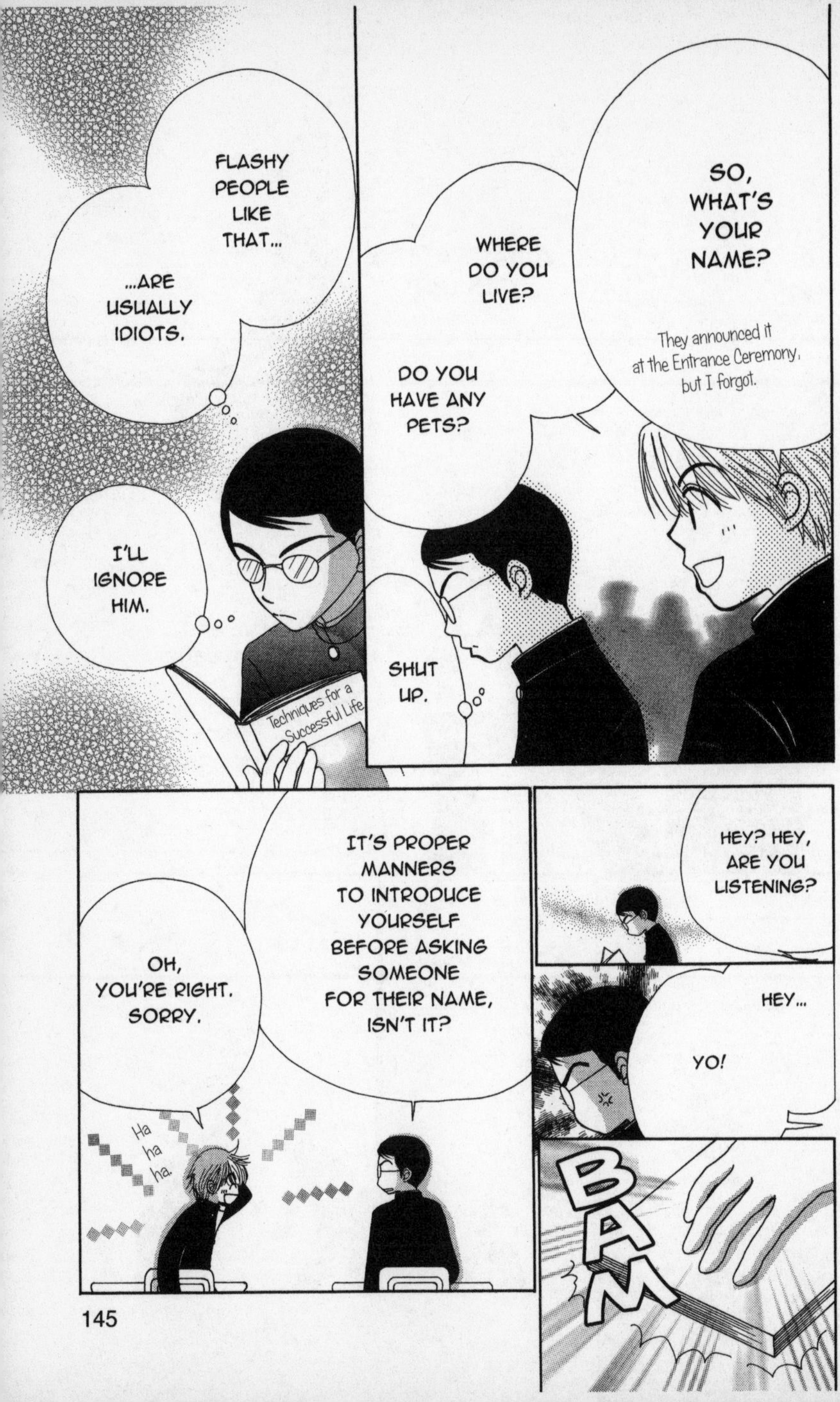
SO, WHAT'S YOUR NAME?
They announced it at the Entrance Ceremony, but I forgot.
WHERE DO YOU LIVE?
DO YOU HAVE ANY PETS?
SHUT UP.
FLASHY PEOPLE LIKE THAT...
...ARE USUALLY IDIOTS.
I'LL IGNORE HIM.
Techniques for a Successful Life
HEY? HEY, ARE YOU LISTENING?
HEY...
YO!
BAM
IT'S PROPER MANNERS TO INTRODUCE YOURSELF BEFORE ASKING SOMEONE FOR THEIR NAME, ISN'T IT?
OH, YOU'RE RIGHT. SORRY.
Ha ha ha.

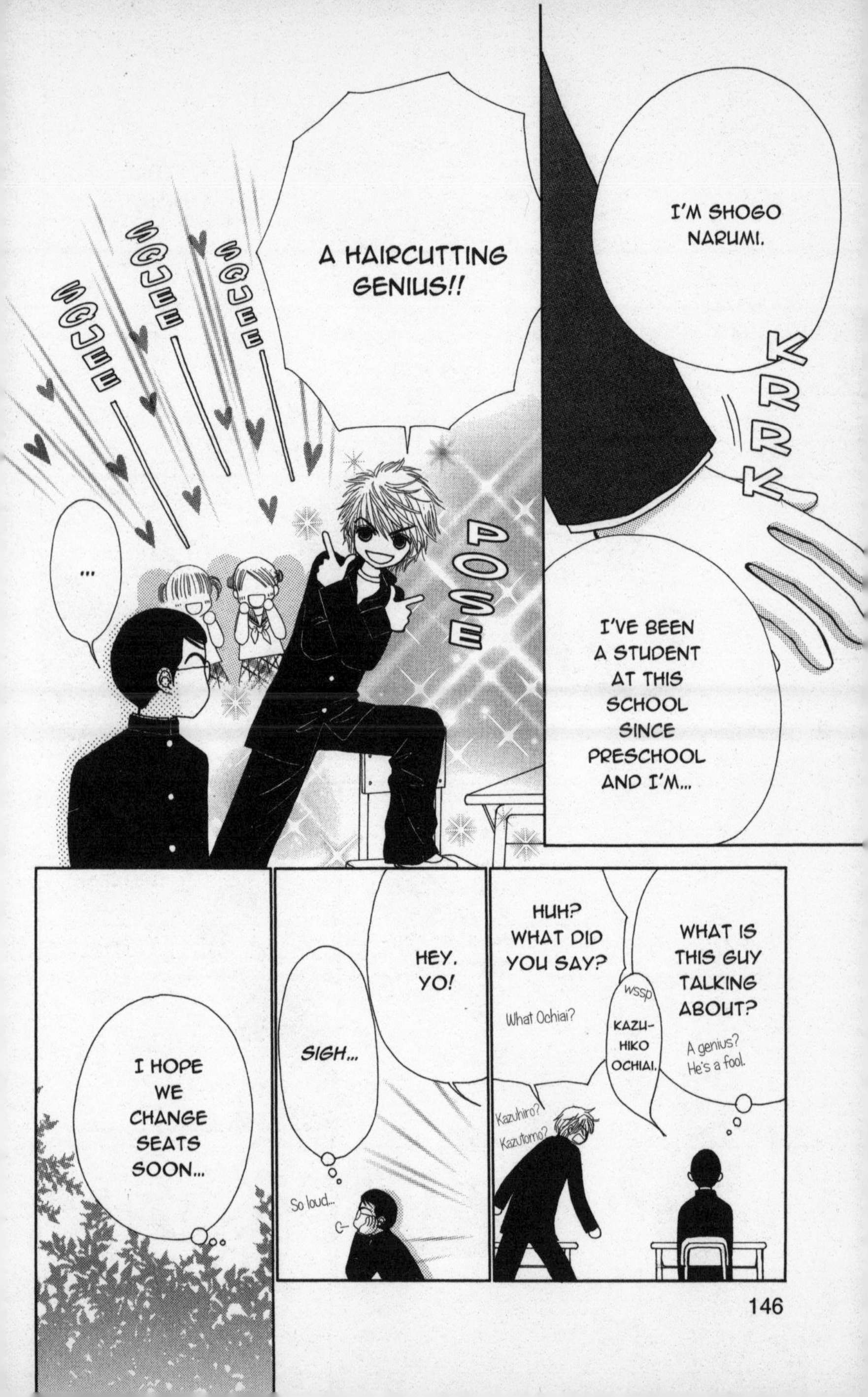
I'M SHOGO NARUMI.
KRRK
I'VE BEEN A STUDENT AT THIS SCHOOL SINCE PRESCHOOL AND I'M...
A HAIRCUTTING GENIUS!!
SQUEE
SQUEE
SQUEE
POSE
...
WHAT IS THIS GUY TALKING ABOUT?
A genius? He's a fool.
wssp
KAZUHIKO OCHIAI.
HUH? WHAT DID YOU SAY?
What Ochiai?
Kazuhiro? Kazutomo?
HEY. YO!
SIGH...
So loud...
I HOPE WE CHANGE SEATS SOON...

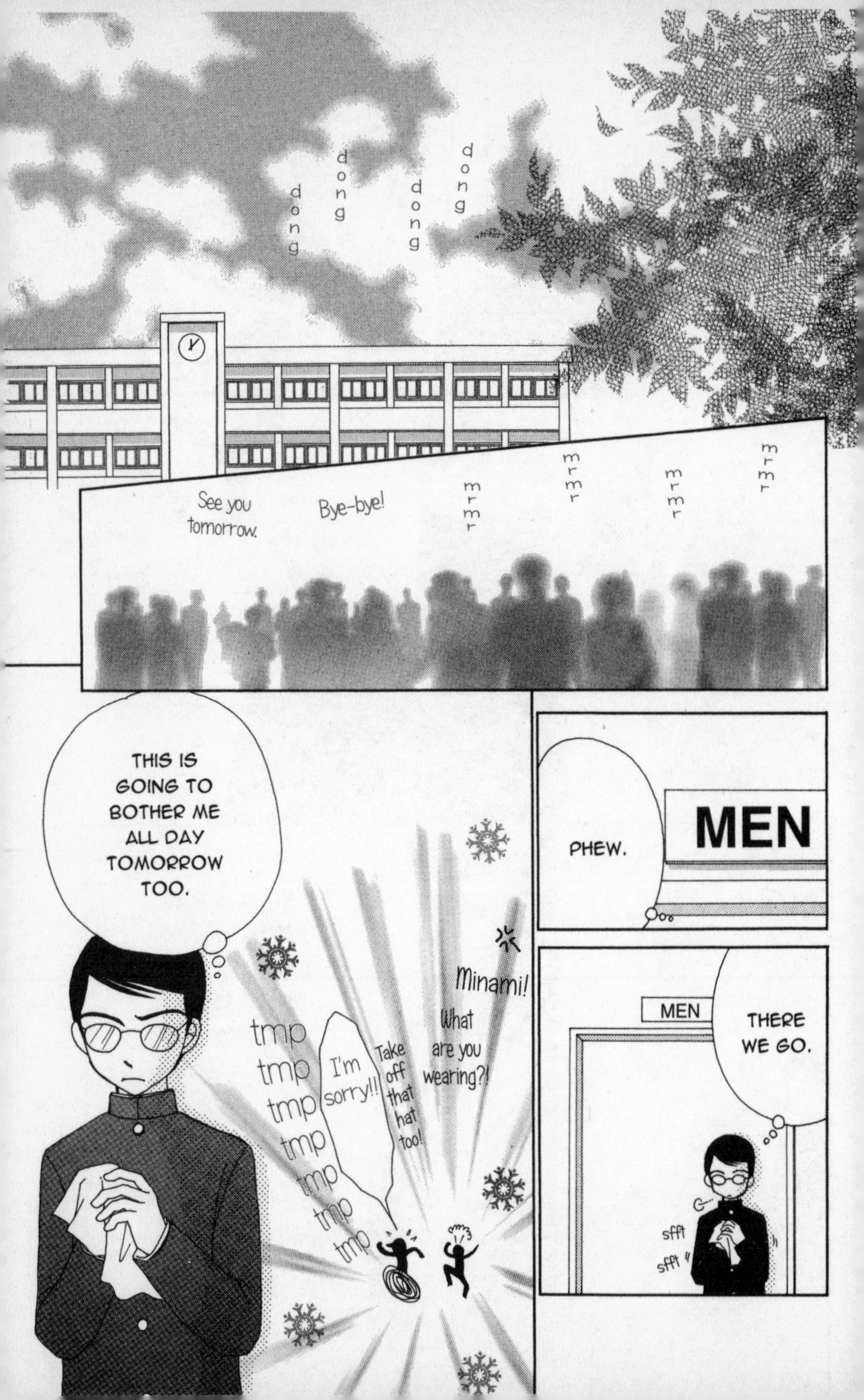
dong
dong
dong
dong
mrmr
mrmr
mrmr
mrmr
Bye-bye!
See you tomorrow.
MEN
PHEW.
THERE WE GO.
MEN
sfft
sfft
Minami!
What are you wearing?!
Take off that hat too!
I'm sorry!!
tmp tmp tmp tmp tmp tmp tmp
THIS IS GOING TO BOTHER ME ALL DAY TOMORROW TOO.

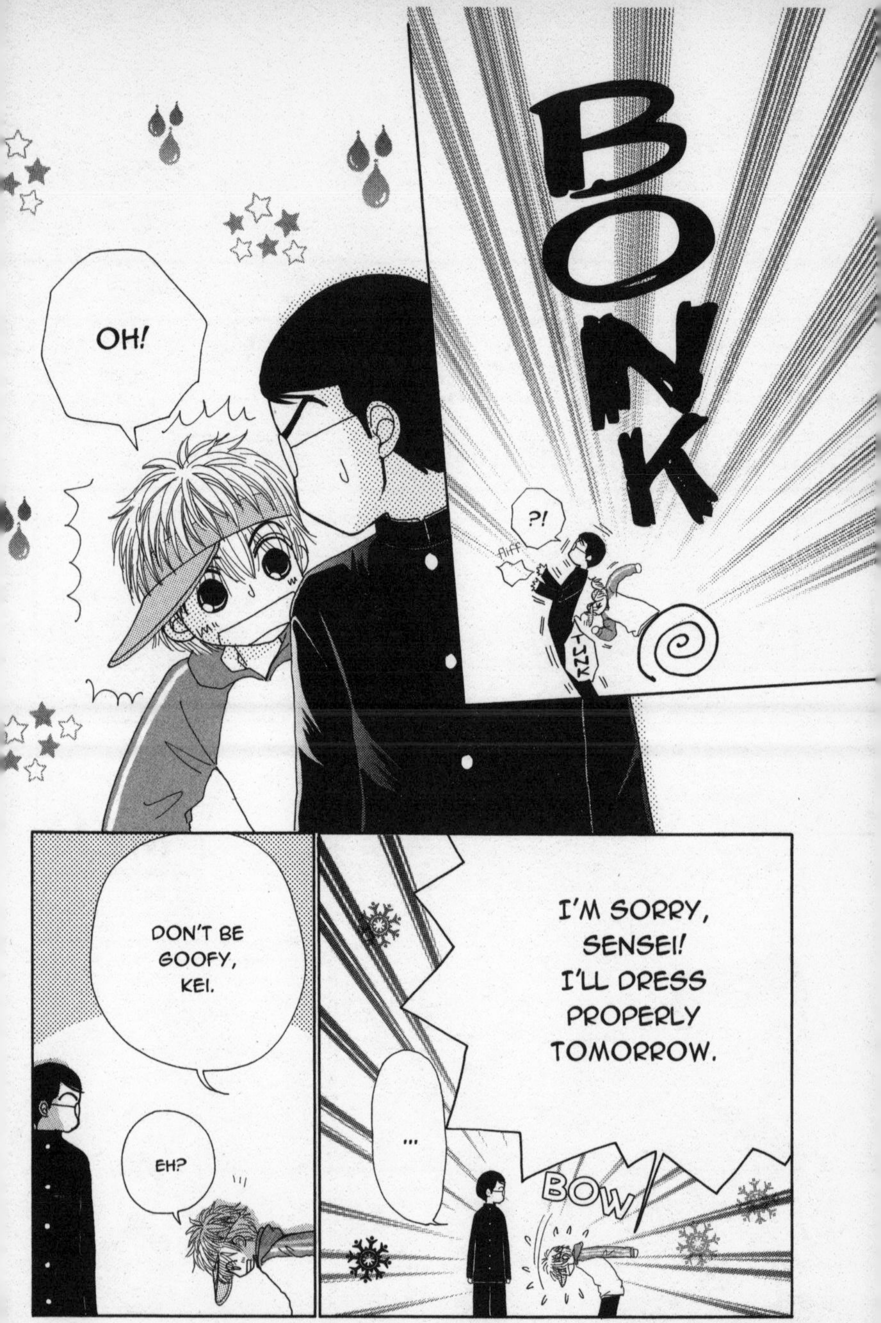
BONK
?!
TINK
OH!
I'M SORRY, SENSEI! I'LL DRESS PROPERLY TOMORROW.
...
BOW
DON'T BE GOOFY, KEI.
EH?

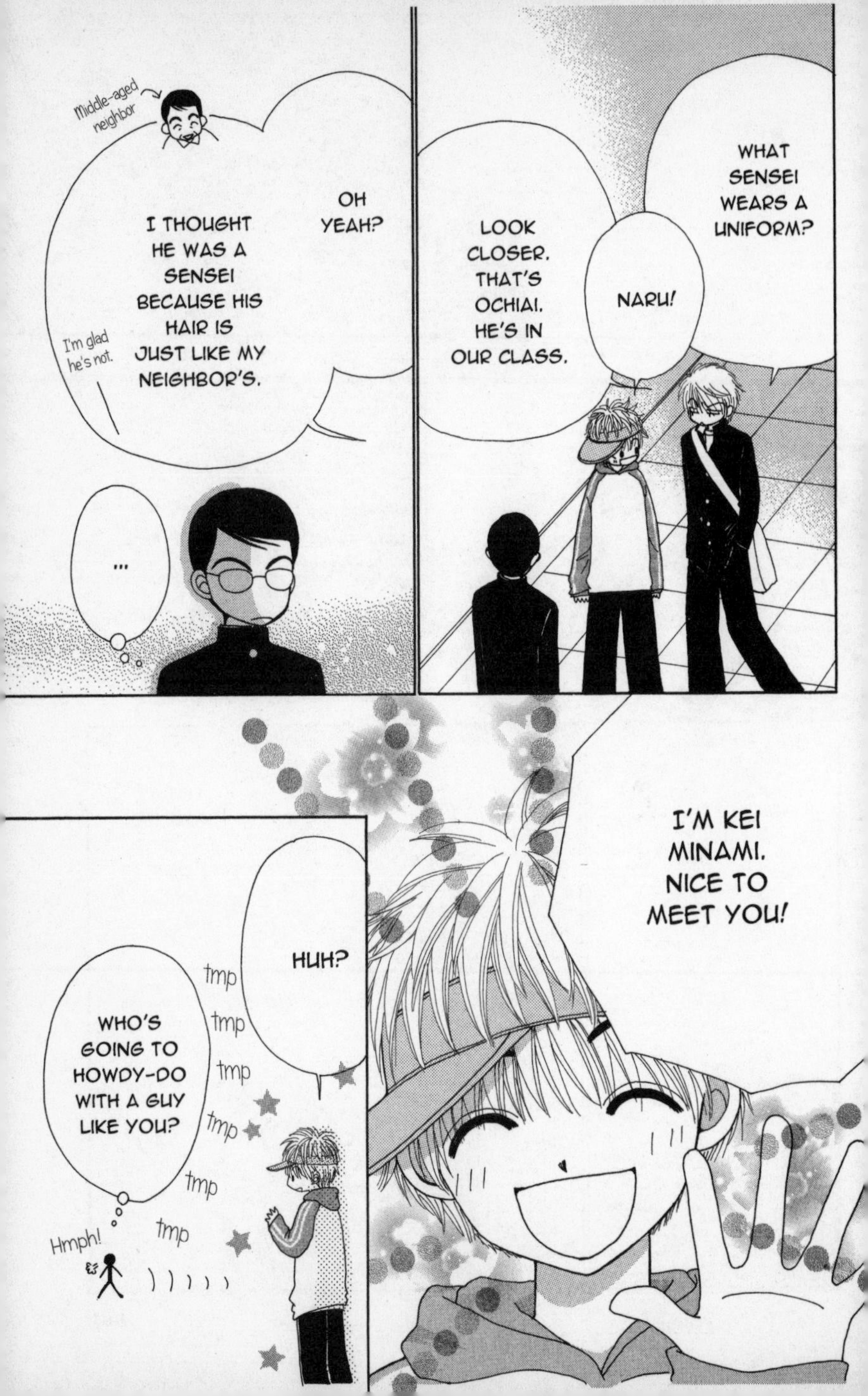
WHAT SENSEI WEARS A UNIFORM?
NARU!
LOOK CLOSER. THAT'S OCHIAI. HE'S IN OUR CLASS.
OH YEAH?
I THOUGHT HE WAS A SENSEI BECAUSE HIS HAIR IS JUST LIKE MY NEIGHBOR'S.
Middle-aged neighbor
I'm glad he's not.
...
I'M KEI MINAMI. NICE TO MEET YOU!
HUH?
tmp tmp tmp tmp tmp tmp
WHO'S GOING TO HOWDY-DO WITH A GUY LIKE YOU?
Hmph!

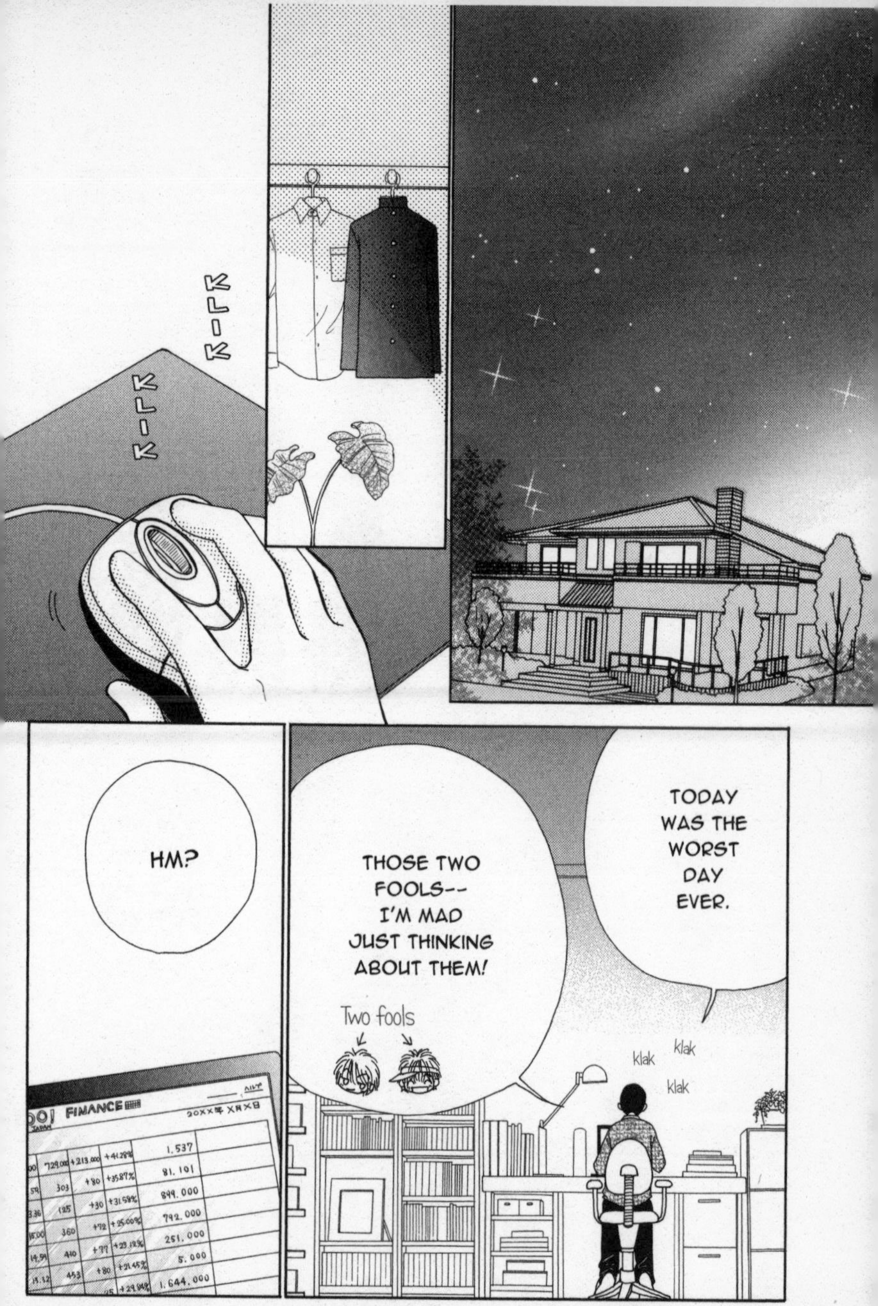
KLIK
KLIK
TODAY WAS THE WORST DAY EVER.
THOSE TWO FOOLS-- I'M MAD JUST THINKING ABOUT THEM!
Two fools
klak
klak
klak
HM?
FINANCE

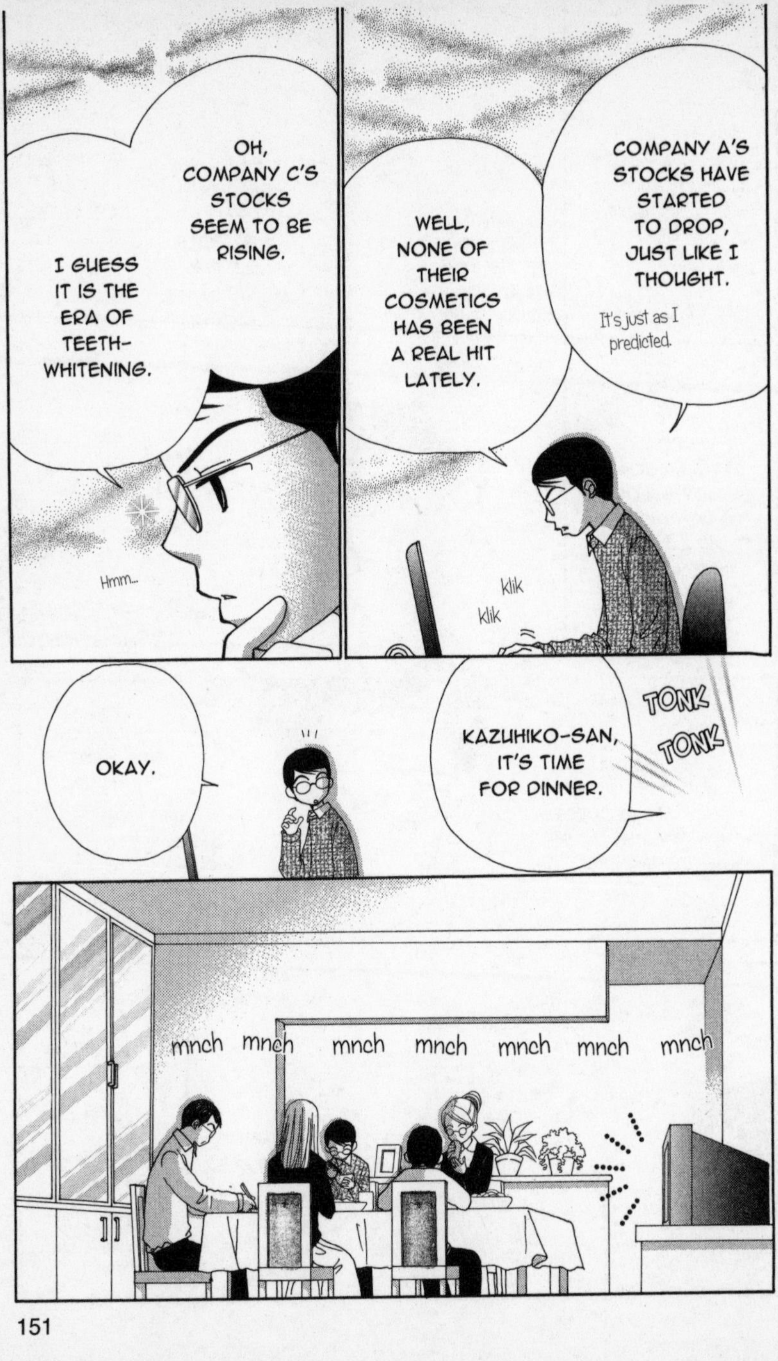
COMPANY A'S STOCKS HAVE STARTED TO DROP, JUST LIKE I THOUGHT.
It's just as I predicted.
WELL, NONE OF THEIR COSMETICS HAS BEEN A REAL HIT LATELY.
klik
klik
OH, COMPANY C'S STOCKS SEEM TO BE RISING.
I GUESS IT IS THE ERA OF TEETH-WHITENING.
Hmm...
TONK
TONK
KAZUHIKO-SAN, IT'S TIME FOR DINNER.
OKAY.
mnch mnch mnch mnch mnch mnch mnch

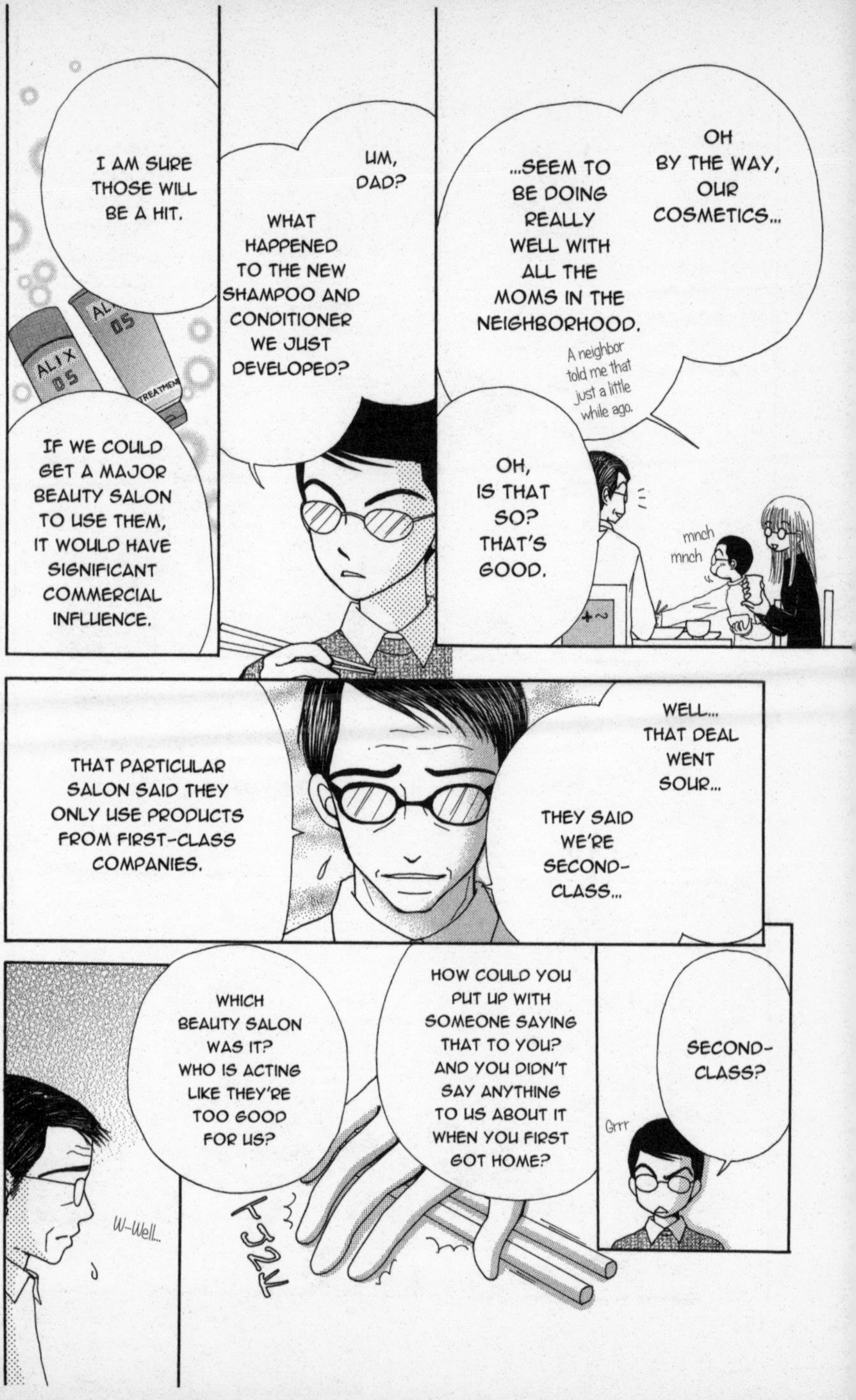
OH BY THE WAY, OUR COSMETICS...
...SEEM TO BE DOING REALLY WELL WITH ALL THE MOMS IN THE NEIGHBORHOOD.
A neighbor told me that just a little while ago.
OH, IS THAT SO? THAT'S GOOD.
mnch mnch
UM, DAD?
WHAT HAPPENED TO THE NEW SHAMPOO AND CONDITIONER WE JUST DEVELOPED?
I AM SURE THOSE WILL BE A HIT.
ALIX 05
ALIX 05
TREATMENT
IF WE COULD GET A MAJOR BEAUTY SALON TO USE THEM, IT WOULD HAVE SIGNIFICANT COMMERCIAL INFLUENCE.
WELL... THAT DEAL WENT SOUR...
THEY SAID WE'RE SECOND-CLASS...
THAT PARTICULAR SALON SAID THEY ONLY USE PRODUCTS FROM FIRST-CLASS COMPANIES.
SECOND-CLASS?
Grrr
HOW COULD YOU PUT UP WITH SOMEONE SAYING THAT TO YOU? AND YOU DIDN'T SAY ANYTHING TO US ABOUT IT WHEN YOU FIRST GOT HOME?
WHICH BEAUTY SALON WAS IT? WHO IS ACTING LIKE THEY'RE TOO GOOD FOR US?
W-Well...

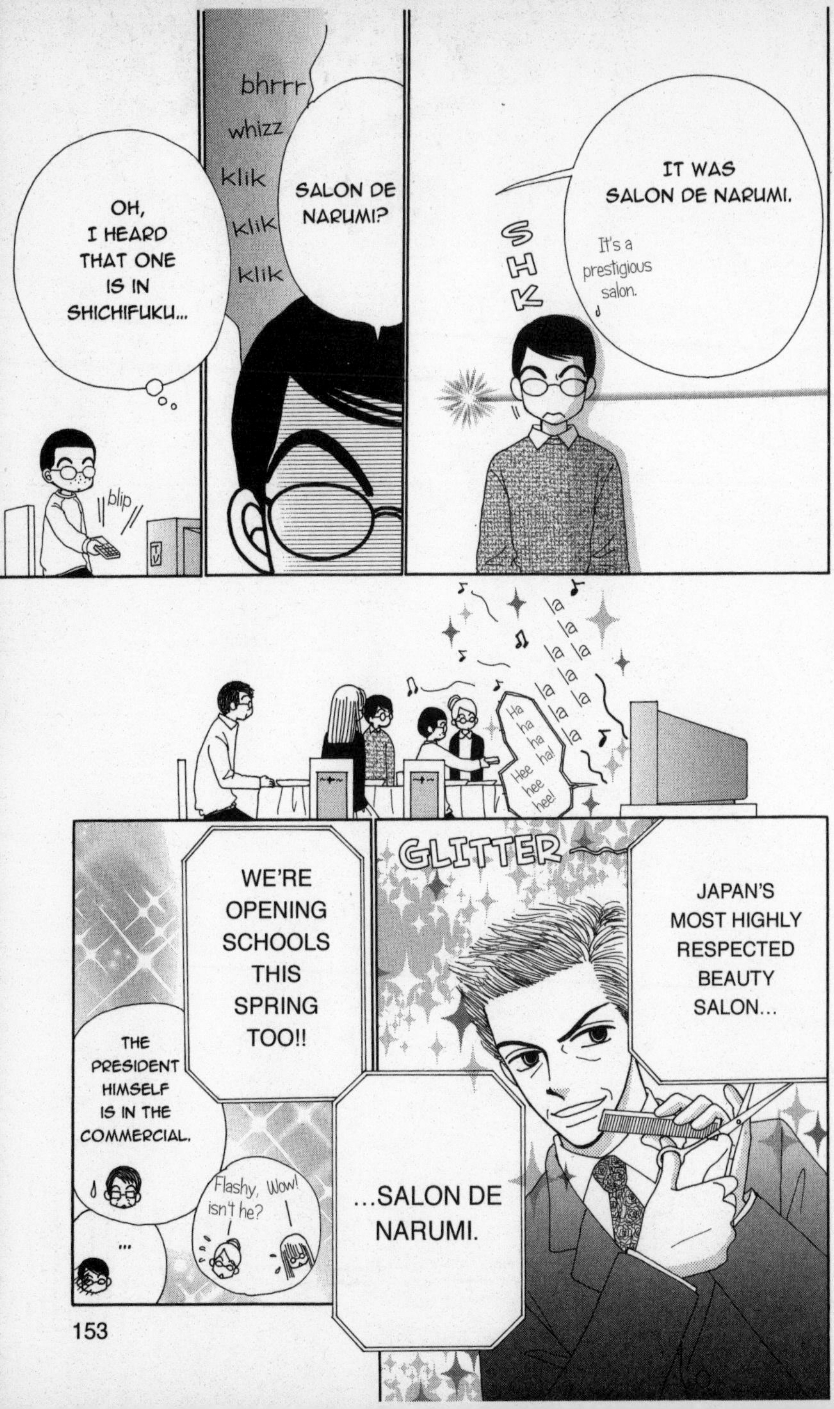
IT WAS SALON DE NARUMI.
SHK
It's a prestigious salon.
bhrrr
whizz
klik
klik
klik
SALON DE NARUMI?
OH, I HEARD THAT ONE IS IN SHICHIFUKU...
blip
la la la la la la la la la la
Ha ha ha ha! Hee hee hee!
GLITTER
JAPAN'S MOST HIGHLY RESPECTED BEAUTY SALON...
...SALON DE NARUMI.
WE'RE OPENING SCHOOLS THIS SPRING TOO!!
THE PRESIDENT HIMSELF IS IN THE COMMERCIAL.
Wow!
Flashy, isn't he?
...

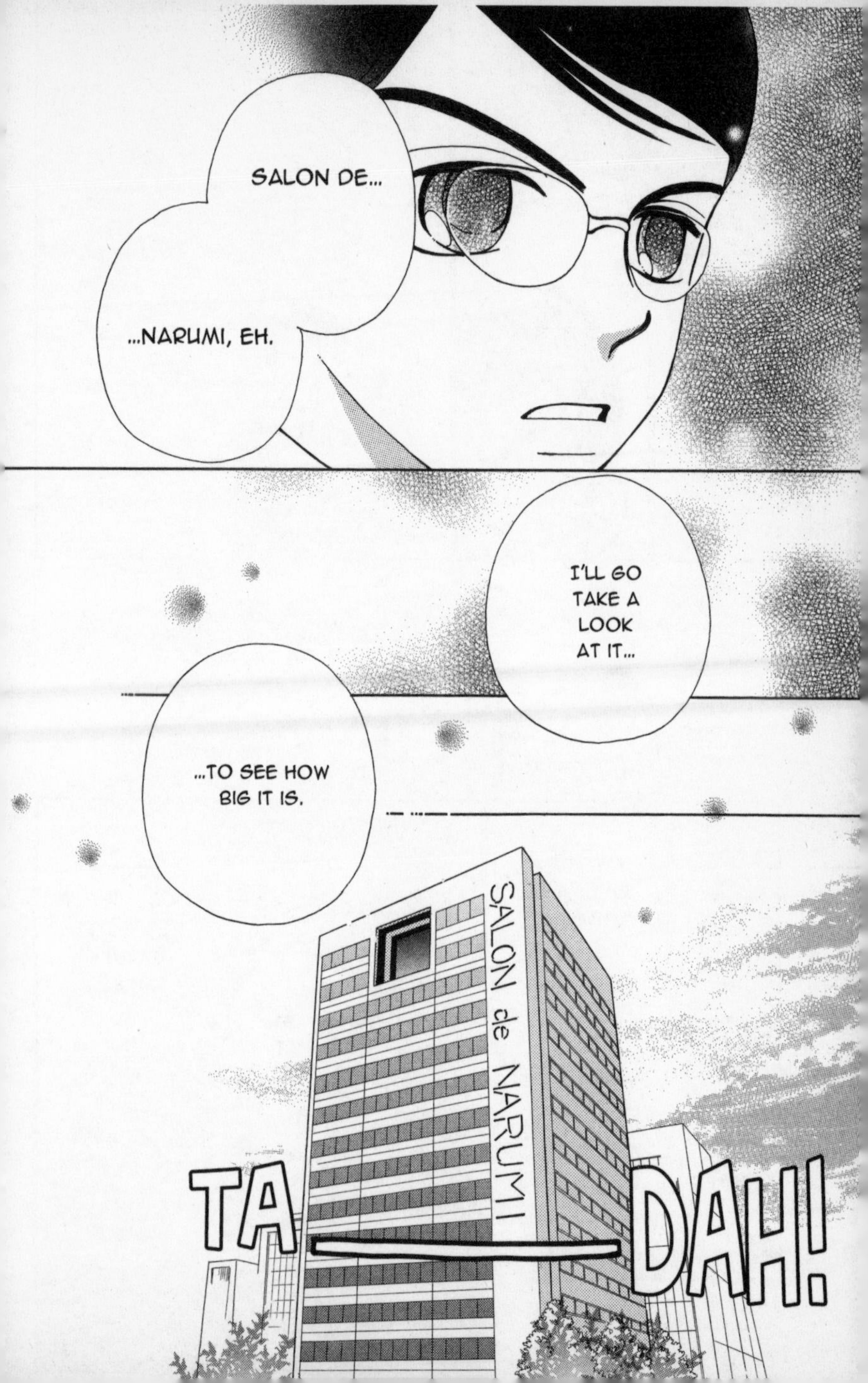
SALON DE...
...NARUMI, EH.
I'LL GO TAKE A LOOK AT IT...
...TO SEE HOW BIG IT IS.
SALON de NARUMI
TA—DAH!

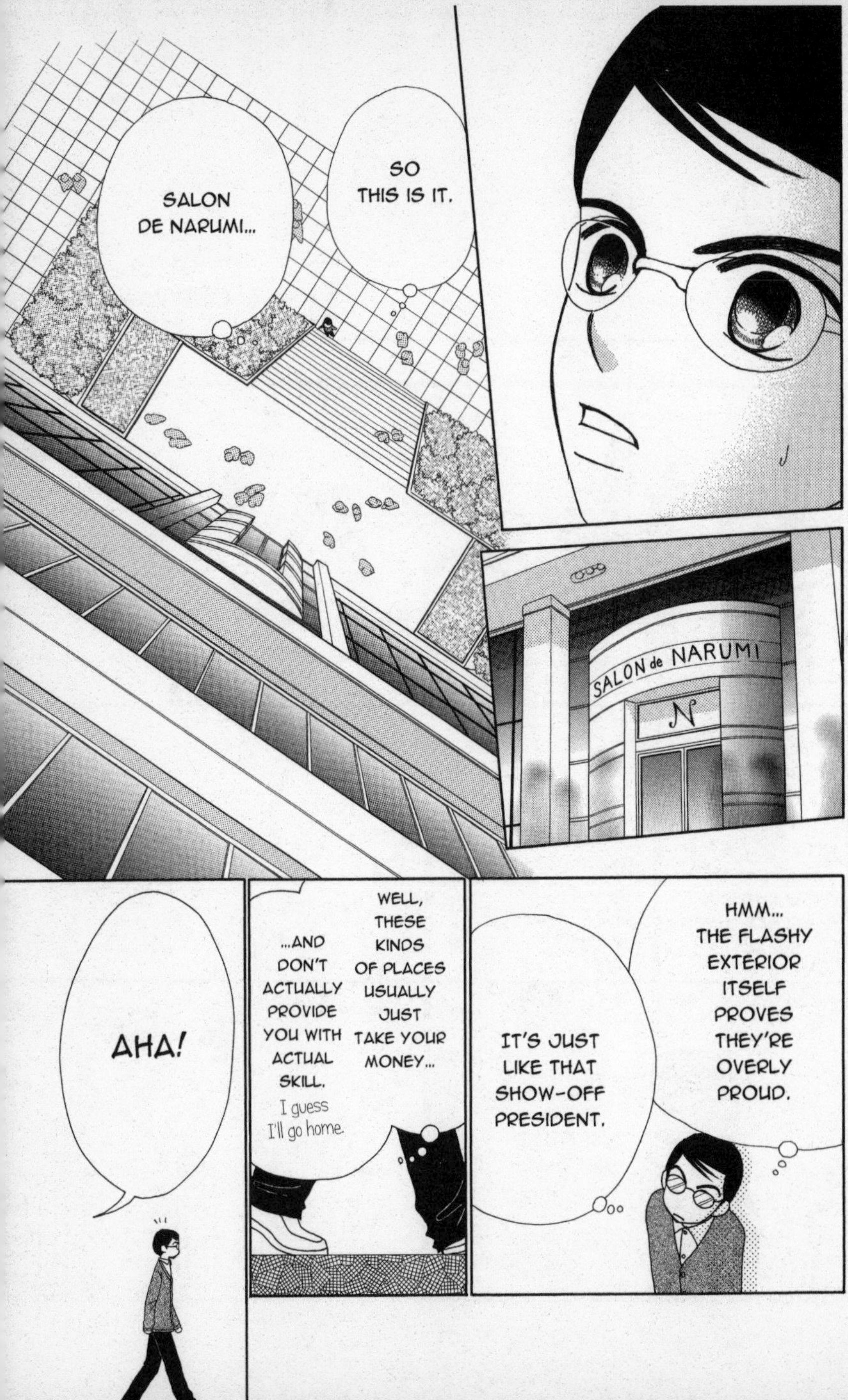
SALON de NARUMI
N
SO THIS IS IT.
SALON DE NARUMI...
HMM... THE FLASHY EXTERIOR ITSELF PROVES THEY'RE OVERLY PROUD.
IT'S JUST LIKE THAT SHOW-OFF PRESIDENT.
WELL, THESE KINDS OF PLACES USUALLY JUST TAKE YOUR MONEY...
...AND DON'T ACTUALLY PROVIDE YOU WITH ACTUAL SKILL.
I guess I'll go home.
AHA!

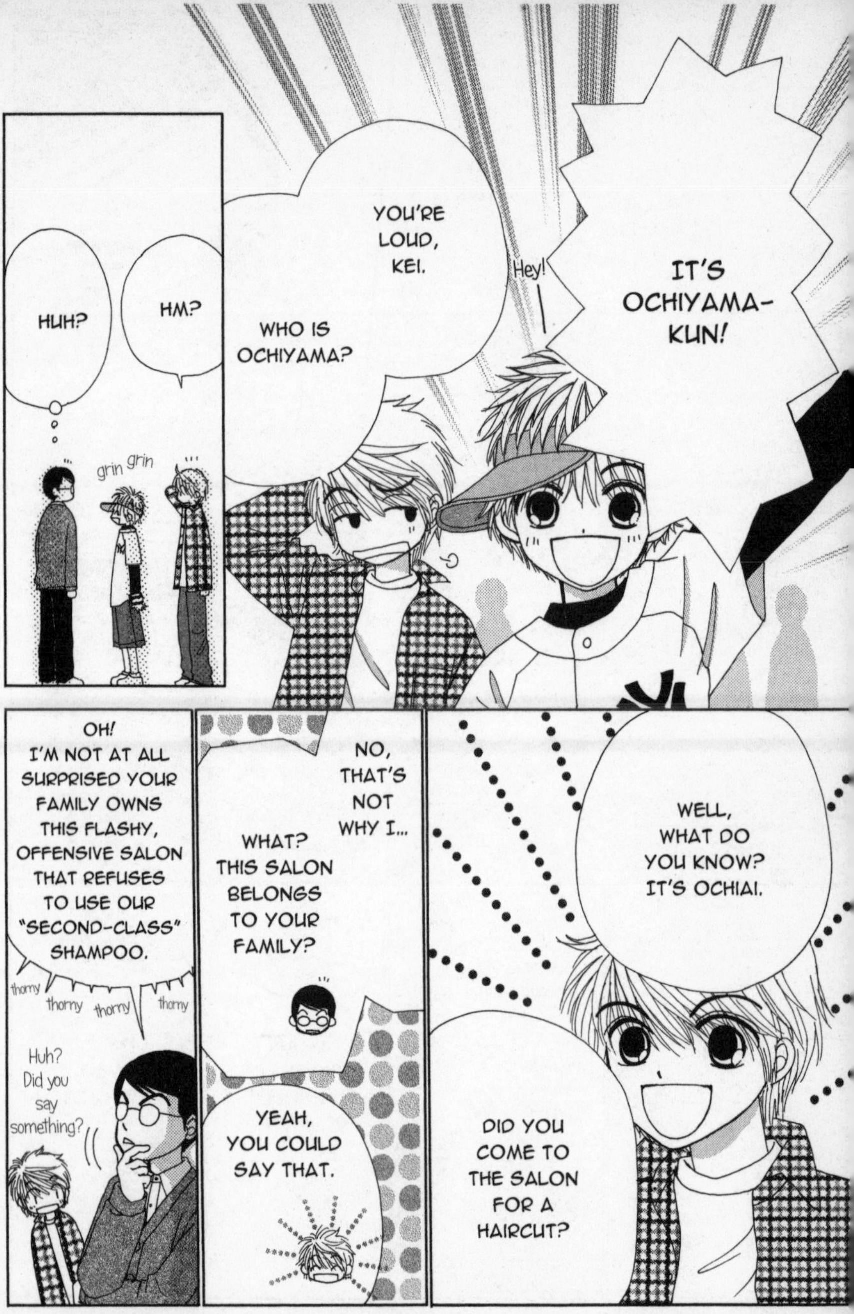
IT'S OCHIYAMA-KUN!
Hey!
YOU'RE LOUD, KEI.
WHO IS OCHIYAMA?
HM?
HUH?
grin grin
WELL, WHAT DO YOU KNOW? IT'S OCHIAI.
DID YOU COME TO THE SALON FOR A HAIRCUT?
NO, THAT'S NOT WHY I...
WHAT? THIS SALON BELONGS TO YOUR FAMILY?
YEAH, YOU COULD SAY THAT.
OH! I'M NOT AT ALL SURPRISED YOUR FAMILY OWNS THIS FLASHY, OFFENSIVE SALON THAT REFUSES TO USE OUR "SECOND-CLASS" SHAMPOO.
thorny thorny thorny thorny
Huh? Did you say something?

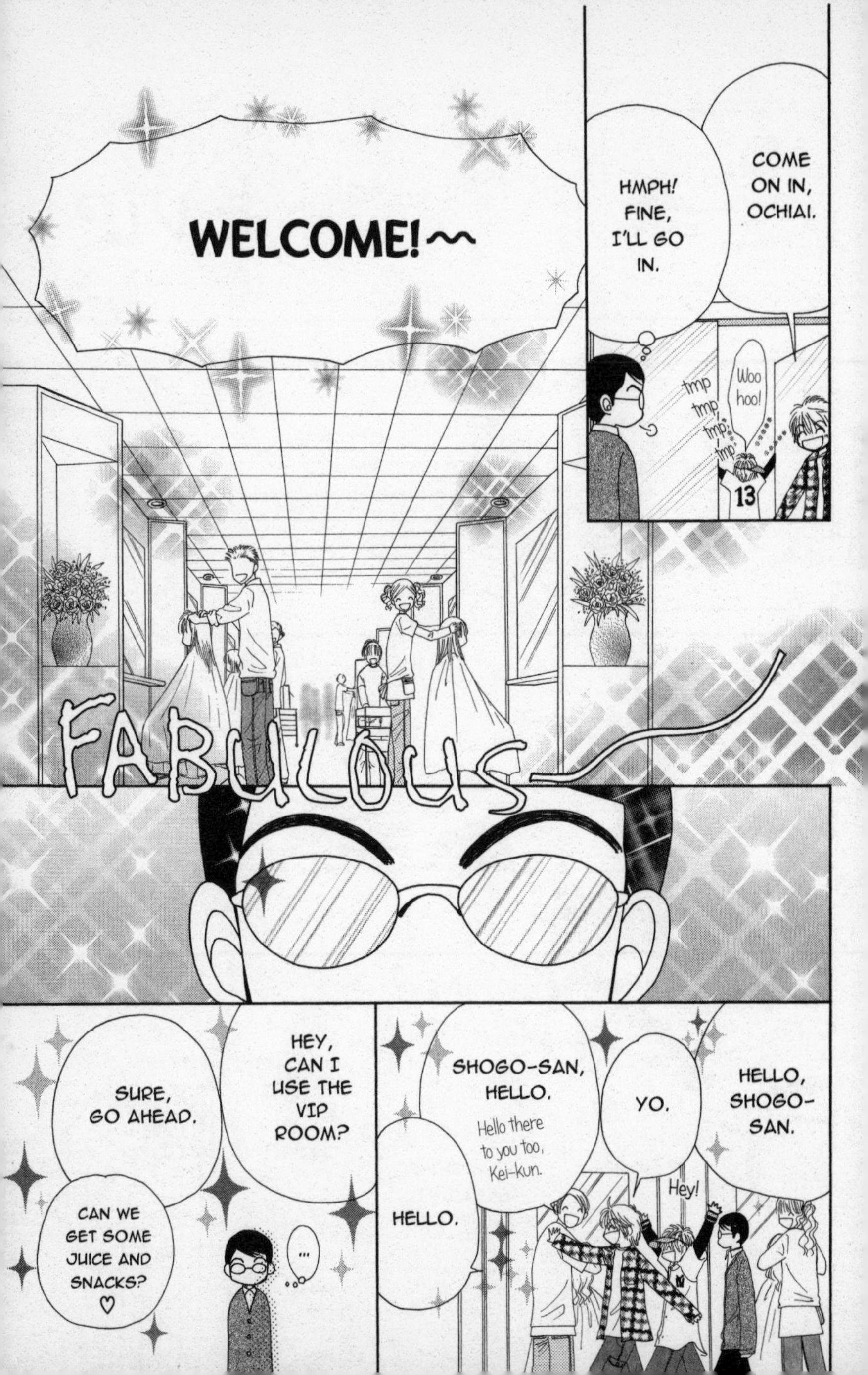
COME ON IN, OCHIAI.
HMPH! FINE, I'LL GO IN.
Woo hoo!
tmp tmp tmp tmp
WELCOME!~
FABULOUS~
HELLO, SHOGO-SAN.
YO.
Hey!
SHOGO-SAN, HELLO.
Hello there to you too, Kei-kun.
HELLO.
HEY, CAN I USE THE VIP ROOM?
SURE, GO AHEAD.
CAN WE GET SOME JUICE AND SNACKS? ♡
...

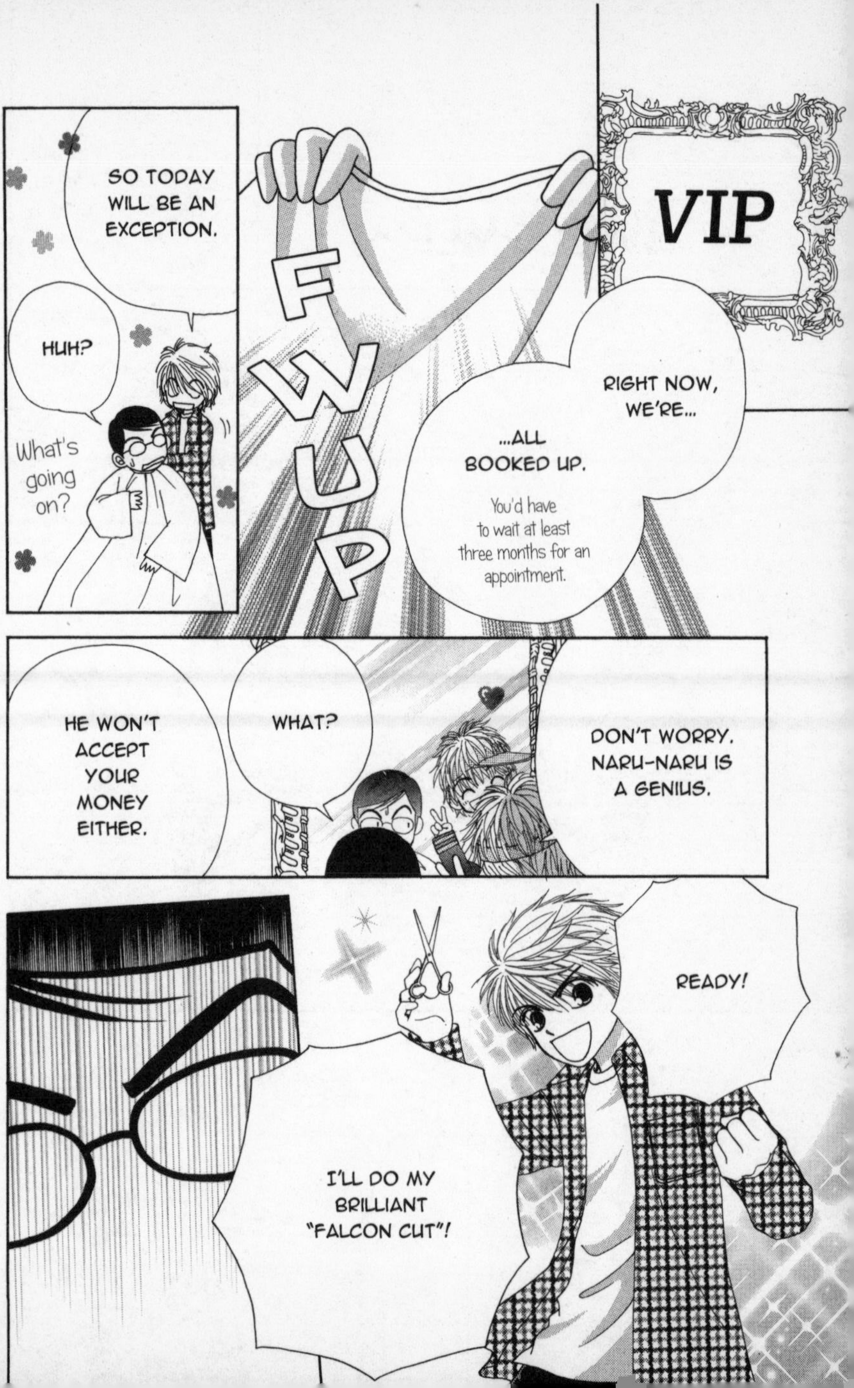
VIP
RIGHT NOW, WE'RE...
...ALL BOOKED UP.
You'd have to wait at least three months for an appointment.
FWUP
SO TODAY WILL BE AN EXCEPTION.
HUH?
What's going on?
DON'T WORRY. NARU-NARU IS A GENIUS.
WHAT?
HE WON'T ACCEPT YOUR MONEY EITHER.
READY!
I'LL DO MY BRILLIANT "FALCON CUT"!

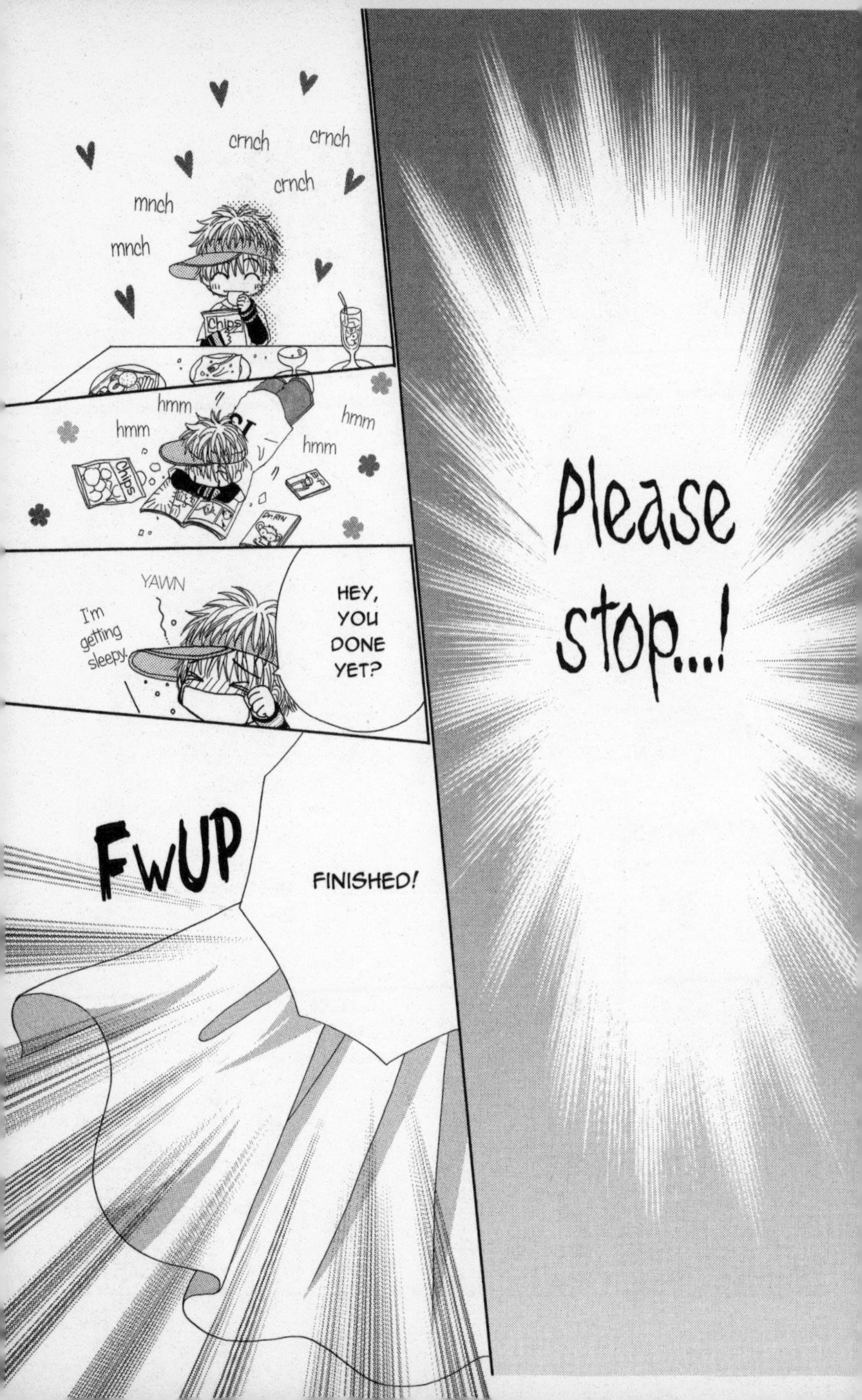
Please stop...!
crnch
crnch
crnch
mnch
mnch
hmm
hmm
hmm
hmm
HEY, YOU DONE YET?
YAWN
I'm getting sleepy.
FINISHED!
FWUP

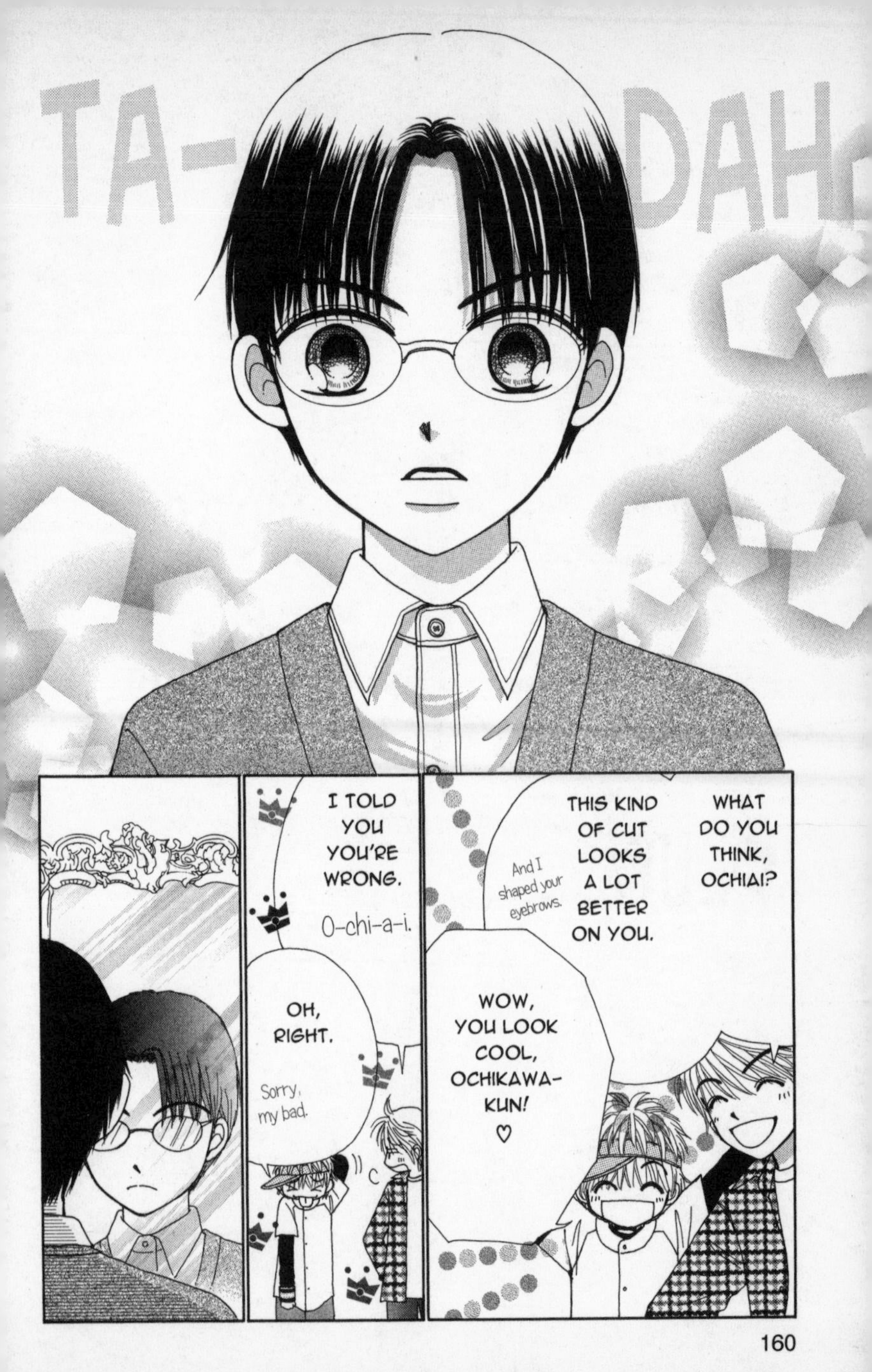
TA-DAH
WHAT DO YOU THINK, OCHIAI?
THIS KIND OF CUT LOOKS A LOT BETTER ON YOU.
And I shaped your eyebrows.
WOW, YOU LOOK COOL, OCHIKAWA-KUN! ♡
I TOLD YOU YOU'RE WRONG.
O-chi-a-i.
OH, RIGHT.
Sorry, my bad.

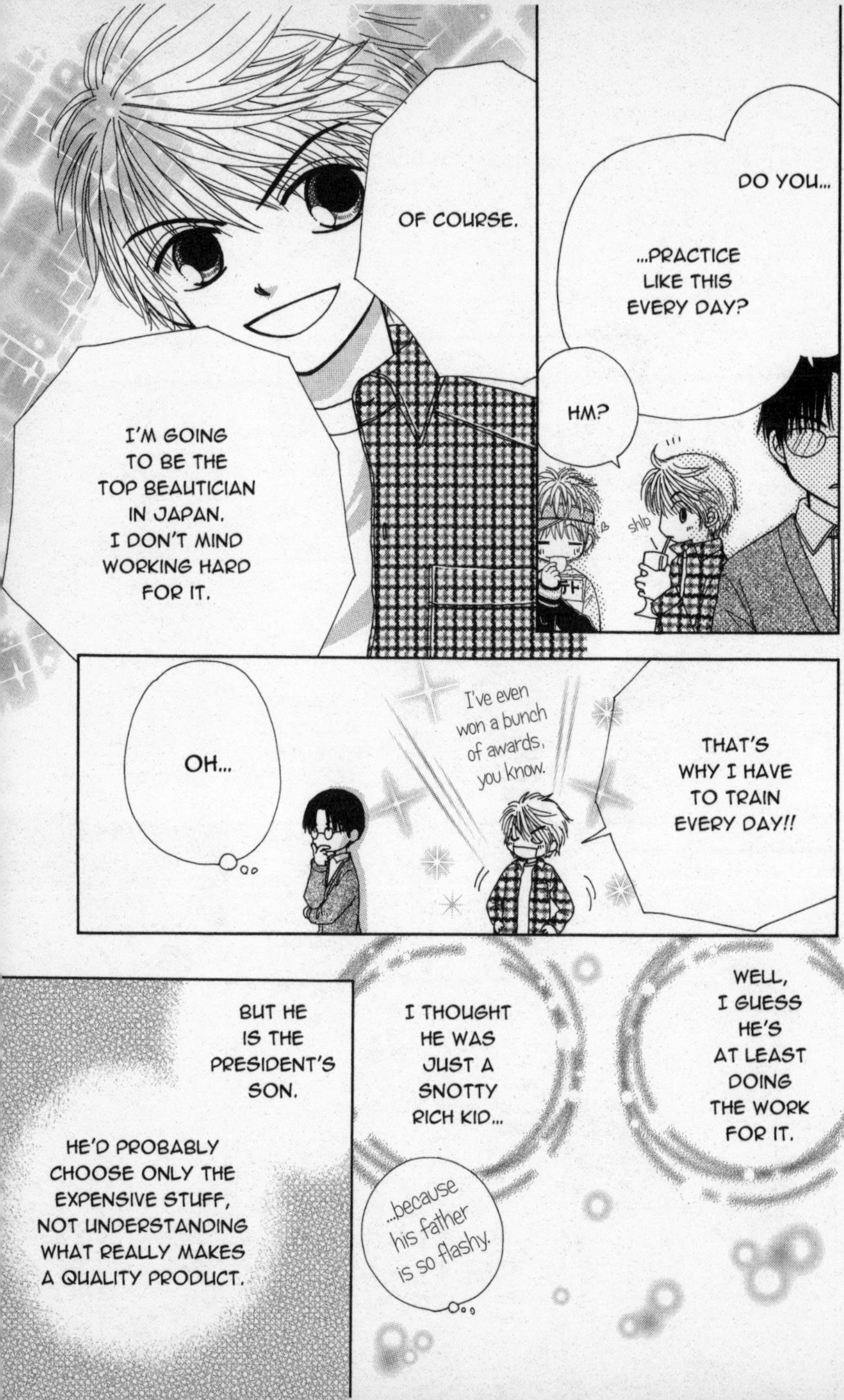
DO YOU...
...PRACTICE LIKE THIS EVERY DAY?
HM?
shlp
OF COURSE.
I'M GOING TO BE THE TOP BEAUTICIAN IN JAPAN. I DON'T MIND WORKING HARD FOR IT.
THAT'S WHY I HAVE TO TRAIN EVERY DAY!!
I've even won a bunch of awards, you know.
OH...
WELL, I GUESS HE'S AT LEAST DOING THE WORK FOR IT.
I THOUGHT HE WAS JUST A SNOTTY RICH KID...
...because his father is so flashy.
BUT HE IS THE PRESIDENT'S SON.
HE'D PROBABLY CHOOSE ONLY THE EXPENSIVE STUFF, NOT UNDERSTANDING WHAT REALLY MAKES A QUALITY PRODUCT.

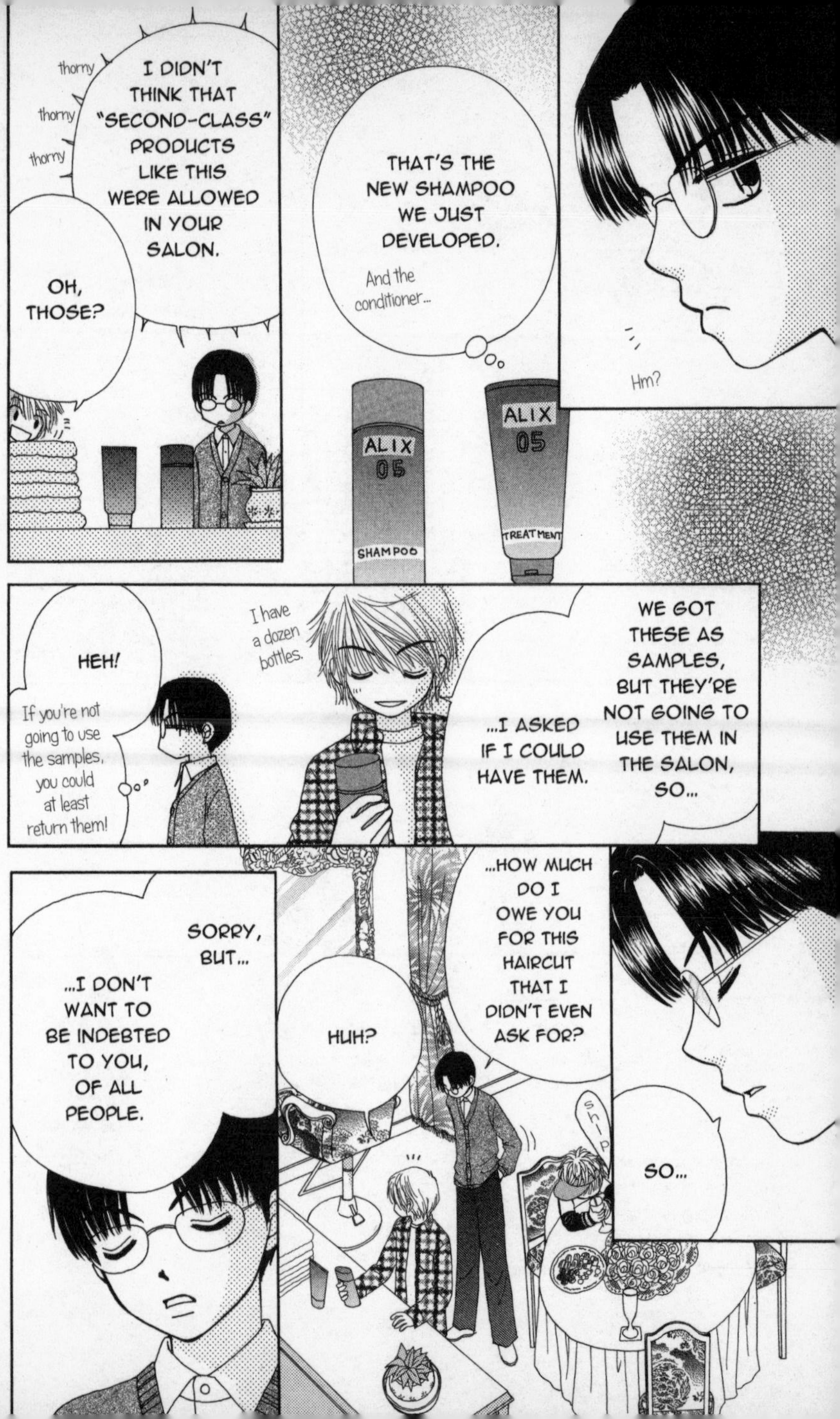
Hm?
THAT'S THE NEW SHAMPOO WE JUST DEVELOPED.
And the conditioner...
ALIX 05
TREATMENT
ALIX 05
SHAMPOO
I DIDN'T THINK THAT "SECOND-CLASS" PRODUCTS LIKE THIS WERE ALLOWED IN YOUR SALON.
thorny
thorny
thorny
OH, THOSE?
WE GOT THESE AS SAMPLES, BUT THEY'RE NOT GOING TO USE THEM IN THE SALON, SO...
...I ASKED IF I COULD HAVE THEM.
I have a dozen bottles.
HEH!
If you're not going to use the samples, you could at least return them!
SO...
...HOW MUCH DO I OWE YOU FOR THIS HAIRCUT THAT I DIDN'T EVEN ASK FOR?
shlp
HUH?
SORRY, BUT...
...I DON'T WANT TO BE INDEBTED TO YOU, OF ALL PEOPLE.

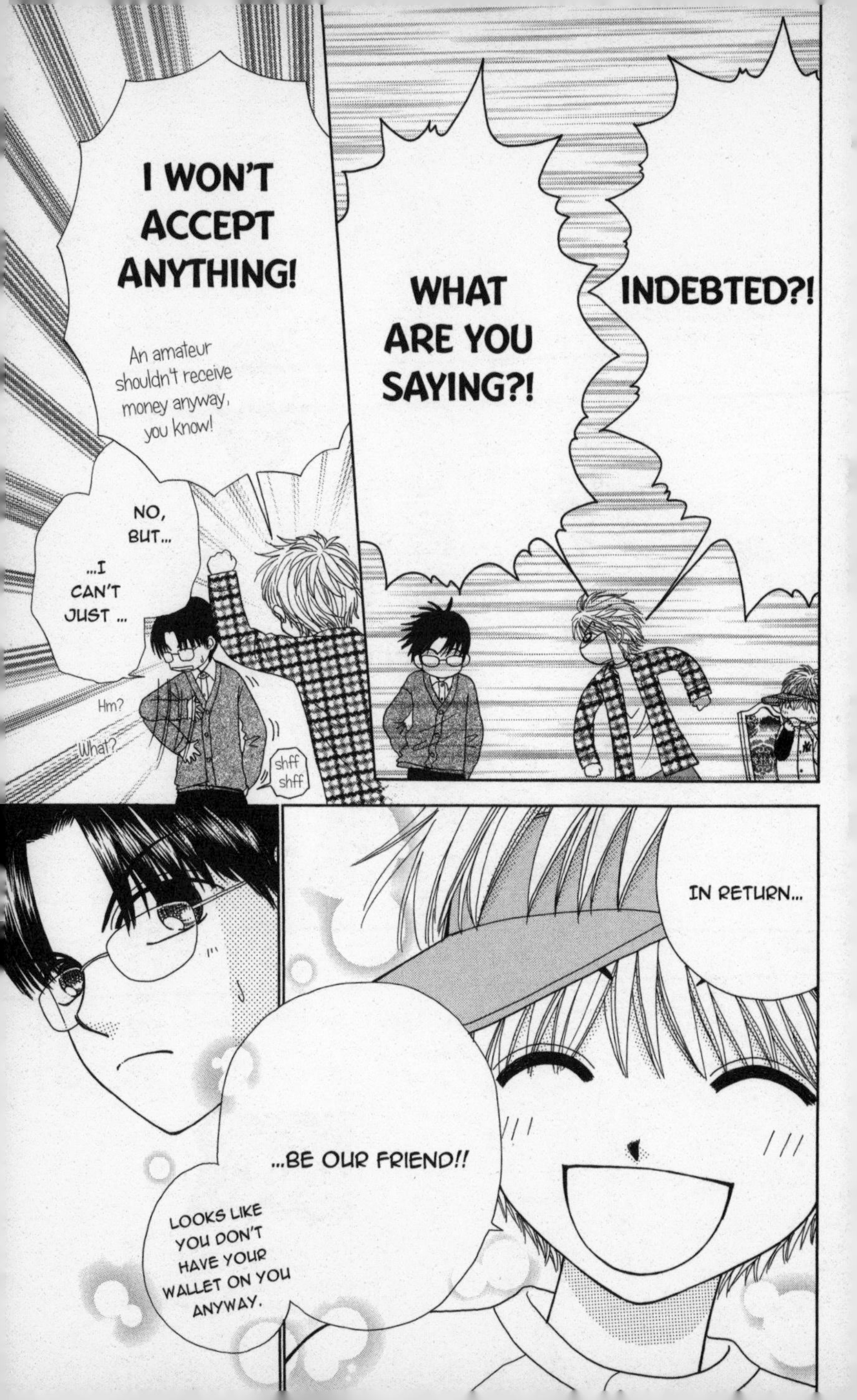
WHAT ARE YOU SAYING?! INDEBTED?!
I WON'T ACCEPT ANYTHING!
An amateur shouldn't receive money anyway, you know!
NO, BUT...
...I CAN'T JUST ...
Hm?
What?
shff shff
IN RETURN...
...BE OUR FRIEND!!
LOOKS LIKE YOU DON'T HAVE YOUR WALLET ON YOU ANYWAY.

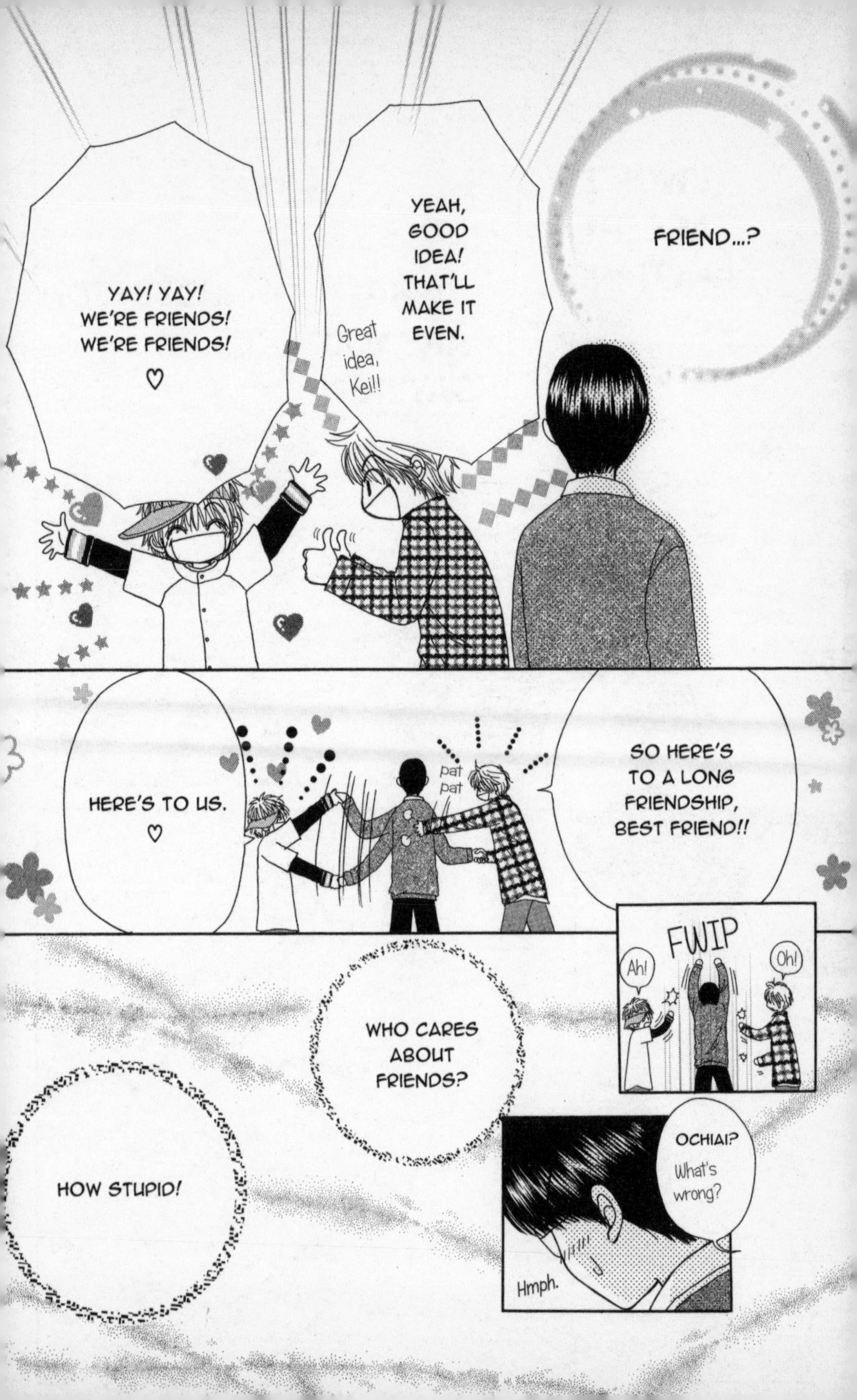
FRIEND...?
YEAH, GOOD IDEA! THAT'LL MAKE IT EVEN.
Great idea, Keil!
YAY! YAY! WE'RE FRIENDS! WE'RE FRIENDS! ♡
SO HERE'S TO A LONG FRIENDSHIP, BEST FRIEND!!
pat pat
HERE'S TO US. ♡
FWIP
Oh!
Ah!
OCHIAI? What's wrong?
Hmph.
WHO CARES ABOUT FRIENDS?
HOW STUPID!

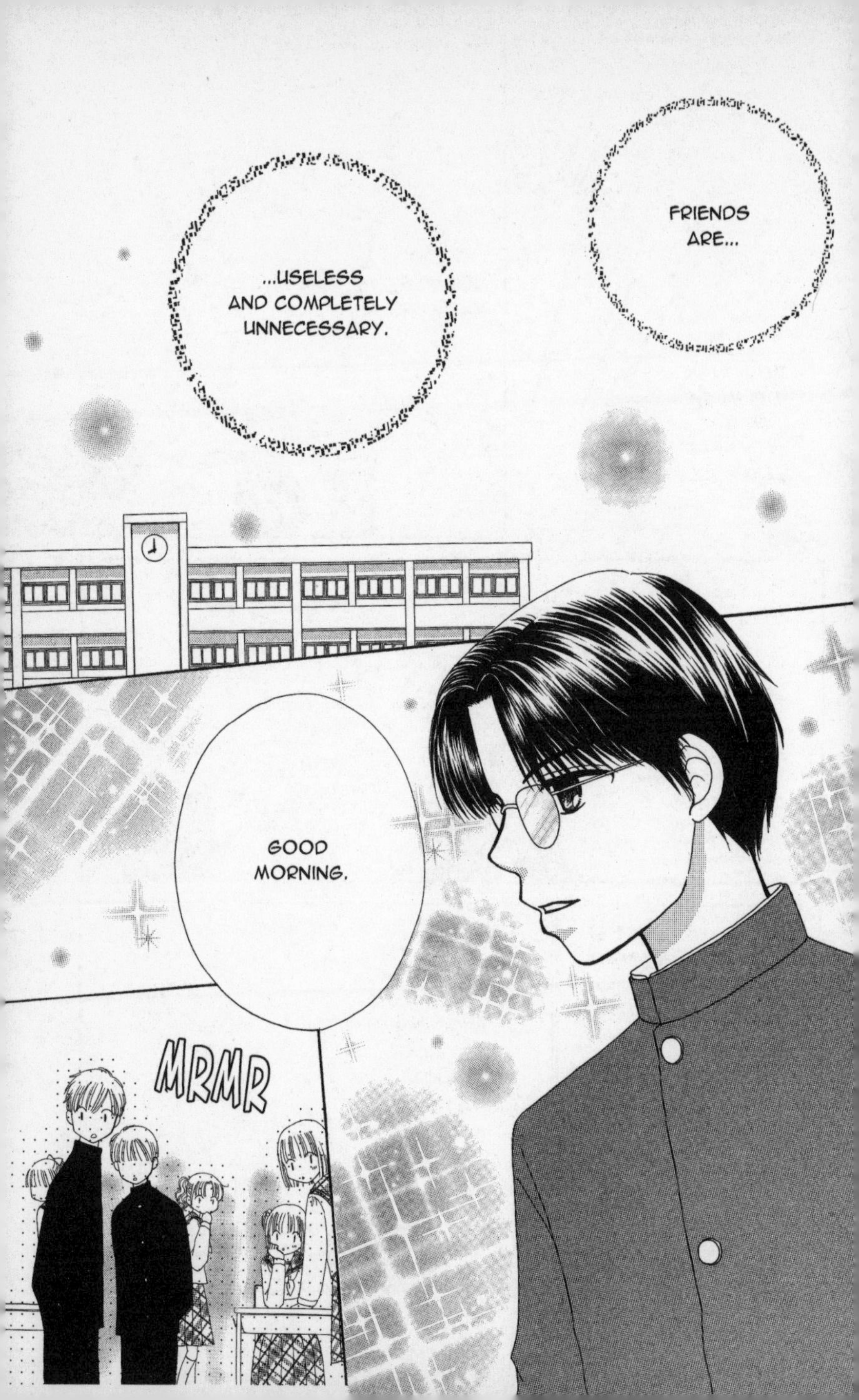
FRIENDS ARE...
...USELESS AND COMPLETELY UNNECESSARY.
GOOD MORNING.
MRMR

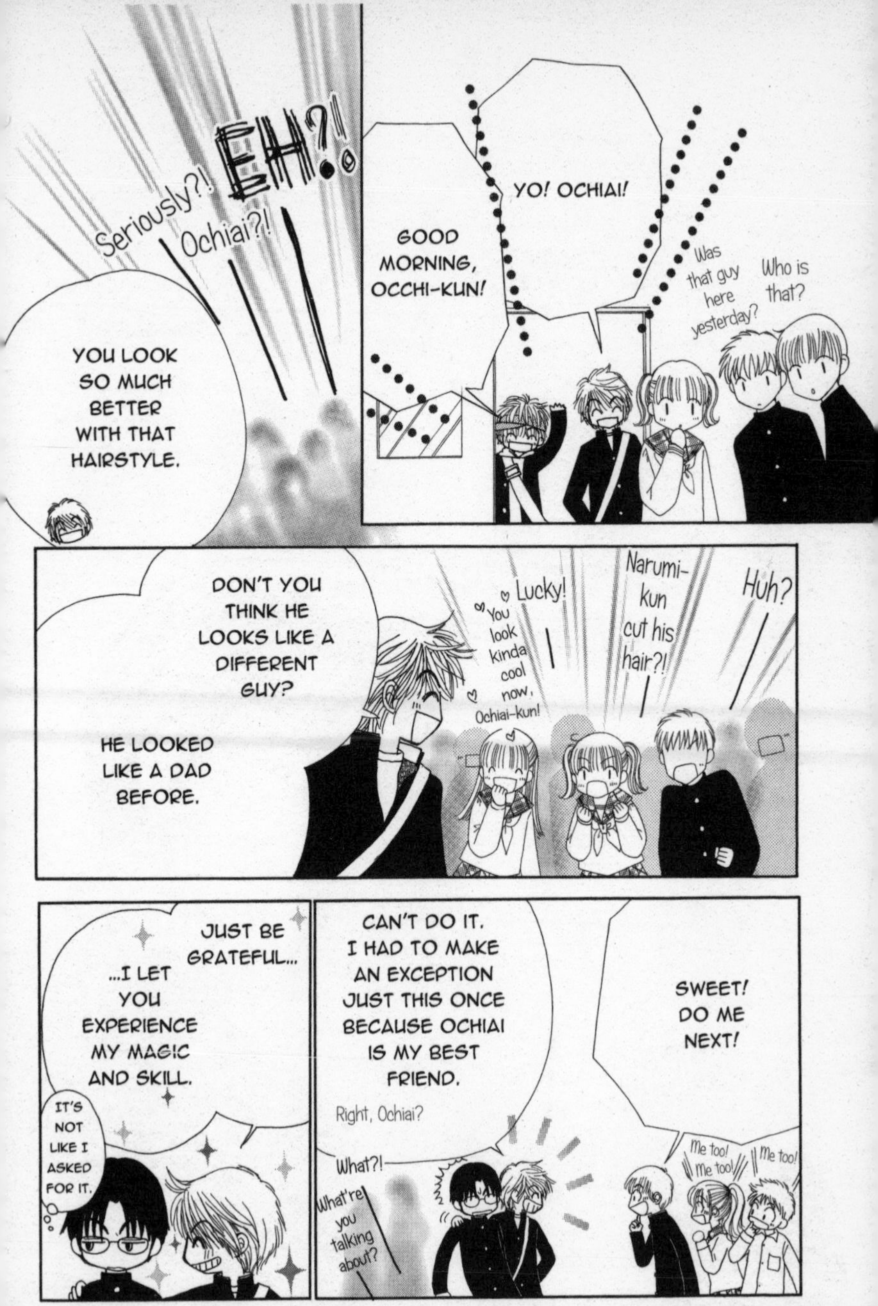
YO! OCHIAI!
GOOD MORNING, OCCHI-KUN!
Who is that?
Was that guy here yesterday?
EH?!
Ochiai?!
Seriously?!
YOU LOOK SO MUCH BETTER WITH THAT HAIRSTYLE.
Huh?
Narumi-kun cut his hair?!
Lucky!
You look kinda cool now, Ochiai-kun!
DON'T YOU THINK HE LOOKS LIKE A DIFFERENT GUY?
HE LOOKED LIKE A DAD BEFORE.
SWEET! DO ME NEXT!
Me too!
Me too!
Me too!
CAN'T DO IT. I HAD TO MAKE AN EXCEPTION JUST THIS ONCE BECAUSE OCHIAI IS MY BEST FRIEND.
Right, Ochiai?
What?!
What're you talking about?
JUST BE GRATEFUL...
...I LET YOU EXPERIENCE MY MAGIC AND SKILL.
IT'S NOT LIKE I ASKED FOR IT.

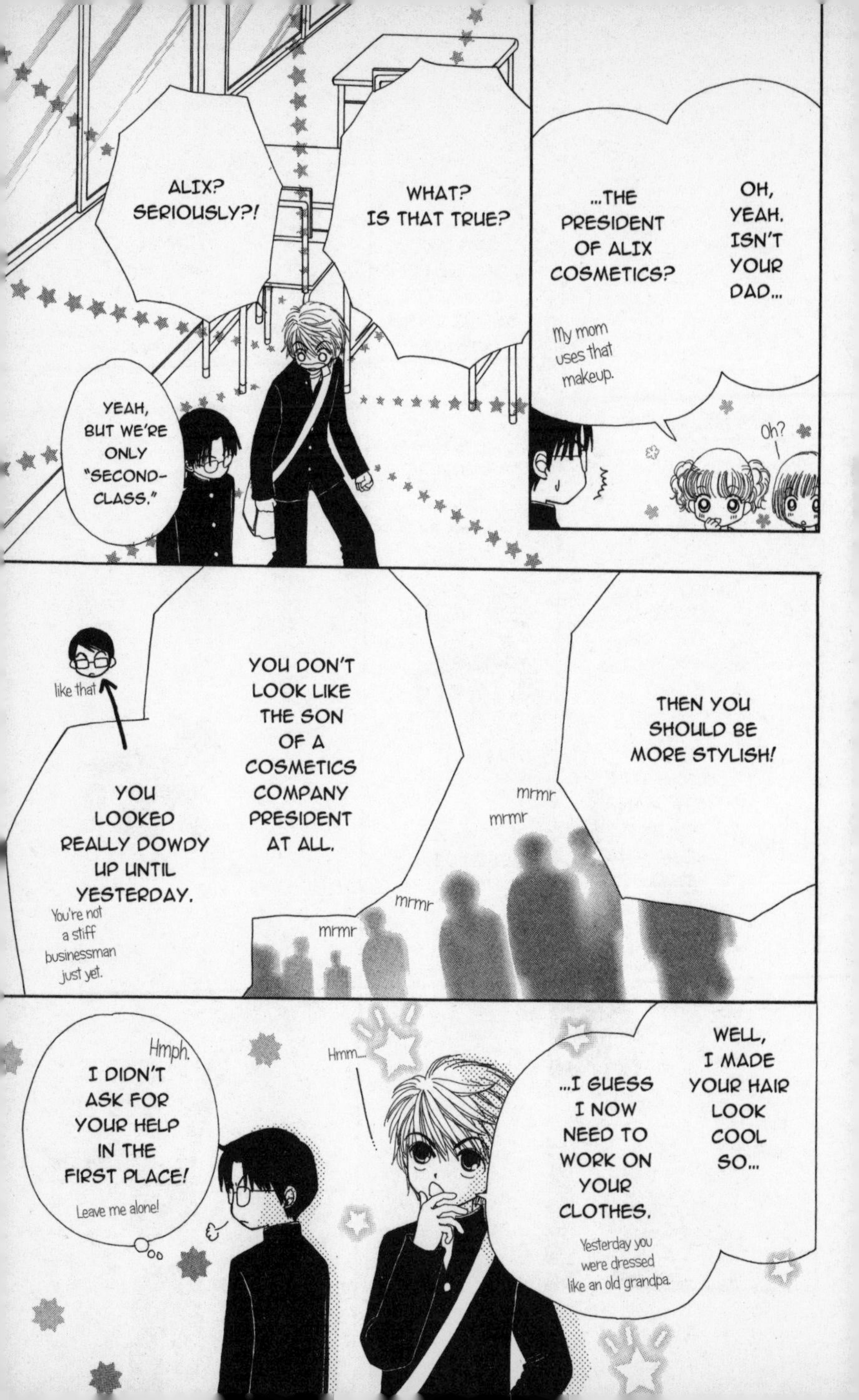
OH, YEAH. ISN'T YOUR DAD...
...THE PRESIDENT OF ALIX COSMETICS?
My mom uses that makeup.
Oh?
WHAT? IS THAT TRUE?
ALIX? SERIOUSLY?!
YEAH, BUT WE'RE ONLY "SECOND-CLASS."
THEN YOU SHOULD BE MORE STYLISH!
mrmr
mrmr
mrmr
mrmr
YOU DON'T LOOK LIKE THE SON OF A COSMETICS COMPANY PRESIDENT AT ALL.
like that
YOU LOOKED REALLY DOWDY UP UNTIL YESTERDAY.
You're not a stiff businessman just yet.
WELL, I MADE YOUR HAIR LOOK COOL SO...
...I GUESS I NOW NEED TO WORK ON YOUR CLOTHES.
Yesterday you were dressed like an old grandpa.
Hmm...
Hmph.
I DIDN'T ASK FOR YOUR HELP IN THE FIRST PLACE!
Leave me alone!

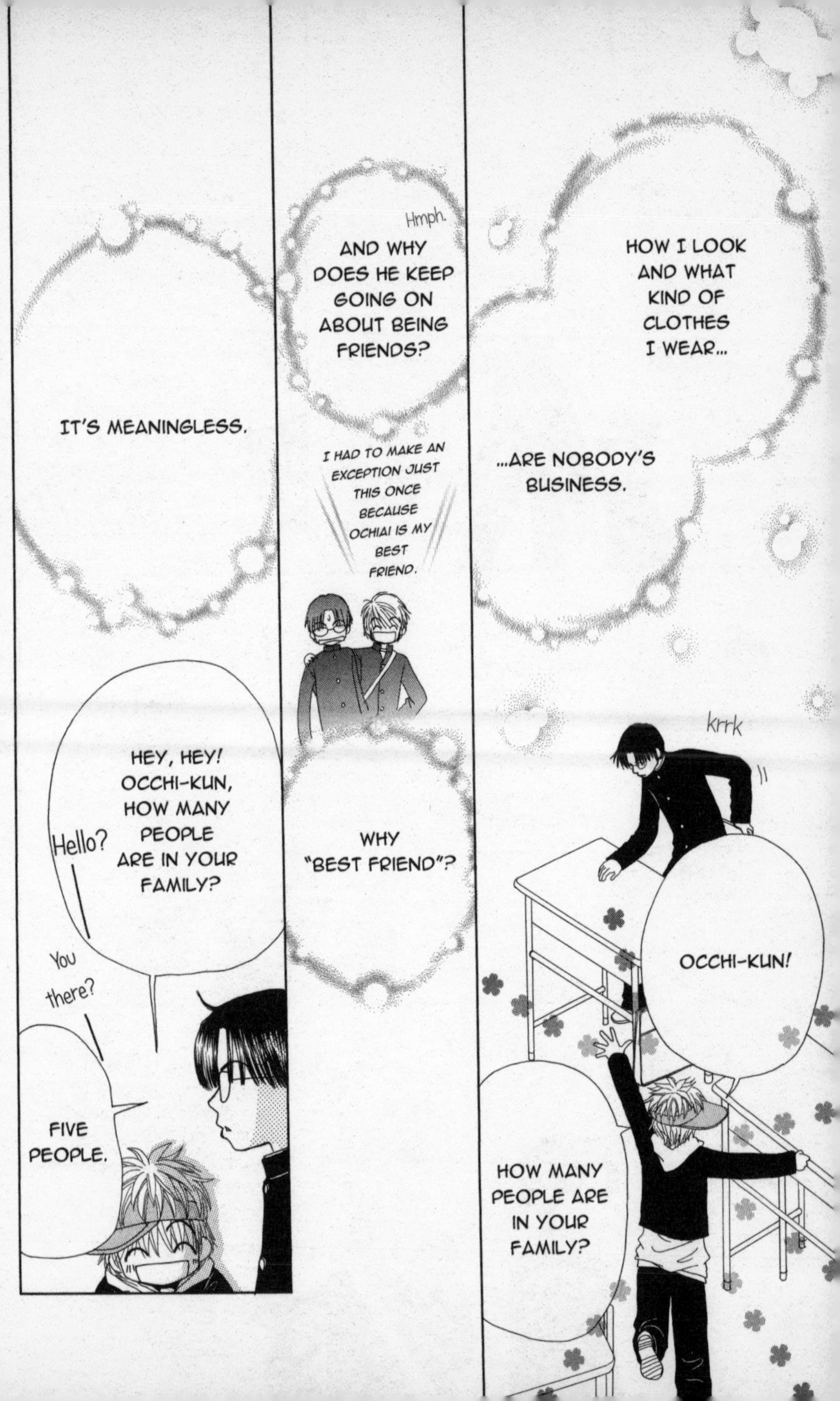
HOW I LOOK AND WHAT KIND OF CLOTHES I WEAR...
...ARE NOBODY'S BUSINESS.
krrk
OCCHI-KUN!
HOW MANY PEOPLE ARE IN YOUR FAMILY?
Hmph.
AND WHY DOES HE KEEP GOING ON ABOUT BEING FRIENDS?
I HAD TO MAKE AN EXCEPTION JUST THIS ONCE BECAUSE OCHIAI IS MY BEST FRIEND.
WHY "BEST FRIEND"?
IT'S MEANINGLESS.
HEY, HEY! OCCHI-KUN, HOW MANY PEOPLE ARE IN YOUR FAMILY?
Hello?
You there?
FIVE PEOPLE.

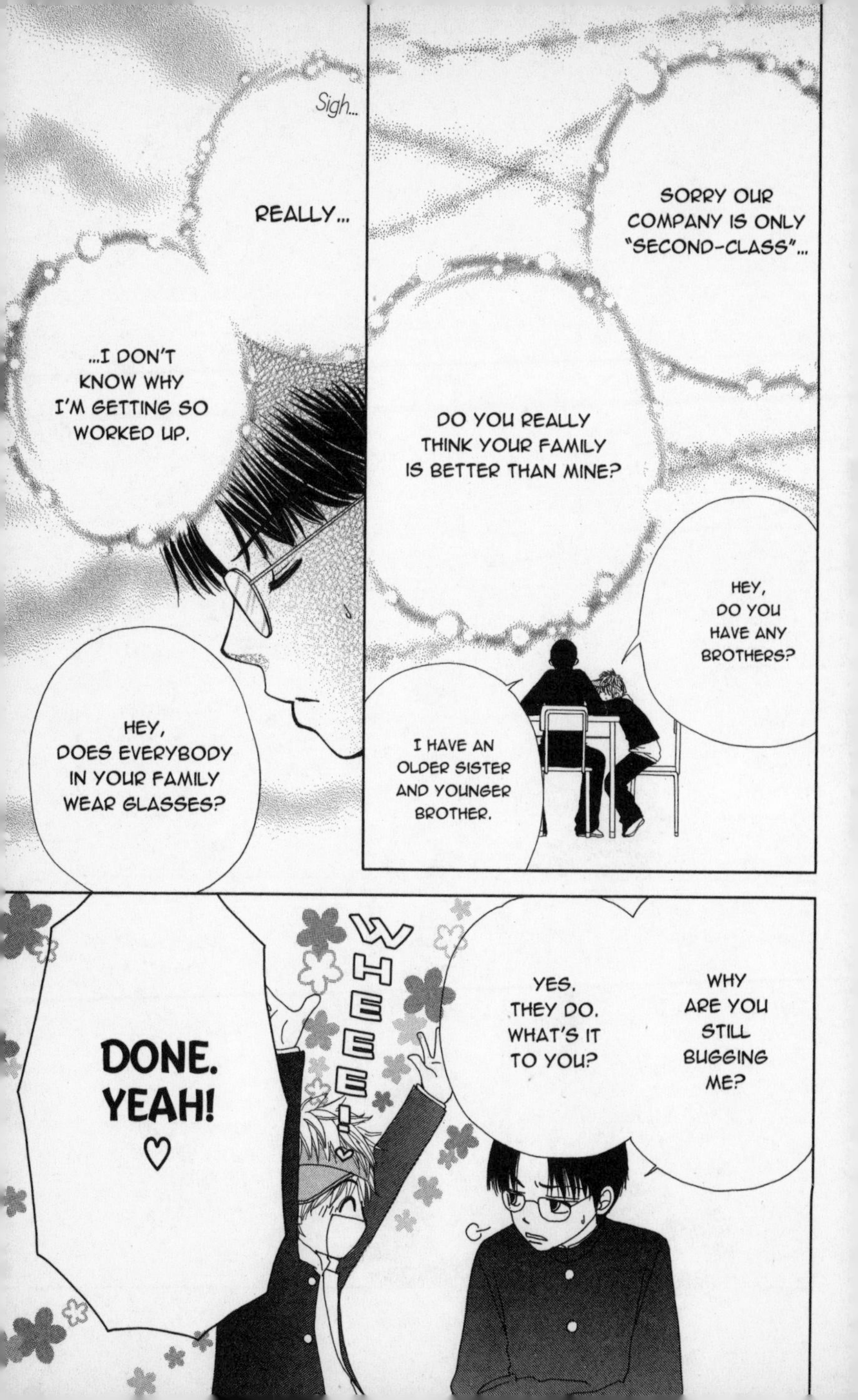
SORRY OUR COMPANY IS ONLY "SECOND-CLASS"...
DO YOU REALLY THINK YOUR FAMILY IS BETTER THAN MINE?
HEY, DO YOU HAVE ANY BROTHERS?
I HAVE AN OLDER SISTER AND YOUNGER BROTHER.
Sigh...
REALLY...
...I DON'T KNOW WHY I'M GETTING SO WORKED UP.
HEY, DOES EVERYBODY IN YOUR FAMILY WEAR GLASSES?
YES. THEY DO. WHAT'S IT TO YOU?
WHY ARE YOU STILL BUGGING ME?
WHEEE!
DONE. YEAH! ♡

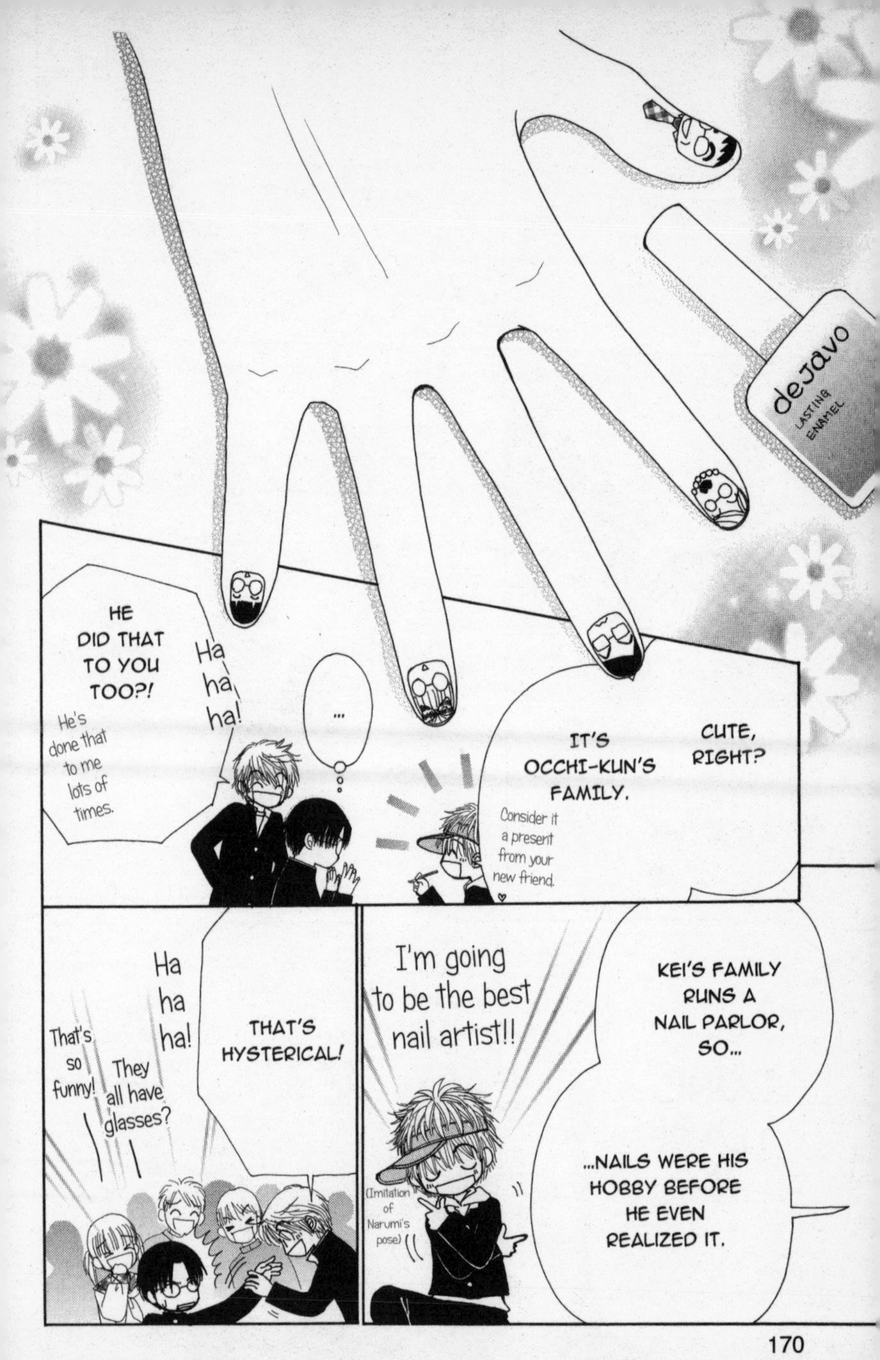
dejavo
LASTING ENAMEL
CUTE, RIGHT?
IT'S OCCHI-KUN'S FAMILY.
Consider it a present from your new friend.
...
Ha ha ha!
HE DID THAT TO YOU TOO?!
He's done that to me lots of times.
KEI'S FAMILY RUNS A NAIL PARLOR, SO...
...NAILS WERE HIS HOBBY BEFORE HE EVEN REALIZED IT.
I'm going to be the best nail artist!!
(Imitation of Narumi's pose)
THAT'S HYSTERICAL!
Ha ha ha!
They all have glasses?
That's so funny!

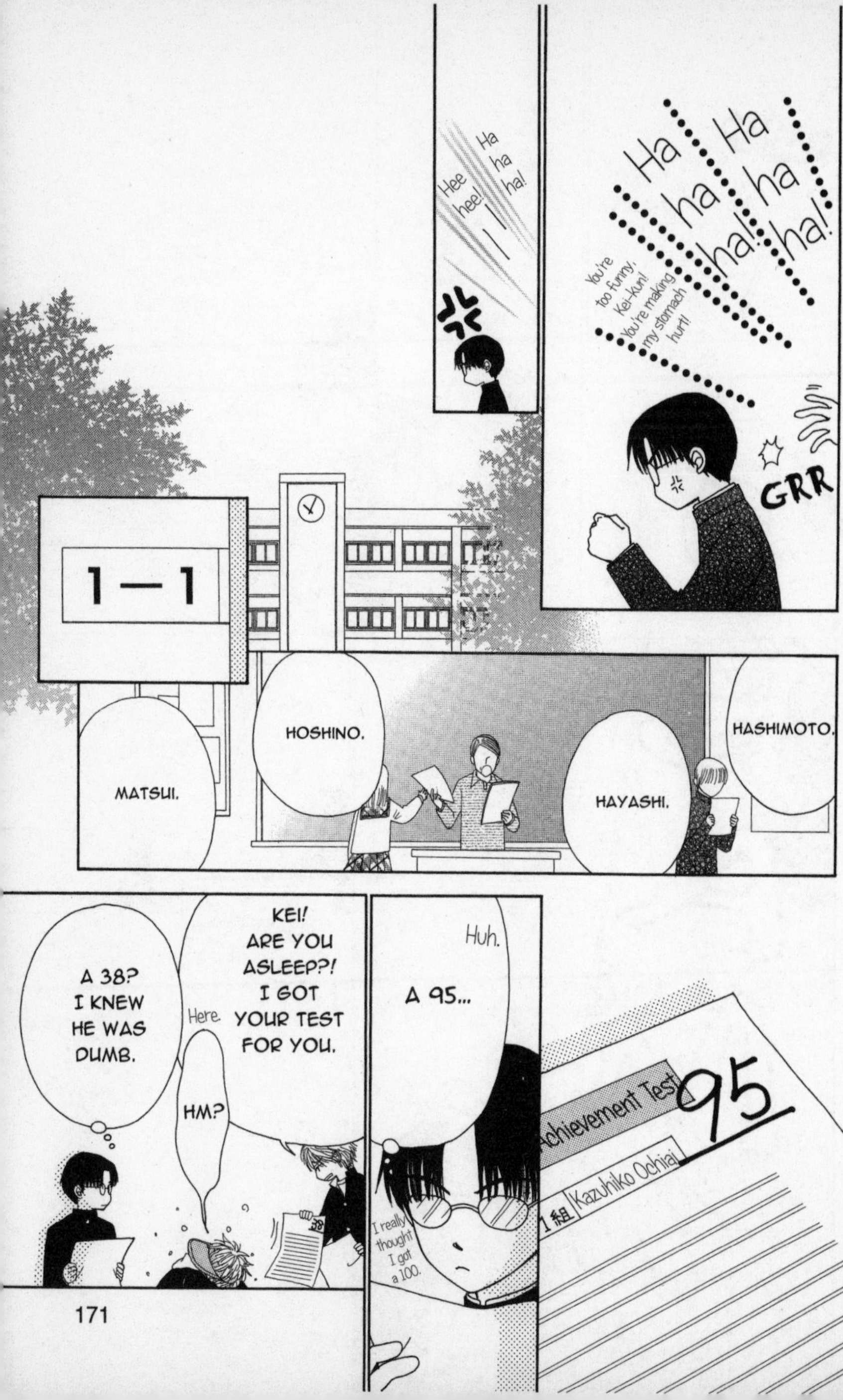
Ha ha ha! Ha ha ha!
You're too funny, Kei-kun! You're making my stomach hurt!
GRR
Ha ha ha!
Hee hee!
1—1
HASHIMOTO.
HAYASHI.
HOSHINO.
MATSUI.
Achievement Test
95
1組 Kazuhiko Ochiai
Huh.
A 95...
I really thought I got a 100.
KEI! ARE YOU ASLEEP?! I GOT YOUR TEST FOR YOU.
Here.
HM?
38
A 38? I KNEW HE WAS DUMB.

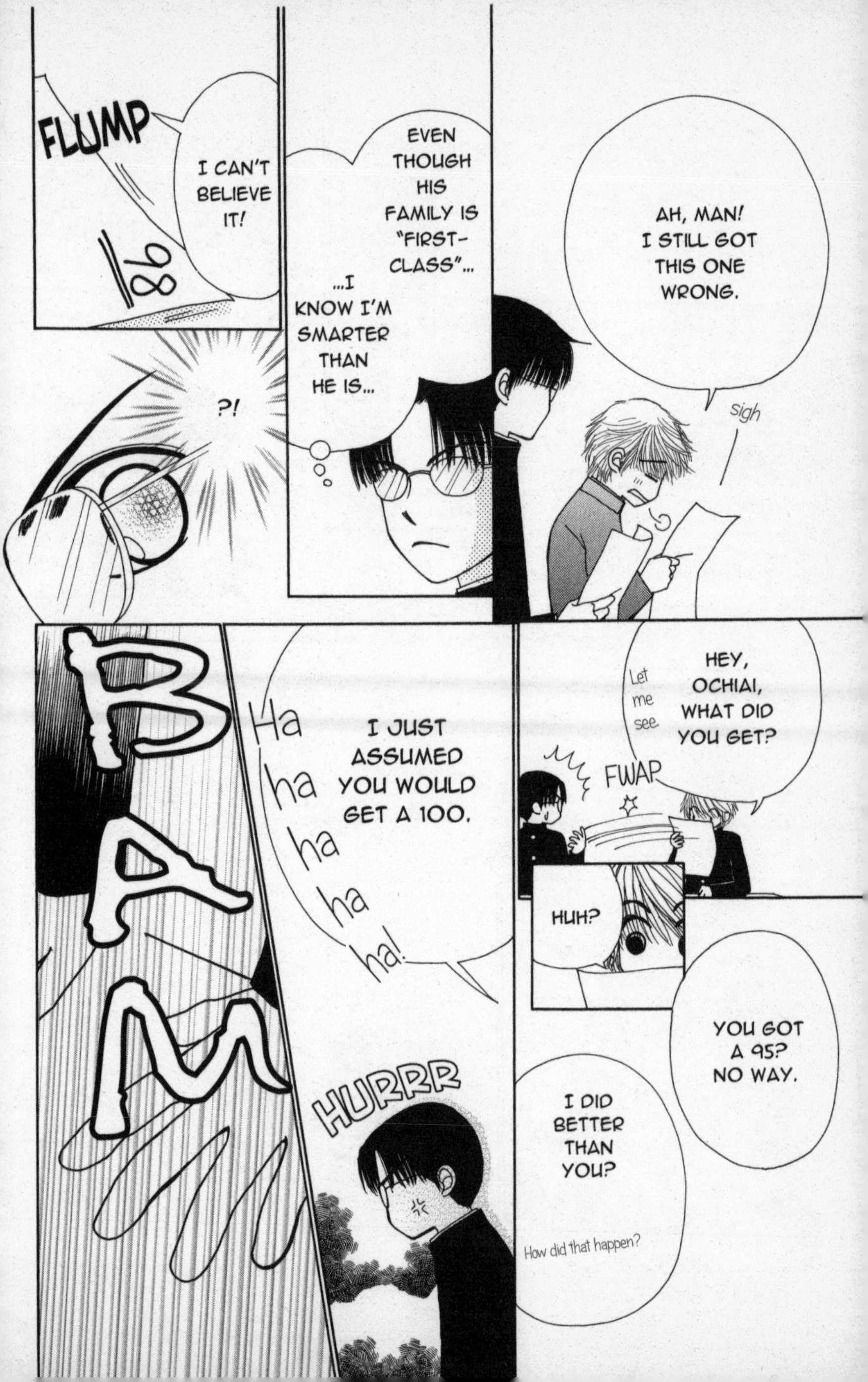
AH, MAN! I STILL GOT THIS ONE WRONG.
sigh
EVEN THOUGH HIS FAMILY IS "FIRST-CLASS"...
...I KNOW I'M SMARTER THAN HE IS...
FLUMP
I CAN'T BELIEVE IT!
98
?!
HEY, OCHIAI, WHAT DID YOU GET?
Let me see
FWAP
HUH?
YOU GOT A 95? NO WAY.
I DID BETTER THAN YOU?
How did that happen?
I JUST ASSUMED YOU WOULD GET A 100.
Ha ha ha ha ha!
HURRR
BAM

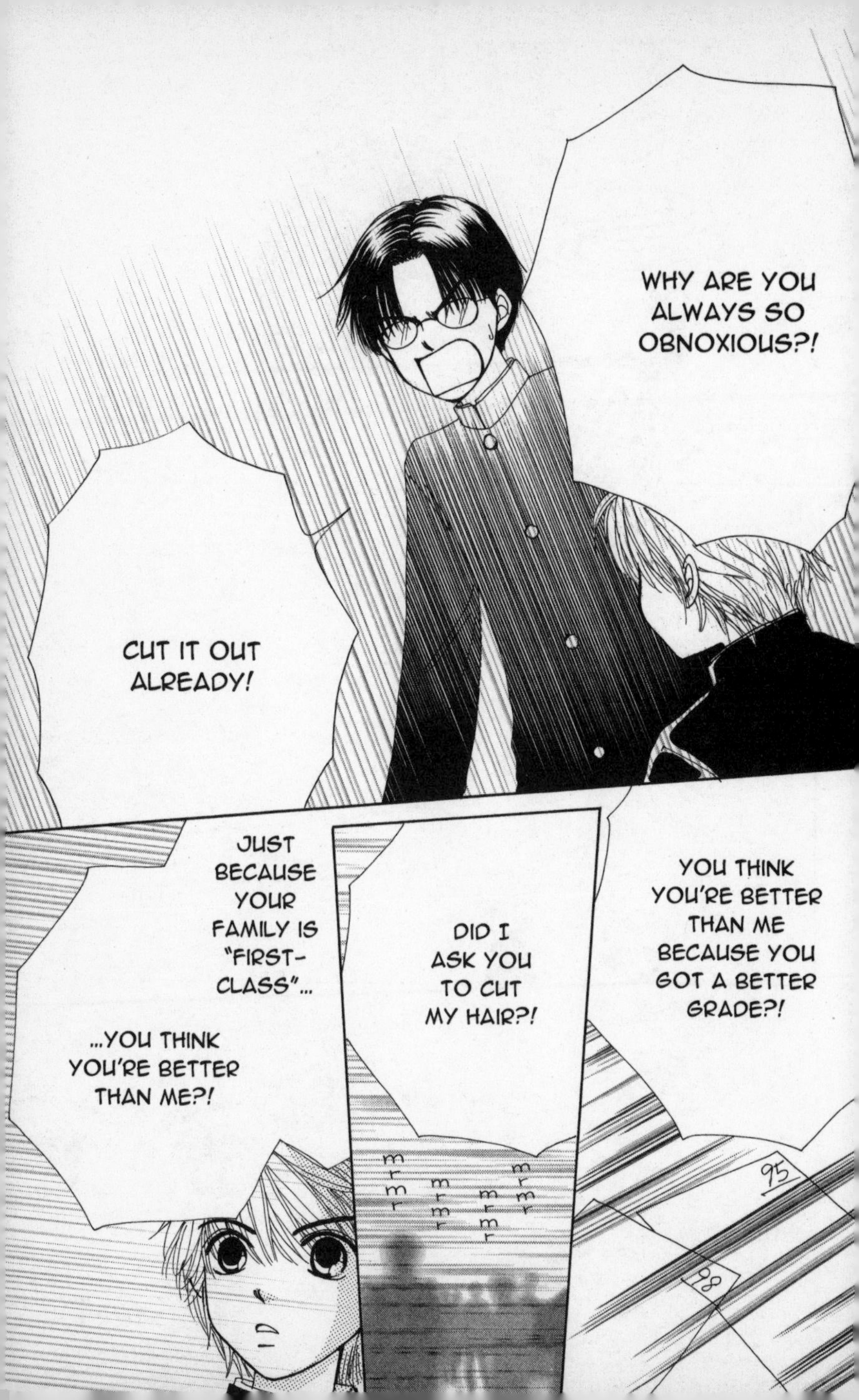
WHY ARE YOU ALWAYS SO OBNOXIOUS?!
CUT IT OUT ALREADY!
YOU THINK YOU'RE BETTER THAN ME BECAUSE YOU GOT A BETTER GRADE?!
DID I ASK YOU TO CUT MY HAIR?!
JUST BECAUSE YOUR FAMILY IS "FIRST-CLASS"...
...YOU THINK YOU'RE BETTER THAN ME?!
95
98

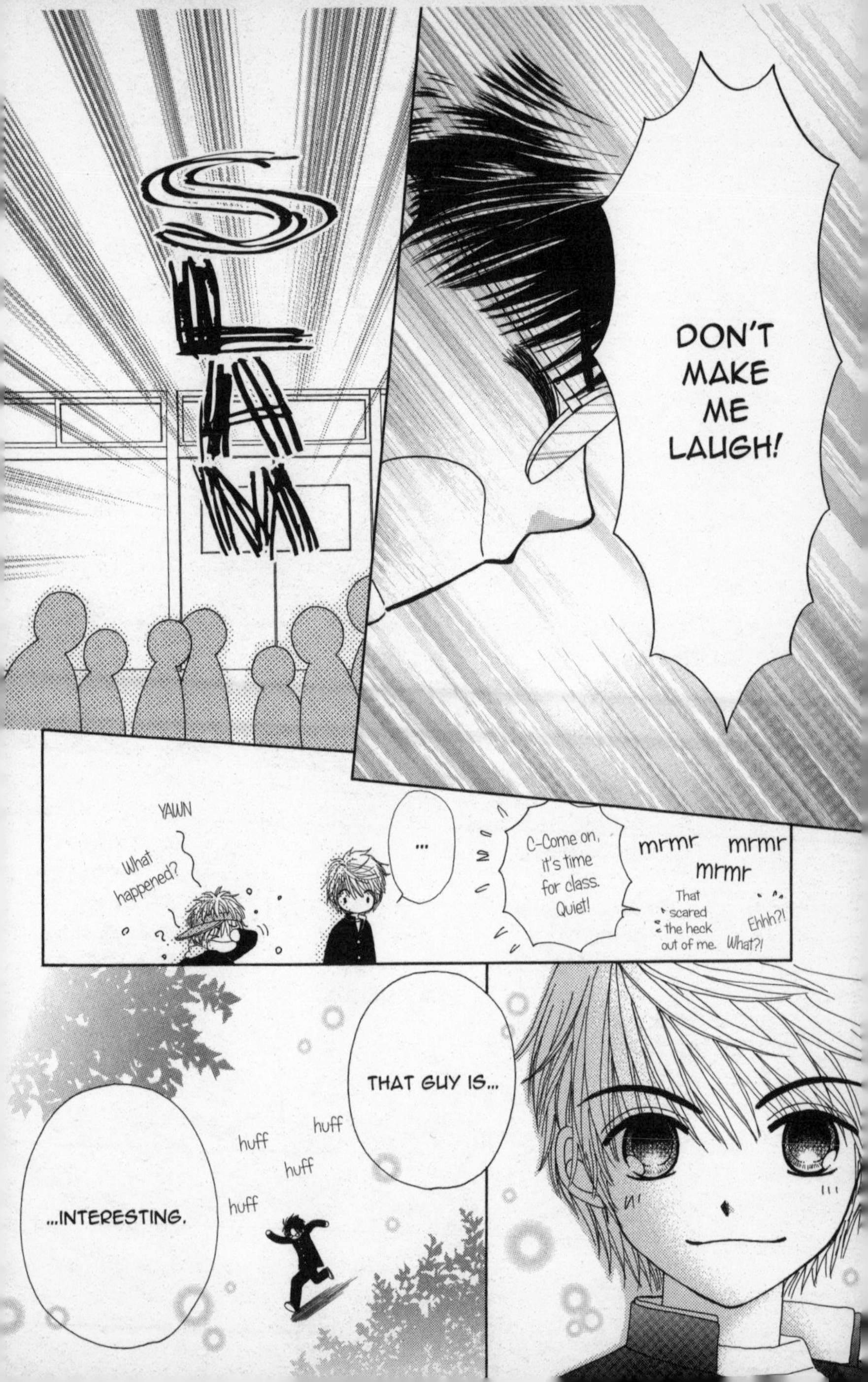
DON'T MAKE ME LAUGH!
SLAM
mrmr mrmr mrmr
That scared the heck out of me.
Ehhh?! What?!
C-Come on, it's time for class. Quiet!
...
YAWN
What happened?
THAT GUY IS...
huff huff huff huff
...INTERESTING.

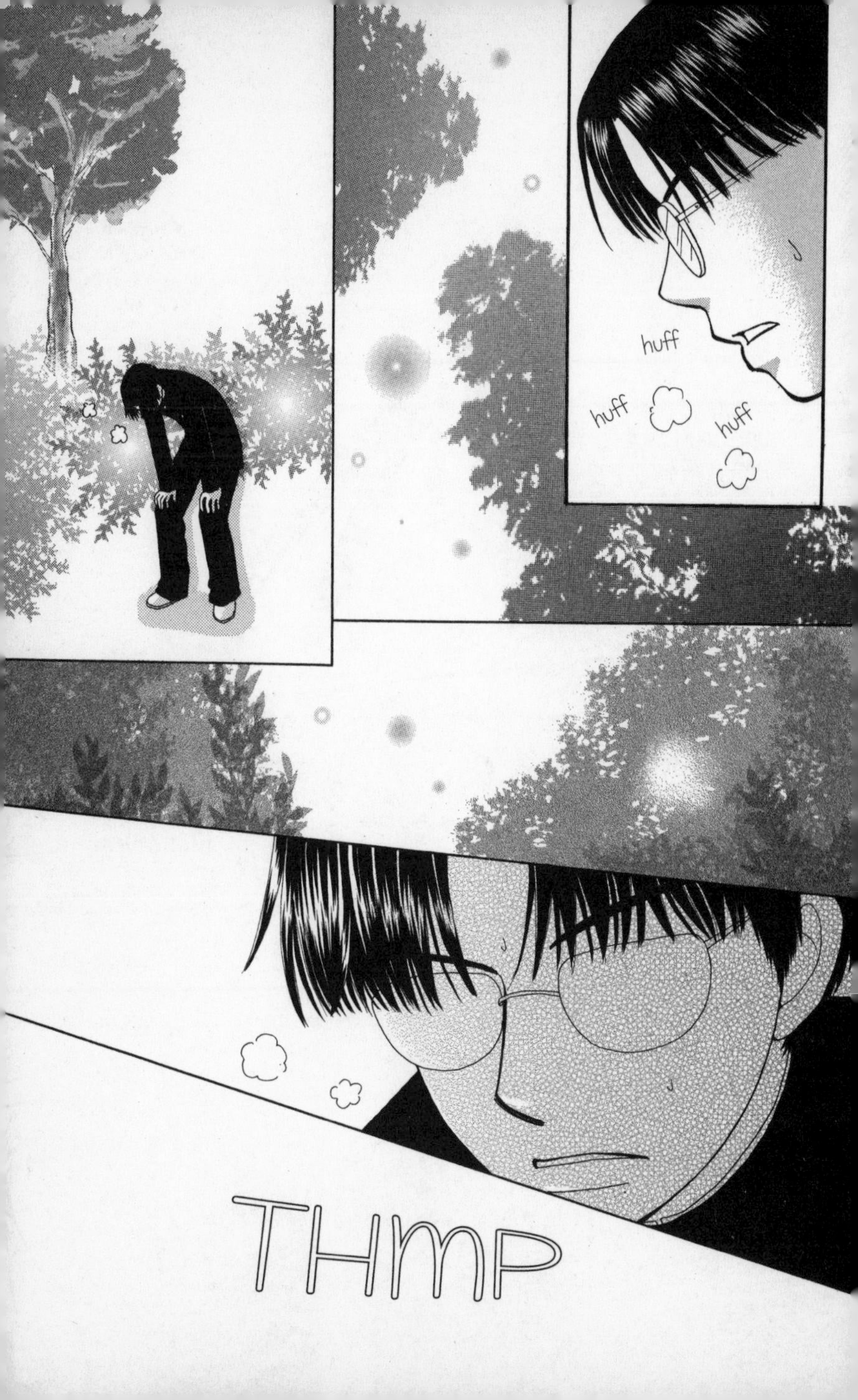
huff
huff
huff
THMP

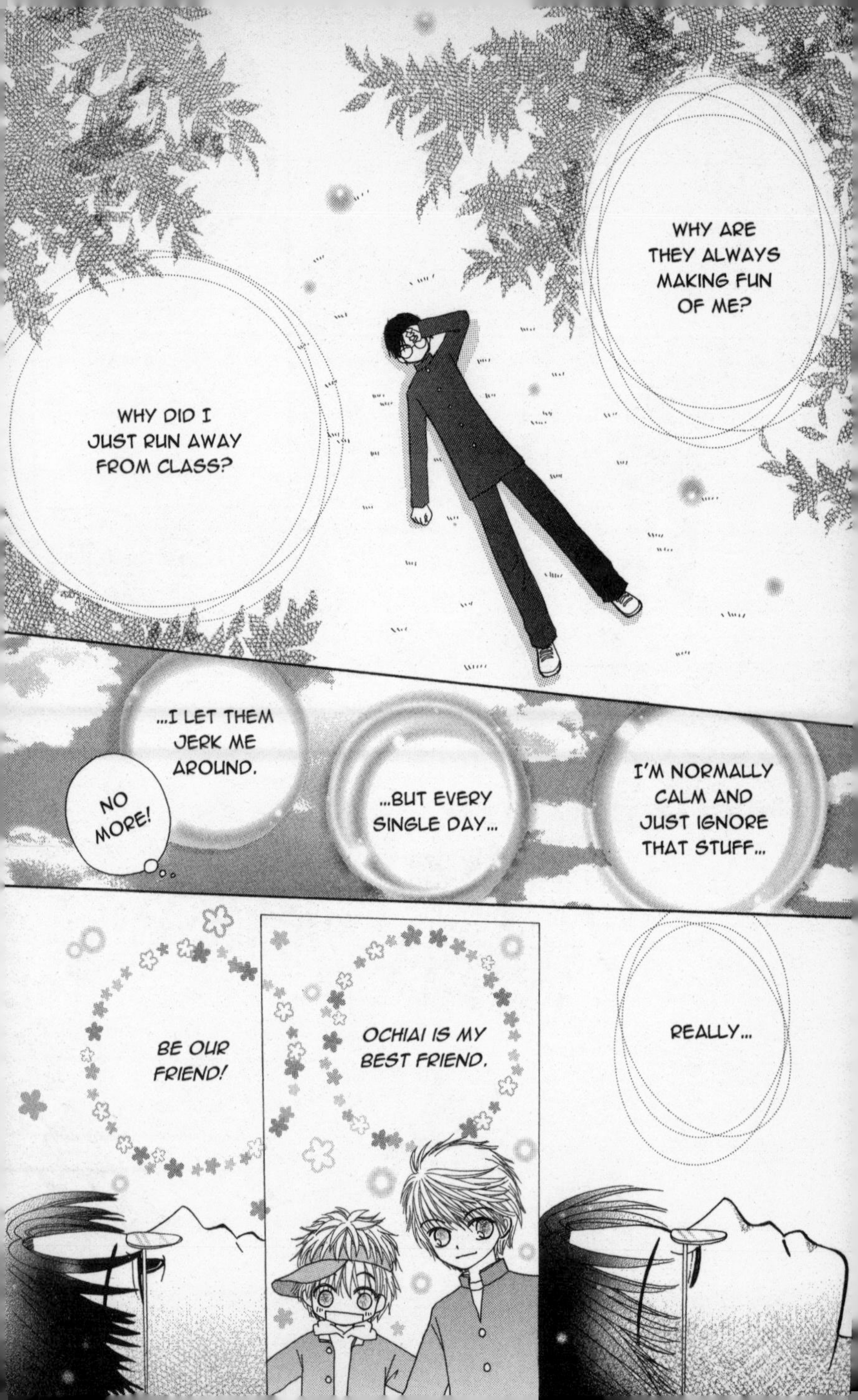
WHY ARE THEY ALWAYS MAKING FUN OF ME?
WHY DID I JUST RUN AWAY FROM CLASS?
I'M NORMALLY CALM AND JUST IGNORE THAT STUFF...
...BUT EVERY SINGLE DAY...
...I LET THEM JERK ME AROUND.
NO MORE!
REALLY...
OCHIAI IS MY BEST FRIEND.
BE OUR FRIEND!

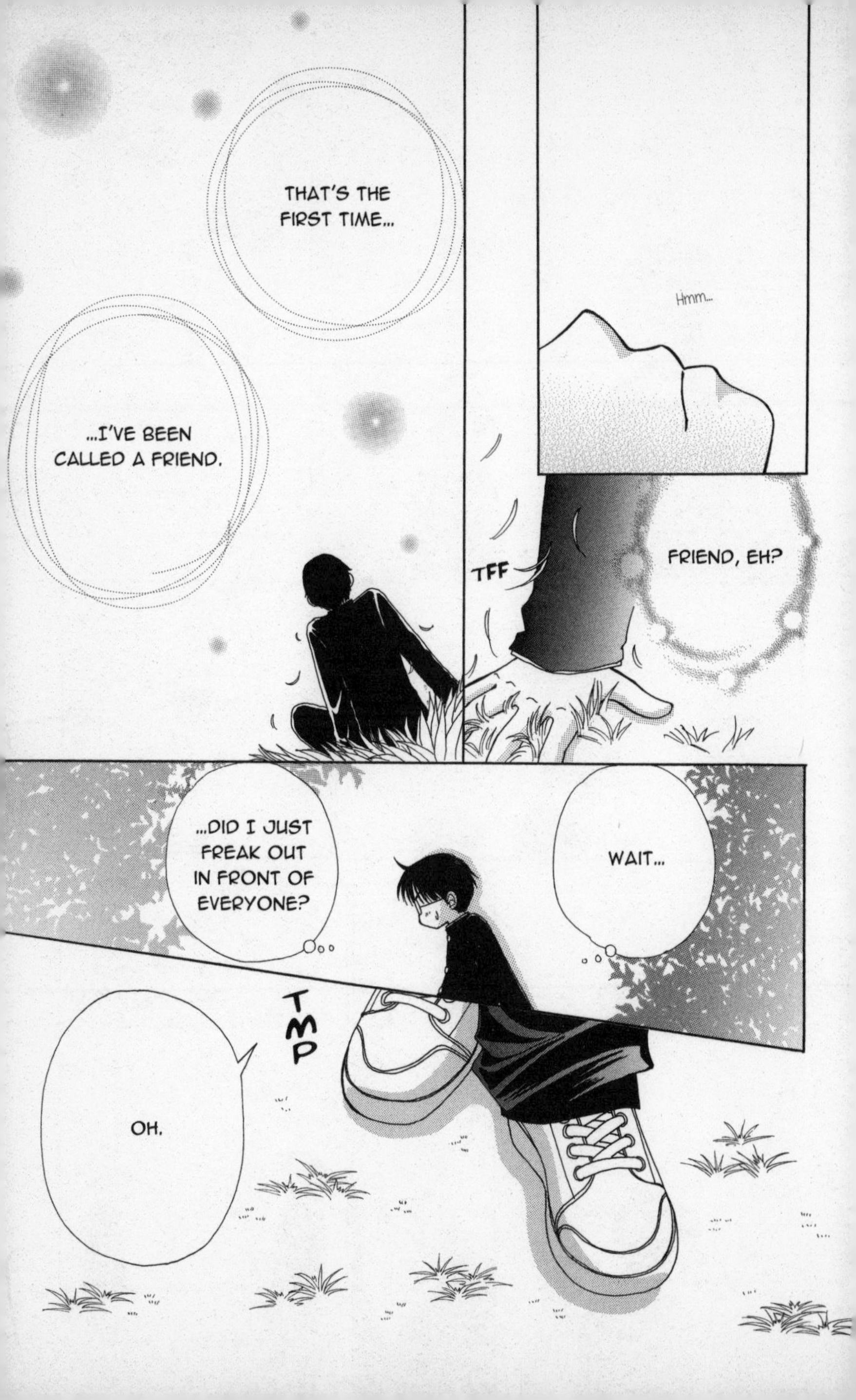
Hmm...
FRIEND, EH?
TFF
THAT'S THE FIRST TIME...
...I'VE BEEN CALLED A FRIEND.
WAIT...
...DID I JUST FREAK OUT IN FRONT OF EVERYONE?
TMP
OH.

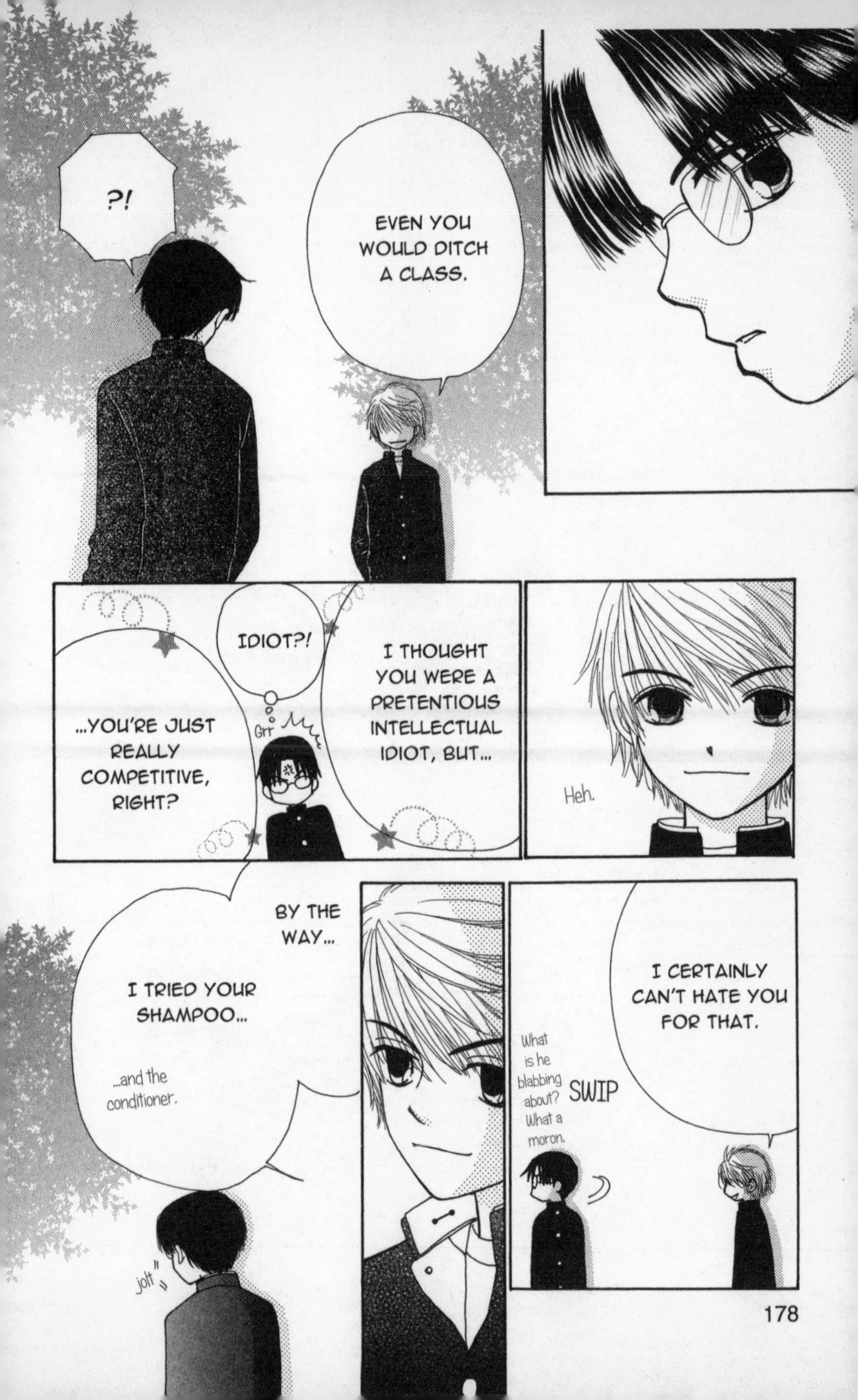
EVEN YOU WOULD DITCH A CLASS.
?!
Heh.
I THOUGHT YOU WERE A PRETENTIOUS INTELLECTUAL IDIOT, BUT...
IDIOT?!
Grr
...YOU'RE JUST REALLY COMPETITIVE, RIGHT?
I CERTAINLY CAN'T HATE YOU FOR THAT.
SWIP
What is he blabbing about? What a moron.
BY THE WAY...
I TRIED YOUR SHAMPOO...
...and the conditioner.
jolt

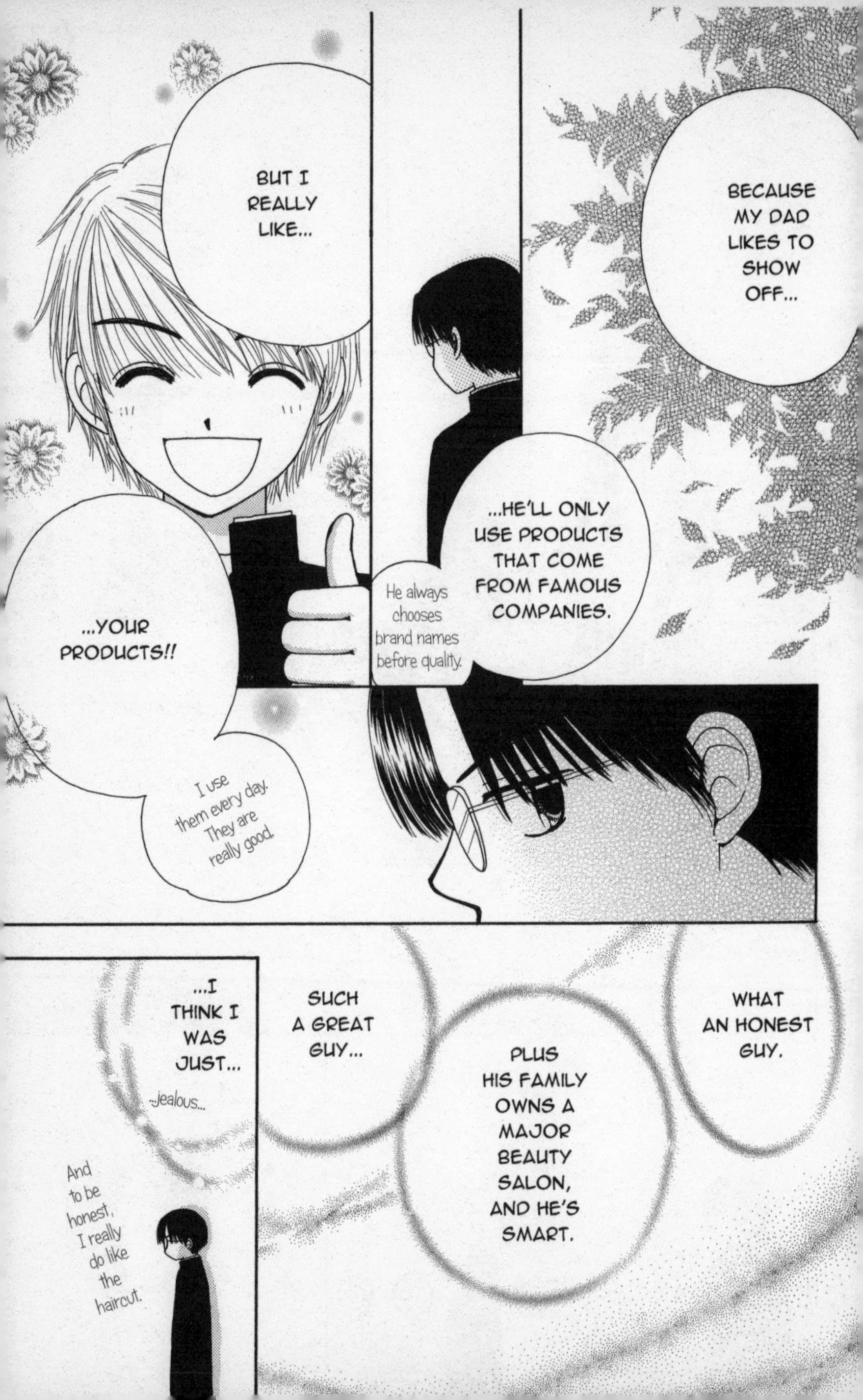
BECAUSE MY DAD LIKES TO SHOW OFF...
...HE'LL ONLY USE PRODUCTS THAT COME FROM FAMOUS COMPANIES.
He always chooses brand names before quality.
BUT I REALLY LIKE...
...YOUR PRODUCTS!!
I use them every day. They are really good.
WHAT AN HONEST GUY.
PLUS HIS FAMILY OWNS A MAJOR BEAUTY SALON, AND HE'S SMART.
SUCH A GREAT GUY...
...I THINK I WAS JUST...
...jealous...
And to be honest, I really do like the haircut.

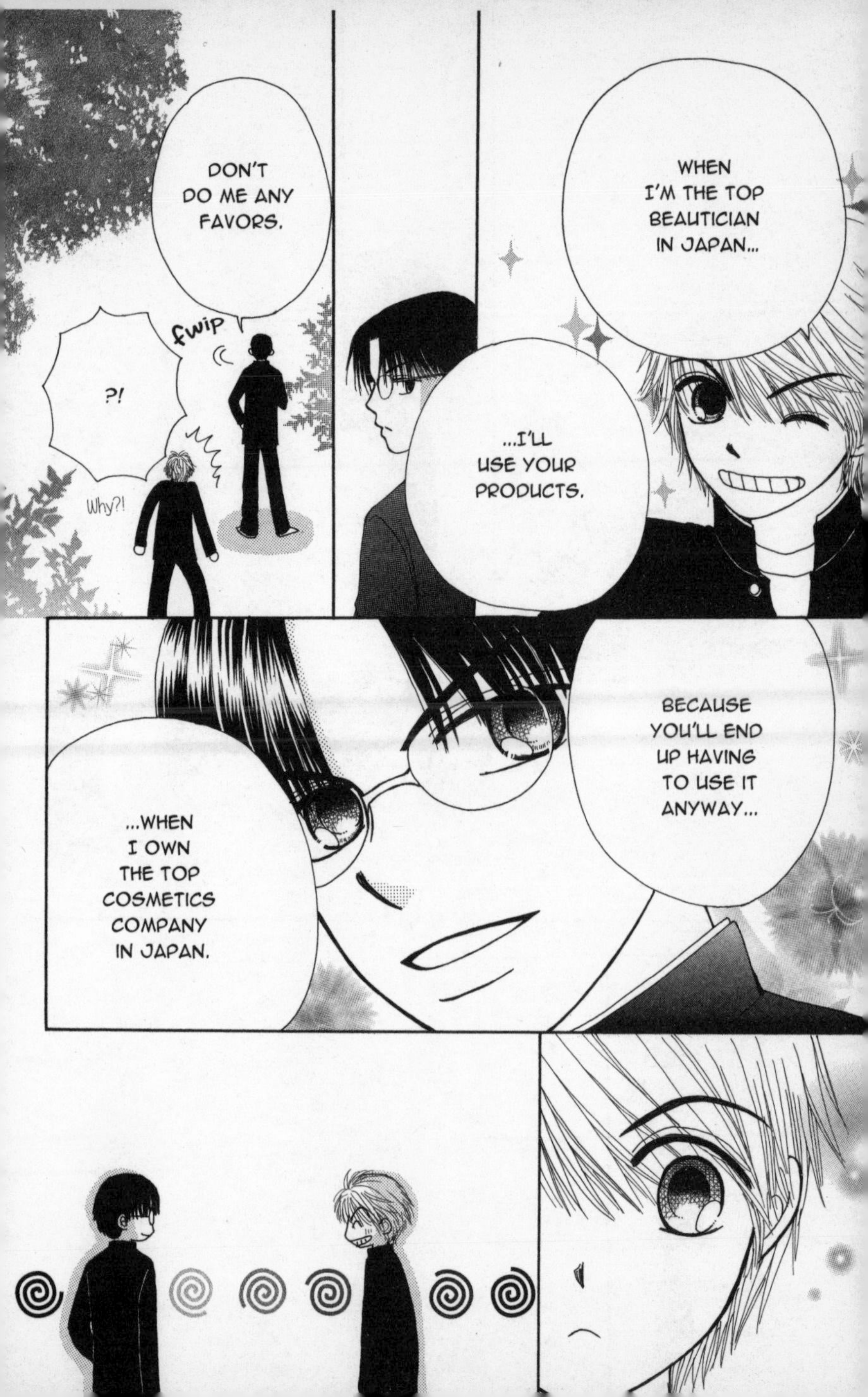
WHEN I'M THE TOP BEAUTICIAN IN JAPAN...
...I'LL USE YOUR PRODUCTS.
DON'T DO ME ANY FAVORS.
fwip
?!
Why?!
BECAUSE YOU'LL END UP HAVING TO USE IT ANYWAY...
...WHEN I OWN THE TOP COSMETICS COMPANY IN JAPAN.

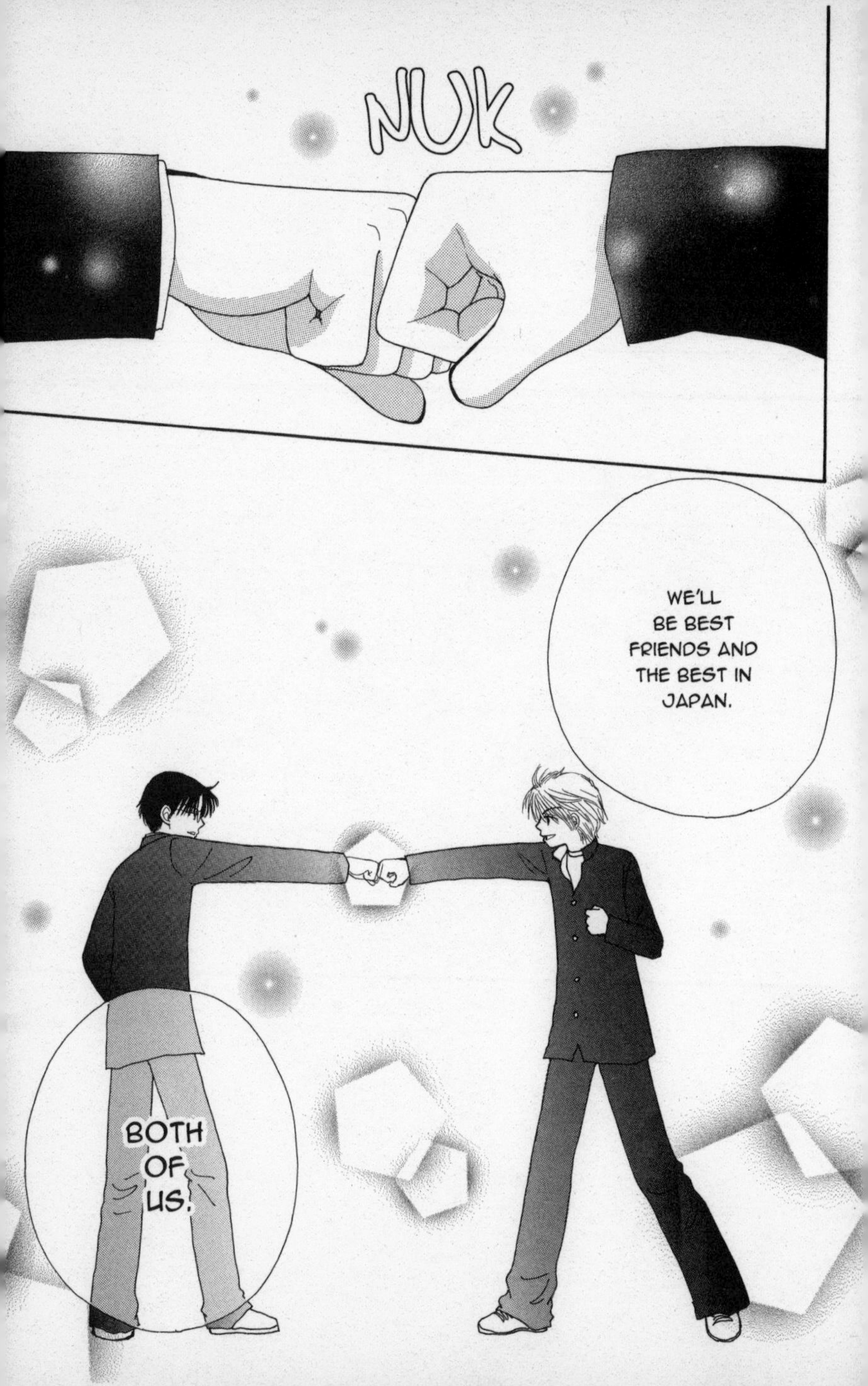
NUK
WE'LL BE BEST FRIENDS AND THE BEST IN JAPAN.
BOTH OF US.

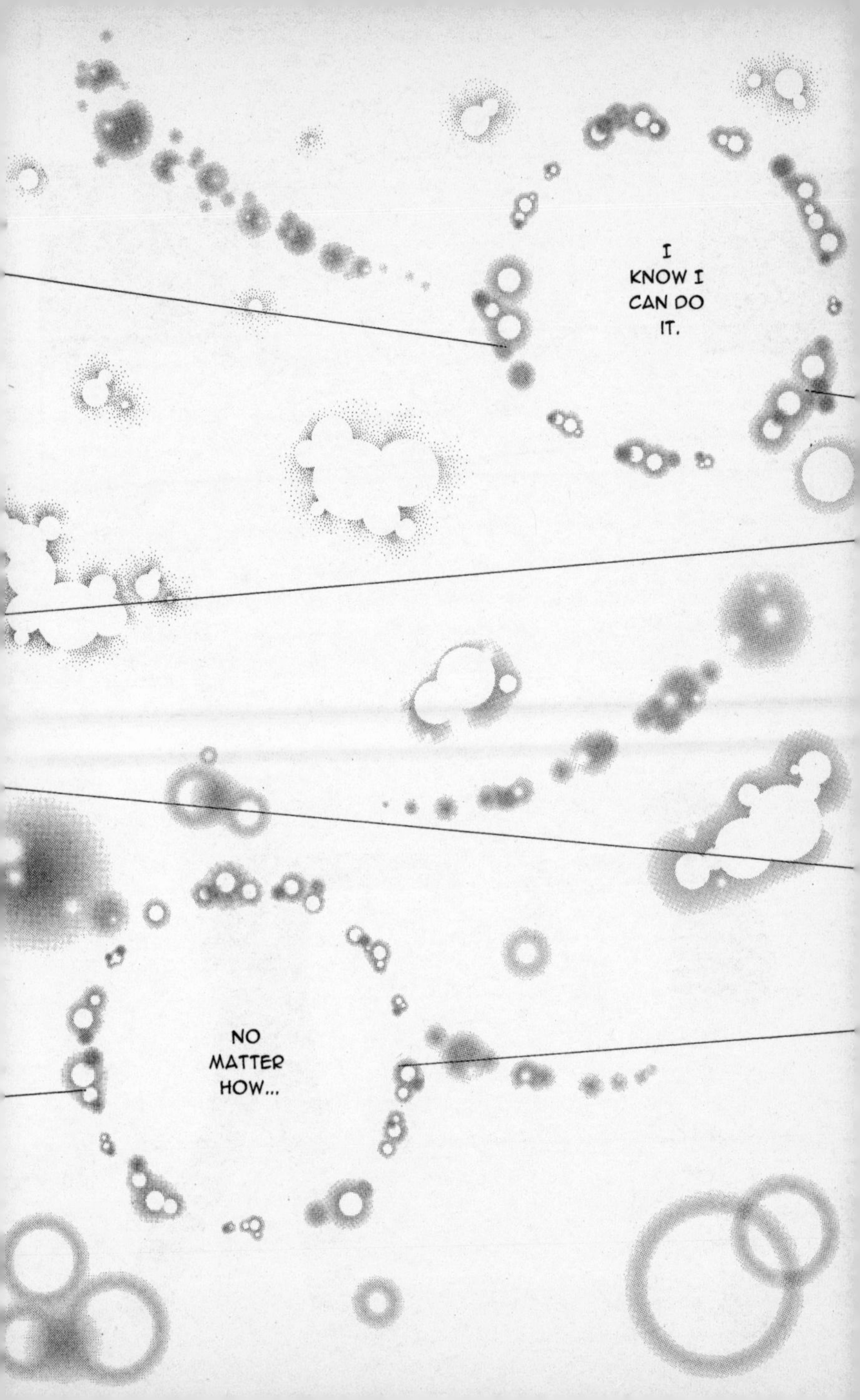
I KNOW I CAN DO IT.
NO MATTER HOW...

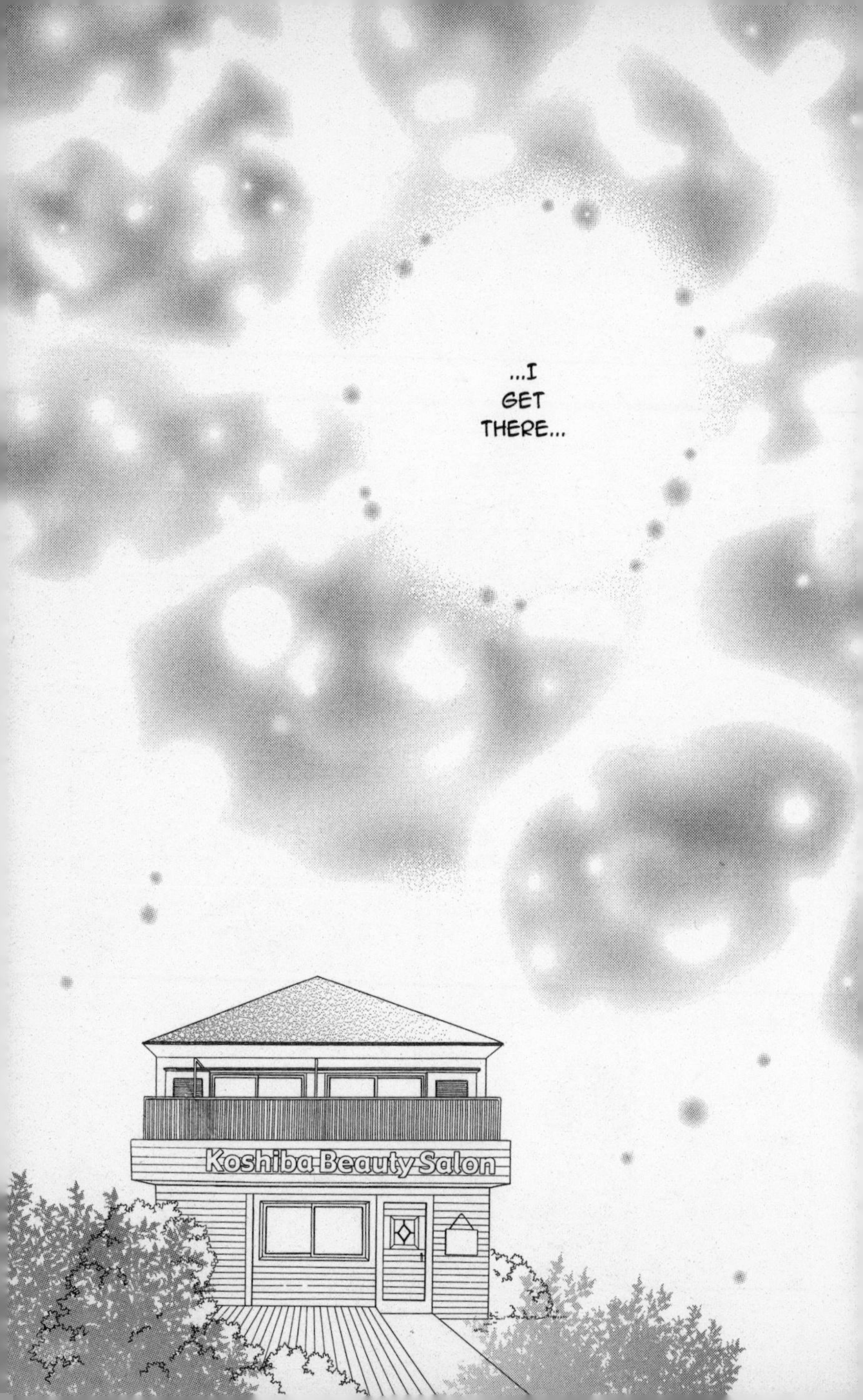
...I GET THERE...
Koshiba Beauty Salon

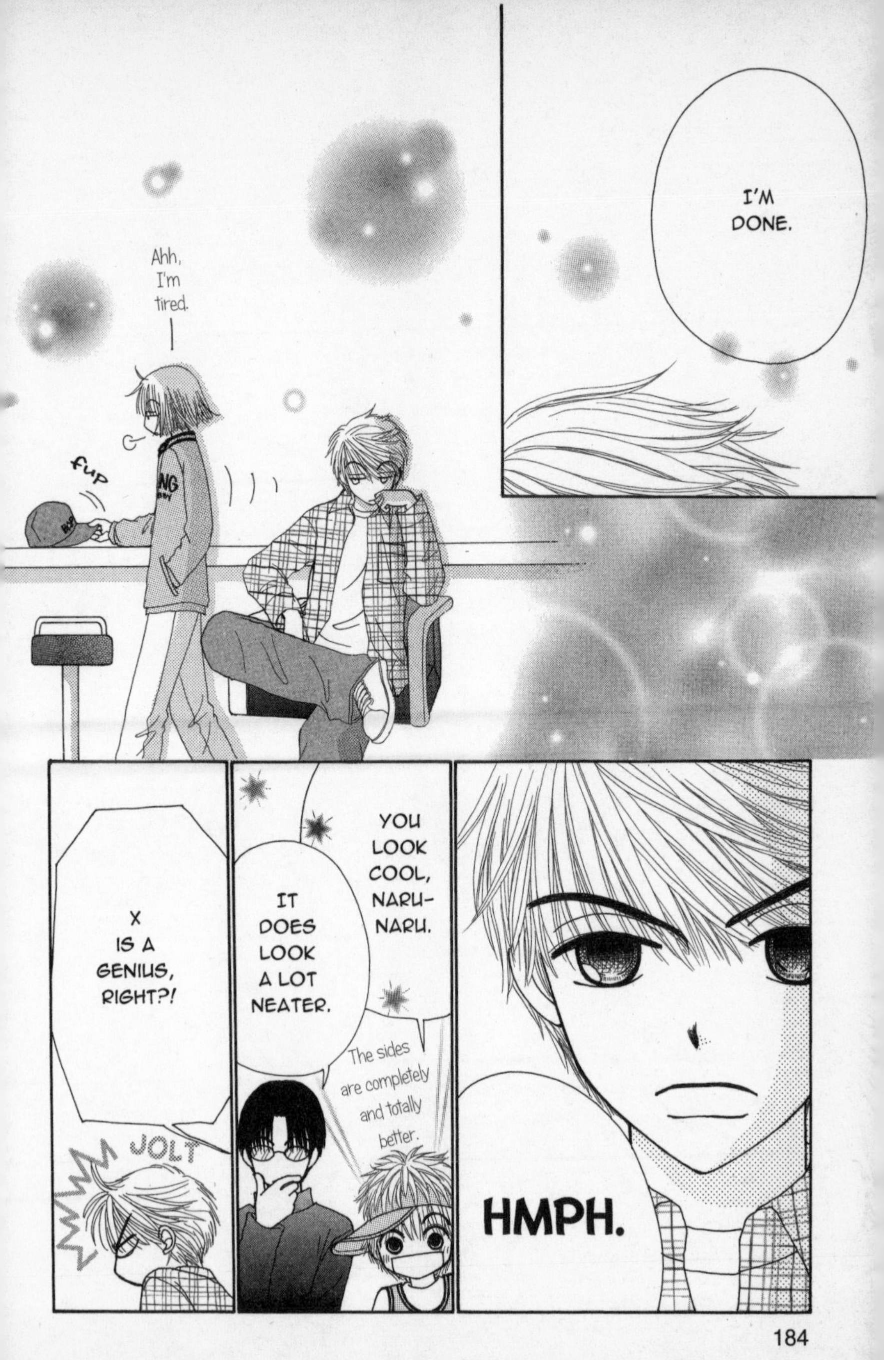
I'M DONE.
Ahh, I'm tired.
fup
HMPH.
YOU LOOK COOL, NARU-NARU.
IT DOES LOOK A LOT NEATER.
The sides are completely and totally better.
X IS A GENIUS, RIGHT?!
JOLT

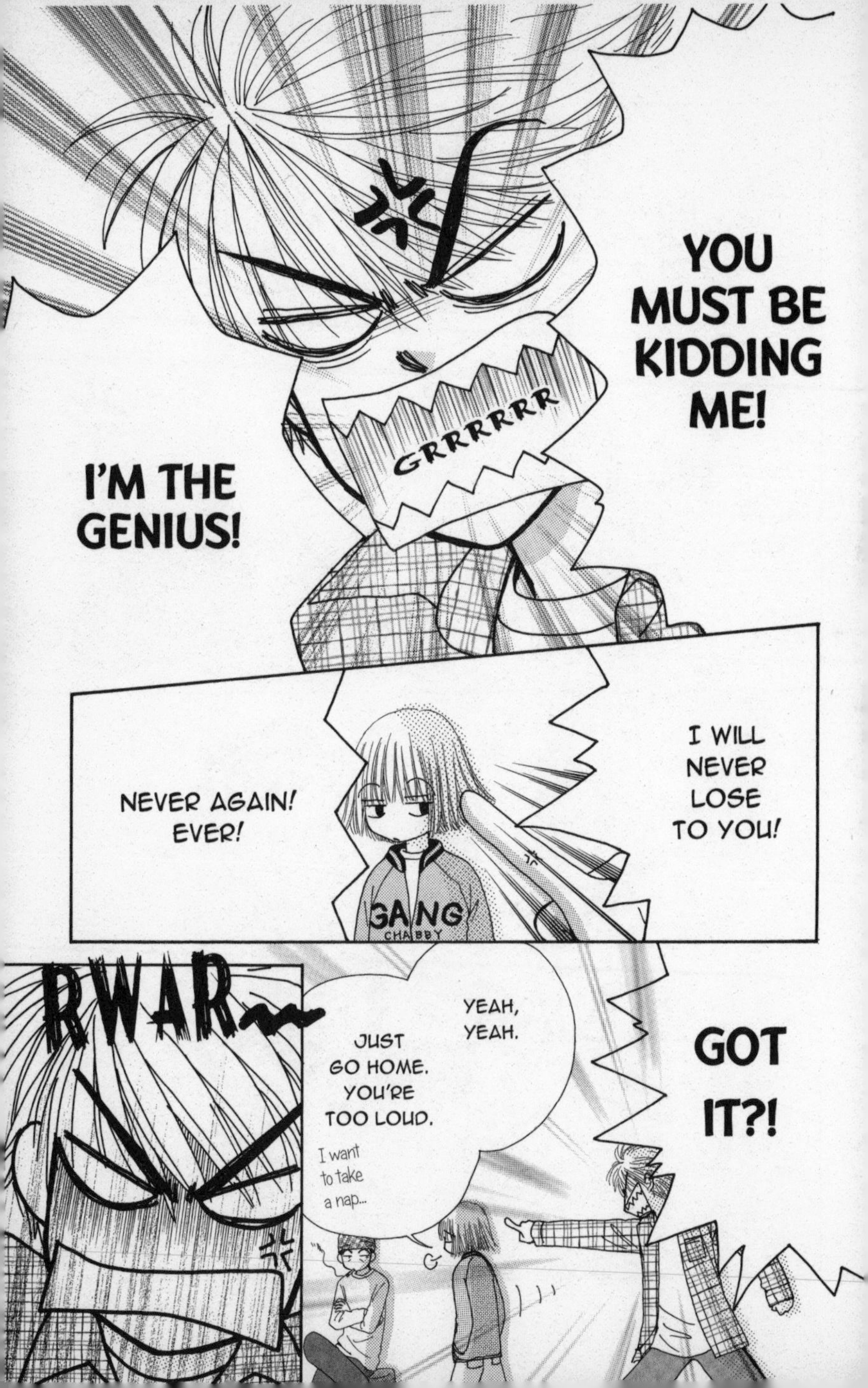
YOU MUST BE KIDDING ME!
GRRRRRR
I'M THE GENIUS!
I WILL NEVER LOSE TO YOU!
NEVER AGAIN! EVER!
GANG
CHABBY
GOT IT?!
YEAH, YEAH.
JUST GO HOME. YOU'RE TOO LOUD.
I want to take a nap...
RWAR

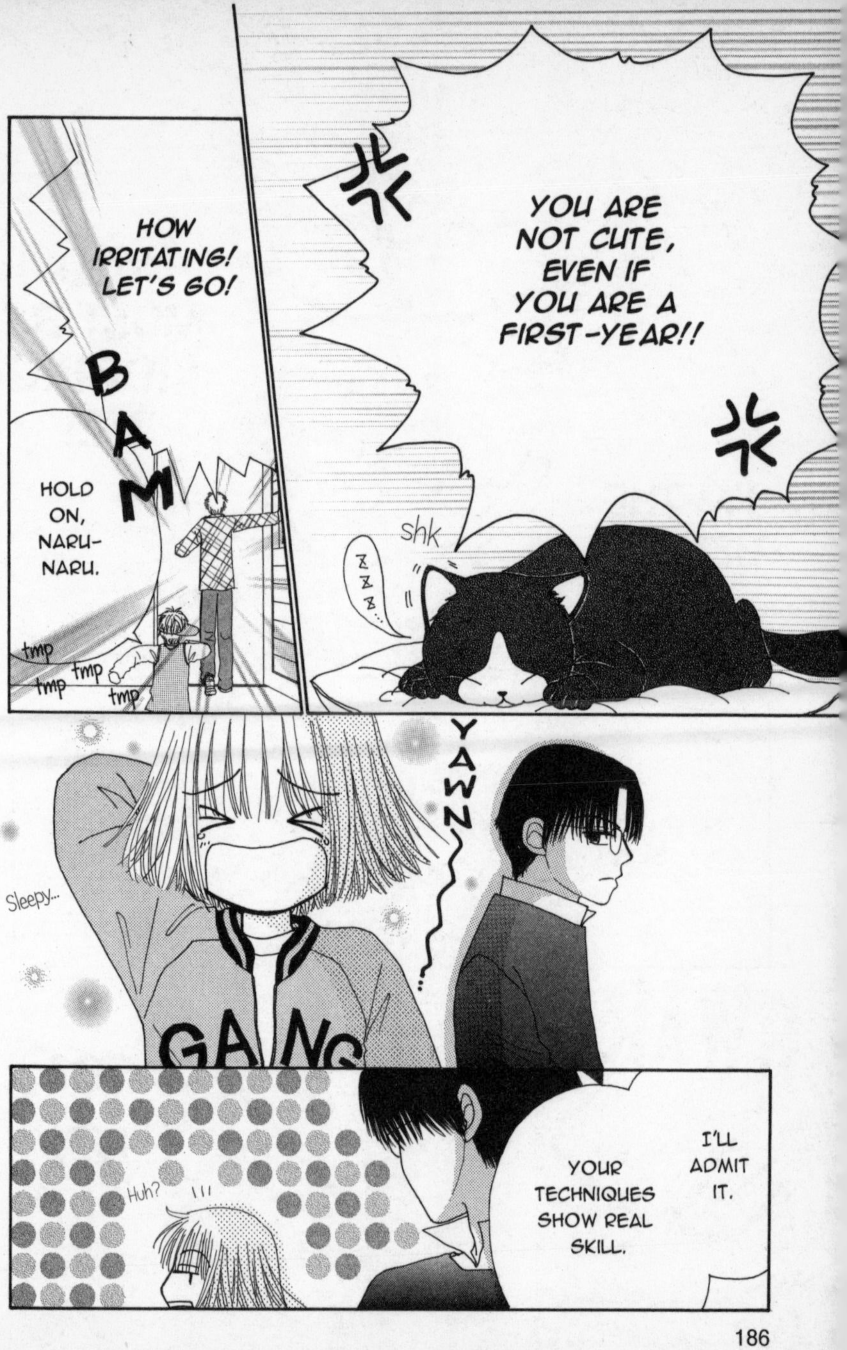
YOU ARE NOT CUTE, EVEN IF YOU ARE A FIRST-YEAR!!
shk
HOW IRRITATING! LET'S GO!
BAM
HOLD ON, NARU-NARU.
tmp tmp tmp tmp
YAWN
Sleepy...
GANG
I'LL ADMIT IT.
YOUR TECHNIQUES SHOW REAL SKILL.
Huh?

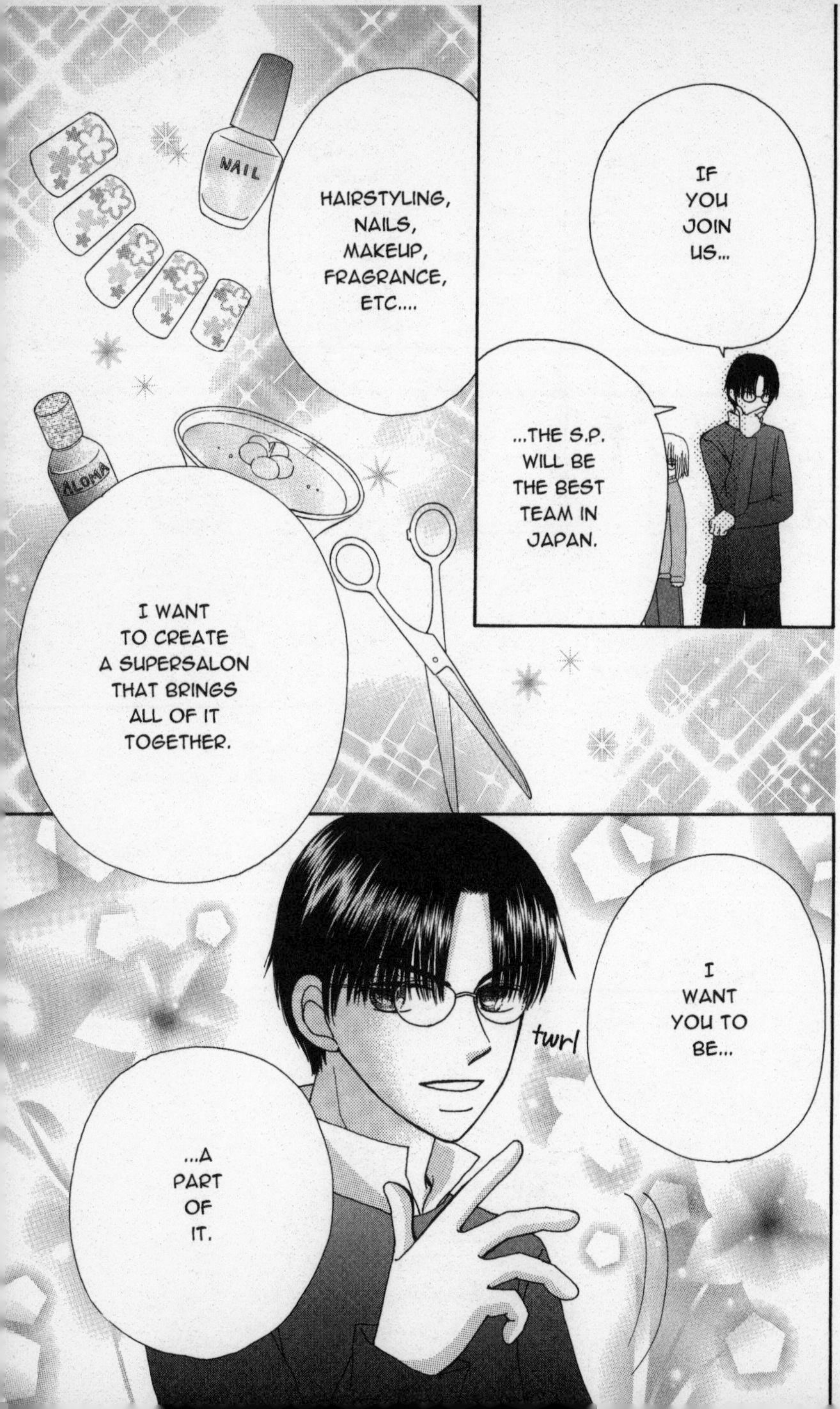
IF YOU JOIN US...
...THE S.P. WILL BE THE BEST TEAM IN JAPAN.
HAIRSTYLING, NAILS, MAKEUP, FRAGRANCE, ETC....
NAIL
ALOMA
I WANT TO CREATE A SUPERSALON THAT BRINGS ALL OF IT TOGETHER.
I WANT YOU TO BE...
twrl
...A PART OF IT.

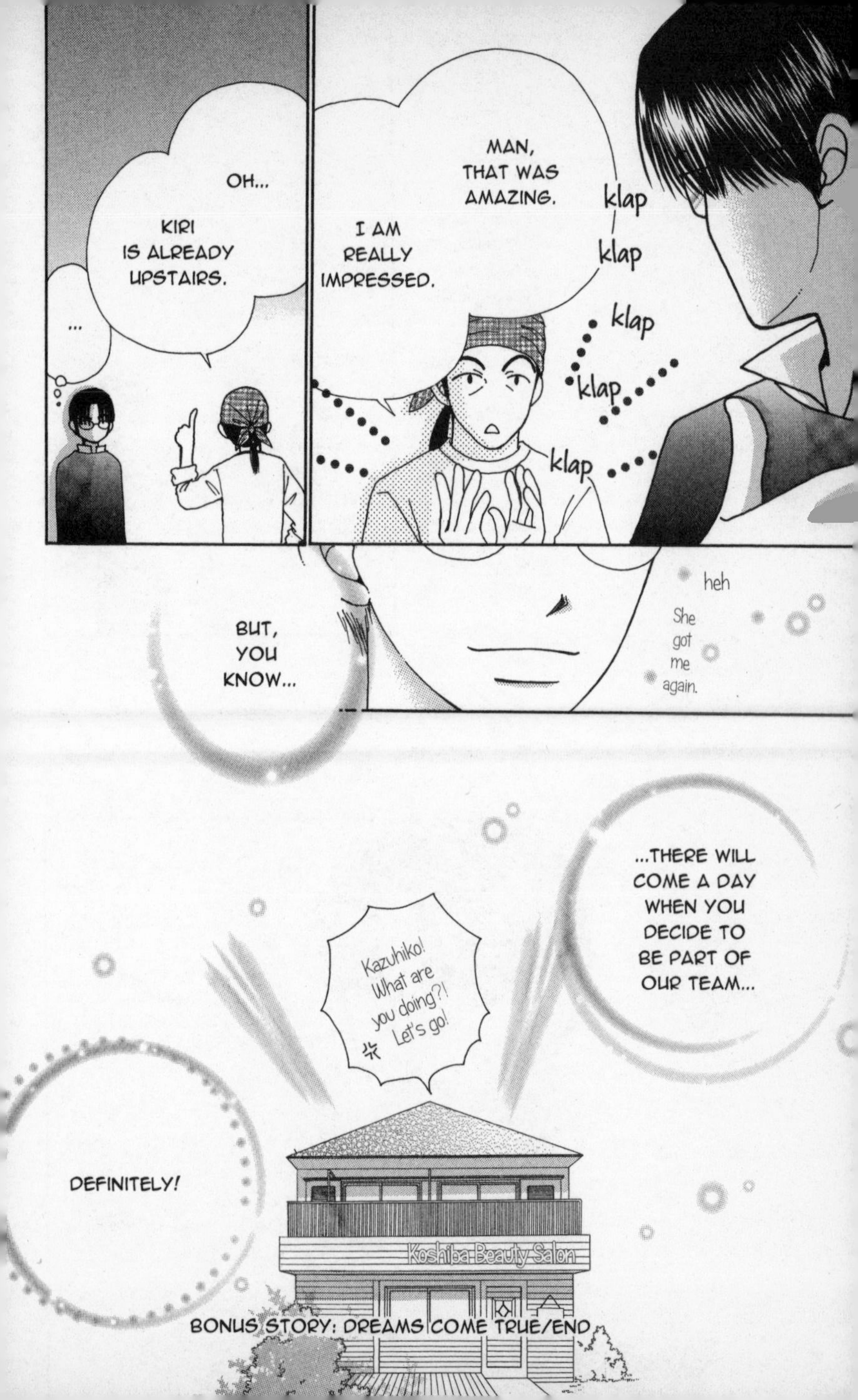

MAN, THAT WAS AMAZING.
I AM REALLY IMPRESSED.
klap
klap
klap
klap
klap
OH... KIRI IS ALREADY UPSTAIRS.
...
heh
She got me again.
BUT, YOU KNOW...
...THERE WILL COME A DAY WHEN YOU DECIDE TO BE PART OF OUR TEAM...
Kazuhiko! What are you doing?! Let's go!
DEFINITELY!
Koshiba Beauty Salon
BONUS STORY: DREAMS COME TRUE/END

Extra

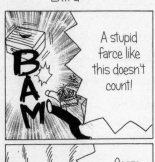

A stupid farce like this doesn't count!
BAM
Geeze. Occhi's makeup box is...
Ack! Sorry, Kazuhiko.
I'll pay you back for whatever broke.
shk
...what the?! They're all glasses!
Yay! Filled to the brim with glasses.
Seriously?!
wipe wipe
...So now,
I'll see you again in volume 3!
Kiyoko Arai

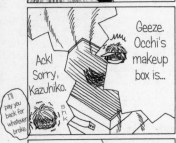

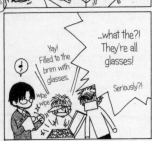

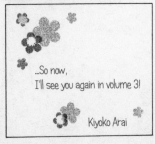

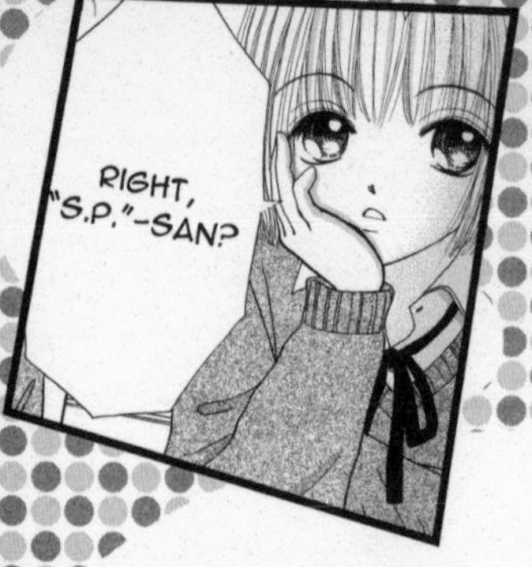
RIGHT, "S.P."-SAN?

Honorifics

In Japan, people are usually addressed by their name followed by a suffix. The suffix shows familiarity or respect, depending on the relationship.

Male (familiar): first or last name + kun
Female (familiar): first or last name + chan
Upperclassman (polite): last name + senpai
Adult (polite): last name + san

+ sama: A deferential suffix that is also used by fan girls when referring to the object of their adoration.

+ sensei: A suffix used for respected professionals, such as teachers, doctors, and mangaka.

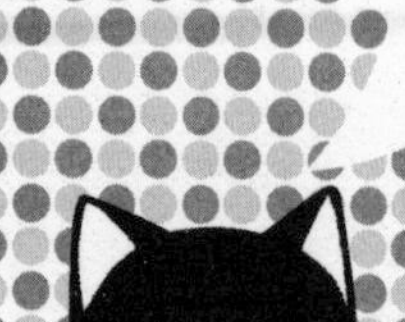

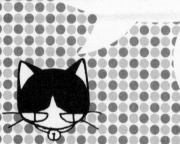

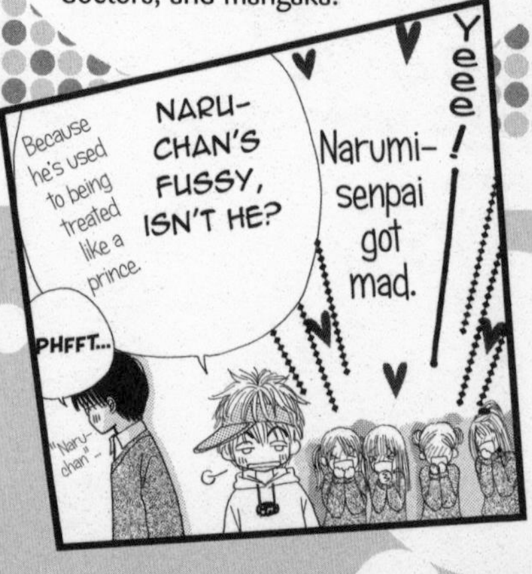
Yeee!
Narumi-senpai got mad.
NARU-CHAN'S FUSSY, ISN'T HE?
Because he's used to being treated like a prince.
PHFFT...
"Naru-chan"...

Author's Note

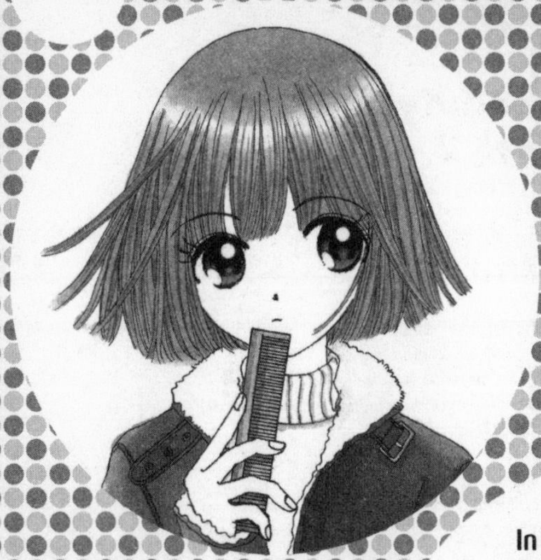

In January 2004, I adopted a toy poodle named Kanon, and she is so very cute! When I first got her, she was so small she could fit in the palm of my hand, but in the last five months, she's grown so fast and so big that it almost seems like a trick! Right now I'm in the middle of trying to "train" her!

Kiyoko Arai was born in Tokyo, and now resides in Chiba Prefecture. In 1999, she received the prestigious Shogakukan Manga Award for *Angel Lip*. The popular *Dr. Rin ni Kiitemite!* (Ask Dr. Rin!) was made into an animated TV show. *Beauty Pop* is her current series running in *Ciao* magazine.

Beauty Pop
Vol. 2
The Shojo Beat Manga Edition

STORY AND ART BY
KIYOKO ARAI

English Adaptation/Amanda Hubbard
Translation/Miho Nishida
Touch-up Art & Lettering/Elena Diaz
Design/Izumi Hirayama
Editor/Nancy Thistlethwaite

Managing Editor/Megan Bates
Editorial Director/Elizabeth Kawasaki
VP & Editor in Chief/Yumi Hoashi
Sr. Director of Acquisitions/Rika Inouye
Sr. VP of Marketing/Liza Coppola
Exec. VP of Sales & Marketing/John Easum
Publisher/Hyoe Narita

© 2004 Kiyoko ARAI/Shogakukan Inc. First published by
Shogakukan Inc. in Japan as "Beauty Pop." New and adapted
artwork and text © 2006 VIZ Media, LLC. The BEAUTY POP
logo is a trademark of VIZ Media, LLC. All rights reserved.
Some scenes have been modified from the original Japanese
edition. The stories, characters and incidents mentioned in this
publication are entirely fictional.

No portion of this book may be reproduced or transmitted in
any form or by any means without written permission from the
copyright holders.

Printed in Canada

Published by VIZ Media, LLC
P.O. Box 77010
San Francisco, CA 94107

Shojo Beat Manga Edition
10 9 8 7 6 5 4 3 2
First printing, December 2006
Second printing, December 2006

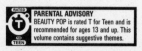

www.viz.com

store.viz.com

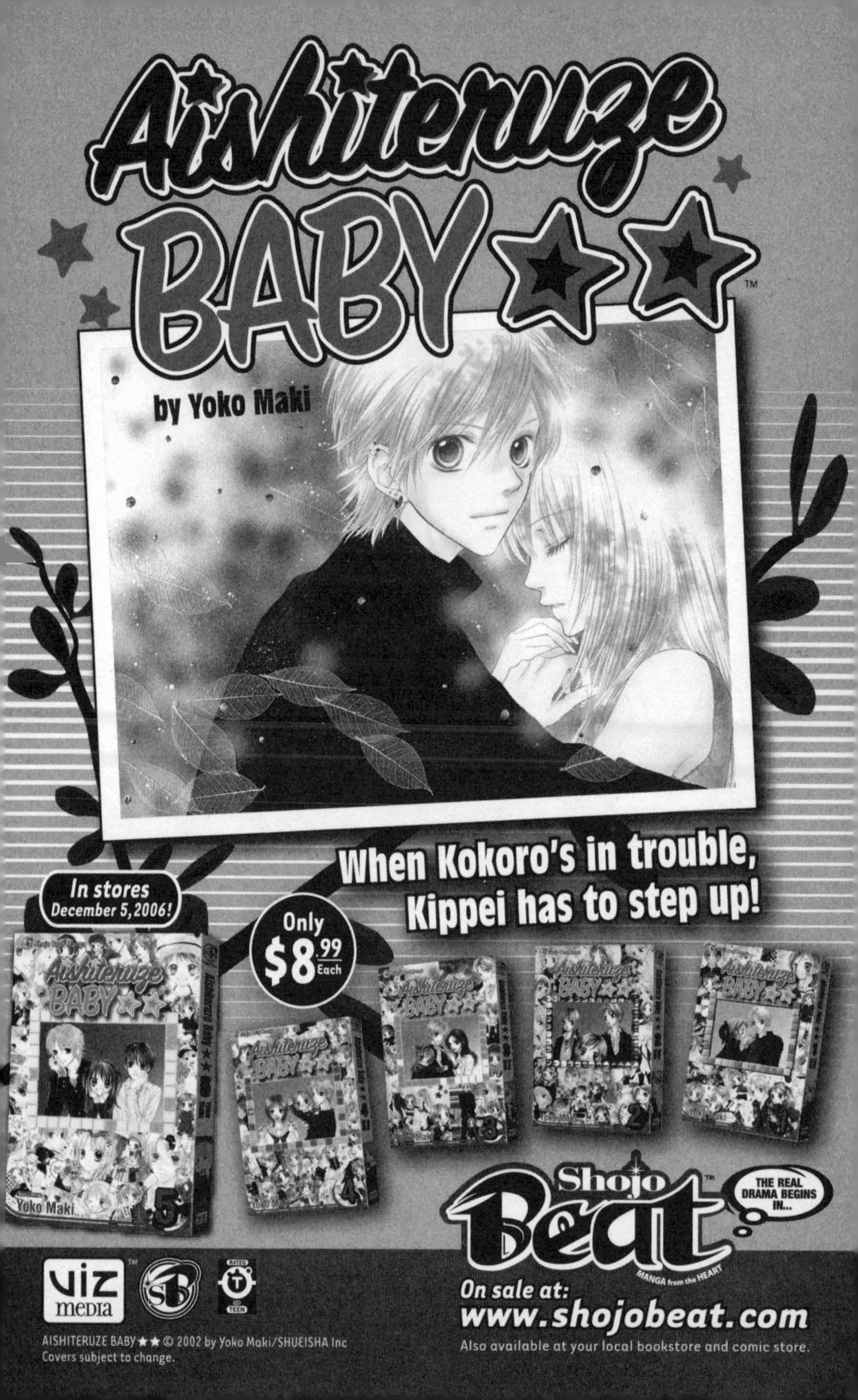
Aishiteruze BABY★★™
by Yoko Maki
When Kokoro's in trouble, Kippei has to step up!
In stores December 5, 2006!
Only $8.99 Each
Shojo Beat™
THE REAL DRAMA BEGINS IN...
MANGA from the HEART
On sale at:
www.shojobeat.com
Also available at your local bookstore and comic store.
viz media
AISHITERUZE BABY★★ © 2002 by Yoko Maki/SHUEISHA Inc
Covers subject to change.

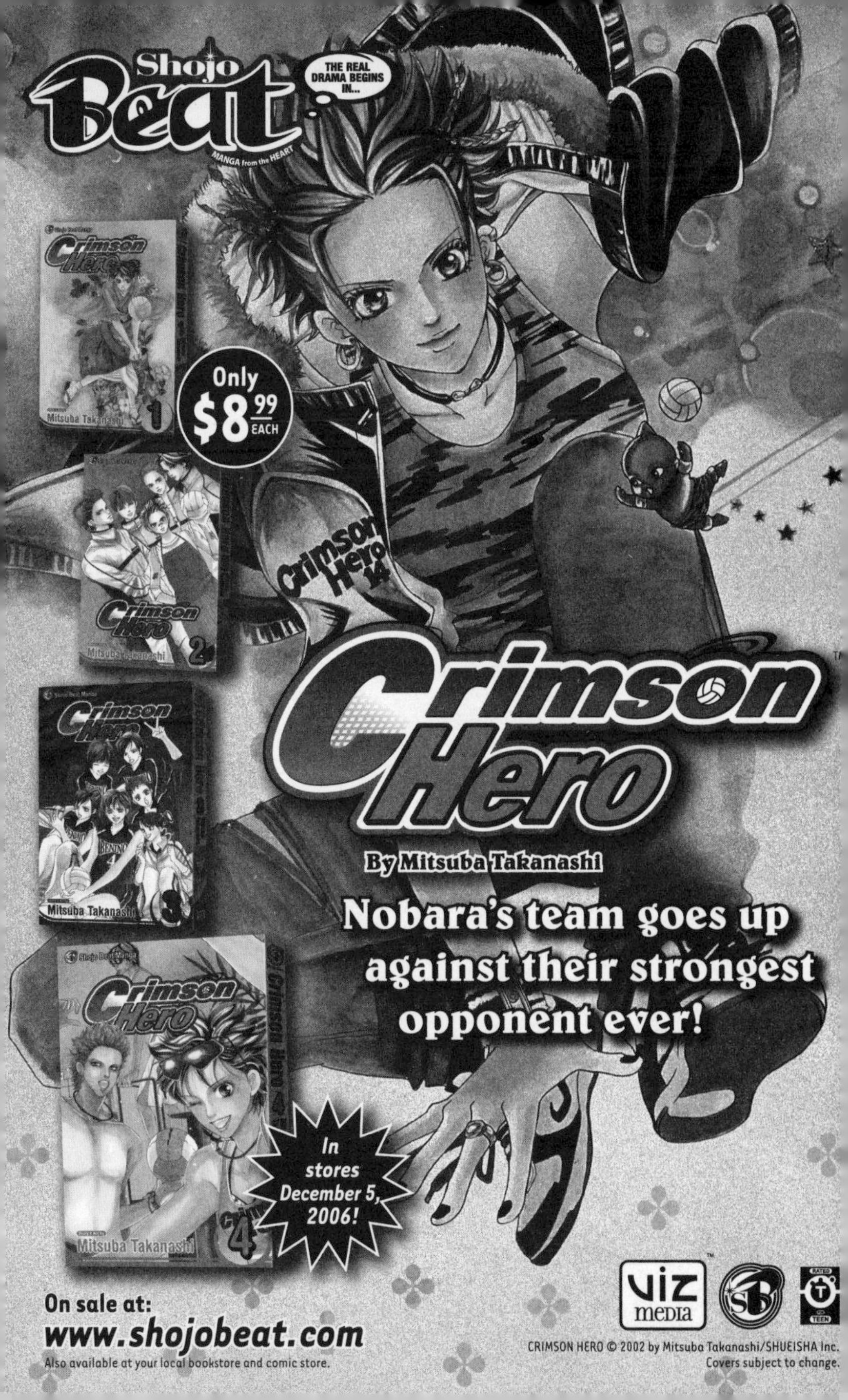
Shojo Beat
MANGA from the HEART
THE REAL DRAMA BEGINS IN...
Only $8.99 EACH
Crimson Hero
By Mitsuba Takanashi
Nobara's team goes up against their strongest opponent ever!
In stores December 5, 2006!
On sale at:
www.shojobeat.com
Also available at your local bookstore and comic store.
VIZ MEDIA
CRIMSON HERO © 2002 by Mitsuba Takanashi/SHUEISHA Inc.
Covers subject to change.

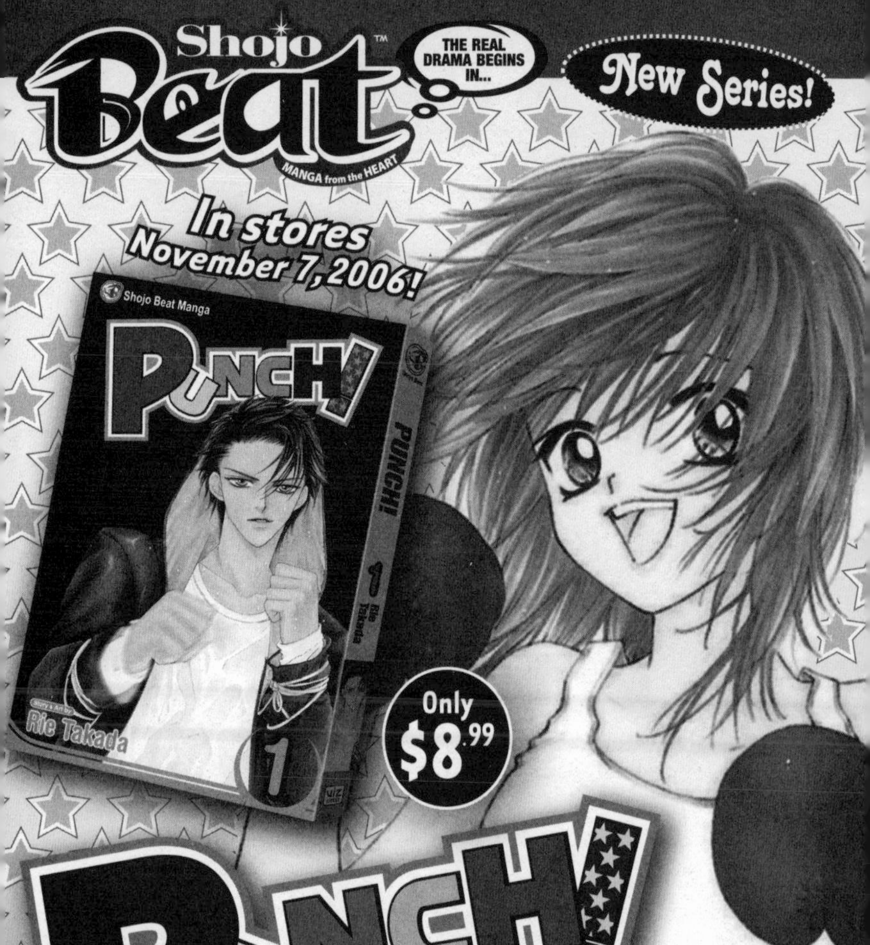

Shojo Beat™
MANGA from the HEART
THE REAL DRAMA BEGINS IN...
New Series!
In stores November 7, 2006!
Shojo Beat Manga
PUNCH!
Story & Art by
Rie Takada
1
Only $8.99
PUNCH!™
by Rie Takada
Sometimes love can feel like a punch in the face!

Tell us what you think about Shojo Beat Manga!

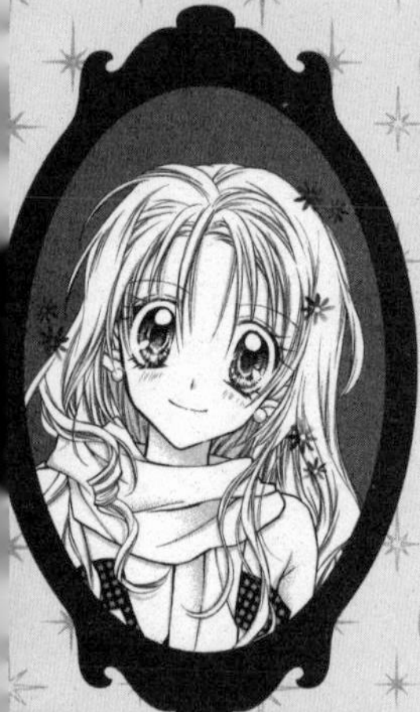

Our survey is now available online. Go to:

shojobeat.com/mangasurvey

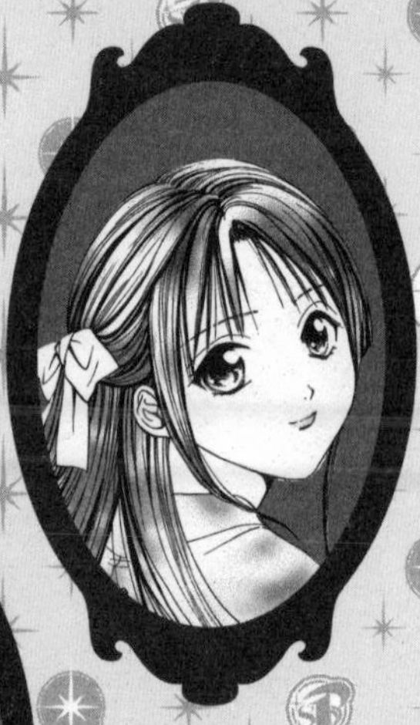

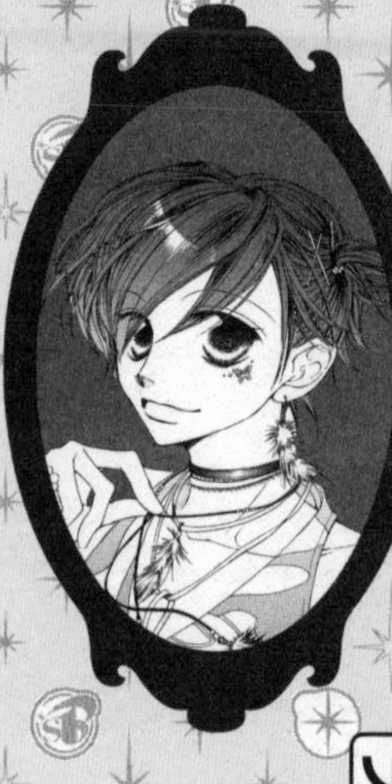

Help us make our product offerings better!

VIZ media

Shojo Beat
MANGA from the HEART
THE REAL DRAMA BEGINS IN...